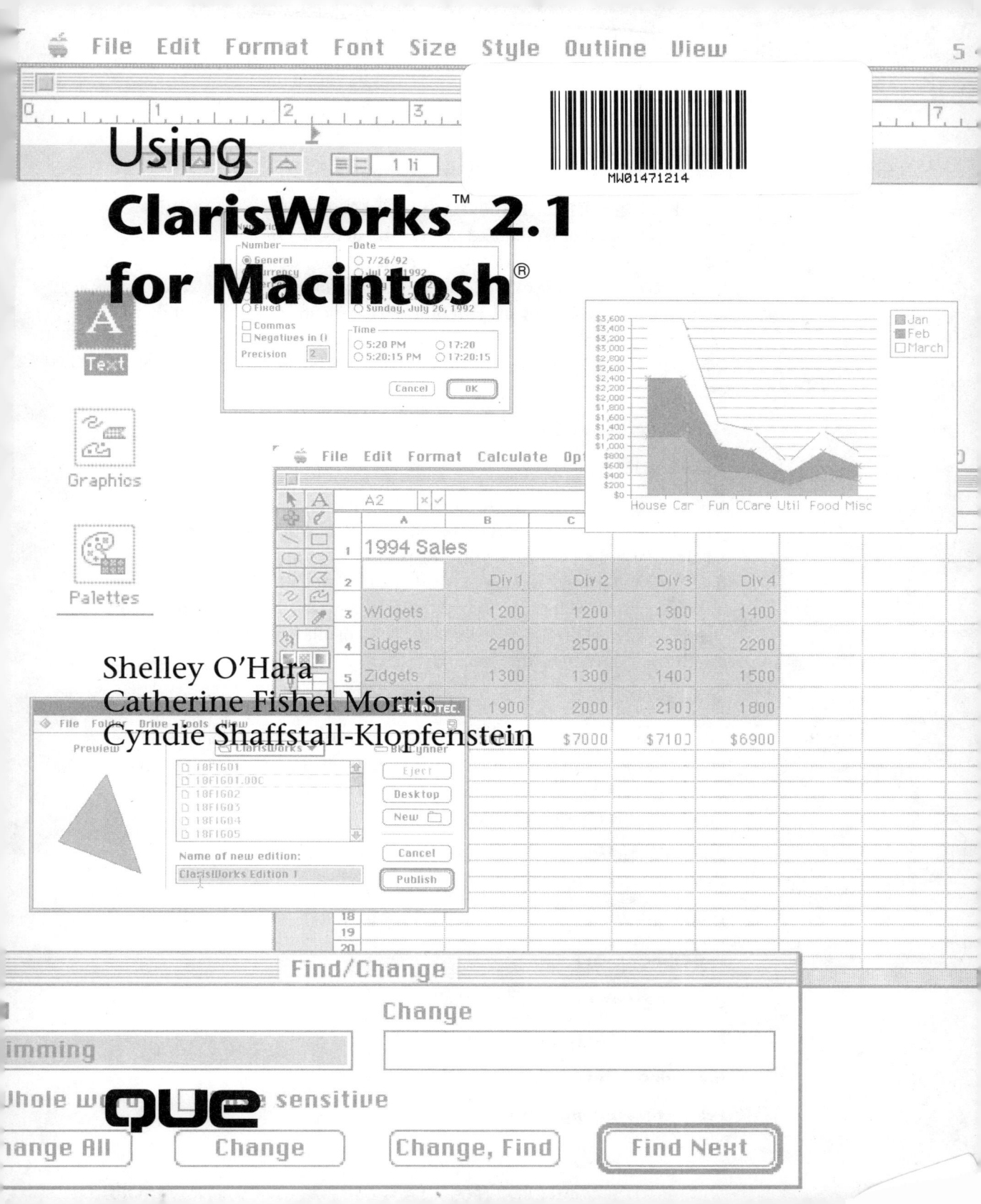

Using
ClarisWorks™ 2.1
for Macintosh®

Shelley O'Hara
Catherine Fishel Morris
Cyndie Shaffstall-Klopfenstein

que

Using ClarisWorks™ 2.1 for Macintosh®

Copyright © 1994 by Que® Corporation.

All rights reserved. Printed in the United States of America. No part of this book may be used or reproduced in any form or by any means, or stored in a database or retrieval system, without prior written permission of the publisher except in the case of brief quotations embedded in critical articles and reviews. Making copies of any part of this book for any purpose other than your own personal use is a violation of United States copyright laws. For information, address Que Corporation, 201 W. 103rd St., Indianapolis, IN 46290.

Library of Congress Catalog No.: 94-65147

ISBN: 1-56529-550-1

This book is sold as is, without warranty of any kind, either express or implied, respecting the contents of this book, including but not limited to implied warranties for the book's quality, performance, merchantability, or fitness for any particular purpose. Neither Que Corporation nor its dealers or distributors shall be liable to the purchaser or any other person or entity with respect to any liability, loss, or damage caused or alleged to have been caused directly or indirectly by this book.

96 95 94   6 5 4 3 2 1

Interpretation of the printing code: the rightmost double-digit number is the year of the book's printing; the rightmost single-digit number, the number of the book's printing. For example, a printing code of 94-1 shows that the first printing of the book occurred in 1994.

Screen reproductions in this book were created using Capture from Mainstay, Camarillo, California.

Using ClarisWorks 2.1 for Macintosh covers ClarisWorks Version 2.1.

Publisher: David P. Ewing

Associate Publisher: Corinne Walls

Publishing Director: Lisa A. Bucki

Managing Editor: Anne Owen

Product Marketing Manager: Ray Robinson

Credits

Publishing Manager
Thomas H. Bennett

Acquisitions Editor
Thomas F. Godfrey III

Product Director
Stephanie D. Gould

Copy Editors
Lorna Gentry
Phil Kitchel

Technical Editor
Lisa M. Lynch

Editorial Assistant
Jill L. Stanley

Book Designer
Amy Peppler-Adams

Cover Designer
Dan Armstrong

Indexer
Charlotte Clapp

Production Team
Gary Adair
Angela Bannan
Anne Dickerson
Karen Dodson
Brook Farling
Teresa Forrester
Joelynn Gifford
Carla Hall
Bob LaRoche
Joy Dean Lee
Beth Lewis
Andrea Marcum
Tim Montgomery
Aren Munk
G. Alan Palmore
Nanci Sears Perry
Linda Quigley
Dennis Sheehan
Amy Steed
Michael Thomas
Johnna VanHoose
Sue VandeWalle
Mary Beth Wakefield
Jennifer Willis
Donna Winter
Michelle Worthington
Lillian Yates

Composed in *Stone Serif* and *MCPdigital*
by Que Corporation

About the Authors

Shelley O'Hara recently started her own technical writing and training company in Indianapolis. She has written more than 25 computer books, including the best-selling *Easy Windows*, *Easy DOS*, *Easy 1-2-3*, and *Easy WordPerfect*. O'Hara has a B.A. in English from the University of South Carolina and an M.A. in English from the University of Maryland.

Catherine Fishel Morris has been involved in education for most of her professional career. Currently, she is coordinator of Project Spark, a program that helps teachers and schools become knowledgeable in the use and integration of technology. She also teaches ClarisWorks and other software programs at the college level and privately.

Cyndie Shaffstall-Klopfenstein, whose roots are deeply seated in the printing and prepress industries, is a renowned speaker on desktop publishing and the producer of a series of videos on printing software. She has spent the past nine years training high-end users of QuarkXPress and supporting programs.

About the Authors

Shelley O'Hara recently started her own technical writing and training company in Indianapolis. She has written more than 25 computer books, including the best-selling *Easy Windows, Easy DOS, Easy 1-2-3*, and *Easy WordPerfect*. O'Hara has a B.A. in English from the University of South Carolina and an M.A. in English from the University of Maryland.

Catherine Fishel Morris has been involved in education for most of her professional career. Currently, she is coordinator of Project Spark, a program that helps teachers and schools become knowledgeable in the use and integration of technology. She also teaches ClarisWorks and other software programs at the college level and privately.

Cyndie Shaffstall-Klopfenstein, whose roots are deeply seated in the printing and prepress industries, is a renowned speaker on desktop publishing and the producer of a series of videos on printing software. She has spent the past nine years training high-end users of QuarkXPress and supporting programs.

Credits

Publishing Manager
Thomas H. Bennett

Acquisitions Editor
Thomas F. Godfrey III

Product Director
Stephanie D. Gould

Copy Editors
Lorna Gentry
Phil Kitchel

Technical Editor
Lisa M. Lynch

Editorial Assistant
Jill L. Stanley

Book Designer
Amy Peppler-Adams

Cover Designer
Dan Armstrong

Indexer
Charlotte Clapp

Production Team
Gary Adair
Angela Bannan
Anne Dickerson
Karen Dodson
Brook Farling
Teresa Forrester
Joelynn Gifford
Carla Hall
Bob LaRoche
Joy Dean Lee
Beth Lewis
Andrea Marcum
Tim Montgomery
Aren Munk
G. Alan Palmore
Nanci Sears Perry
Linda Quigley
Dennis Sheehan
Amy Steed
Michael Thomas
Johnna VanHoose
Sue VandeWalle
Mary Beth Wakefield
Jennifer Willis
Donna Winter
Michelle Worthington
Lillian Yates

Composed in *Stone Serif* and *MCPdigital*
by Que Corporation

Acknowledgments

Shelley O'Hara: Thanks to Kathy Simpson for a clean, perfect, painless edit on this book. Thanks also to Tom Godfrey for his sensibleness and sense of humor.

Catherine Fishel Morris: I would like to thank Van Cleve Morris for his support and always being there when I needed him.

Cyndie Shaffstall-Klopfenstein: I can't possibly let my contributions to this book be recorded as though I achieved them on my own. Because Gene Wolff would not let me give up on myself and because Joann Harriss would not let me give up on my dream of a career with words, I thank them. I also thank BK, Coy Boy, Mom, and Dad.

Trademark Acknowledgments

Que Corporation has made every effort to supply trademark information about company names, products, and services mentioned in this book. Trademarks indicated below were derived from various sources. Que Corporation cannot attest to the accuracy of this information.

Claris is a registered trademark and ClarisWorks is a trademark of Claris Corporation.

Apple and Macintosh are registered trademarks and Balloon Help and System 7 are trademarks of Apple Computer, Inc.

dBASE is a registered trademark of Borland International Inc.

Contents at a Glance

Introduction	1
Getting Started with ClarisWorks	**7**
1 What Is ClarisWorks?	9
2 Learning the Essentials	25

Creating Documents	**55**
3 Working with Text	57
4 Enhancing Your Text	79
5 Working with Outlines	107
6 Drawing	117
7 Painting	143
8 Spreadsheet Basics	169
9 Enhancing a Worksheet	197
10 Using Spreadsheet Functions	213
11 Creating Charts	227

Creating Databases	**243**
12 Database Basics	245
13 Creating Layouts	269
14 Enhancing the Presentation of Data	291

More on Integration	**313**
15 Creating Integrated Documents	315
16 Sharing Data with Other Documents and Applications	343

Communications	**353**
17 Communications Basics	355
18 Working with the Communications Tools	373

Advanced Topics	**387**
19 Automating Your Work	389
20 Customizing ClarisWorks	405
Appendix	423
Index	447

Contents

Introduction   **1**

    Versions Past and Present 1
    Why You Should Use This Book 4
        The Business World 4
        The School Environment 5
        The Home 5
    How the Book Is Organized 6

I Getting Started with ClarisWorks   7

1 What Is ClarisWorks?   9

    Understanding Equipment Requirements 10
    Installing ClarisWorks 10
    Starting the Program 11
    Understanding the Benefits of Integration 12
    Understanding Document Types and Environments 14
        Word Processing 14
        Spreadsheet 16
        Database 17
        Drawing 17
        Painting 18
        Communications 19
    Using Frames for Integration 20
    Understanding the Tools 21
        Environment Tools 22
        Drawing Tools 22
        Painting Tools 23
        Fill and Pen Palettes 23
    From Here… 24

2 Learning the Essentials   25

    Working with Documents 25
        Creating a Document 26
        Opening a Document 28
        Saving a Document 29
        Making a Backup Copy 30
        Going Back to the Last Saved Version 31
        Closing a Document 32
    Getting Help 32
        ClarisWorks Help 32
        Balloon Help 33

Working with Windows 34
    Showing or Hiding Tools and Rulers 34
    Zooming to Rescale the Contents of a Window 34
    Using Multiple Document Views 36
    Splitting Windows 36
    Tiling Several Open Windows 37
    Stacking Several Open Windows 38
Working with Pages 39
    Viewing Pages 39
    Moving Directly to a Page 39
    The Page Settings 40
    Ruler Settings 41
    Page and Column Breaks 42
    Headers and Footers 43
    Automatically Adding the Date, Time,
      or Page Number 44
The Printing Process 44
    Selecting the Printer 44
    Selecting Page Options 45
    Printing the Document 46
Cutting, Copying, and Pasting 47
Importing, Inserting, and Exporting Documents 48
    Importing a Document 48
    Inserting a Document 49
    Exporting a Document 50
Using the Stationery Option to Create Templates 51
Quitting ClarisWorks 52
From Here… 52

II Creating Documents   55

3 Working with Text   57

Understanding the Screen Display and Tools 57
    Changing the View 58
    Using the Shortcuts Palette 59
Creating a Document 60
    Typing Text 61
    Moving Around 61
    Inserting Page Breaks 62
    Saving the Document 62
Editing Text 63
    Selecting Text 63
    Moving Text 65
    Copying Text 65
    Deleting Text 66
Finding and Changing Text 67
    Finding Text 67
    Changing Found Text 69
    Finding Invisible Characters 71

Checking Spelling 72
    Performing a Spell Check 72
    Adding Words to the User Dictionary 74
    Creating a User Dictionary 75
Using the Thesaurus 75
Setting Preferences 76
From Here... 78

4 Enhancing Your Text   79

Formatting Characters 79
    Defining a Font 79
    Changing Fonts 81
    Adjusting Type Size 81
    Using Type Styles 81
    Adding Color 82
Formatting Paragraphs 83
    Changing the Alignment 84
    Indenting a Paragraph 84
    Changing Line Spacing 86
    Changing Paragraph Spacing 87
    Setting Tabs 87
    Copying Paragraph Formats 89
Formatting Pages 90
    Setting Margins 91
    Inserting Headers and Footers 92
    Adding Page Numbers 93
Hyphenating a Document 93
Inserting the Date and Time 94
Inserting Graphics 94
    Moving and Deleting a Picture 96
    Wrapping Text around an Object 96
    Layering Text and Graphics 98
Working with Columns 99
    Creating Columns with the Ruler 100
    Creating Columns with the Columns Dialog Box 100
    Typing in Columns 101
Working with Tables 102
Adding Footnotes 103
    Inserting a Footnote 103
    Customizing a Footnote 104
From Here... 105

5 Working with Outlines   107

Creating an Outline 107
Rearranging an Outline 108
    Changing the Level of a Topic 108
    Changing the Order of an Outline 109
Viewing an Outline 110
Formatting an Outline 112

Changing the Symbol for a Topic 112
Changing the Outline Format 112
Creating a Custom Outline Format 114
From Here... 116

6 Drawing   117

Understanding the Drawing Window 117
Drawing Objects 120
    Drawing a Line, Rectangle, Rounded Rectangle,
        or Oval 121
    Drawing an Arc 123
    Drawing a Polygon 124
    Drawing a Regular Polygon 125
    Drawing Freehand 126
    Drawing with the Bezigon Tool 127
    Using the Eyedropper 128
Editing Objects 128
    Selecting Objects 128
    Moving Objects 129
    Deleting Objects 129
    Rearranging Overlapping Objects 130
    Copying Objects 130
    Moving Objects 131
    Grouping Objects 134
Changing Colors, Patterns, and Borders 135
    The Color Editor 135
    The Pattern Editor 136
    The Gradient Editor 137
Working with Multiple-Page Drawings 140
From Here... 141

7 Painting   143

Opening a Painting Document 143
Using the Tools 144
Painting a Picture 145
    Using the Fill Indicator Palette 146
    Using the Pen Indicator Palette 147
    Painting Images 147
Using the Painting Tools 149
    The Pencil 149
    The Brush 150
    The Spray Can 151
    The Paint Bucket 152
Editing an Image with the Painting Tools 154
    The Selection Rectangle 154
    The Lasso 155
    The Magic Wand 155
    The Eraser 156
    The Eyedropper 156

Creating Special Effects 157
    Changing the Size of a Painting Document 164
    Changing the Resolution in a Painting Document 165
    Displaying Overlapping Graphics 166
From Here… 167

8 Spreadsheet Basics   169

Understanding the Screen and Tools 169
    Understanding Cells, Columns, and Rows 170
    Using the Shortcuts Palette 171
Entering Data 172
    Entering Text, Numbers, and Dates 173
    Saving Your Worksheet 174
Entering Formulas 175
    Understanding the Parts of a Formula 175
    Entering a Formula 176
    Understanding Cell References 177
    Understanding the Calculation Order 178
    Calculating the Worksheet 178
    Understanding the Parts of a Function 179
    Entering a Function 179
    Understanding Error Messages 181
Editing Data 182
    Editing a Cell 183
    Moving to a Cell 183
    Selecting a Range 183
    Deleting Cell Contents 185
    Moving Cell Contents 185
    Copying Cell Contents 186
    Filling a Range 187
    Transposing a Range 188
    Freezing Values 189
    Protecting Cells 190
Editing the Worksheet Layout 191
    Inserting Cells, Rows, and Columns 191
    Deleting Cells, Rows, and Columns 192
Setting Display Options 192
Locking Row and Column Titles On-Screen 193
Sorting Worksheet Data 194
From Here… 196

9 Enhancing a Worksheet   197

Changing the Number Format 197
Changing Fonts, Type Size, Style, and Color 199
    Changing Fonts 199
    Adjusting Type Size 201
    Using Type Styles 202
    Adding Color 203

Adding Borders 204
Aligning Data 205
Copying Formatting 207
Changing Column Width and Row Height 207
    Changing the Column Width 208
    Changing the Row Height 208
Adding Graphics 209
Printing the Worksheet 210
    Entering a Page Break 210
    Setting the Print Range 211
From Here… 212

10 Using Spreadsheet Functions   213

Expanding Basic Skills 214
    Using Date Functions 215
    Using Statistical Functions 217
    Calculating and Auto Calc 218
Using Logical Functions 219
Using Financial Functions 220
    Using Functions for Investment Planning 220
    Using Functions to Compare Loan Payments 222
Using Lookup Functions 225
From Here… 226

11 Creating Charts   227

Creating a Chart 227
Understanding Chart Types 230
Editing a Chart 233
    Moving a Chart 233
    Resizing a Chart 233
    Deleting a Chart 234
Formatting a Chart 234
    Changing the Chart Type 234
    Changing the Formatting of Chart Data 235
    Formatting the Chart Series 235
    Changing the Chart Colors 237
    Formatting the Chart Title 238
    Formatting the Chart Legend 239
    Formatting the Chart Axes 240
From Here… 242

III Creating Databases   243

12 Database Basics   245

Understanding Database Concepts 245
Planning a Database 246

Creating a Database 246
    Understanding Field Types 247
    Defining Fields 248
    Defining a Calculation Field 249
    Customizing Fields 250
    Saving the Database 254
Editing the Database 254
    Changing Field Definitions 255
    Adding Fields 255
    Deleting Fields 255
Entering Data 256
Working with Records 259
    Adding Records 259
    Duplicating a Record 259
    Scrolling through Records 260
    Going to a Particular Record 260
    Editing a Record 260
    Selecting a Record 261
    Hiding Records 262
    Deleting Records 262
Finding Records 262
    Searching the Database 263
    Using Multiple Find Requests 265
    Matching Records 265
Sorting Records 266
From Here… 268

13 Creating Layouts   269

Planning a Layout 270
Working with Views 271
    The Browse View 272
    The Find View 272
    The Layout View 272
Working with Layouts 272
    Using the Standard Layout 273
    Using Columnar Report Layouts 274
    Creating Label Layouts 277
    Using Blank Layouts 279
    Using Duplicate Layouts 279
    Renaming Layouts 280
    Deleting a Layout 281
Editing a Layout 281
    Using Browse and Layout Views 281
    Editing Field Shapes, Sizes, and Positions 284
    Deleting Fields 285
    Adding Fields to a Layout 285
    Changing the Size of the Record 286

Printing Layouts 288
    Printing Labels 288
    Removing Space between Fields 289
From Here… 290

14 Enhancing the Presentation of Data   291

Formatting Function Fields 292
    Formatting Numbers 293
    Formatting Dates 294
    Formatting Times..295
Performing Calculations and Summaries 296
Understanding the Parts of a Layout 298
    Adding Headers and Footers 299
    Using a Sub-Summary...301
    Using Grand Summary 304
    Deleting Parts 304
Using the Graphics Tools in a Layout 305
    Shading Fields 306
    Outlining Fields 306
Making Changes to Text 307
    Changing Text Attributes 307
    Changing the Tab Order of the Fields 311
From Here… 312

IV More on Integration   313

15 Creating Integrated Documents   315

Using Frames in a Document 315
    Adding a Frame to a Document 316
    Moving between the Frame and Document 317
    Working with an Open Frame 318
    Creating a Chart from a Spreadsheet Frame 318
Linking Frames...321
    Linking Text Frames 322
    Linking Spreadsheet or Painting Frames 324
Combining Text, Graphics, and Spreadsheets
    in a Document 327
    Working with More Than One Document.........................327
    Combining Graphics and Spreadsheets with
        Text Documents 329
    Using Graphics from Another Source 331
    Using Graphics from the Apple Menu 331
Making a Slide Presentation 334
Using Form Letters and Mail Merge 336
    Setting up the Database 336
    Creating the Form Letter 337
From Here… 341

16 Sharing Data with Other Documents and Applications   343

   Publishing an Item 343
   Subscribing to a Published Item 347
   Changing Publisher and Subscriber Options 349
      The Publisher Options Dialog Box 349
      The Subscriber Options Dialog Box 350
      Rules for Using Editions 351
   From Here... 352

V Communications   353

17 Communications Basics   355

   Setting Up 356
      Using the Hardware and Software 356
      Learning the Menus 358
      Adjusting the Settings 358
      Making a Connection 371
   Sending Files to Remote Computers 372
   From Here... 372

18 Working with the Communications Tools   373

   Understanding the Communications Window 373
      Accessing the Phone Book 374
      Watching the Clock 376
      Using the Optional Status Bar 376
      Using the Tab Ruler 377
   Receiving Calls 378
      Capturing Data 378
      Putting Scrollback to Work 379
   Using Captured Data 381
      Using Captured Data in a Spreadsheet 381
      Printing Data 381
   Automating Communications 382
      Using Macros 382
      Using Other Shortcuts 384
   From Here... 385

VI Advanced Topics   387

19 Automating Your Work   389

   Using ClarisWorks Shortcuts 389
      Finding Your Way around the Shortcuts Palette 390
      Using the Shortcut Palette 391
      Editing the Shortcut Palette 393

Using Macros 396
    Practicing Macro Making 396
    Choosing Macro Options 399
    Using Macros from the Menu 400
    Editing a Macro 401
    Removing Macros 401
    Using Macro Wait 402
From Here... 404

20 Customizing ClarisWorks 405

Setting Preferences 405
    Setting Text Preferences 406
    Setting Graphics Preferences 409
    Setting Palette Preferences 411
    Setting Communications Preferences 416
Using Custom Text Styles 419
    Choosing Styles to be Defined 419
    Defining Styles 419
    Applying Stored Styles 421
    Modifying Styles 421
    Deleting Styles 421
From Here... 422

A Functions 423

Function Reference 424
    Business and Financial 424
    Date and Time 427
    Information 431
    Logical 433
    Numeric 435
    Statistical 438
    Text 441
    Trigonometric 444

Index 447

Introduction

by Catherine Fishel Morris

ClarisWorks is one software package with six modules that have stand-alone capabilities, yet each module can be used in another module's environment. The software is designed to be a good introduction for people who have limited experience with technology and to provide enough advanced features for users who are ready to go further.

The ClarisWorks logo, regardless of the version, is a box containing a telephone, a clipboard, a grid sheet, a pen, and a pencil, all ready to be plucked out of the package. Opening the software is like opening one wonderful present with many parts. ClarisWorks gives you just what you need to create text documents, make spreadsheets, develop databases, add graphics, and connect your computer with the outside world.

Versions Past and Present

The first version of ClarisWorks consisted of five basic modules: word processing, spreadsheet, database, graphics, and communications. The program did the job but had few frills to perform much more than perfunctory tasks.

In the past year, Claris came out with ClarisWorks Version 2.0, which was a major upgrade. The upgrade also provided another graphics module. The following list describes the features of Version 2.0.

General Enhancements

- Custom text styles
- Capability to go directly to a specified page
- Capability to view or hide Fill and Pen palettes
- 256 editable colors
- Customized colors, patterns, and gradients

More Preferences settings

A Shortcuts palette that can display icons or text

Capability to play a macro by clicking a palette button

Capability to create slide-show presentations

Capability to open a stationery document by default

System 7 Publish and Subscribe capability

Capability to play QuickTime movies

Word Processing Module

Capability to outline text in documents and frames

Column controls that can alter the number of columns in a document

Capability to resize columns manually

Capability to check spelling in highlighted text only

A Show/Hide Invisible Characters toggle command

Soft returns to permit text-block formatting

Capability to customize the amount of space before and after paragraphs

Drawing Module

New tools (Bezigon, Polygon, and Eyedropper)

A dialog box for specifying the size and placement of objects

Capability to frame the edges of an arc to make pie-shaped objects

Capability to select multiple objects of the same kind for editing

Painting Module

Eight new drawing tools

Spreadsheet Module

Capability to add custom borders or solid lines

Capability to lock a column or row to repeat a title on each page

Capability to copy and paste the format of a cell

Greater variety of charts and chart formats

Database Module

Capability to create pop-up menus that automatically place information in a specified field in every record of the database

Preset Avery label formats

Capability to insert the contents of another document into the correct fields of a database

Capability to share data with DBF-format (dBASE) files

Communications Module

Automation of often-used communications settings

Capability to open an overflow area for incoming data that will not fit in the working area

Capability to conduct multiple communications sessions, each in its own window

Capability to print from the communications module

A customized phone book

With Version 2.1, ClarisWorks goes one step further. Version 2.1 has two new features: hyphenation and electronic mail.

As part of the dictionaries you can install in the System folder on your hard drive, ClarisWorks adds the US Hyphenation dictionary. This feature enables you to include automatic hyphenation in any text you create, whether in a word processing document, a text frame, or a database field. You can purchase and install other hyphenation dictionaries, and you can customize the existing one to meet your needs.

Electronic mail, or *e-mail*, enables you to communicate with compatibly networked computers. Instead of using a phone, you can use the e-mail software on your computer to send and receive messages.

Using e-mail is optional, but if using e-mail is necessary right now, you need to make sure that your system is System 7 Pro. The e-mail program, PowerTalk (which comes only in System 7 Pro), must be installed in the System folder. To upgrade to System 7 Pro, call Apple or your local computer dealer, or look through discount catalogs. You also will need to be *networked* (electronically connected) with other computers that have the same system and software.

Why You Should Use This Book

It is hard to find a business in this country that does not use technology in some way. The same can be said for the educational system; technology may not be in every classroom, but most schools are using some kind of technology. Also, the number of computers bought for home use increases every year. As multimedia grows, so will purchases of home computers.

ClarisWorks is a perfect software package for business, school, and home users. The purpose of this book is to help you learn how to create professional-looking, appealing documents for clients, co-workers, teachers, children, and friends.

People are always finding new ways to use ClarisWorks. The following suggestions are some of the many effective, efficient ways you can use ClarisWorks 2.1 in the business world, in school, or at home.

The Business World

Businesses have put technology (calculators, copying machines, robots, computers, and so on) to use for many years. It is the business world that first understood the impact of technology in the workplace and how to use it effectively. Software has been developed, and continues to be developed, primarily to meet the needs of the business world. The following uses for ClarisWorks are just a small sample of the kinds of work you can do to meet business needs:

- Create templates for forms and letterhead documents
- Set up standardized styles for different kinds of letters
- Create a database of client or employee information
- Create mailing labels

- Create mail-merge forms
- Create a company logo
- Chart yearly sales progress
- Chart business costs
- Create designs for a new product
- Research product information

The School Environment

In most traditional learning situations, a teacher expects students to take in new information and to apply that information correctly on the first try. Technology has a different approach—one that involves a good deal of trial and error, much questioning, and multiple ways to get a job done. That approach makes technology a wonderful learning tool. Following are just a few of the ways that you can use ClarisWorks in schools:

- Write reports, research papers, and essays
- Illustrate reports and newsletters
- Create a literary magazine
- Set up seating charts
- Set up weekly schedules
- Create a classroom database
- Create charts from scientific data
- Communicate with other schools
- Create databases on social-studies topics (for example, early explcrers)
- Create presentations
- Keep statistical data on student scores to track progress and compare student groups

The Home

Many uses for ClarisWorks in the home are similar to those in businesses and schools. The difference is that the focus is on personal needs—such as setting up a budget or stock portfolio for one person or for a club—as opposed to clients or students. Following are some of the ways you can use ClarisWorks in the home:

- Write individual letters
- Write form letters that can be combined, or *mail merged*, with a database so that the letters are individually addressed
- Set up a budget
- Set up a stocks-and-bonds portfolio
- Create an address book
- Do work at home and send it via modem to the office
- Do research for a school project
- Create greeting cards
- List all the albums, tapes, and CDs in the house
- Keep track of family members' schedules
- Pay bills electronically
- Create invitations
- Create flyers

How the Book Is Organized

This book gives you an overall picture of ClarisWorks 2.1 and then explains how to use each module and its menus and tools. The book is organized into the following parts:

Part I: Getting Started with ClarisWorks

Part II: Creating Documents

Part III: Creating Databases

Part IV: More on Integration

Part V: Communications

Part VI: Advanced Topics

Part I

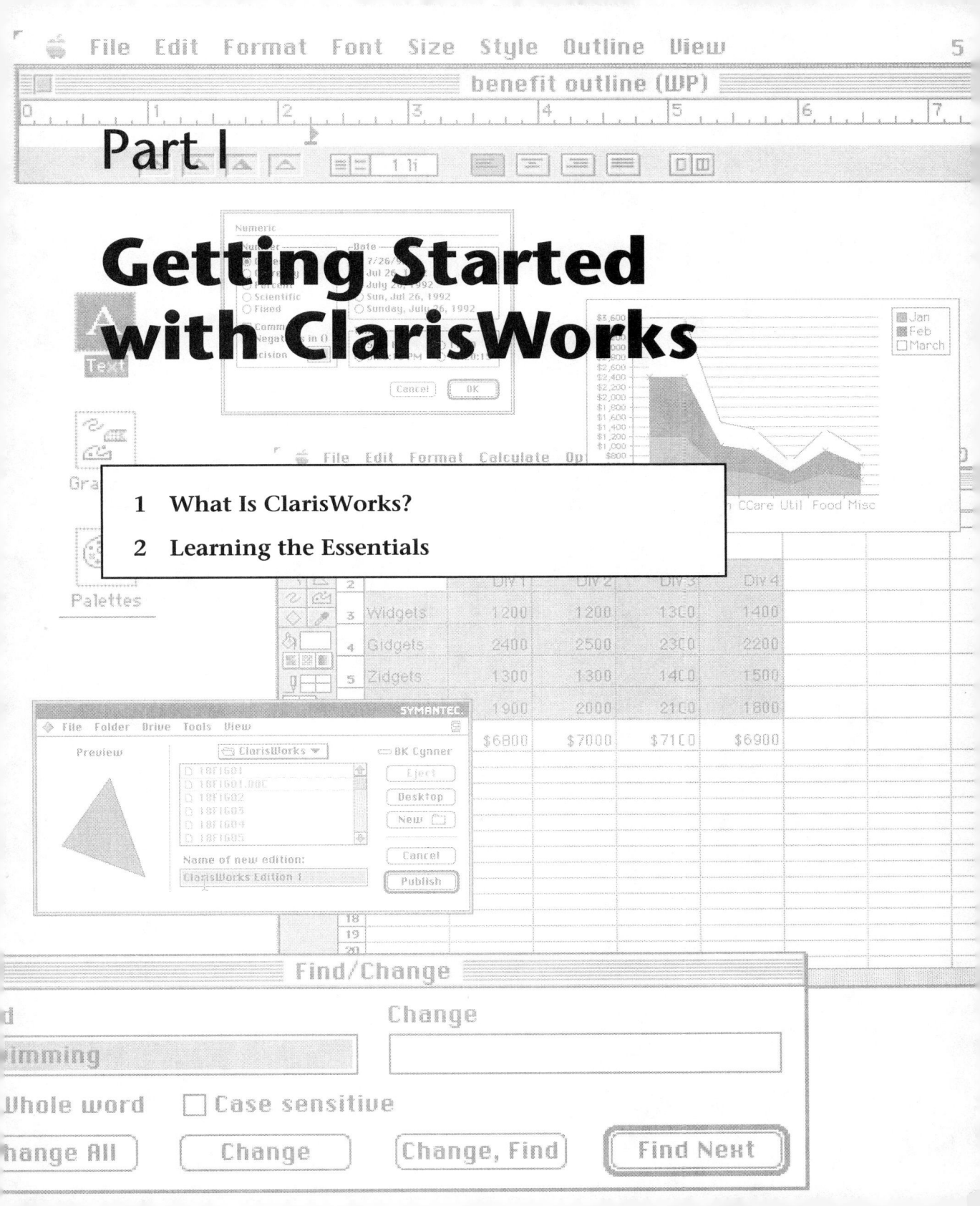

Getting Started with ClarisWorks

1. What Is ClarisWorks?
2. Learning the Essentials

File Edit Format Font Size Style Outline View

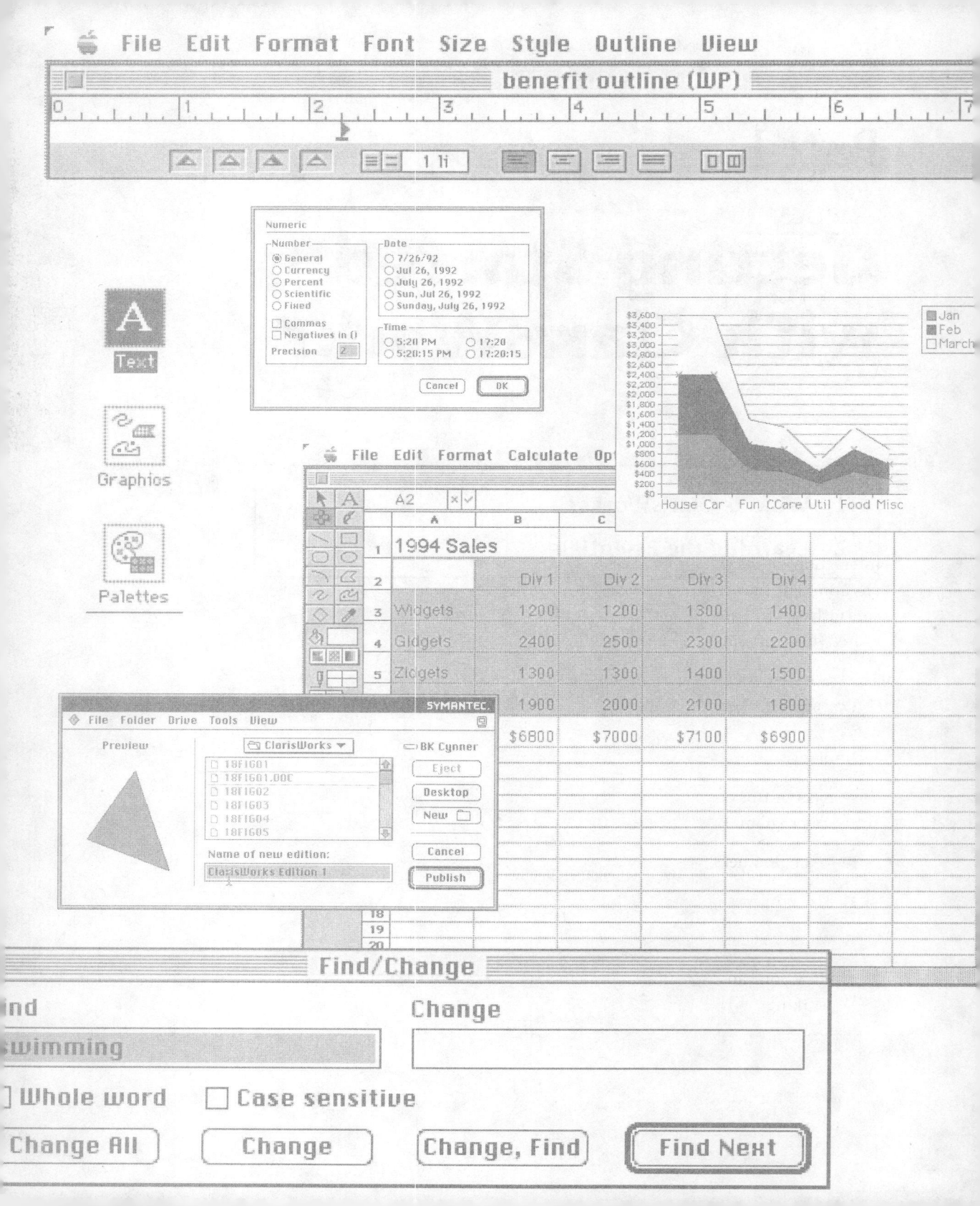

benefit outline (WP)

0 | 1 | 2 | 3 | 4 | 5 | 6 | 7

1 li

Numeric

- Number -
  - ● General
  - ○ Currency
  - ○ Percent
  - ○ Scientific
  - ○ Fixed
  - ☐ Commas
  - ☐ Negatives in ()
  - Precision [2]

- Date -
  - ○ 7/26/92
  - ○ Jul 26, 1992
  - ○ July 26, 1992
  - ○ Sun, Jul 26, 1992
  - ○ Sunday, July 26, 1992

- Time -
  - ○ 5:20 PM   ○ 17:20
  - ○ 5:20:15 PM   ○ 17:20:15

[Cancel] [OK]

A Text

Graphics

Palettes

Jan
Feb
March

$3,600
$3,400
$3,200
$3,000
$2,800
$2,600
$2,400
$2,200
$2,000
$1,800
$1,600
$1,400
$1,200
$1,000
$800
$600
$400
$200
$0

House Car Fun CCare Util Food Misc

File Edit Format Calculate Op

A2

	A	B	C	D	E
1	1994 Sales				
2		Div 1	Div 2	Div 3	Div 4
3	Widgets	1200	1200	1300	1400
4	Gidgets	2400	2500	2300	2200
5	Zidgets	1300	1300	1400	1500
		1900	2000	2100	1800
		$6800	$7000	$7100	$6900

SYMANTEC

File Folder Drive Tools View

Preview

📁 ClarisWorks ▼   💾 BK Cynner

- 18F1G01
- 18F1G01.DOC
- 18F1G02
- 18F1G03
- 18F1G04
- 18F1G05

[Eject]
[Desktop]
[New 📁]

Name of new edition:
ClarisWorks Edition 1

[Cancel]
[Publish]

18
19
20

Find/Change

ind

swimming

Change

☐ Whole word   ☐ Case sensitive

[Change All]   [Change]   [Change, Find]   [[Find Next]]

Chapter 1

What Is ClarisWorks?

by Catherine Fishel Morris

ClarisWorks 2.1 is one software program composed of six individual applications, or *modules*: word processing, spreadsheet, database, drawing, painting, and communications. These modules can operate separately or interact. This interaction, or *integration*, makes ClarisWorks seamless in its flow from one environment into another within one document. The capability to use spreadsheet tools and data in a word processing document makes ClarisWorks an especially efficient software program.

The basic elements of ClarisWorks are easy to understand and learn. The software is varied and powerful enough for experienced, knowledgeable users as well as for those who are taking their first steps into the world of technology.

The object of this chapter is to give you an overview of the ClarisWorks 2.1 software program. In this chapter, you learn the following things:

- What you need to run ClarisWorks 2.1 on your computer
- The purposes of the six modules
- What you can do within each module
- How you can add a different module to the one in which you are working

Understanding Equipment Requirements

You need the following equipment to install the ClarisWorks 2.1 software:

- A Macintosh Plus or any later Macintosh model.
- An internal or external hard drive.
- One 800K floppy disk drive or one 1.4M (megabyte) SuperDrive floppy disk drive.
- Macintosh System software, Version 6.05 or later.
- At least 1M of memory if you have System 6.
- At least 2M of memory if you have System 7. If you use System 7.0 or System 7.01, you also must have System 7 Tune-up Version 1.1.1 installed. This program is available from Apple.

If you decide to install the ClarisWorks electronic-mail feature (optional), you need the following additional equipment:

- A Macintosh II or any later Macintosh model with a minimum of 4M RAM (8M is suggested for smoother operation)
- Macintosh System 7 Pro or a later version that incorporates PowerTalk System software

Installing ClarisWorks

Before you install ClarisWorks 2.1 on your hard drive, you need to lock each original disk. You can lock a disk by sliding the tab in the top-left corner of the disk so that the square hole is open. Locking a disk prevents you from accidentally deleting or saving any information to the original disk. It is also a good idea to make a backup copy of the originals and to use the backups to install ClarisWorks 2.1 on your hard drive.

To install ClarisWorks, follow these steps:

1. Insert the Installer disk into the 3.5-inch floppy disk drive. The disk opens on-screen automatically.
2. Double-click the Installer icon. The welcome screen appears.

3. Click OK to open the Easy Install dialog box.

4. If the name of your hard drive does not appear next to the drive icon, click the Switch Disk button to find it.

5. If you click the Install button, ClarisWorks will install everything on the floppy disks. ClarisWorks will also check to ensure that there is enough space on the hard drive. Read the screen, and place the proper disk in the floppy drive when told to.

   If you click the Customize button, you must manually select only those parts of ClarisWorks 2.1 that you want to install on the hard drive. For example, you may want to install the Minimum Translator set rather than All Translators so that less space is used on the hard drive.

   > **Note**
   >
   > If you decide to customize the installation of the program, be sure to include the U.S. Hyphenation dictionary so you can use the automatic-hyphenation option that is new to this version of ClarisWorks.

6. When you see the message Installation was successful, click the Restart button to leave the Installer and restart your computer. Restarting the computer will cause the final disk to eject automatically.

After you install ClarisWorks, store all the installation disks in a safe place so that you will have them in case you need to reinstall the program on your hard drive.

Starting the Program

After you install ClarisWorks 2.1 on the hard drive, a folder icon appears in the Finder screen (the Desktop). Double-click the ClarisWorks folder to open it. Then double-click the ClarisWorks program icon to open the registration screen.

The first time you use the installed ClarisWorks software, you see the dialog box shown in figure 1.1. This dialog box enables you to personalize the software by typing your name, your company's name (if applicable), and the registration number (listed on the ClarisWorks registration card). Check your entries carefully before clicking the OK button, because the only way to change this information after you click OK is to reinstall the ClarisWorks software.

Figure 1.1
Use this dialog box to register your copy of ClarisWorks 2.1.

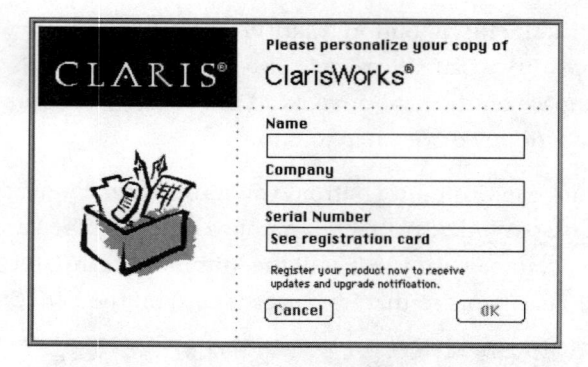

After you register your software, you see the New Document dialog box (see fig. 1.2), which lists the modules available in the program. Hereafter, every time you open the ClarisWorks program, this dialog box appears.

Figure 1.2
The New Document dialog box appears when you start ClarisWorks.

To open a document in the word processing module, which is selected by default, click OK. To open a document in a different module, click the appropriate radio button and then click OK.

If you want to open an existing file, either on a floppy disk or in the ClarisWorks folder on the Desktop, double-click the icon for that file.

Understanding the Benefits of Integration

Certain aspects of the screen remain the same in all ClarisWorks modules (see fig. 1.3).

Understanding the Benefits of Integration 13

Figure 1.3
A new document screen in the word processing module.

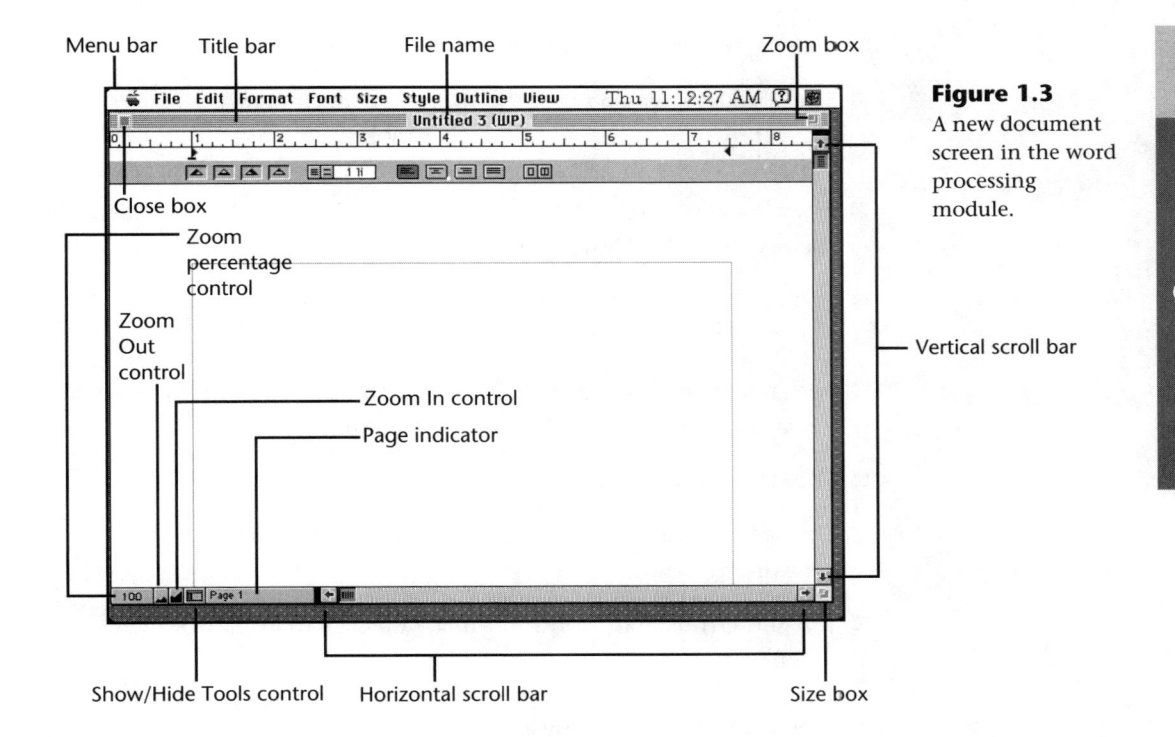

Labels on figure: Menu bar, Title bar, File name, Zoom box, Close box, Zoom percentage control, Zoom Out control, Zoom In control, Page indicator, Vertical scroll bar, Show/Hide Tools control, Horizontal scroll bar, Size box

The menu bar lists the names of individual menus. When you click a menu name, such as File, and hold down the mouse button, you see a list of commands and options that affect the file in some way. Some of the commands and options in a menu appear in light gray, which means that they are available only after you do something else within the document. For example, to use the Copy and Paste commands in word processing, spreadsheet, and database documents, you first must select the data you want to copy. Then the command appears in black, meaning that it is available. After you use the Copy command, the Paste command becomes available.

Four menus listed in the menu bar of figure 1.3—File, Edit, Format, and View—appear in all the modules except the communications module, in which Settings replaces Format. Within each module, not all the commands and options listed in a menu are available. For example, the Date, Time, and Page # commands in the Edit menu of the word processing module are not available in the Edit menu of the drawing module.

Following are the other parts of the window that are the same in all modules:

- The close box, which you click to close the document
- The title bar
- The file-name area, which displays the name under which you saved the document (or Untitled, if you have not yet saved the document)
- The horizontal and vertical scroll bars, which help you move to portions of a document that are not visible on-screen
- The zoom controls and percentage box, which enable you to make the document larger and smaller for easier editing
- The size box, which you use to resize the document window
- The page indicator, which lists the number of the page in which you are working
- The Show/Hide Tools control, which you click to display or hide the tool palette

ClarisWorks 2.1 makes it as easy as possible for you to go from one module to another. If you know how to use the Copy and Paste commands in a drawing document, you also know how to use those commands in word processing, spreadsheet, database, and painting documents. This arrangement reduces your "new" learning to those parts of the menus and tools that are specific to each module.

Understanding Document Types and Environments

There are six different kinds of documents you can create in ClarisWorks 2.1. Each module allows you to create a document specific to its environment. For example, if you want to write a letter, you open a word processing document; if you are going to set up a household budget, you use a spreadsheet document. This section gives you an overview of the primary uses of each module.

Word Processing

The purpose of word processing is to create and format text. You can perform the same five processes in any word processing program you use: create a text document, add to it, delete all or part of it, save it, and print all or part of it.

The differences among word processing programs are the "bells and whistles" added to the basic capabilities.

The ClarisWorks word processing module now incorporates most of the extra features provided in stand-alone programs, such as text styles, outlining, text-importing capability, and saving documents in a template format.

Whenever you start a new word processing document or open an existing one, you see the screen features shown in figure 1.4. The menu bar contains the word processing menus as well as the apple menu, the Balloon Help icon, and the program icon. Below the title bar is the text ruler (which is different from the graphics ruler); below that is the ribbon, which contains controls for setting margins, spacing, justification, tabs, and number of columns. The large empty space is the work area, where you will type the text. You can click the Show/Hide Tools control to bring the tool palette into view. Clicking any of the drawing tools lets you use a drawing tool within a text document.

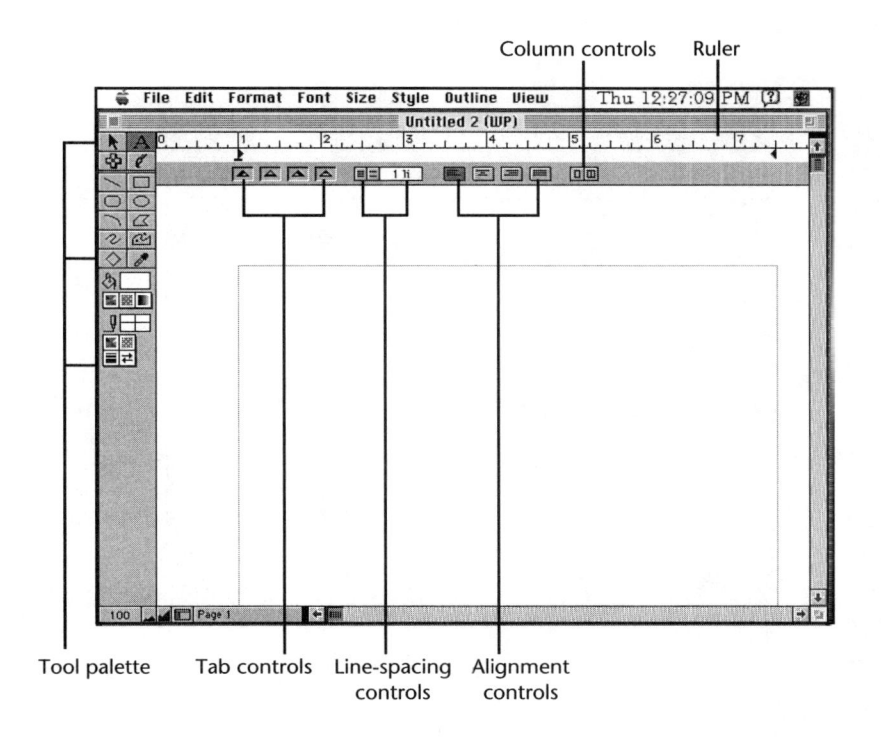

Figure 1.4
A word processing document with the tool palette visible.

New in Version 2.1 of ClarisWorks is automatic hyphenation. When a word needs to be hyphenated, ClarisWorks searches the System folder for the hyphenation dictionary called US Hyphenation to apply the rules of hyphenation to the word. US Hyphenation is automatically installed when you use the Easy Install method of installing ClarisWorks 2.1 on the hard drive.

Spreadsheet

Many people think that a spreadsheet's use is limited to crunching numbers and doing scientific calculations. It is true that the primary function of a spreadsheet is to organize numeric information, but at times, the spreadsheet format is the best way to present information. If you want to make a schedule—home and away games, work schedule, weekly schedule, who's responsible for which chores, and so on—a spreadsheet document, or *worksheet*, is the fastest and easiest way to set it up. Whenever a document calls for many columns of varying sizes, spreadsheet is the ideal format, whether or not numbers are involved.

Figure 1.5 shows a traditional use for a worksheet.

Figure 1.5
Spreadsheet data and the resulting chart.

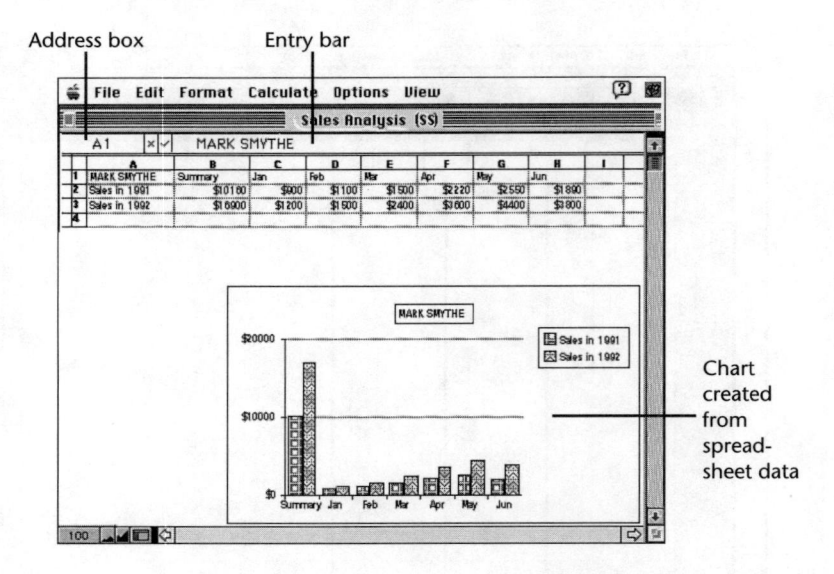

As the figure shows, you can make a chart from spreadsheet information. After you highlight the data you want to chart, you can click an icon or make various choices in a dialog box, and ClarisWorks does the rest of the work to create the chart. Because ClarisWorks 2.1 is an integrated software package, you can use the drawing or painting tools to change the colors in the chart; you also can enter a comment about the chart.

The work area in a worksheet consists of rows and columns. You don't type information in those rows and columns, however; you type information into the entry bar and then press the Return key. When you press Return, the information appears in the *active cell* (the outlined cell in the work area). The address box shows the location of the active cell.

Database

A database stores information on a certain subject, such as clients, students in a school district, or people invited to a wedding. You can search databases to find out specific information, such as which clients are in arrears, which students have Mrs. Brown as their adviser, and which wedding guests are out-of-towners who will need hotel accommodations. The usefulness of a database depends on whether you can extract this kind of information easily.

Figure 1.6 shows an example of the kinds of categories, or *fields*, you might use to store information in a database.

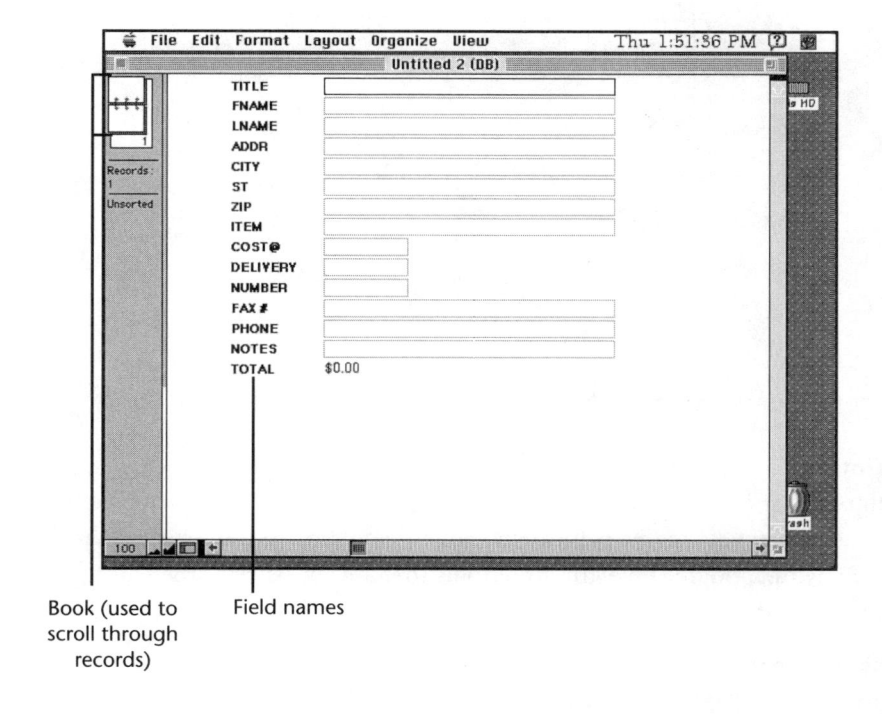

Figure 1.6
A database document in Browse view.

Book (used to scroll through records)   Field names

Drawing

This module is one of two graphics modules in ClarisWorks 2.1. The tools that appear when you open a drawing document are the same tools that are available in the word processing, spreadsheet, and database modules.

Chapter 1—What is ClarisWorks?

Whenever you open a drawing document, you see a graphics ruler. It differs from a text ruler in that the graphics ruler appears horizontally and vertically. Also, a drawing document has two new menus: Arrange and Options. The commands in those menus enable you to perform certain drawing tasks, such as making objects overlap, turning the graphics grid on or off, and grouping several objects into one object.

You use the drawing module primarily for creating and importing graphics as well as for creating page layouts. Figure 1.7 shows how a tree can be drawn in this module. Anything you create in a drawing document—text, a spreadsheet, or a graphic—is an *object*. An object has handles that allow you to move it, resize it, and even change its color, pattern, or gradient. You can easily edit text or a spreadsheet inside a frame in this environment.

Figure 1.7
You may not put yourself in the "artist" category, but the drawing tools can help you create graphics you did not think possible.

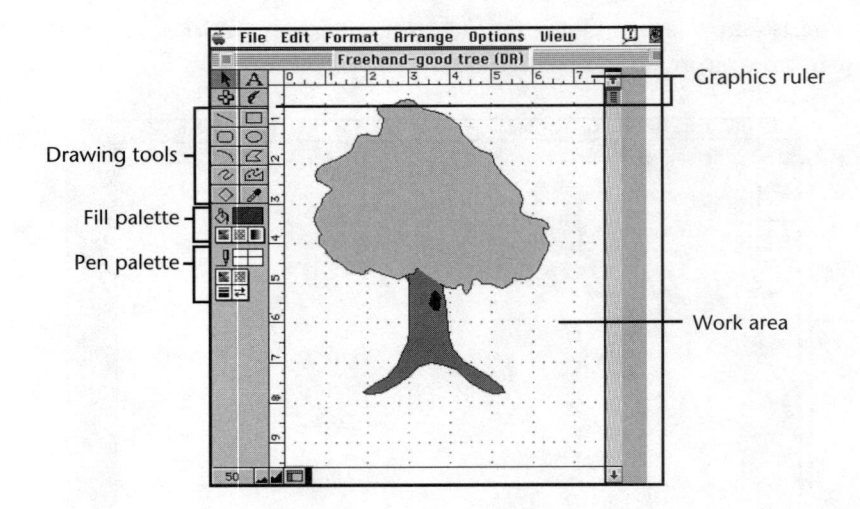

Painting

Painting is the second graphics module in ClarisWorks 2.1. The tool palette you see when you open a painting document contains all the tools that are in the drawing module and eight other tools that are exclusive to the painting environment.

Any picture you create in the painting module, or any graphic you import into this module, is an *image*. An image consists of many small squares, called *pixels*, that you can edit one at a time.

Figure 1.8 shows a portion of a painting image magnified 800 percent for easy editing. Editing may take a little longer in the painting module than in the drawing module, but it gives you more control of the image.

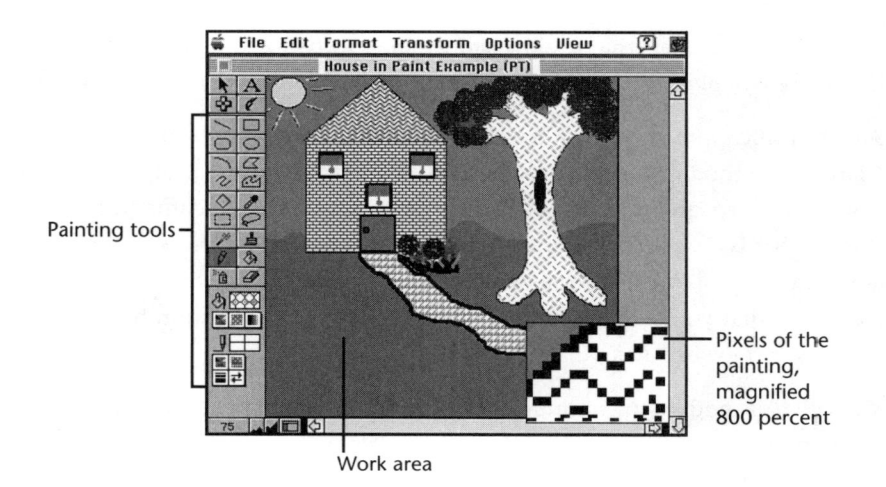

Understanding Document Types and Environments **19**

Figure 1.8
A painting document with a group of pixels magnified 800 percent.

Painting tools

Pixels of the painting, magnified 800 percent

Work area

You can create text and spreadsheet frames in the painting module, so this is the best module to use when you need to create illustrations for newsletters, brochures, or reports.

Communications

The opening screen of the communications module (see fig. 1.9) is somewhat different from the opening screens of the other modules. The menus are different, and the tool palette is not available in the communications module.

Status bar

Scrollback pane

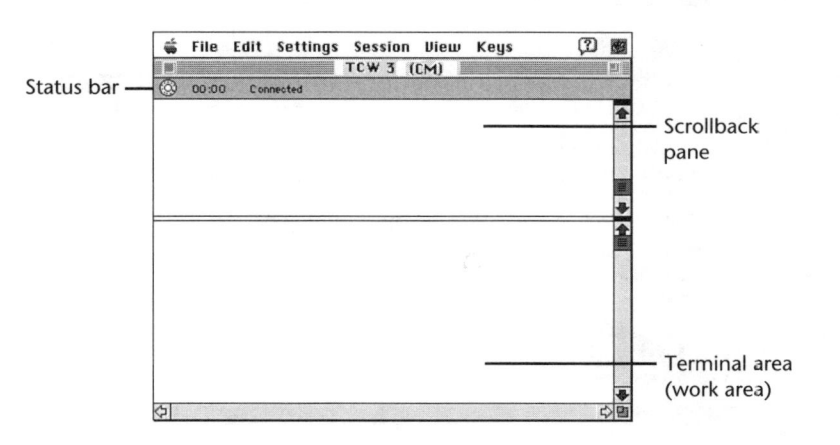

Terminal area (work area)

Figure 1.9
A ClarisWorks communications document.

The communications environment consists of two parts: telecommunications and electronic mail. Telecommunications requires a computer, a telecommunications software program, and a modem that connects with telephone lines. Electronic mail requires a computer that is electronically connected with other computers that use the same e-mail software. If you want to send or receive e-mail outside a networked area, you also need a modem.

A communications document looks different from documents in other ClarisWorks modules. The menu bar lists two new menus—Settings and Session—and there are no control icons at the bottom of the document. Below the title bar is a status bar that reports the status of a connection to another computer. The scrollback pane, which is the top half of the window, keeps a record of what you communicate during the session. The bottom half of the window is the work area.

You use this module to communicate with other computers by sending and receiving messages.

Using Frames for Integration

As you learned earlier in this chapter, the ClarisWorks modules are integrated, meaning that you can use one module's features in another module's document. You can accomplish integration by using frames (see fig. 1.10).

Figure 1.10
A word processing document containing spreadsheet, painting, and text frames.

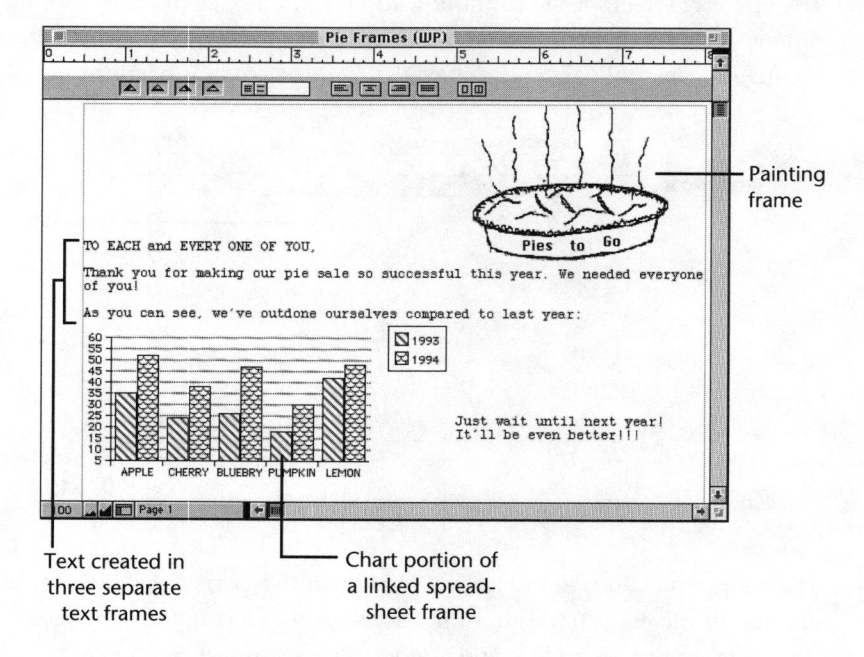

A *frame* is an object that you can insert anywhere in a document. For example, while you are working in a spreadsheet document, you can create a text or painting frame so that you don't have to leave the spreadsheet module to create an annotation or an illustration.

You can link some kinds of frames. For example, you may want certain data from a spreadsheet to appear on page 2 of a word processing document, and you may want page 4 to contain the chart that you made from the spreadsheet data. You can accomplish these tasks by creating linked frames and then placing the necessary information in them.

Understanding the Tools

Using ClarisWorks to the fullest means learning to use all the available tools (see fig. 1.11).

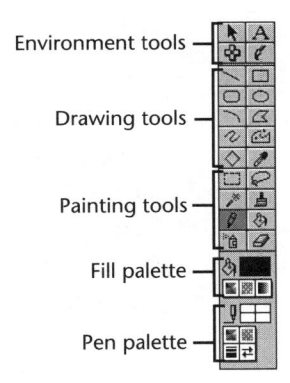

Figure 1.11
The complete tool palette.

These tools are available in almost every module of ClarisWorks 2.1. (Tools are unavailable in the communications module; they are available in the database module only in documents displayed in Layout view.) The tool palette automatically appears when you open a drawing or painting document. To display the tool palette in word processing, spreadsheet, and (Layout view) database documents, click the Show/Hide Tools control at the bottom of the document window.

In any module, you have the choice of displaying or hiding the tool palette. Keeping the tools visible in the drawing and painting modules makes sense. In the other three modules, you can make the tools visible only when you want to draw a frame or import data from a different module; hiding the tools at all other times gives you more screen space for the main document.

Environment Tools

You should constantly be aware of the shape of the mouse pointer, because each shape denotes a special function. You want to be sure that you are about to use the proper tool for the job you want to accomplish.

When you click one of the environment tools (see fig. 1.12), the mouse pointer changes shape. The text tool makes the pointer an I-beam, which indicates that a word processing function is active. The spreadsheet tool changes the pointer to a crossbar, meaning that you can draw a spreadsheet frame and then use the spreadsheet tools. When you click the painting tool, the pointer changes to a brush, and all the tools and menus of the painting module become available. The workhorse environment tool is the drawing tool, which changes the mouse pointer to an arrow. In every ClarisWorks 2.1 module, the mouse pointer becomes an arrow when you choose menu commands, click tools, or use the scroll bars.

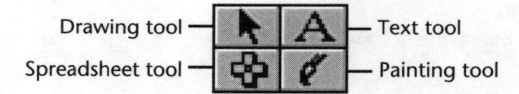

Figure 1.12
The environment tools.

Drawing tool — ▶   A — Text tool
Spreadsheet tool — ✥   ✎ — Painting tool

You also can use the environment tools to create a frame or linked frames in a document. In most modules, after you make a frame, it becomes an object that you can resize and move. In the painting module, however, the contents of a frame become an image as soon as you click outside the frame. Like any image, it needs to be selected before it can be moved. Resizing is done by altering individual pixels.

Drawing Tools

Figure 1.13 shows the drawing tools, which are available in most modules of ClarisWorks 2.1.

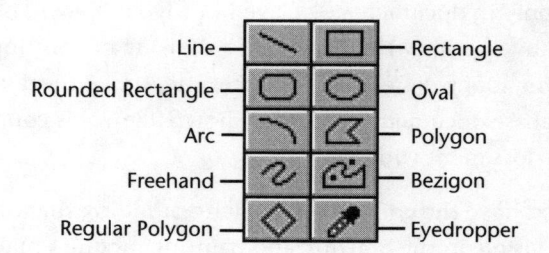

Figure 1.13
The drawing tools.

Line — ╲   ▭ — Rectangle
Rounded Rectangle — ▢   ◯ — Oval
Arc — ⌒   ◺ — Polygon
Freehand — ∿   ✍ — Bezigon
Regular Polygon — ◇   ⚲ — Eyedropper

Painting Tools

In addition to the drawing tools, you can use eight other tools in a painting document, frame, or linked frame (see fig. 1.14). Whenever you create a picture, text frame, or spreadsheet frame in the painting module, ClarisWorks treats that entity as an image.

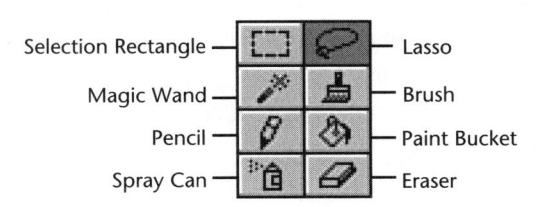

Figure 1.14
Additional tools available only in the painting module.

Fill and Pen Palettes

At the bottom of the tool palette are two smaller palettes. When you click the color, pattern, or gradient box in the Fill palette, your choice affects objects such as circles, rectangles, and polygons. When you click the color, pattern, or line-size box in the Pen palette, you can change the size, shape, color, and pattern of lines and borders. The default colors and patterns are the same in the Fill and Pen palettes. Figure 1.15 shows these default colors, patterns, and gradients, as well as the choices for line width and arrows.

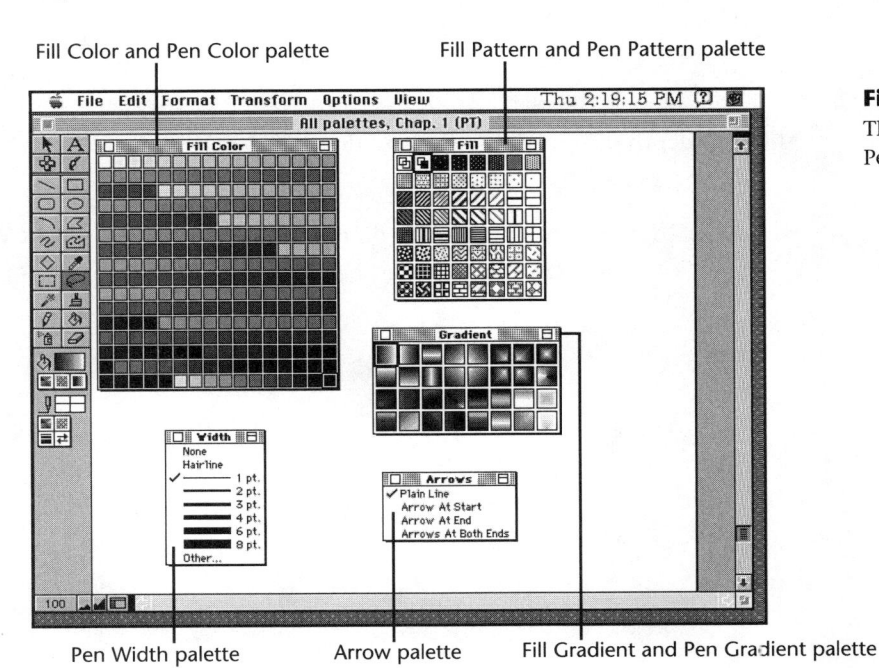

Figure 1.15
The Fill and Pen palettes.

You can *tear off* (click and drag to a new location) a palette to keep that palette open. For example, if you need to change the Fill Indicator frequently, tearing off the palette makes the work simpler by eliminating several steps. You can move the open palette anywhere in the document and close it by clicking its close box. If you want the palette to be readily available but do not want it to take up document space on-screen, collapse the palette by clicking the box in the top-right corner (opposite the close box). To reopen the palette, click the same box again.

From Here...

This chapter introduced the various aspects of ClarisWorks 2.1. The remainder of the book explains in detail how to use this versatile software program.

- For in-depth information on the word processing module, see Part II, chapters 3–5.

- For in-depth information on the drawing and painting modules, see Part II, chapters 6 and 7.

- For in-depth information on the spreadsheet module, see Part II, chapters 8–11.

- For in-depth information on the database module, see Part III, chapters 12–14.

- For in-depth information on integration, see Part IV, chapters 15 and 16.

- For in-depth information on the communications module, see Part V, chapters 17 and 18.

Chapter 2
Learning the Essentials

by Catherine Fishel Morris

This chapter takes you through the basic operations of ClarisWorks 2.1. The chapter begins with opening the ClarisWorks folder on the Desktop and ends with exiting the ClarisWorks program.

Access to ClarisWorks is a hierarchical process: First, you open the software program's folder icon; then you open the program icon; and finally, you can create a document.

If you are familiar with the Macintosh environment, you will recognize the commands—Open, Close, Save, Print, and so on—as standard fare for the Macintosh operating system. This chapter takes the commands one step further by explaining not only what each one accomplishes, but also the slight (yet important) differences between similar commands. You must know, for example, when to use the Save command and when to use the Save As command. You also must understand what happens when you opt for the Close command instead of the Quit command, and vice versa.

This chapter provides an overall picture of how to use the ClarisWorks software.

Working with Documents

A *document* is a file of information you create in any one of the six modules available in ClarisWorks 2.1. When you work in any module of the ClarisWorks program—word processing, spreadsheet, database, drawing, painting, or communications—you are working within a document. In any of these modules, you can open a document, save it, print it, and close it. You also can reopen a document whenever you need to edit it.

26 Chapter 2—Learning the Essentials

You choose a ClarisWorks module based on the kind of work you need to do. If you have to write a letter to a client, you use the word processing module. If you want a sales report to compare this quarter's performance to last quarter's, spreadsheet is the best module to use. If you need to design a company logo, you may choose the drawing module.

You can create a document when you start ClarisWorks. You also can create a new document after you open the ClarisWorks program.

Creating a Document

ClarisWorks 2.1 is installed on the hard drive (either internal or external), and the program folder appears in the Finder or on the Desktop. Follow these steps to open a ClarisWorks document:

1. Double-click the ClarisWorks folder to open the folder.

2. Double-click the ClarisWorks program icon to open the program. The New Document dialog box appears (see fig. 2.1).

Figure 2.1
The New Document dialog box.

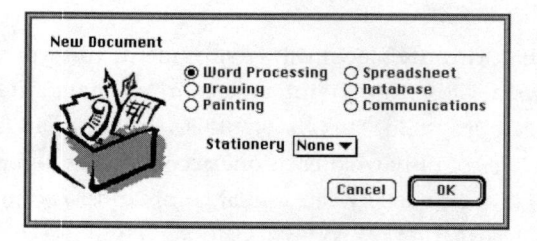

Tip
You also can open a module by double-clicking that module's button in the New Document dialog box.

3. Click the button next to the name of the module you want to use; then choose OK. The document opens with the default name (Untitled 1 is the first document you open; Untitled 2 is the second, and so on), followed by the initials of the current module in parentheses—for example, Untitled 1 (WP). When you save the document the first time, you can give it a meaningful name. (See "Saving a Document" later in this chapter.)

Figure 2.2 shows how a word processing window looks when you open a new document.

Working with Documents   27

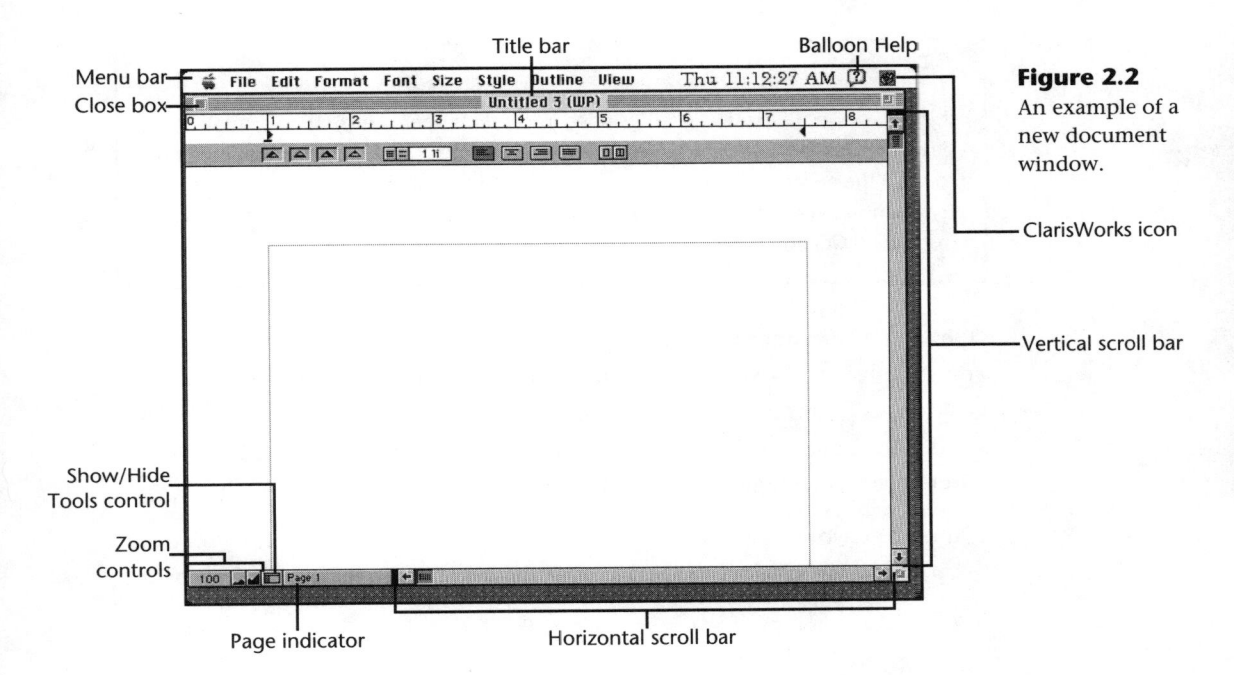

Figure 2.2
An example of a new document window.

Labels on figure: Menu bar, Close box, Title bar, Balloon Help, ClarisWorks icon, Vertical scroll bar, Show/Hide Tools control, Zoom controls, Page indicator, Horizontal scroll bar

The following list explains the initials ClarisWorks uses in the title bar of a document to identify the module in which you are working:

- (WP) = word processing
- (DR) = drawing
- (PT) = painting
- (SS) = spreadsheet
- (DB) = database
- (CM) = communications

Follow these steps to open a new document while the ClarisWorks program is running:

1. Choose New from the File menu. The New Document dialog box appears.
2. Click the button preceding the type of document you want to create.
3. Choose OK.

Tip
In the New Document dialog box, you can use the Tab and arrow keys to move from one module to another. You also can press ⌘-1 to choose word processing, ⌘-2 to choose drawing, and so on.

28 Chapter 2—Learning the Essentials

> **Caution**
>
> If you have word processing and painting documents open, and you open another painting document, you are likely to get a message that there is not enough memory to open the new document. Save and close one of the other documents, and then try again. Another option is to increase the memory allocation (see the ClarisWorks Installation Guide).

Opening a Document

You can place a ClarisWorks document in the ClarisWorks folder on the Desktop, or you can store the document on a floppy disk. To retrieve a document from either location, double-click the document icon. The ClarisWorks program starts and opens the document.

You may be working in one ClarisWorks document and decide that you need to open an existing document. To accomplish this task, follow these steps:

1. Choose Open from the File menu. The Open dialog box appears (see fig. 2.3).

Figure 2.3
The Open dialog box.

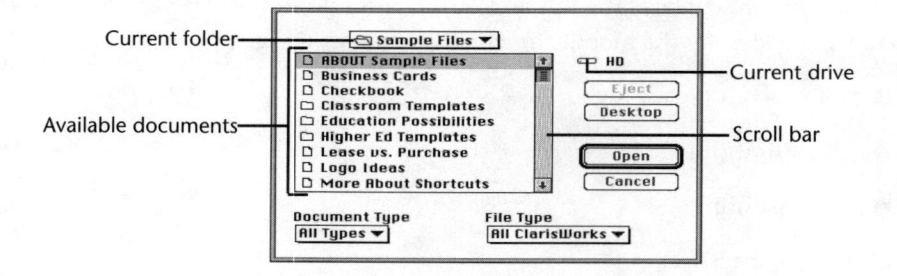

Current folder
Available documents
Current drive
Scroll bar

2. Click the name of the file you want to open, and then choose Open. Alternatively, you can double-click the name of the file.

> **Note**
>
> If you don't see the name of the file you want when the dialog box opens, you may have to switch folders or disks (depending on where the document is stored) or scroll through the names in the list box. To scroll the list, click the up or down arrow in the scroll bar.

The pop-up menus at the bottom of the dialog box enable you to access different kinds of documents. For more information, see "Importing a Document" later in this chapter.

Saving a Document

You may be working on one document and decide to open another. While you go on to edit the second document, the first document remains in the background. The first document is in the computer's memory and will stay there until you quit ClarisWorks, turn off the computer, or experience an interruption in the power source. To protect the file from inadvertent loss, you need to save the document and give it a meaningful name.

Even after an initial save, if you do not perform save operations periodically, the chances of losing all or some of a document are higher than you may like to think. Expect a painful experience if you lose hours of work because you decide not to save until the document is complete. You need to have that experience only once to learn that saving frequently is much easier than reconstructing an entire document.

The first time you save a document, you can use either the Save or the Save As command, each of which has a specific function.

Before you can save a document, the document must be active. To save a document for the first time, click anywhere in the document to make it active, and then follow these steps:

1. Choose Save As from the File menu. The Save As dialog box appears (see fig. 2.4).

2. Look carefully at the current folder and the current disk. You may want to save the document to a different location. To see other options, click the arrow in the Current Folder box or click the Desktop button.

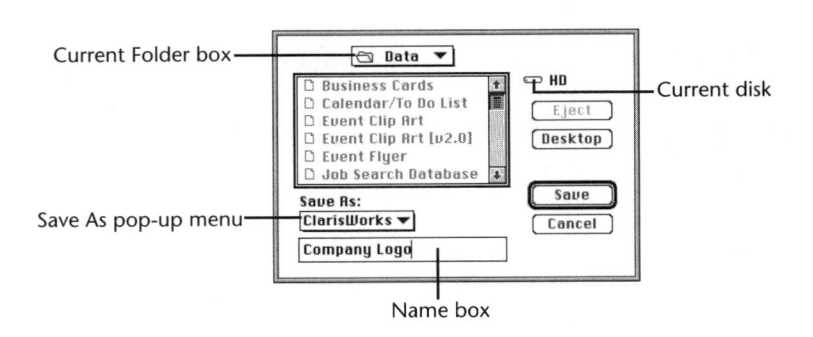

Tip
As a practice, always save the current document before you open another document.

Figure 2.4
The Save As dialog box.

3. In the Save As text box, type a name that describes the current document. (Because the default name is highlighted, you can simply type the new name; you need not delete the text first.)

4. Choose Save.

When you want to save a document that has been saved before, choose Save from the File menu. While the computer is saving the document, the mouse pointer becomes a clock icon, indicating that the computer is working. You cannot work within the document until the clock changes back to the mouse pointer you were using before the save.

Sometimes you make changes in a document and decide that you want to keep the original as well as a copy with changes. You can have both documents if you use the Save As command and give a new name to the copy of the document with changes. The original document remains, with no changes, under its original name. Follow the preceding steps to save a document with another name.

Making a Backup Copy

The purpose of making a backup copy of a document is to ensure that you have a duplicate in case the original is lost or destroyed. Unfortunately, damage can occur on a hard disk as well as on a floppy. Backups, therefore, are stored separately from originals. If an original document is located on the hard drive, you want to back it up on a floppy. If the document first appears on a floppy, you can back it up on another floppy or on the hard drive.

Follow these steps to make a backup copy on a floppy disk:

1. Insert the floppy disk into the drive. The floppy disk's icon appears on the Desktop.

2. Double-click the hard disk icon to open it.

3. Click the document icon for the file you want to copy, and, without releasing the mouse button, drag the document icon to the floppy disk's icon. Then release the mouse button. A copy of the document is placed on the floppy disk.

> **Note**
>
> If an earlier copy of this document already exists (with the same name) on the floppy disk, a message box appears, asking whether you want to replace the existing copy with the new version. Click OK to approve the replacement.

Sometimes, you need to place a copy of a document on the hard drive temporarily—for example, to copy a document from one floppy disk to another on a computer with a single floppy disk drive. In that situation, you first copy the document from the floppy disk to the hard drive and then from the hard drive to the second floppy disk. To copy a document from a floppy disk to the hard drive, follow these steps:

1. Double-click the floppy disk's icon to open that disk.

2. Double-click the hard drive's icon to open the hard drive.

3. Click the document icon for the file you want to copy, and drag it to the folder on the hard drive in which you want to place the document.

> **Note**
>
> Save those documents you create but do not access often to floppy disks, and reserve the hard drive primarily for programs, such as ClarisWorks. Accessing documents from a floppy does take longer than accessing them from the hard drive, but if the drive crashes, you still have the original program disks as well as all the data on floppy disks.

Going Back to the Last Saved Version

If you make changes in a saved document, you can eliminate those changes and restore the preceding version of the document by choosing Revert from the File menu. This command is particularly helpful in a drawing or painting document if you want to experiment with a picture. If you don't like the result of the experiment, Revert eliminates the need to undo all the changes by hand. Revert also is useful in a spreadsheet document, in which you may want to try a series of "what if" questions.

Alternatively, you can eliminate changes by closing the document and choosing not to save the altered version. When you try to close a document without saving it, ClarisWorks asks you to confirm the fact that you want to discard the latest changes.

Closing a Document

When you choose to close a document, you are saying, in effect, that you are finished with the document and no longer need it in the computer's memory. Closing a document is different from quitting the program. The following list helps you understand what happens and the options you have for saving when you decide to close a document.

Tip
If you have several documents open and want to close all of them at the same time, hold down the Option key while you click the close box of any open document.

- To close a ClarisWorks document, you can click its close box or choose Close from the File menu. The closed document is no longer available for use until you open it again.

- When you close a document that you have changed since performing the last save operation, a dialog box appears, offering you the opportunity to save the document. Saving before you close ensures that all changes from the current session are saved in your document.

- When you click the close box of a ClarisWorks document, the ClarisWorks icon remains in the menu bar at the top of the screen. This icon shows that the ClarisWorks program is still running.

Getting Help

There are several places where you can find answers to questions about the ClarisWorks software. You can get on-screen help from the ClarisWorks Help command and the Apple Balloon Help feature. In addition, the ClarisWorks software includes sample documents that explain the various kinds of documents you can create. These documents are templates that act as springboards to get you working on documents quickly.

ClarisWorks Help

While you are working on a ClarisWorks document, you can access on-screen help. You can activate the Help dialog box for instructions and reference information while the active document remains open.

When you access the ClarisWorks Help while you are working on a document, you see information that is relevant to the current module. If you are working in the spreadsheet module, for example, you get the help pages that pertain to spreadsheets.

Figure 2.5 shows the general ClarisWorks Help screen. You can select any specific information area, or use the icons at the top right to move from one piece of information to another.

You can choose Help from the apple menu. The opening screen varies, depending on what you are working on in ClarisWorks when you choose Help.

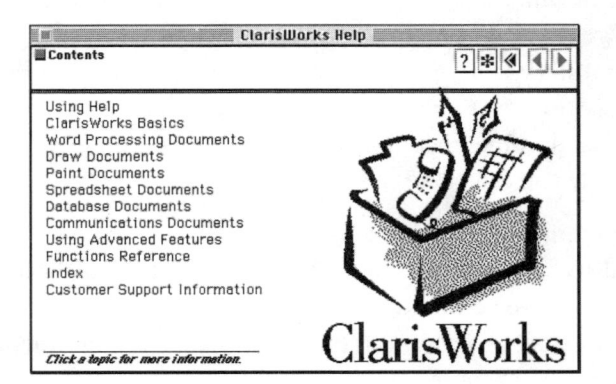

Figure 2.5
The ClarisWorks Help screen.

You can move the ClarisWorks Help window around on-screen by clicking and dragging the title bar. To close the Help window, click the close box.

Balloon Help

If your computer uses System 7 or later, the Balloon Help pop-up menu is present at every screen level. Balloon Help gives short descriptions of tools, icons, and menus. These descriptions are reminders of what a tool does, or what the icon stands for; they are not explanations of how to use the tools, icons, and menus.

To use Balloon Help, click the question mark at the right end of the menu bar, holding down the mouse button. The Balloon Help menu appears (see fig. 2.6). Drag down to choose Show Balloons from the menu. Subsequently, you see a description of any icon, tool, or menu simply by pointing at it with your mouse pointer. Every time your mouse pointer passes over or rests on one of these items, a description of the item appears on-screen. To turn Balloon Help off, click the question mark again, holding down the mouse button, and then choose Hide Balloons from the menu.

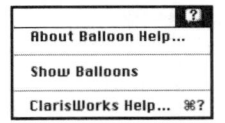

Figure 2.6
The Balloon Help pop-up menu.

Working with Windows

The document window is the world in which you do your work. By default, the window shows a portion of a document page. You can customize or change that display temporarily to see multiple views of a document, to see an entire page, to view more than one part of the document at a time, or to arrange several document windows on-screen. The purpose of this section is to explain how you can alter the view of your window.

Showing or Hiding Tools and Rulers

The tool palette and either the text ruler or the graphics ruler can be visible in a document when you need them for your work. When they are not necessary to the work at hand, they can be hidden so there is more actual working area available in the window.

To show or hide the rulers, choose the Show Rulers/Hide Rulers command from the View menu. Because this command is a toggle switch, the inactive command is the option in the menu (in other words, if rulers currently appear on-screen, the View menu offers the Hide Rulers option, and so on). In the word processing module, the text ruler is set to appear automatically whenever you open a document.

The tools are visible when you open a drawing or painting document. To show them in any other module (except communications), choose Show Tools or Hide Tools from the View menu, or click the Show/Hide Tools control at the bottom of the document window.

Zooming to Rescale the Contents of a Window

In ClarisWorks, you frequently may need to *rescale* (make larger or smaller) the contents of a window. Sometimes you need to view an entire page of a document to make sure it looks right before you print it. To view an entire page, you *zoom out,* or reduce the contents. *Zooming in* (making the contents larger) helps you see details better when editing, especially in the drawing and painting modules. Zooming does not change the size of the window; it changes the size of the window's contents. Further, zooming in or out does not alter the printout. You change the size of the printout only by changing the scale percentage in the Page Setup dialog box.

To rescale the contents of a window, use the zoom controls at the lower-left corner of the document window (see fig. 2.7).

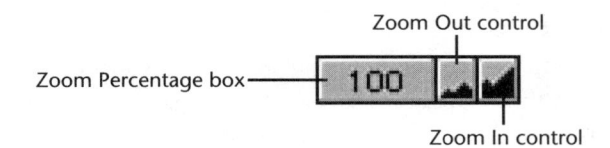

Working with Windows **35**

Figure 2.7
The zoom controls.

Zoom Out control
Zoom Percentage box
Zoom In control

You use these controls in the following ways:

- Click the Zoom Out control to decrease the size of the document. Repeatedly clicking this control reduces your document to as small as 3.13 percent of the original size of the document.

- Click the Zoom Out control to enlarge the size of the document. Repeatedly clicking this control enlarges your document to a maximum of 3,200 percent of the original size of the document.

- Use the Zoom Percentage box for a more precise, and sometimes faster, method of enlarging or decreasing the size of the document. Click the box, and the Percentage pop-up menu appears (see fig. 2.8). Choose a percentage of increase or decrease from the menu.

Tip
Press the Option key and click the Zoom Out control to reduce the scale by 50 percent. Press the Option key and click the Zoom In control to double the size of the document.

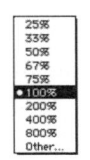

Figure 2.8
The Percentage pop-up menu.

If the menu doesn't list the percentage you want, choose Other to customize. The dialog box shown in figure 2.9 appears. Enter a percentage of increase or decrease in the View Scale text box, and then choose OK.

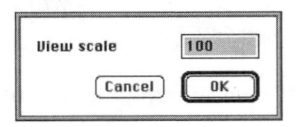

Figure 2.9
The Custom Percentage dialog box.

You can return the document to actual size at any time. Choosing 100 in the Custom Percentage dialog box immediately returns your document to actual size. Alternatively, you can click the Zoom In or Zoom Out control until you reach the 100 percent level.

Using Multiple Document Views

Seeing a document in multiple views has many advantages, but you must use this option carefully. Although it's nice to see different parts of the document at the same time, with each view in its own window, you need to keep in mind that any change you make in any view changes your original document.

Multiple views of documents in the database module are especially helpful. Displaying your document in both Layout view and Browse view makes designing the look of the database—the size and placement of field names and field variables—much easier than toggling back and forth between the views.

To open a second view, choose New View from the View menu. A new window appears, with the document name followed by the number 2 in the title bar. If you open another view, the document name in its title bar is followed by 3, and so on. If you have several views on-screen, you may want to return to a previous view. Each view is listed at the bottom of the View menu; choose the view you want to see.

Be alert as to which view you are saving. Regardless of which view contains your original document, whatever view is *active* when you use the Save command becomes the original document and is saved to the storage area (disk or hard drive).

Splitting Windows

Sometimes (especially when you work in the spreadsheet module), the top or far left portion of your document contains labeling information that gives meaning to the information on the right side or bottom of the document. If you scroll to the right or down, the labels disappear. To solve this problem, you can split the window to display the labels while you scroll horizontally or vertically through the rest of the information.

Figure 2.10 shows a window split horizontally to produce a top pane and bottom pane (such as a house's windowpane). The top pane of the split window provides a constant display of the column header information, while you scroll through the columns' figures in the lower pane.

Working with Windows 37

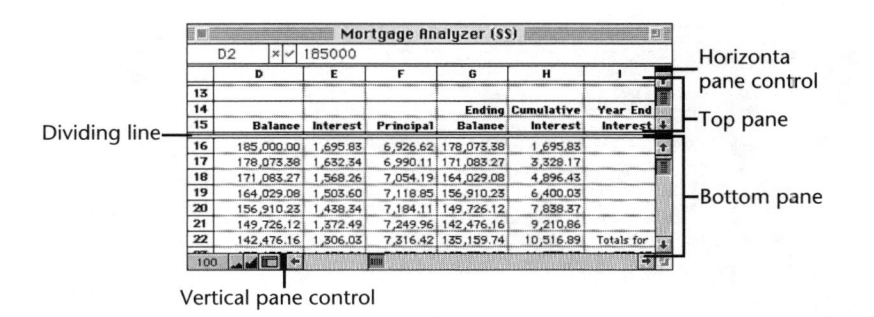

Figure 2.10
A spreadsheet document with a split window.

(Figure shows a Mortgage Analyzer spreadsheet with labels: Dividing line, Horizontal pane control, Top pane, Bottom pane, Vertical pane control)

The pane controls are the small black rectangles at the top (horizontal) and to the left (vertical) of the arrows on the scroll bars. Drag the appropriate pane control to split a window horizontally into top and bottom panes, or vertically into left and right panes. To remove the panes and return to a single window, drag the vertical pane control all the way left or the horizontal pane control all the way to the top.

You can also lock a column or row you use for titles so the rest of the information moves while the titles stay visible in the same place. Select the row or the column you want to lock, and choose Lock Title Position from the Options menu. A checkmark appears next to the option name, showing that it is selected. Similar to the split-window option, locking a row or column gives you a better understanding of all the data you see when the titles are constant. To unlock the row or column, choose Lock Title Position from the Options menu again. The checkmark disappears, and the column or row is like any other in the document.

Tiling Several Open Windows

You might open several windows when you are working in ClarisWorks and then need to see all of them individually. You can see all open windows on-screen at once by *tiling* the windows. Figure 2.11 shows three open windows tiled on-screen. Notice that the windows do not overlap. To see a tiled view of several documents, choose Tile Windows from the View menu. The documents appear top to bottom, as if in rows.

Figure 2.11
A tiled view of documents.

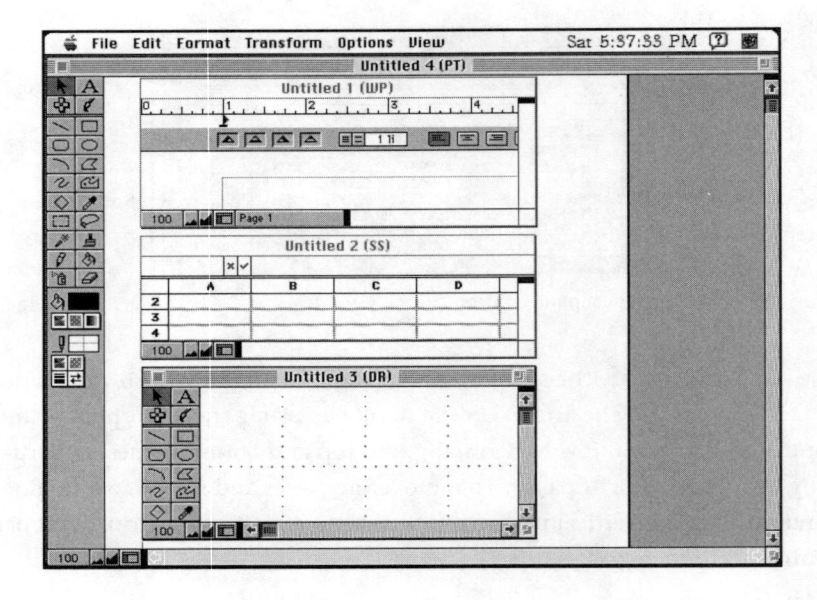

Stacking Several Open Windows

Figure 2.12 shows how you can stack several open windows so the top one is full-size. You easily can make any of the other windows the active document by clicking the window's title bar. To stack windows, choose Stack Windows from the View menu.

Figure 2.12
A stacked view of documents.

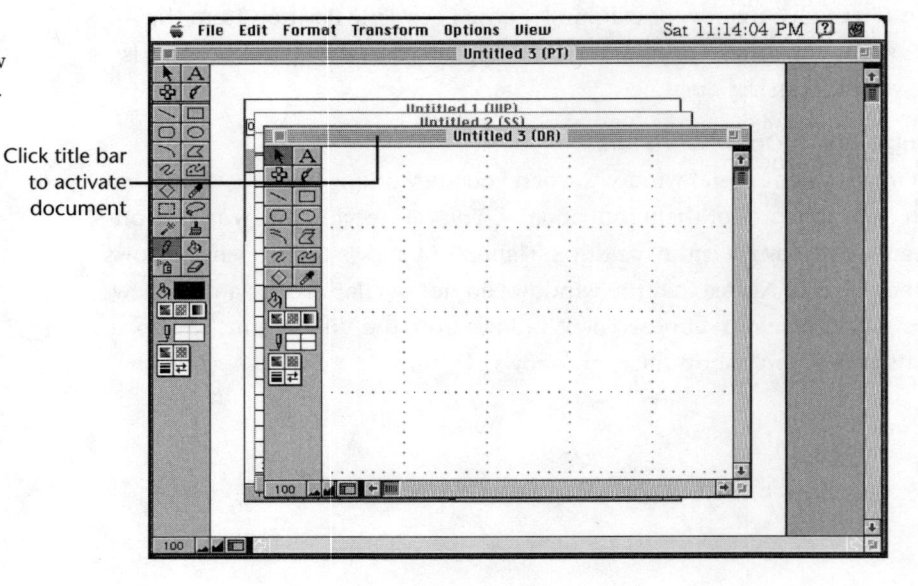

Click title bar to activate document

Working with Pages

ClarisWorks divides a document into pages. The default size of one page is 8.5 inches wide by 11 inches long. Each page consists of margins and a working area. In some circumstances (for example, in a drawing or painting opening screen), the margins, marked by a light gray border called *page guides*, do not show automatically. You can see the page guides if you choose the Page View option from the View menu.

The purpose of this section is to go through the general aspects that involve how a page looks. It explains how you can change default settings. You learn how to create page breaks so information can flow the way you want. You also learn how to add a header or footer for a title to appear on each page or for pages to be numbered.

Viewing Pages

ClarisWorks can display your documents in *WYSIWYG* (What You See Is What You Get). You see WYSIWYG when you choose Page View from the View menu. Page View gives you an opportunity to see what a printout of the document will look like before you actually print it out. The only area where this does not apply is in the database module. In the Layout view of a database, you can set the fields so there are no unwanted empty spaces between pieces of information. When you look at the information in Browse view, unwanted empty spaces may still appear between a first and last name or a city and state. The printout should print with none of the unwanted spaces.

In a word processing document, Page View is the default view in any document, but the page guides are dimmed. You can turn off this default by choosing Document from the Format menu. The Document dialog box appears. Deselect the Show Margins and Show Page Guides options.

When you work in modules other than word processing, keep Page View turned off. You then can work in the full-screen view, and you don't sacrifice space to margins.

Moving Directly to a Page

When you are working in a long document, scrolling between pages can be inconvenient. ClarisWorks has an option with which you can move directly to any page in the document. To use the Go To Page feature, follow these steps:

   1. Double-click the page indicator at the bottom of the document screen. The dialog box shown in figure 2.13 appears.

Figure 2.13
The Go To Page dialog box.

2. Key in the number of the page you want to go to.

3. Click OK.

The Page Settings

Each ClarisWorks module has its own dialog box for formatting the overall look of the document. Each module also has its own default settings. Figure 2.14 is an example of the word processing module's Document dialog box, showing the default page settings. As the figure demonstrates, when you open a new word processing document, all margins are set to 1 inch, and the page numbering begins with 1. The page display shows one page at a time, with the margin and page guides visible. The document has no title page.

Figure 2.14
The Document dialog box for word processing.

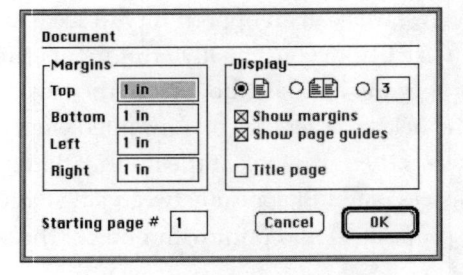

Although the defaults represent the common choice of the majority of word processing module users, you can customize any and all of the page settings to suit your individual needs or preferences.

To change the page settings, follow these steps:

1. Choose Document from the Format menu. The Document dialog box appears.

2. Key in the margin widths you want. If you want a fraction of an inch, key in a decimal amount such as .5 or .75. To go from one margin setting to the next, use the Tab key.

Working with Pages   **41**

3. Click the button preceding the page display of your choice. You can display more than two pages at a time by clicking the far-right button and keying in the number of pages you want to display. If you do not want the margins and page guides to show, deselect them. Choose Title Page if you want the first page to appear without a header or footer. This option is available only in word processing and database module documents.

4. Key in a Starting Page #.

5. Click OK.

Ruler Settings

ClarisWorks provides two kinds of rulers. For any document or frame that contains text, you use the text ruler. For any document or frame that contains an image or object, you use the graphics rulers. Except in the word processing module (where the ruler appears when you open a document), you use a command to access and specify which ruler is to be part of the document screen.

The text ruler extends horizontally across the top of the document. The text ruler has settings for indenting, tabs, line spacing, justification, and number of columns. The graphics rulers extend horizontally across the top and vertically down the left side of the document. The graphics rulers are there to help you place and line up your objects and images. You can change the ruler settings by following these steps:

1. Choose Rulers from the Format menu. The Rulers dialog box appears (see fig. 2.15).

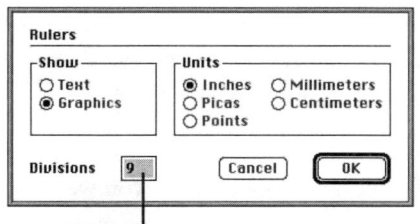

Figure 2.15
The Rulers dialog box.

The number you enter here affects the spacing in the graphic rulers as well as the grid in the drawing and painting modules.

2. Click either the Text or Graphics button, depending on which ruler you need.

3. To change the unit of measurement from inches (the default) click the appropriate button in the Units section. (One inch contains 72 points, or 6 picas; 1 pica contains 12 points.)

4. Key in a number if you want to change the default number of *divisions*, or the size of each Autogrid unit. The graphics ruler and number of dots in each grid unit reflect the number of divisions in the document. If you plan to turn off the Autogrid, do not bother changing this number.

5. Click OK.

Page and Column Breaks

Page breaks are determined by the length of the document and the size of the margins. When one page fills up, a page break occurs, and the information continues on the next page. The same is true when you work in columns; as one column fills, the information flows into the next column.

Sometimes the page and column breaks come at awkward places for your set of information. You can change where a page breaks or column ends by using the appropriate commands.

If you need to change the page or column break in a text document, use the mouse to click and place the insert cursor (a thin flashing line) where you want the break to occur. The new break must occur before (or above) the normal break. Choose Insert Break from the Format menu. That point is now the end of that page.

If you edit your work after you add a page break, you may need to get rid of that page break because it is no longer a good breaking point. To remove a page or column break from a text document, click at the beginning of the line that follows the break, then press Delete.

Adding a page break in a spreadsheet document is a little different. You need to select the cell to the left and above where you want the break to occur. Then choose Add Page Break from the Options menu. The break is marked with a dashed line.

To remove an added page break in a spreadsheet document, click the cell immediately to the left and above the break. Choose Remove Page Break from the Options menu. The break is no longer there.

Headers and Footers

You use a header or footer to place information—text, a graphic, date, time, or page number—on every page in the document. Figure 2.16 shows what a document can look like with both a header and footer appearing on each page. If you use the Insert commands for date and time, those categories are set to always show the current date or time, not the date or time you create the document.

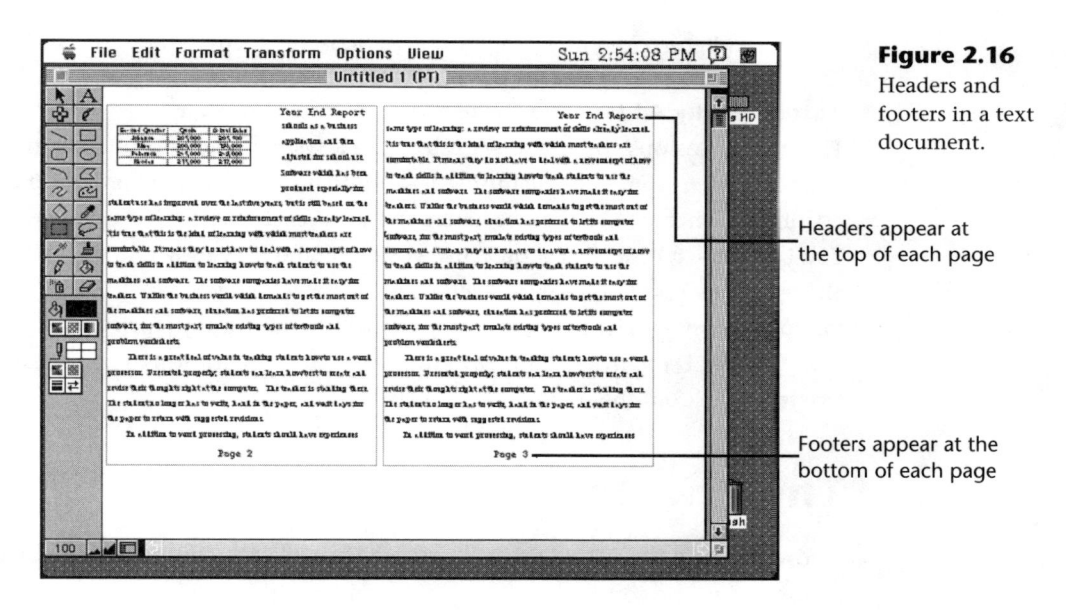

Figure 2.16
Headers and footers in a text document.

Headers appear at the top of each page

Footers appear at the bottom of each page

When you add a header or footer to a document, a light gray box, the length of the document, appears at the top or bottom of the page. In most cases, this line consumes one line of document space. The line can be larger, however, to accommodate pictures; you can increase the height of the header or footer by pressing the Return key. A header or footer can take up as much as one-third of the height of your working area.

You can add a header or footer to a document at any time. As a rule, however, wait until you finish the document to add headers and footers. Before you check all the page break positions or do other editing checks, add one or both. The space consumed by the header or footer alters the formatting of the rest of the document.

To add a header or footer, follow these steps:

1. Choose Insert Header or Insert Footer from the Format menu. A light gray box, one line deep, running the length of the document, appears at the top or bottom of the page.

2. Type the header or footer text; or use the Paste command to position the information that is to appear on each page of the document.

3. Press Return, or click in any other area of the document.

Automatically Adding the Date, Time, or Page Number
There are occasions when you want to place a system date and/or time in your document so it will be automatically updated whenever you open the document. There are also times when you want each page to be numbered. You can place a header or footer into your document as shown in the steps above (or have both appear on each page). Click where you want the information to appear. Then choose from the Edit menu the appropriate command (Insert Date, Insert Time, Insert Page #), and the information appears where you clicked the mouse.

The Printing Process

Before you begin trying to print, check to ensure that the printer is properly connected to the computer; all the cables and plugs must be in the right places. Verify that the printer is on and that you have enough paper in the tray to complete the job.

Selecting the Printer
Next on the checklist is to ensure that in the apple menu, the Chooser is set up to recognize the printer that receives the data. This step is necessary to print out the information. In most cases, you only need to go through this procedure once. If you switch between printers or have a fax/modem connected to your computer, however, you go through this procedure on a regular basis. The following takes you through the necessary steps to enable you to print out documents.

1. Choose Chooser from the apple menu. The Chooser dialog box opens. The look and options available in a Chooser menu depend on the installed drivers. Figure 2.17 is a sample of how one Chooser menu appears.

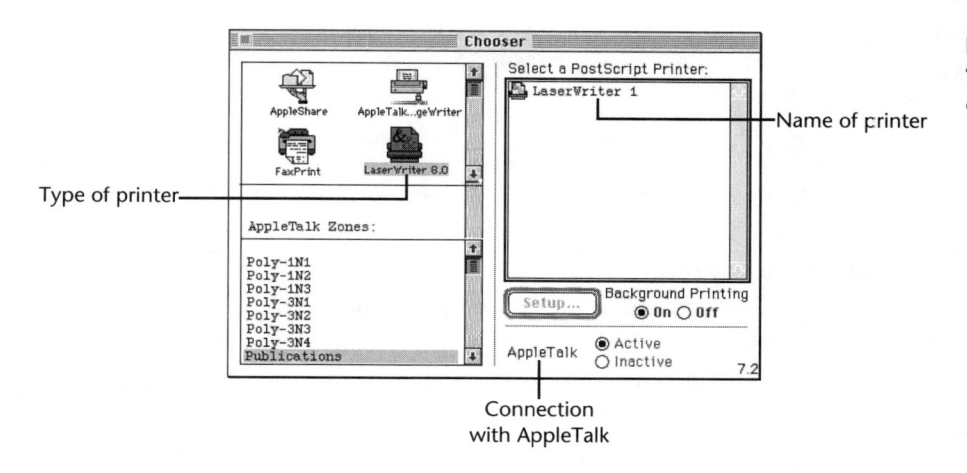

Figure 2.17
The Chooser dialog box.

Type of printer

Name of printer

Connection with AppleTalk

2. Click the icon for the printer that you use. These icons appear on the left side of the Chooser dialog box.

3. Click your printer name on the right side of the Chooser dialog box to highlight it.

4. Click the Background Printing button of your choice (with Background Printing On, you can continue working while the printer is in operation).

5. Click the AppleTalk Active button if your printer needs it to be active. You need to check your printer manual to know if AppleTalk should be active or inactive.

6. Click the close box.

Selecting Page Options

Once you finish with the Chooser, you want to select Page Setup in the File menu. Basically, the Page Setup gives you options for printing your document and envelopes. The Page Setup dialog box is slightly different for each printer; therefore, the look and options you get depend on the kind of printer you are using. Most Page Setup dialog boxes, however, offer choices for the size of paper, the size of envelope, enlarging or decreasing the size of the document, and font formats.

Another standard option is whether to print the information vertically (*portrait* orientation) or horizontally (*landscape* orientation). Figure 2.18 shows the orientation icons.

Figure 2.18
Page Setup icons.

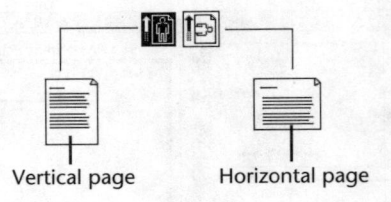

Vertical page   Horizontal page

Printing the Document

After you take care of identifying your printer to your system and making the necessary Page Setup choices, you are ready to actually print a document. Again, the Printer dialog box information will depend on the kind of printer you are using. The example in figure 2.19 may look different from your Printer dialog box (note the 8.0 directly to the left of the Print button, indicating the version of the laser driver), but it holds similar information. Most printers default to printing one copy of the entire document, with no cover page, and feeding directly from the paper cassette. You can change any of those defaults. If you want to check the printed "look" of a large document, you can print a single page or just a few pages by using the Pages option.

Figure 2.19
The Printer dialog box.

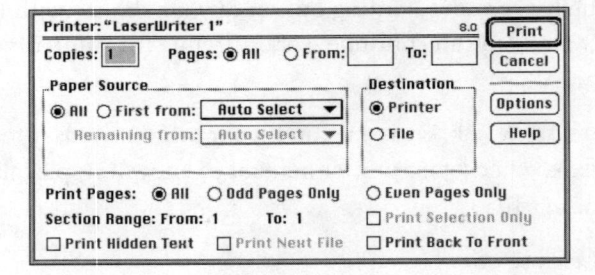

1. With the document open, choose Print from the File menu. The Printer dialog box appears.

2. Choose from among the available options:

   - If you want more than one copy, in the Copies text box, key in the number of copies you want.

   - If you want to print less than the entire document, in the From and To boxes, key in the range of pages to be printed.

   - Change the No option of Cover Page to First Page or Last Page if that is part of the document.

- Change the color designation if you are printing on a color capable printer.

- If you are printing envelopes, change the Paper Source designation.

- Make additional choices if you are printing a spreadsheet (not wanting the cell grid, row, and column headings to print) and database (printing a single record or all visible records).

3. Click Print. If you chose Print In Background from the Chooser, you can continue working on a document or send another document to the printer after all printing messages go off the screen.

Cutting, Copying, and Pasting

Cutting, copying, and pasting are three extremely useful steps for moving information around in a document, to a frame, or to a different document altogether. The information is temporarily placed on the Clipboard, an area of RAM set aside to hold this kind of data. You can access the Clipboard by selecting Show Clipboard in the Edit menu. The following explains what each command, Cut, Copy, and Paste, is capable of doing with text and graphics.

- *Cutting* text, an object, an image, or a number removes it from its position in the document. The information is placed on the Clipboard until something else is put there or the computer is turned off.

- *Copying* text, an object, an image, or a number places a copy of the information on the Clipboard. The original information remains in the document. The copy remains on the Clipboard until something else is placed there or the computer is turned off.

- *Pasting* inserts a copy of the information from the Clipboard into the document at the insertion point.

All of these commands work in the various modules of ClarisWorks except in a communications document. You can copy text, but you cannot cut it. In a communications document, copied text can be sent to the remote computer with which you are in communication and pasted there.

Follow these steps to cut or copy, then paste information:

1. Select the information you want to cut or copy (highlight it by clicking and dragging the mouse over the information).

2. Choose Cut or Copy from the Edit menu. The information, or a copy of the information, is placed on the Clipboard temporarily.

3. Locate the insertion point where you want to place the information, then click (on a spreadsheet cell, for example, or database field variable).

4. Choose Paste from the Edit menu. A copy of the information appears in the document at the insertion point.

Importing, Inserting, and Exporting Documents

With ClarisWorks 2.1, you can import a document from another program into a ClarisWorks document. Similarly, you can export a ClarisWorks document into another program's document. You may have information in a Word 5.0 document, for example, that you want to add to a document you are creating in ClarisWorks. Or you can take information from most of the ClarisWorks modules and place it in a Word, Excel, or FileMaker document.

Importing, inserting, and exporting documents from one program to another is possible because of the translators installed on the hard drive as part of the ClarisWorks program. Regardless of whether you bring the information into ClarisWorks or send it to another program, the original document remains in the format in which it is created.

Importing a Document

When you import a document from a different program, you are not taking the actual document, you are taking a copy of that document. As a result, the original document remains unchanged.

To import a document into ClarisWorks, follow these steps:

1. With ClarisWorks as the active program, select Open from the File menu. The dialog box shown in figure 2.20 appears.

Importing, Inserting, and Exporting Documents **49**

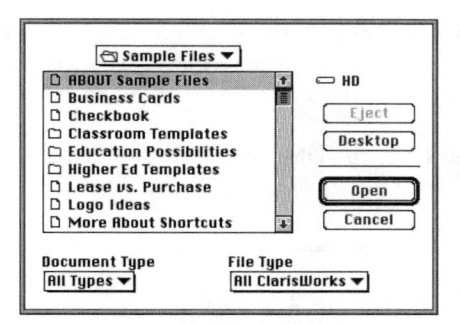

Figure 2.20
Open dialog box showing all available documents.

2. From the Document Type pop-up menu, choose the type of document you want to import (see fig. 2.21).

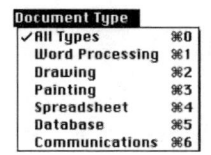

Figure 2.21
Document Type pop-up menu.

3. Choose a file format from the File Type pop-up menu (see fig. 2.22). This list is dependent on the file format you select. If the file format is Word Processing, the File Type pop-up menu is much longer.

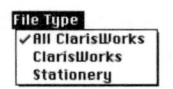

Figure 2.22
File Type pop-up menu.

4. Double-click the name of the document you want to open (or click the name, then the Open button). The word Converted is added to the title. When you close the document, you will be prompted to save changes. Then you can save a converted file to whatever location you want.

Inserting a Document

You use the Insert command from the File menu when you want an entire document brought into an active document. The Insert command can be used with text and graphics documents, but not with data from a database. The following steps explain how to insert an existing document into the one you are presently working on.

50 Chapter 2—Learning the Essentials

1. In the document that is to receive the information, place the cursor, highlight the cell, or click at the location where you want to place the new information.

2. Choose Insert from the File menu. The Insert dialog box appears (see fig. 2.23).

Figure 2.23
Insert dialog box.

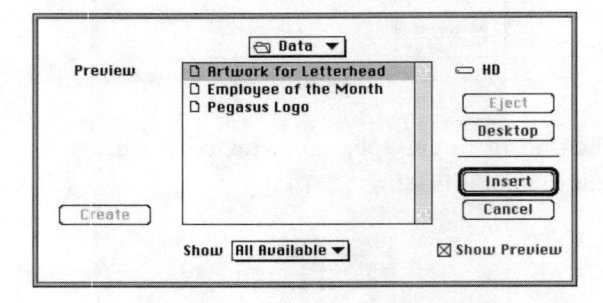

3. Click the Show pop-up menu if you need to select a different document type.

4. Double-click the name of the document you want to open, or click the name, then the Open button. A copy of the document is inserted into the ClarisWorks document.

   If you initially did not place the insertion point where you want the new information to begin, before doing anything else, choose Undo from the Edit menu. The inserted document is deleted and you can try again, following the steps.

Exporting a Document

You can export a ClarisWorks document into a different program. Exporting does not change the original ClarisWorks document, because you export only a copy of the original. To export a document, follow these steps:

1. From the ClarisWorks document you want to export, choose Save As from the File menu. The dialog box shown in figure 2.24 appears.

2. Use the Eject and Desktop buttons, as well as the scroll bar, to locate the disk and folder into which you want to export the ClarisWorks document.

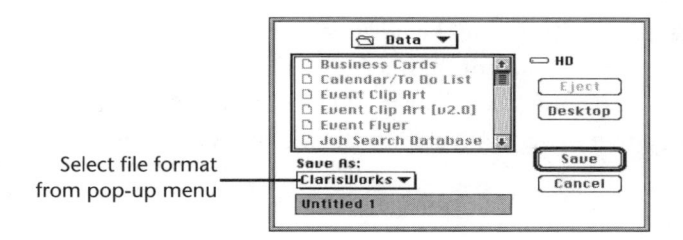

Figure 2.24
Save As dialog box to export a document.

Select file format from pop-up menu

3. Key in a name for the export document.

4. Select the file format type from the Save As pop-up menu.

5. Click Save. A copy of the ClarisWorks document now resides with the new name in the folder and on the disk you chose.

Using the Stationery Option to Create Templates

You can create a template document that customizes the format of a document and then save it as a Stationery document. This is helpful if you need the same choice of font, font size, number of columns, or margin widths frequently when you create word processing documents.

Alternately, ClarisWorks provides you with a number of templates, ready for you to use. You access these templates by clicking Stationery in the New Document screen and selecting one of the several options. Click on the document name, and the template is opened. Put in your own text and graphics in the designated areas, and save the document as a regular ClarisWorks document or as another Stationery document. In either case, save it with a new name. The following steps show how you can save a template (one you create or one of the ClarisWorks templates) as a Stationery document.

1. Create the document, or use one from the ClarisWorks Stationery documents, with all the settings that you want to appear each time you open a copy.

2. Choose Save As from the File menu.

3. Name the document with a meaningful name, and possibly the initials of the module used to create it (for example, WP for word processing).

4. Locate the disk and folder where the document is to be saved. If you want the name of the document to be a choice in the New dialog box under Stationery, save this document to the ClarisWorks Stationery folder (in the System folder), and change the file type to ClarisWorks Stationery.

5. Click Save.

Quitting ClarisWorks

In order to leave ClarisWorks and close everything down, including the program, you need to choose Quit from the File menu. Always go though this procedure before you shut down your computer.

If you click on the close box of a document, that closes the document, not the program itself. If you then work in another software program, the ClarisWorks program software continues to take up memory space. You may not be able to do as much work in the other program for lack of available RAM (Random Access Memory). If you finish your work in ClarisWorks, go through the Quit procedure to get ClarisWorks completely shut down for the time being.

You can use the Quit command to close several open documents at one time. The command checks to see if each document has been saved. If a document was not saved prior to the Quit command, you receive a message that asks whether or not you want to save the document.

For all the above reasons, take the time to use the Quit command when you are ready to leave ClarisWorks.

From Here...

This chapter gives you an overall view of the essential parts of the ClarisWorks 2.1 software program. The following chapters provide more information on specific modules.

- Chapter 3, "Working with Text." Read this chapter for more detailed information regarding word processing.

- Chapter 6, "Drawing," and Chapter 7, "Painting." These chapters describe the ClarisWorks 2.1 graphics modules.

- Chapter 8, "Spreadsheet Basics." Read this chapter for information about spreadsheets.

- Chapter 12, "Database Basics." This chapter introduces you to databases.

- Chapter 17, "Communications Basics." This chapter describes the communications module.

Part II

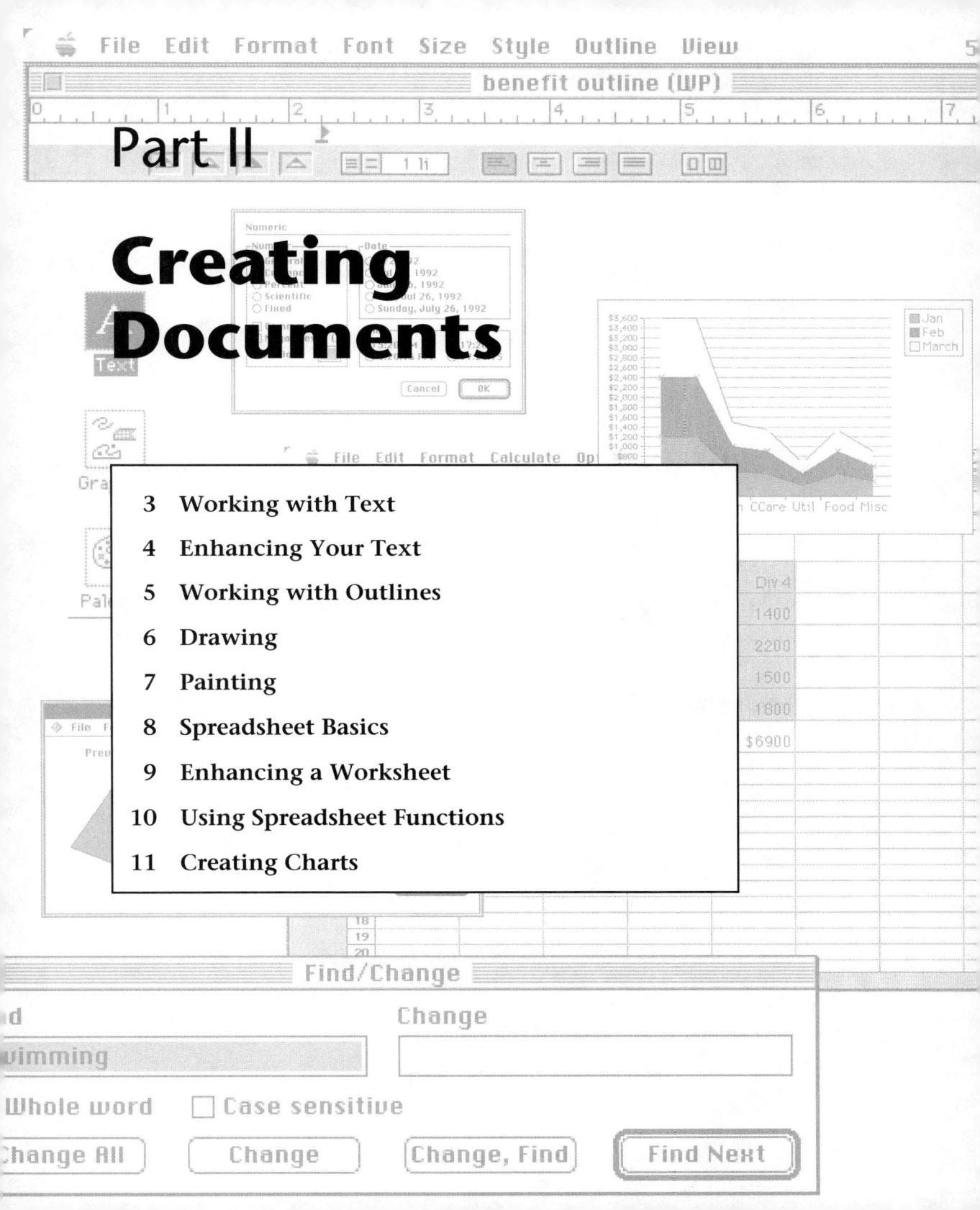

Creating Documents

3 Working with Text

4 Enhancing Your Text

5 Working with Outlines

6 Drawing

7 Painting

8 Spreadsheet Basics

9 Enhancing a Worksheet

10 Using Spreadsheet Functions

11 Creating Charts

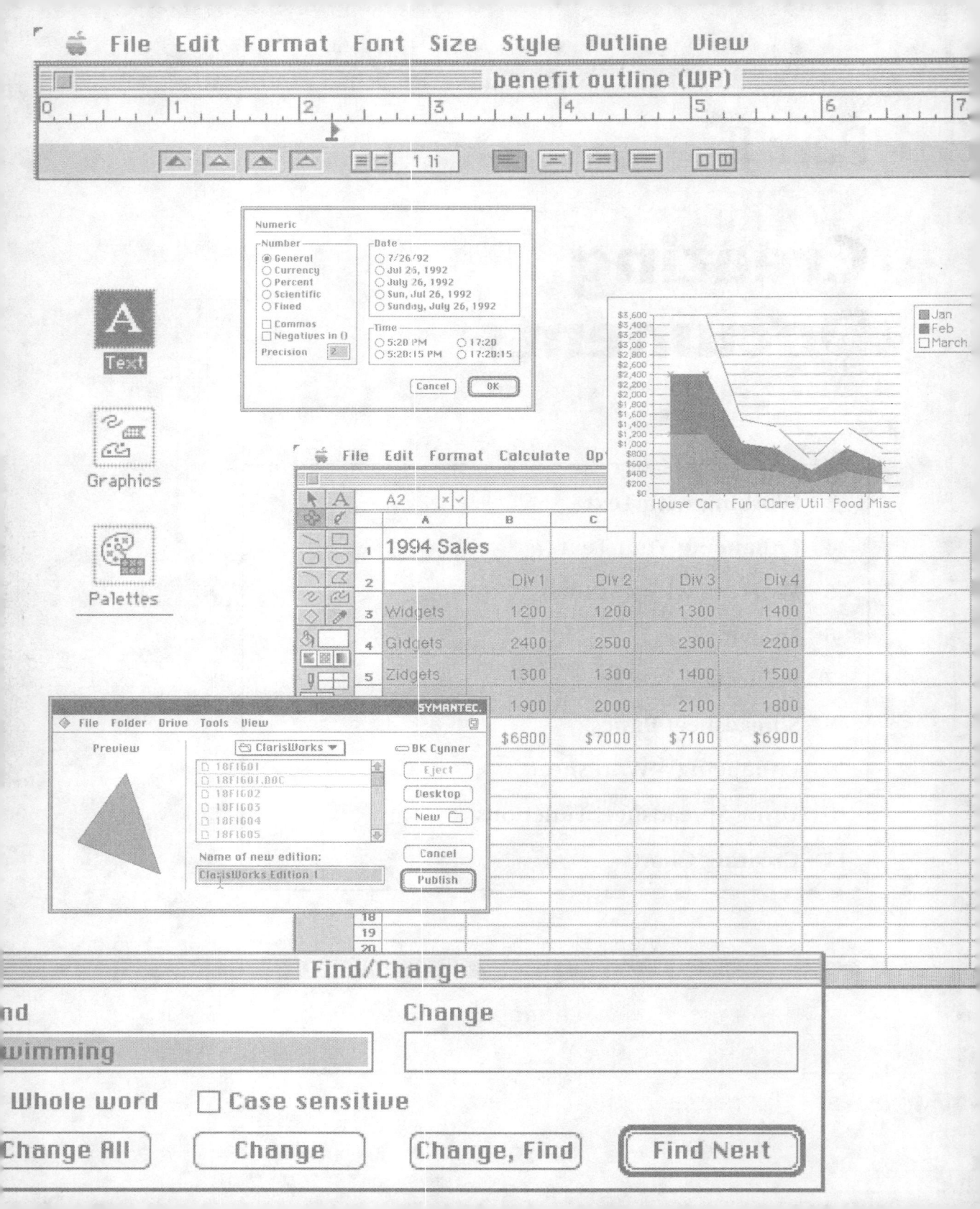

Chapter 3
Working with Text

by Shelley O'Hara

Many of the documents that you create with ClarisWorks will be text documents, such as reports, letters, memos, and newsletters. To work with text, you use the word processing module.

In this chapter, you learn the basics of typing and editing text. You also learn some editing shortcuts.

This chapter covers the following topics:

- How to type text
- How to delete, move, and copy text
- How to find and replace text
- How to check spelling
- How to look up a word in the Thesaurus

Note
For more information on creating a new document, see Chapter 2, "Learning the Essentials." Chapter 2 also covers saving and opening documents.

Understanding the Screen Display and Tools

When you click the Word Processing button in the New Document dialog box, a blank document appears. Figure 3.1 identifies the key screen elements.

The *menu bar* lists the names of the menus. Choosing a menu command is covered in Chapter 1, "What Is ClarisWorks?"

The *ruler* includes the tab, alignment, column, and line-spacing controls, and enables you to make indent and formatting changes. Chapter 4, "Enhancing Your Text," covers these formatting options.

The *page guides* indicate the space where you can type text. The areas outside the page guides are the page margins. For information on changing margin settings, see Chapter 4, "Enhancing Your Text."

The *insertion point* is a flashing vertical line. This line indicates where text will appear when you start typing. Moving the insertion point is covered in "Moving Around" later in this chapter.

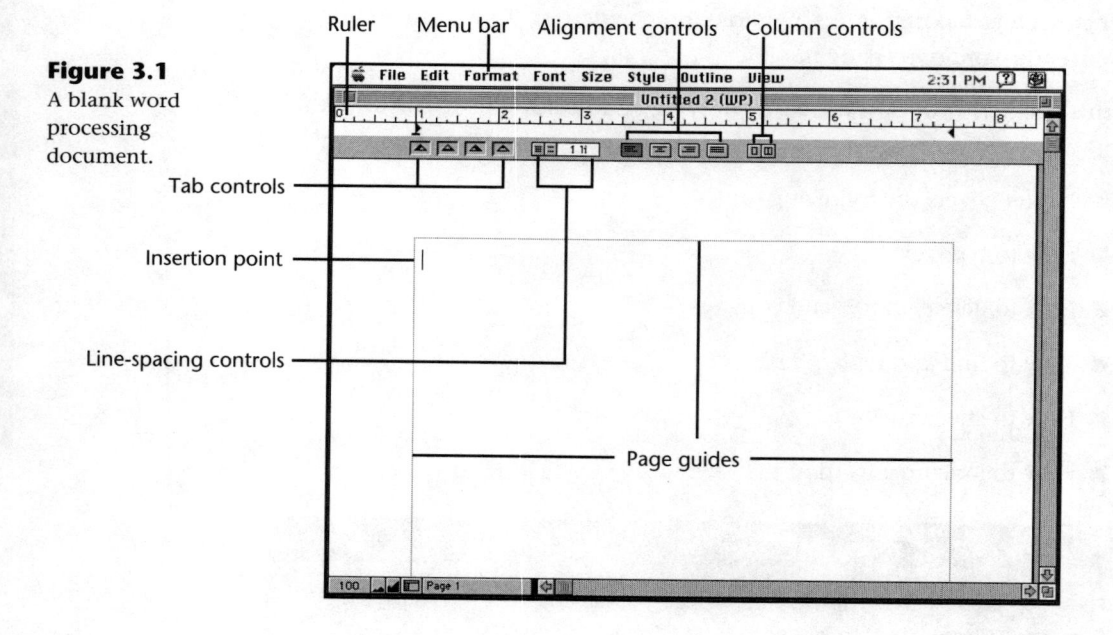

Figure 3.1
A blank word processing document.

Changing the View

If you prefer, you can turn off the display of the ruler or turn on the display of the tool palette. To hide the ruler, choose Hide Rulers from the View menu. Hiding the ruler provides more room for text on-screen. To display the tool palette, choose Show Tools from the View menu. Display the tool palette when you want to insert frames or objects.

You also can change the view of the document—for example, show an enlarged view. Chapter 2, "Learning the Essentials," covers changing the view.

Using the Shortcuts Palette

In addition to the tool palette and ruler, you can display a palette of shortcut buttons. To display the palette, choose Shortcuts from the File menu, and then choose Show Shortcuts from the submenu. You can add buttons to or delete buttons from this palette (see Chapter 20, "Customizing ClarisWorks"). To close the palette, click the close box. To move the palette, click and drag it to the new location.

> **Tip**
> You also can press Shift-⌘-X to display the Shortcuts palette.

Table 3.1 describes the shortcut buttons.

Table 3.1 Word Processing Shortcut Buttons

Button	Description
	Open a document
	Save a document
	Print a document
	Undo
	Cut
	Copy
	Paste
	Bold
	Italic
	Underline
	Show/hide invisible characters
	Make table

(continues)

Table 3.1 Continued

Button	Description
	Make custom style
	Copy ruler
	Apply ruler
	Increase font size
	Decrease font size
	Align left
	Align center
	Align right

Troubleshooting the Display

On my screen, I see something different from what's shown in the figures. Why?

Keep in mind that you can hide certain display elements (the ruler, the tool palette, and the Shortcuts palette). Your display will be different if you have different items displayed.

I don't see the Shortcuts palette. Why?

The Shortcuts palette does not appear by default. To display this palette of icons, choose Shortcuts from the File menu, and then choose Show Shortcuts from the submenu.

Creating a Document

Creating a document is as simple as typing on the keyboard. The characters appear on-screen as you type. After you have typed some words, you may need to move around—for example, to the top of the screen to make a change. As you work, it is important that you remember to save the document. This section covers these topics.

Typing Text

To type text, just type on the keyboard. The characters appear on-screen as you type. If you make a mistake while typing, you can press Delete to delete the characters to the left of the insertion point.

> **Note**
>
> Your keyboard may have two Delete keys. One may appear above the backslash (\) key on the right side of the keyboard. You also may have a key labeled Del, with an arrow pointing to the right. Pressing the Del key erases characters to the right of the insertion point.

Tip
If you want to delete a lot of text, select the text and then press Delete. (See "Deleting Text" later in this chapter.)

On a typewriter, you need to press the return key at the end of each line. In ClarisWorks, if a word doesn't fit on a line, the program wraps the word to the next line. If you need to add or delete text, you can do so, and ClarisWorks adjusts the line breaks accordingly. In a word processing document, press Return only when you want to end a paragraph or when you want to insert a blank line.

Moving Around

As you type, the insertion point moves along the screen. When you want to return to an earlier part of the document—for example, to make a change—you first move the insertion point to that spot.

The easiest way to move the insertion point is to move the mouse pointer (which appears as an I-beam) to the spot you want and then click the mouse button. The insertion point moves to the new location.

If you prefer to keep your hands on the keyboard, you can use the keys listed in Table 3.2 to move around the document.

Table 3.2 Movement Keys

To Move...	Press
One character right	→
One character left	←
One line up	↑

(continues)

Table 3.2 Continued

To Move...	Press
One line down	↓
To the beginning of a line	⌘-←
To the end of a line	⌘-→
To the beginning of a paragraph	Option-↑
To the end of a paragraph	Option-↓
To the top of the document	⌘-↑
To the end of the document	⌘-↓

Inserting Page Breaks

If you type more than one page of text, ClarisWorks shows you the text continuing onto a new page. You can add or delete text, and ClarisWorks adjusts the text on the pages. If you need to move to a new page before reaching the end of the preceding page, you can insert a manual page break.

Tip
If you want to experiment with a document (such as making formatting changes), save the document first. If the change doesn't come out the way you want, you then can revert to the last saved copy of the document by choosing Revert from the File menu.

From the Format menu, choose the Insert Break command. ClarisWorks inserts a new page with the insertion point in the top left corner. To remove a page break, place the insertion point in that top left corner and press the Delete key.

Saving the Document

Keep in mind that everything you type is stored only temporarily in the computer's memory. To make a permanent copy of your work, you need to save the document to the hard disk. Saving to the hard disk copies the on-screen version to the disk and stores the data in a file. You then can open and edit the document again.

Don't wait until you finish a document to save it. If something happens—for example, the power goes off—while you are working on an unsaved document, you will lose all your work. Instead, save frequently by choosing Save from the File menu. (Saving documents is covered in Chapter 2, "Learning the Essentials.")

> **Troubleshooting Document Creation**
>
> *I have a document on-screen. How do I create a new document?*
>
> To create a new document, choose New from the File menu. When the New Document dialog box appears, click the radio button for the type of document you want to create.
>
> *How do I correct mistakes?*
>
> As you type, you can press the Delete key to delete characters to the left of the insertion point. If you need to delete a lot of text, select it first and then press Delete.

Editing Text

If all your writing comes out perfect as you type it, you're a lucky writer. Most of the time, you will need to make changes. You may need to delete and rewrite text, copy text, or move text. With a typewriter, you have to use whiteout to delete text and then type over it, or you may literally cut and paste to make changes. You might even have to retype the entire document. With a word processing program, you can make editing changes easily.

Knowing that you can move or delete text should free you from worrying about getting the words just right the first time. You can write freely and then go back to make editing changes.

The first step in making most editing changes is selecting the text you want to work with. Selecting text is covered in the following section.

Selecting Text

Selecting text means highlighting the text you want to change. You select text when you want to make editing or formatting changes.

To select text, follow these steps:

1. Move the insertion point to the start of the text you want to select.
2. Press and hold down the mouse button, and then drag across the text.

   As you drag, the text is displayed in reverse video or in a different color so that you know it is selected.

3. When you have highlighted all the text you want, release the mouse button.

> **Note**
>
> You also can place the insertion point at the end of the text and drag forward to select.

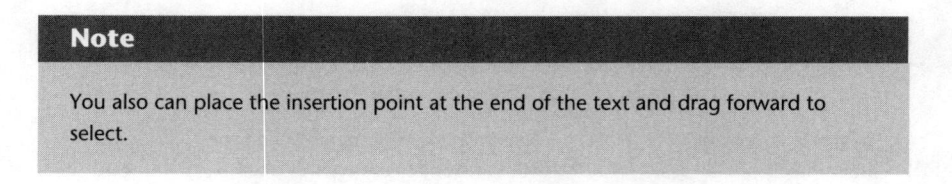

Figure 3.2 shows an example of selected text.

Figure 3.2
To select text, drag across it with the mouse. The text appears in reverse video, indicating that it is selected.

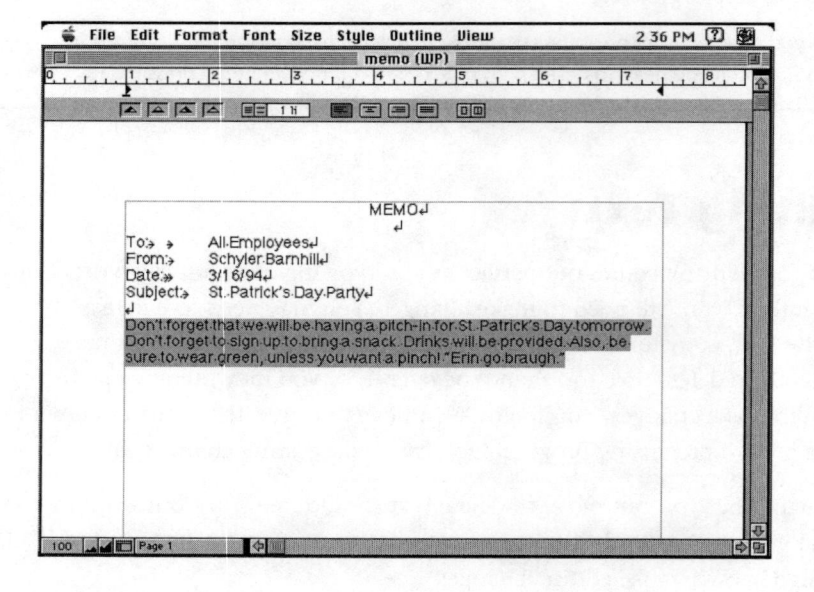

In addition to using this method, you can use any of the following shortcut methods of selecting text:

- To select a word, double-click in the word.

- To select a line, triple-click in the line.

- To select a paragraph, click in the paragraph four times.

- To select all the text in the document, choose Select All from the Edit menu or press ⌘-A.

- To select a large amount of text, click at the beginning of the text you want to select, press and hold down the Shift key, move the mouse pointer to the end of the text, and then click the mouse button. This process is called *Shift-clicking*.

- To select text with the keyboard, press and hold down the Shift key and then use the arrow keys to highlight the text.

Moving Text

As you revise a document, you may decide that the text would work better in a different order. Perhaps a point you made at the end would work better as an opening. You can move text easily in ClarisWorks.

To move text, follow these steps:

1. Select the text you want to move.

2. Choose Cut from the Edit menu. The text is removed from the document and stored in the Clipboard.

3. Move the insertion point to where you want the text to appear. This location can be in the current document or in a different document (not necessarily a ClarisWorks document).

4. Choose Paste from the Edit menu. The text moves to the new location.

If you accidentally pick the wrong location, choose Undo from the Edit menu; then move the insertion point to the right location and choose Paste from the Edit menu. You also can choose Undo to undo the move entirely.

Copying Text

Copying text is useful when you want to repeat information or to use similar information and edit it to make it new. Moving and copying text are similar processes. When writing this chapter, I copied the steps for moving text and then edited them so that they were appropriate for copying.

To copy text, follow these steps:

1. Select the text you want to move.

   Figure 3.3 shows text about to be copied.

2. Choose Copy from the Edit menu. The text remains in the document, and a copy is stored in the Clipboard.

3. Move the insertion point to where you want the text to appear. (This location can be in the current document or in a different document.)

Tip
As alternatives to step 2, you can press ⌘-X or click the Cut button in the Shortcuts palette.

Tip
As alternatives to step 4, you can press ⌘-V or click the Paste button in the Shortcuts palette.

Tip
To move text quickly, select the text, move the insertion point to where you want to move the text, press ⌘-Option, and click the mouse button.

Tip
Alternatively, press ⌘-C or click the Copy button in the Shortcuts palette.

Chapter 3—Working with Text

Tip
Alternatively, press ⌘-V or click the Paste button in the Shortcuts palette.

Tip
To undo the copy operation, choose Undo from the Edit menu or click the Undo button in the Shortcuts palette.

Tip
A quick way to replace existing text with new text is to select the text you want to replace and then type the new text.

4. Choose Paste from the Edit menu.

You now have two copies of the selected text (see fig. 3.4).

Deleting Text

If you have a few characters to delete, the fastest method is to press Delete. You can undo the text deletion by choosing Undo from the Edit menu. You cannot paste the deleted text.

If you have a lot of text to delete, select the text and then press Delete. You can undo the deletion, but you cannot paste the text.

Troubleshooting Document Creation

I selected too much text. How do I unselect text?

To unselect text, click outside the selection, and then drag across the text you *do* want to select.

I copied something to the Clipboard, but when I pasted it, something different appeared. What happened?

The Clipboard stores only the last item you copied or cut. If you copied or cut something else, that item replaces what you first copied or cut. Be sure to copy and cut and then immediately paste the item you want to copy.

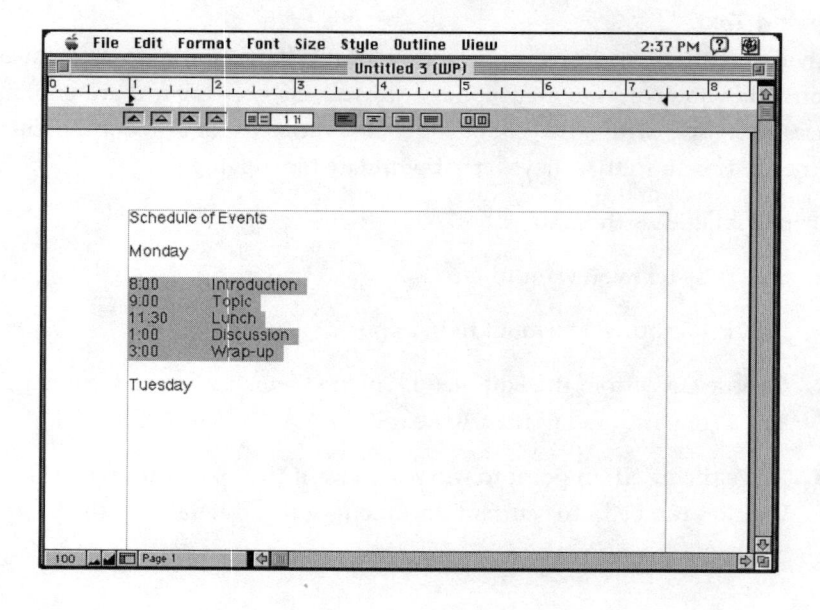

Figure 3.3
This selected text is ready to be copied.

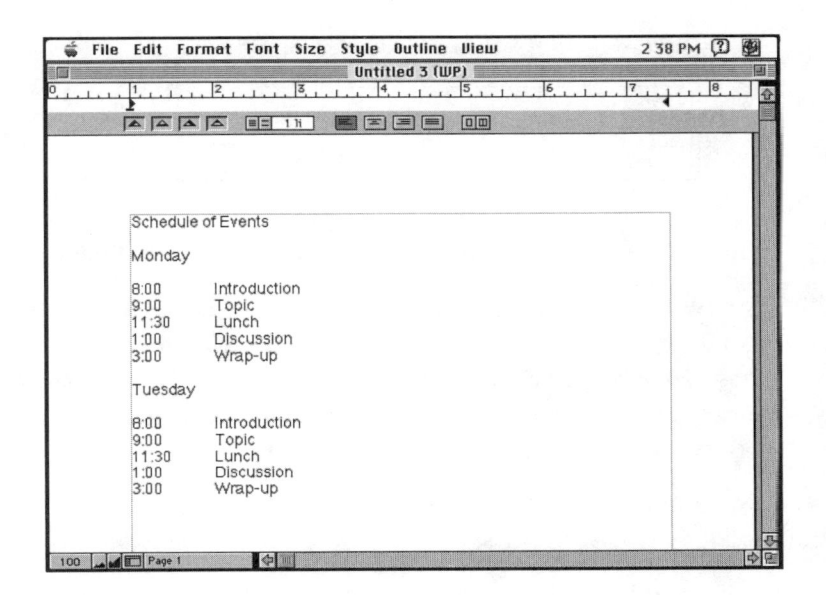

Figure 3.4
Two copies of
the same text.

Finding and Changing Text

In a long document, finding a specific piece of text is difficult when you have to scan through page after page. Instead of scanning through several pages for a section of a document, you can search for it.

A variation on searching for text is finding and changing. This feature is useful when you make a mistake in a document or when you want to make a wholesale change. Suppose that you use the term *spokesman* in a document and then decide to use *spokesperson* instead. You can scroll through the document, finding each location and then making the change manually, or you can have ClarisWorks do the finding and changing automatically.

This section covers both finding and changing text.

Finding Text
When you want to find a particular word or phrase in your document, use the Find/Change command. Follow these steps:

1. Choose Find/Change from the Edit menu.

2. The first time you choose the Find/Change command, a submenu appears. Choose the command name again to display the Find/Change dialog box (see fig. 3.5).

Tip
You also can press ⌘-F to choose the Find/Change command.

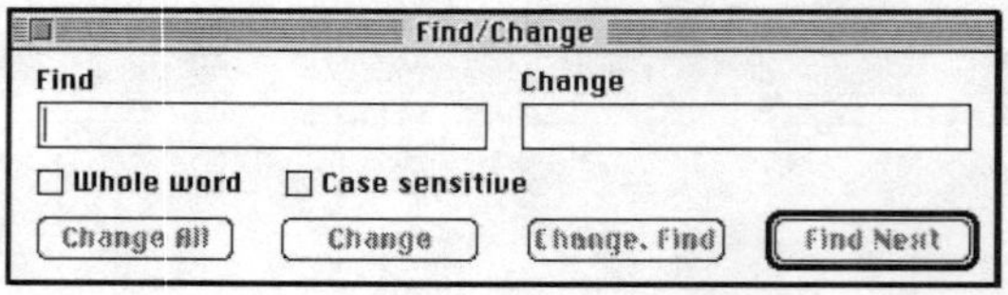

68 Chapter 3—Working with Text

Figure 3.5
Use the Find/Change dialog box to search for a particular word or phrase in a document.

3. In the Find text box, type the word or phrase you want to find.

    Try to search for a unique phrase or word. If you search for a common word or phrase, the program stops at each occurrence of that word or phrase. For example, if you have a document that deals with company benefits, and you want to find text on insurance benefits, the best method is to search for *insurance* rather than *benefits*.

4. If you want, choose either of these options:

    ■ *Whole Word.* If you want ClarisWorks to find only whole words, check this box. If you type **heal** in the Find box, for example, ClarisWorks will stop on *heal* but not on *health*.

    ■ *Case Sensitive.* If you want ClarisWorks to match the case of the text as you typed it, check this box. If you want to find the text no matter what the case (uppercase or lowercase), leave this box unchecked.

5. Choose the Find Next button. ClarisWorks moves to and highlights the first occurrence of the text (see fig. 3.6). The dialog box remains open.

6. Do one of the following things:

    ■ If the highlighted text is the spot you wanted, click in the document to close the Find/Change dialog box. (Alternatively, click the dialog box's close box.)

    ■ If the highlighted text isn't the right location, choose the Find Next button again until you find the spot you want. If ClarisWorks finds no more matches, the program sounds the alert sound.

    ■ If no matches are found, an alert box appears, telling you so. Click OK. Then double-check the text you typed in step 3. If you made a mistake, try again.

Tip
You can select a word or phrase in the document and then choose Find/Change, Find Selection from the Edit menu to have ClarisWorks find the next occurrence of this text.

Tip
ClarisWorks remembers the last Find/Change entries. If the dialog box is closed and you want to Find/Change with the same entries, press ⌘-E.

Finding and Changing Text   **69**

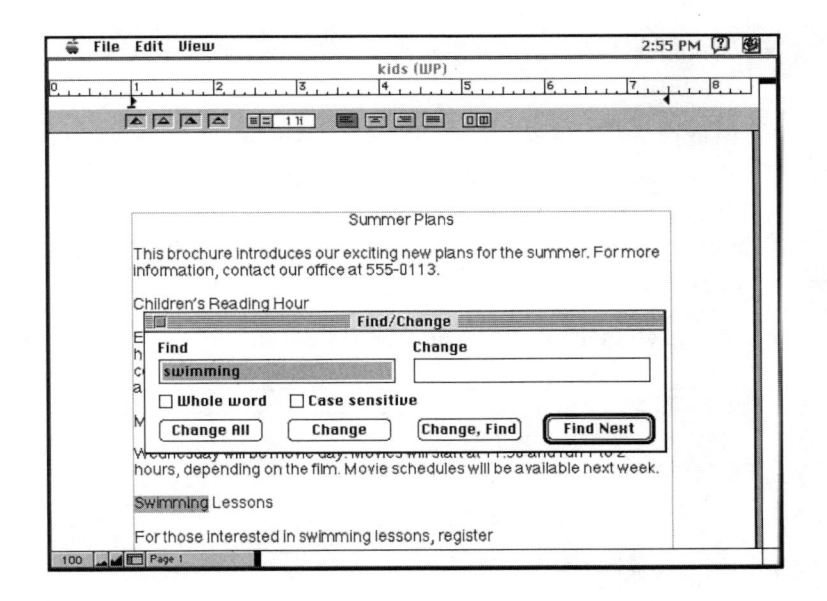

Figure 3.6
When you search for text, ClarisWorks highlights the found text and keeps the dialog box open so that you can search again, if necessary.

Changing Found Text

To search for and replace text in a document, follow these steps:

1. Choose Find/Change from the Edit menu, and then choose Find/Change from the submenu. The Find/Change dialog box appears.

2. In the Find text box, type the word or phrase you want to find.

3. In the Change text box, type the word or phrase you want to use as the replacement.

4. If you want to replace only whole words, check the Whole Word check box. If you want ClarisWorks to match case, check the Case Sensitive check box.

5. Choose the Find Next button. ClarisWorks moves to and highlights the first occurrence of the text (see fig. 3.7). The dialog box remains open so that you can tell ClarisWorks what to do with the found text.

6. Do one of the following things:

    ■ To skip this occurrence and move to the next one, click the Find Next button.

    ■ To change this occurrence but not find the next one, click the Change button.

Chapter 3—Working with Text

- To change this occurrence and move to the next one, click the Change, Find button.

- To change all occurrences without confirming the change, click the Change All button. An alert message appears, telling you that changing all the occurrences cannot be undone. Click OK. Another message appears, telling you the number of replacements made. Click OK.

- To cancel the procedure, click the close box.

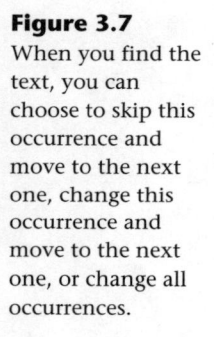

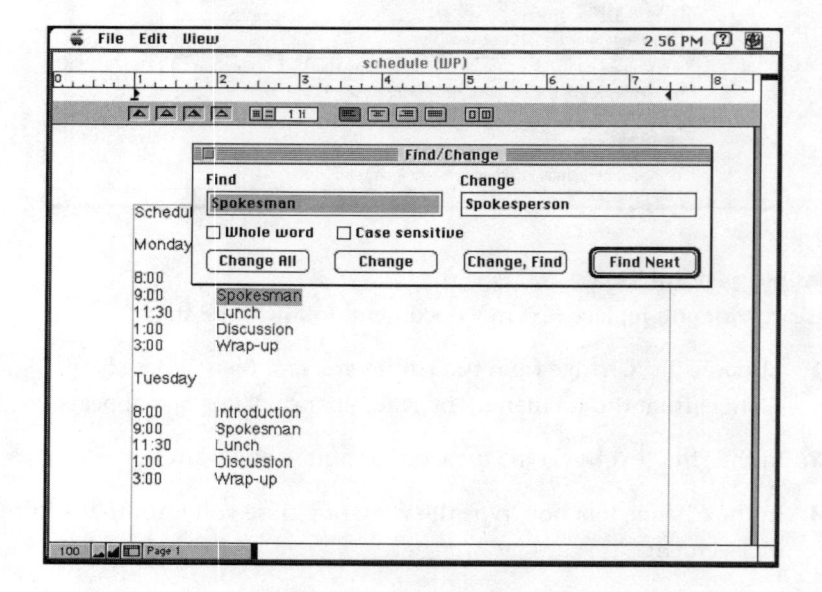

Figure 3.7
When you find the text, you can choose to skip this occurrence and move to the next one, change this occurrence and move to the next one, or change all occurrences.

Caution

Make sure that the Find/Change operation is working the way you want before you click Change All. You can easily make changes you didn't intend. For example, if you blindly change all occurrences of *fig* to *figure*, the following would happen:

Original Word	Changed Word
fig	figure
figure	figureure
configuration	configureuration

If you search occurrence by occurrence, ClarisWorks continues to flag each match. When the program can find no more matches, an alert box appears to tell you so. Click OK.

Finding Invisible Characters

Some characters do not appear on-screen by default—for example, tabs, paragraph returns, and page breaks. ClarisWorks still considers these characters to be characters, which means that you can find and change them. To do so, you enter a special code in the Find text box. If you want to replace the found character with another character, you can enter a special code in the Change text box.

Table 3.3 lists the codes that help you find invisible characters.

> **Note**
>
> You must press \ on the keyboard, not /. Also, the keystrokes are case-sensitive—that is, you must type **\t**, not **\T**, for Tab.

Table 3.3 Finding Invisible Characters

To Find This	Press This
Tab	\t
Paragraph return	\p
Line break	\n
Page or column break	\c
Automatic date	\d
Automatic time	\h
Automatic page number	\
Backslash	\\
Footnote	\f

Chapter 3—Working with Text

> **Troubleshooting Find/Change Operations**
>
> *I get an error message when I try to find text. Why?*
>
> If ClarisWorks can't find the text that you entered in the Find text box, you see an alert box. Try the find operation again, and this time, double-check your spelling. Also, if you are searching for a long phrase, try typing only part of the phrase.
>
> *I accidentally made replacements I didn't want to make. What can I do?*
>
> To undo a Find/Change operation, immediately choose Undo from the Edit menu.

Checking Spelling

Even if you are a perfect speller, you can easily make a mistake in typing. To ensure that your document does not contain any errors, you can use ClarisWorks' built-in Spelling Checker.

The Spelling Checker works by comparing the words in your document with the words in its dictionary (more than 100,000 words). If the Spelling Checker doesn't find a match, it flags the word. Keep in mind that a flag doesn't necessarily mean that the word is misspelled. Personal names, medical or scientific language, and other terms may not be included in the ClarisWorks dictionary. You can choose to ignore the word, edit the word, or replace the word.

> **Caution**
>
> The Spelling Checker isn't a replacement for good proofreading of your document. ClarisWorks doesn't know the difference among *two*, *too*, and *to*; it only knows if the word is spelled correctly. Read your document carefully to catch and correct any usage or grammatical errors.

Performing a Spell Check

Tip
You also can check spelling in the spreadsheet module.

To perform a spell check, follow these steps:

1. If you want to check only part of the document, select that part. Otherwise, ClarisWorks checks the entire document.

2. Choose Writing Tools from the Edit menu. When the pop-up menu appears, choose Check Document Spelling.

ClarisWorks checks the document, comparing the words in the document with its dictionary. The Spelling dialog box appears on-screen.

If the document contains no misspellings, only one button in the dialog box is available: Done. Click Done to close the dialog box.

If ClarisWorks finds a misspelling, it highlights the word and displays alternative spellings in the Spelling dialog box (see fig. 3.8).

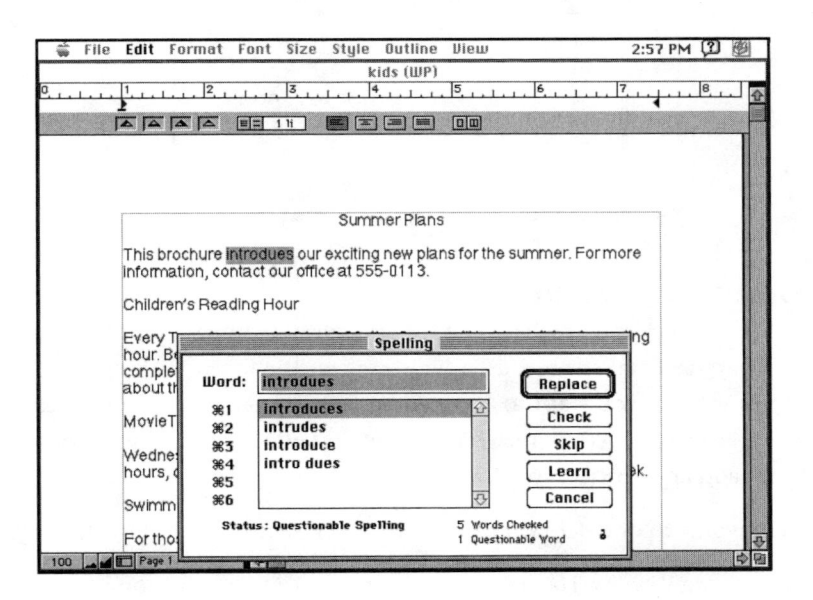

Tip
You also can press ⌘-= to choose the Check Document Spelling command.

Figure 3.8
When you check spelling, you can choose to replace a word, skip the word, or add the word to the user dictionary.

3. Whenever the program flags a misspelling, do one of the following things:

   ■ Click a replacement word in the spelling list, and then click the Replace button. If the correct replacement isn't listed, type it in the Word text box before you click Replace.

   ■ To skip the word and move to the next misspelling, click the Skip button.

   ■ To add the word to your user dictionary, click the Learn button. (See the following section for information on this dictionary.)

   ■ To cancel the spell check, click the Cancel button.

74 Chapter 3—Working with Text

When all the words have been checked, the dialog box tells you that the status of the check is `Finished Spelling`. The bottom of the dialog box indicates the number of words checked and the number of words flagged as questionable. Only the Done button is available (see fig. 3.9).

4. Click the Done button. The spell check is complete.

Figure 3.9
The status of the spell check.

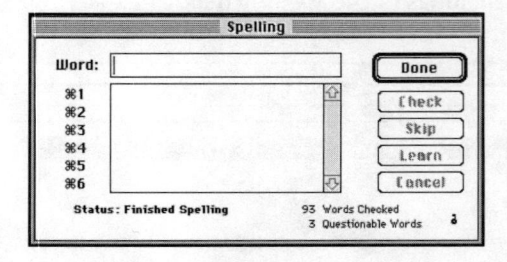

Adding Words to the User Dictionary

When you check spelling, you can use the main dictionary and one user dictionary. You can create a user dictionary on the fly by clicking the Learn button for terms you want to add; ClarisWorks automatically adds these words to the user dictionary. You also can add words manually. If you mistakenly add an incorrect word, you can delete it.

To add words to or delete words from the user dictionary, follow these steps:

1. Choose Writing Tools from the Edit menu. When the pop-up menu appears, choose Install Dictionaries. The Select Dictionary dialog box appears, listing the folders in your system.

2. In the Select Dictionary drop-down list, choose User Dictionary.

3. Click User Dictionary in the folder and file list.

4. Click the Edit button. You see a list of words in the dictionary (see fig. 3.10).

5. To remove a word, click the word in the list and then click the Remove button.

    To add a word, type it in the Entry text box, and then click the Add button.

6. When you finish adding and deleting words, choose OK.

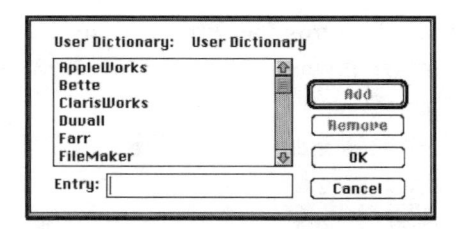

Figure 3.10
You can add words to or delete words from the user dictionary.

Creating a User Dictionary

You can create more than one user dictionary and switch among them. To create a user dictionary, follow these steps:

1. Choose Writing Tools from the Edit menu, and then choose Install Dictionaries from the pop-up menu. You see a dialog box that lists the folders in your system.

2. In the Select Dictionary drop-down list, choose User Dictionary.

3. Click the New button. You are prompted to type the dictionary name (see fig. 3.11).

4. Type the dictionary name, and then click the Save button.

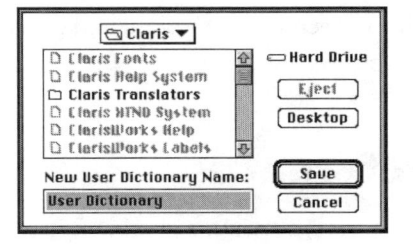

Figure 3.11
Type the name you want to use for the dictionary.

Using the Thesaurus

Finding just the right word can be difficult. Does *magnificent, splendid, awesome, glorious,* or *grand* convey the exact meaning? You can fine-tune your writing by using ClarisWorks' Thesaurus to find the right word.

To look up a word in the Thesaurus, follow these steps:

1. Select the word.

2. Choose Writing Tools from the Edit menu. When the pop-up menu appears, choose Thesaurus.

Tip
You also can press Shift-⌘-Z to choose the Thesaurus command.

Chapter 3—Working with Text

The Word Finder Thesaurus dialog box appears, listing the word you selected and synonyms for the word (see fig. 3.12).

Figure 3.12
When you look up a word in the Thesaurus, you see synonyms for the selected word. You can replace the word with another word or look up another word.

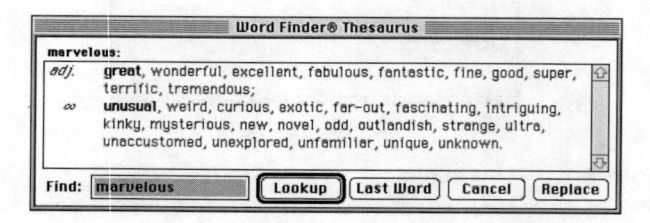

3. Do one of the following things:

- If you see a word that you'd rather use, click the word, and then click the Replace button.

- If you want to look up a synonym for one of the listed synonyms, click the word, and then click the Lookup button.

- If you have looked up several words, you can move back to a previous list by clicking the Last Word button. Select the word you want to return to, and then click the Lookup button.

- If you want to keep the same word and cancel the command, click the Cancel button.

Setting Preferences

Customizing ClarisWorks is covered in Chapter 20. Two customize options that deal with text and that you might be interested in using are displaying formatting characters and using "smart" quotation marks.

To set those preferences, follow these steps:

1. Choose Preferences from the Edit menu. The Preferences dialog box appears.

2. If it's not already selected, select the Text icon. You see the options that deal with text (see fig. 3.13).

3. If you want to see invisible characters, such as hard returns and tabs, check the Show Invisibles check box.

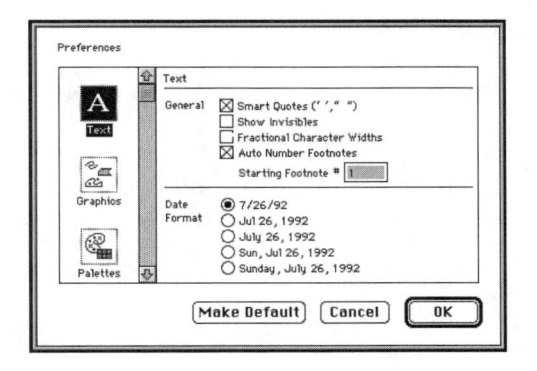

Setting Preferences **77**

Figure 3.13
You can set text preferences so that invisible characters are displayed and smart quotes are used.

4. If you don't want to use smart quotes, click the Smart Quotes check box to remove the x.

5. Choose OK.

Figure 3.14 shows a document with special characters displayed.

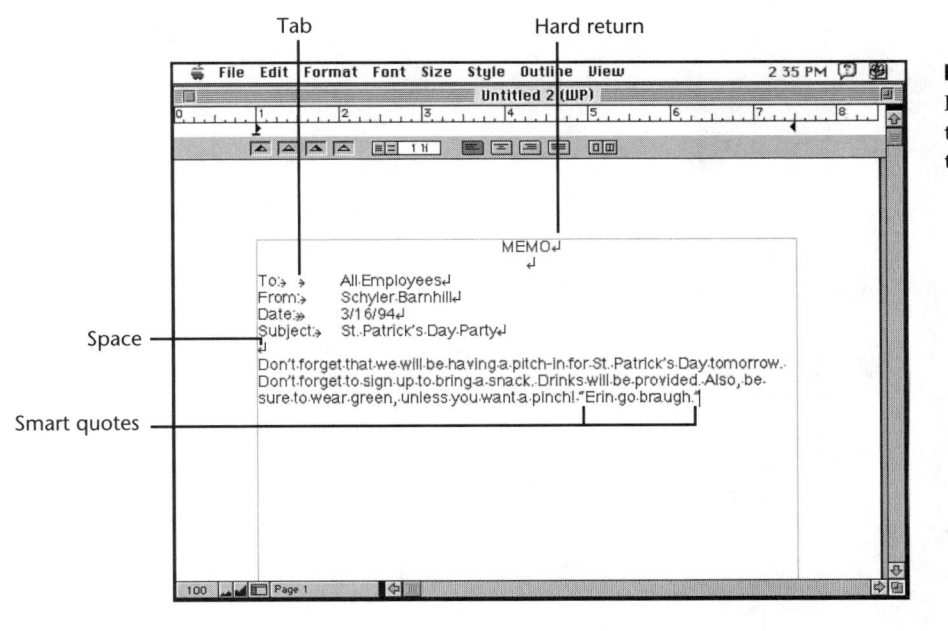

Figure 3.14
Invisible characters are visible in this document.

From Here...

You now know the basics of working with text. As you build on your skills, the following chapters may be of interest to you:

- Creating a document isn't just getting the words right—it's also about getting the appearance right. Chapter 4, "Enhancing Your Text," explains the formatting options you can use to affect the appearance of the document.

- If you work with outlines, investigate the outline feature, which is covered in Chapter 5, "Working with Outlines."

- Creating form letters (mail merge) is covered in Chapter 15, "Creating Integrated Documents."

Chapter 4
Enhancing Your Text

by Shelley O'Hara

In a polished document, getting the words right is the first goal. Getting the look right is the second goal. Using ClarisWorks' formatting features, you can enhance your text to create a professional, attractive document.

In this chapter, you learn the following:

- How to format characters—change the font, font size, and font style
- How to format paragraphs—indent text, center text, and work with tabs
- How to format pages—change margins and insert headers and footers
- How to work with graphics
- How to create tables
- How to create and work in columns

Formatting Characters

The most basic element you can work with in a word processing document is a *character*. A character can be a letter, a number, or a symbol. Your entire document is composed of characters. You can change the look of the text by changing the font, type size, type style, or color.

Defining a Font
A *font* is a set of letters, numbers, and symbols in a certain typeface. All characters in the font have a similar appearance. There are two types of fonts: *serif* and *sans-serif*. Serif fonts feature decorative strokes; sans-serif fonts do not. The default font in ClarisWorks word processing documents is Helvetica.

Figure 4.1
Examples of serif and sans-serif fonts.

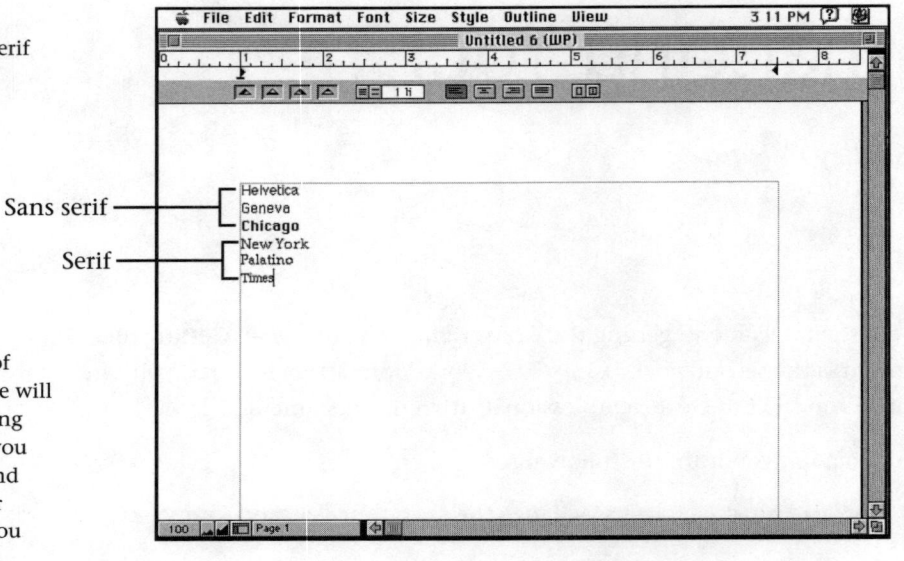

Figure 4.1 shows some sample fonts.

```
Sans serif ——  Helvetica
               Geneva
               Chicago
Serif ——       New York
               Palatino
               Times
```

Tip
The number of fonts you have will vary, depending on the fonts you have added and the fonts your printer has. You can purchase additional fonts to add to your system.

Fonts come in different sizes. The type size is measured in *points*. One point equals 1/72 of an inch; 72 points equal 1 inch.

Figure 4.2 shows examples of type sizes.

Figure 4.2
You can use small type, medium type, or really big type in your documents.

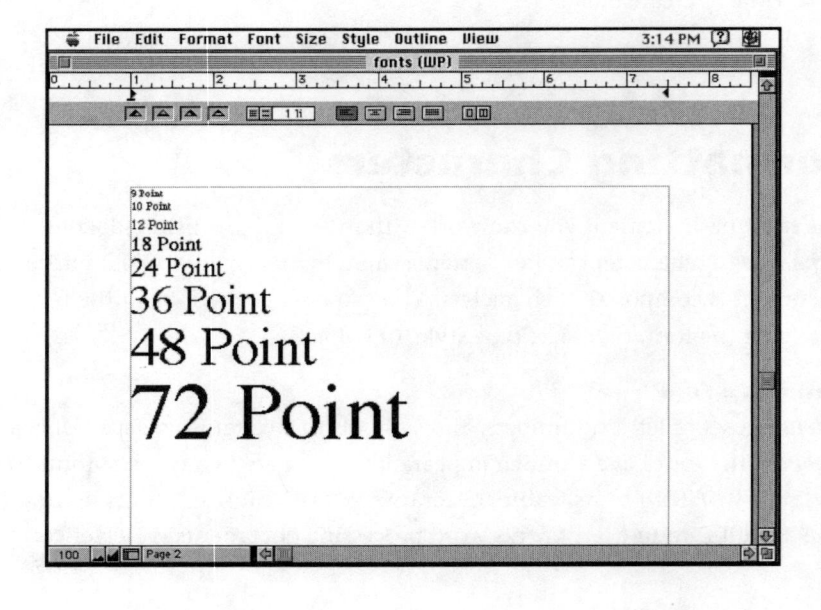

```
9 Point
10 Point
12 Point
18 Point
24 Point
36 Point
48 Point
72 Point
```

In addition to the font and type size, you can change the type styles. The most common styles are bold, italic, and underline. You also can use strikethrough, outline, and other type styles.

The following sections explain how to select a font, type size, type style, and color for your text.

Changing Fonts

Different fonts convey different meanings. A decorative, flowery font would be appropriate for a love letter, but not for a business report. A solid, professional font would work for a memo, but maybe not for an invitation. You can change the font for any amount of text you choose.

To change the font, follow these steps:

1. Select the text you want to change.

2. Open the Font menu and select the font you want. The selected text appears in the new font.

Tip
If you want to change the font for the entire document, choose Select All from the Edit menu.

Adjusting Type Size

The size of your type also is significant to your document. Really large text jumps off the page and is appropriate for flyers or advertisements, but probably not for memos or letters. Small text might be useful when you want to fit a lot of information on the page, perhaps in a scholarly article. The default type size for ClarisWorks word processing documents—12 points—is a good size for most documents.

You can change the size of any text in the document. You may, for instance, want to make headings large and keep the body text in 12-point type.

Tip
Limiting yourself to two or three fonts in a document is a good idea. If you use more fonts than that, your document may start to look like a ransom note.

To change the type size, follow these steps:

1. Select the text you want to change.

2. Open the Size menu and select the size you want. The selected text appears in the new size.

Tip
To use a custom size, choose Other from the Size menu, enter the size you want, and click OK.

Using Type Styles

As mentioned earlier in this chapter, the most common type styles are bold, italic, and underline. Bold is useful for making text stand out. You should use it sparingly; otherwise, your document may appear to be screaming. Italic is another good way to add emphasis. Bear in mind that too much italic is difficult to read.

Chapter 4—Enhancing Your Text

Tip
You also can use the Increase Type Size and Decrease Type Size buttons in the Shortcuts palette. For information on using this palette, refer to Chapter 3, "Working with Text."

ClarisWorks offers some additional type styles. To change the type style, follow these steps:

1. Select the text you want to change.
2. Open the Style menu and choose a type style:

Style	Shortcut Keys
Bold	⌘-B
Italic	⌘-I
Underline	⌘-U
Strikethrough	none
Outline	none
Shadow	none
Condense	none
Extend	none
Superscript	Shift-⌘-+
Subscript	Shift-⌘-–

You can select more than one style. A checkmark appears next to each selected style. To return to normal style, select the text and then choose Plain Text from the Style menu or press ⌘-T. Figure 4.3 shows examples of type styles.

Adding Color

You can change the color of text. If you have a color printer, the document will print in color. If you don't have a color printer, you still may want to use color for documents that will be read on-screen or used in a slide show. (For more information on slide shows, see Chapter 15, "Creating Integrated Documents.")

Tip
You also can use the Bold, Italic, and Underline buttons in the Shortcuts palette. For information on using this palette, refer to Chapter 3, "Working with Text."

To change the color of text, follow these steps:

1. Select the text you want to change.
2. Choose Text Color from the Style menu, and hold down the mouse button so that you can see the color palette.
3. Choose the color you want.

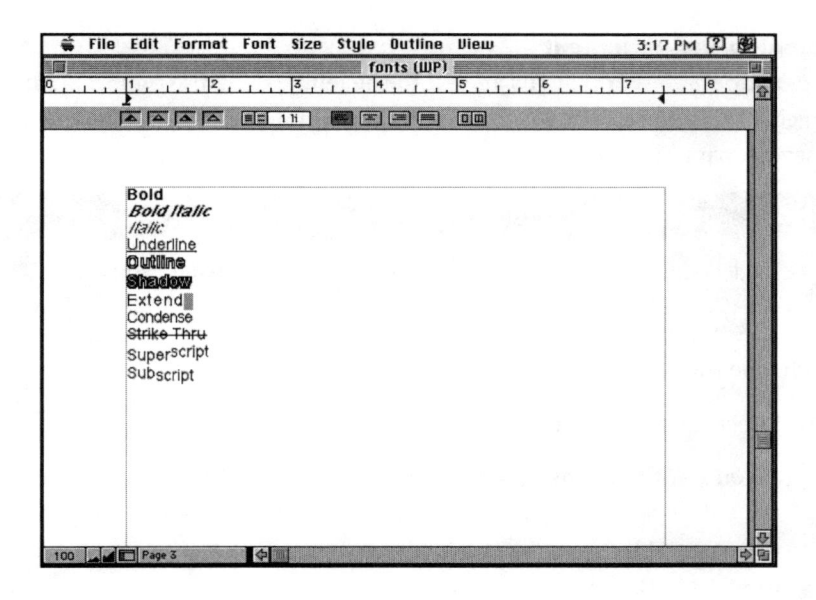

Figure 4.3
ClarisWorks offers several type styles. The most commonly used are bold, italic, and underline.

Troubleshooting Character Formatting

I applied several font styles, but I want to undo them. Is there a quick way to return to normal?

To delete all styles applied to text, select the text and then choose Plain Text from the Style menu.

I don't have the same fonts as mentioned in this chapter. Also, one of my co-workers has different fonts. Why?

The fonts you have depend on your printer and on your System setup. You can add fonts to your system by purchasing and installing font packages.

Tip
You can save formatting—for example, the size, style, and font—in a custom style and then apply that style to other text in the document. For details on using custom text styles, see Chapter 20, "Customizing ClarisWorks."

Formatting Paragraphs

Each time you press Return, you create a paragraph. Each paragraph in a document can have its own spacing, alignment, and tab settings. You may want to center the document title or to right-align a return address; you also can indent the first line or all lines of a paragraph. The following sections explain paragraph-formatting tasks.

Changing the Alignment

By default, ClarisWorks aligns all text to the left, leaving the right margin ragged. You can use the ruler to change the alignment of one paragraph or of several paragraphs at once.

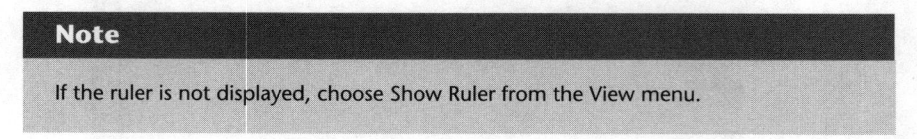

> **Note**
>
> If the ruler is not displayed, choose Show Ruler from the View menu.

To change the alignment, follow these steps:

1. Select the paragraph or paragraphs that you want to change.

   If you want to change only one paragraph, you don't need to select the entire paragraph; simply put the insertion point somewhere in the paragraph. If you want to change several paragraphs, you have to select part of each paragraph.

2. Click one of the following alignment icons:

Icon	Description
	Left-align
	Center
	Right-align
	Justify

Figure 4.4 shows examples of alignments.

Indenting a Paragraph

ClarisWorks provides two ways to indent a paragraph: the ruler and the Paragraph dialog box. The ruler is useful if you want to see the change; as you drag the appropriate markers, the text moves to the new settings. The dialog box is useful when you want to enter an exact measurement.

Indenting with the Ruler. Figure 4.5 identifies the indent markers that you can use to indent paragraphs.

To indent the entire paragraph from the left, drag the left indent marker to the spot you want. (The first-line indent marker moves with it.) To indent the

Formatting Paragraphs **85**

entire paragraph from the right, drag the right indent marker. To indent only the first line, drag the first-line indent marker.

Figure 4.4
You can change the placement of the text on the page by changing the alignment.

Left indent marker

First-line indent marker   Right indent marker

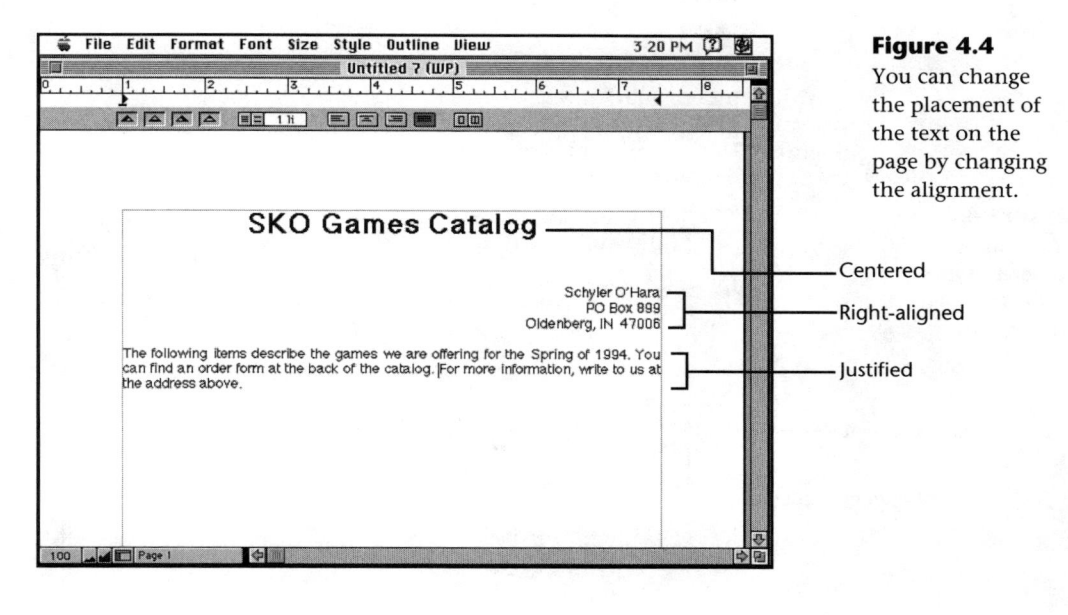

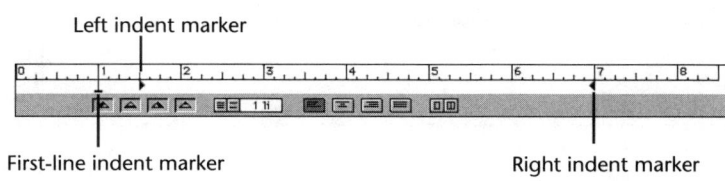

Figure 4.5
You can use the ruler to indent a paragraph. Drag the marker to a new location.

Indenting with the Paragraph Dialog Box. If you have trouble dragging the indent markers, or if you want to enter a precise value, use the dialog box. Follow these steps:

1. Select the paragraph(s) that you want to change.

2. Choose Paragraph from the Format menu. The Paragraph dialog box appears (see fig. 4.6).

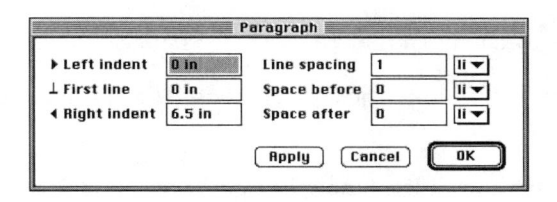

Figure 4.6
You can enter indents and spacing values for the selected paragraphs in this dialog box.

3. Enter values for the left indent, first line, and right indent.

4. Choose OK.

To create a hanging indent, drag the left indent marker right, and drag the first-line indent marker left.

Figure 4.7 shows examples of indents.

Figure 4.7
You can use different types of indents in your documents.

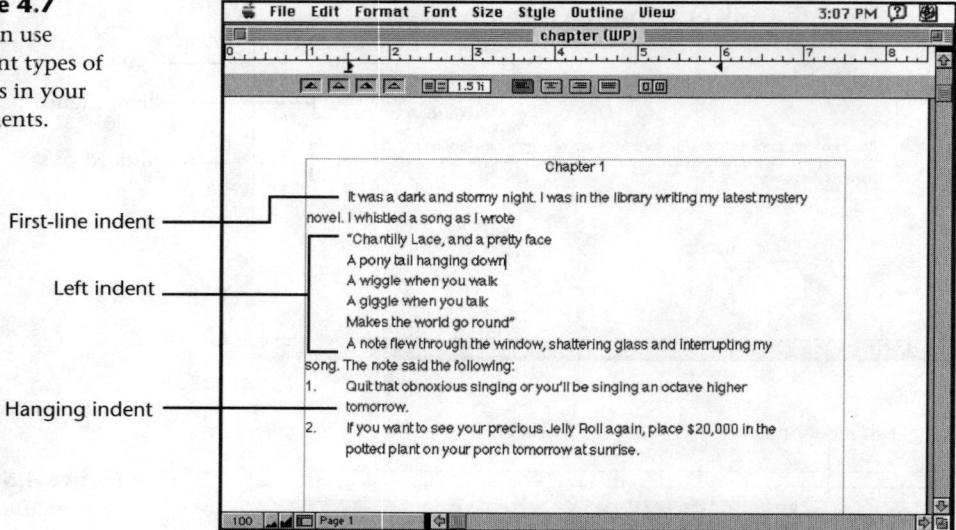

First-line indent
Left indent
Hanging indent

Changing Line Spacing

Line spacing controls the amount of space between lines in a paragraph. Double-spacing is a common line-spacing change. You can use the ruler or the Paragraph dialog box to change spacing.

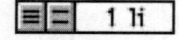

To use the ruler, click a line-spacing control. The control on the left decreases the line spacing by a half line; the control on the right increases the spacing by a half line.

To use the dialog box, follow these steps:

1. Select the paragraph(s) that you want to change.

2. Choose Paragraph from the Format menu. The Paragraph dialog box appears.

3. Enter a new value in the Line Spacing text box, and then choose OK.

Figure 4.8 shows an example of a double-spaced document.

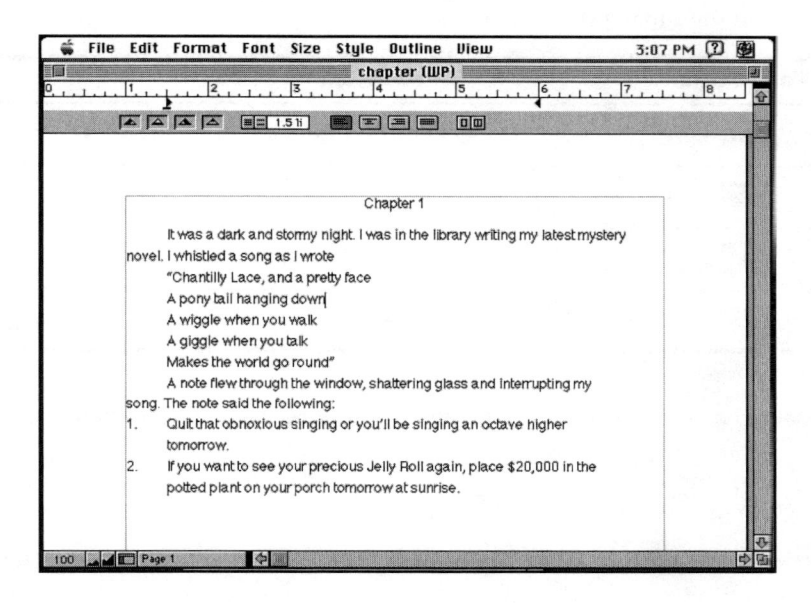

Figure 4.8
Double spacing is useful for reports, manuscripts, and other types of documents.

Changing Paragraph Spacing

Paragraph spacing controls the amount of space above and below paragraphs. You use the Paragraph dialog box to change paragraph spacing. This feature is useful when you want to add some space above or below text—for example, a document heading.

To change paragraph spacing, follow these steps:

1. Select the paragraph(s) that you want to change.

2. Choose Paragraph from the Format menu. The Paragraph dialog box appears.

3. Enter a new value in the Space Before and/or Space After text box.

4. Choose OK.

Tip
If you want to enter data in columns and rows in a document, create a table. For details, see "Working with Tables" later in this chapter.

Setting Tabs

ClarisWorks sets up default left-aligned tabs every half-inch. You can change the placement and the type of tabs by using the ruler or the Tab dialog box. When you use the ruler, you see the changes immediately. The Tab dialog box is useful when you want to enter a precise measurement or when you want to use a fill character.

Setting Tabs with the Ruler. The following table shows the different tab types and their markers on the ruler.

Tab Marker	Description
▲	Left-align tab
▲	Center-align tab
▲	Right-align tab
▲	Align-on tab

To set a tab, drag the appropriate tab marker onto the ruler, and then drag the marker to the position you want.

To remove a tab, drag it off the ruler.

> **Tip**
> If you used the ruler to set tabs, you can double-click a tab marker to display the Tab dialog box.

Setting Tabs with the Tab Dialog Box. The Tab dialog box enables you to specify a *fill character*—a character that is repeated between tabs. Fill characters are useful for creating dotted lines, as in a table of contents, or for creating blank lines, as in a form.

To set tabs with the Tab dialog box, follow these steps:

1. Select the paragraph(s) that you want to change.

   Each paragraph can have its own tab settings. If you want to apply the tab settings to the entire document, choose Select All from the Edit menu.

2. Choose Tab from the Format menu. The Tab dialog box appears (see fig. 4.9).

Figure 4.9
Using the Tab dialog box, you can enter precise measurements for the tab and select a fill character.

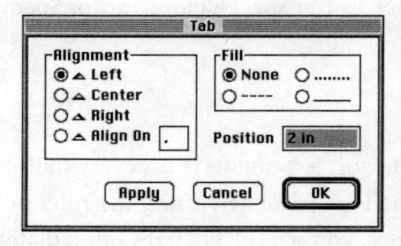

Formatting Paragraphs **89**

3. In the Alignment area, select the type of tab you want.

4. In the Position text box, type the position for the tab.

5. If you want a fill character, select it in the Fill area.

6. To see the changes before closing the dialog box, click Apply.

7. To apply the changes and close the dialog box, choose OK.

Figure 4.10 shows examples of right-aligned tabs with a dotted fill.

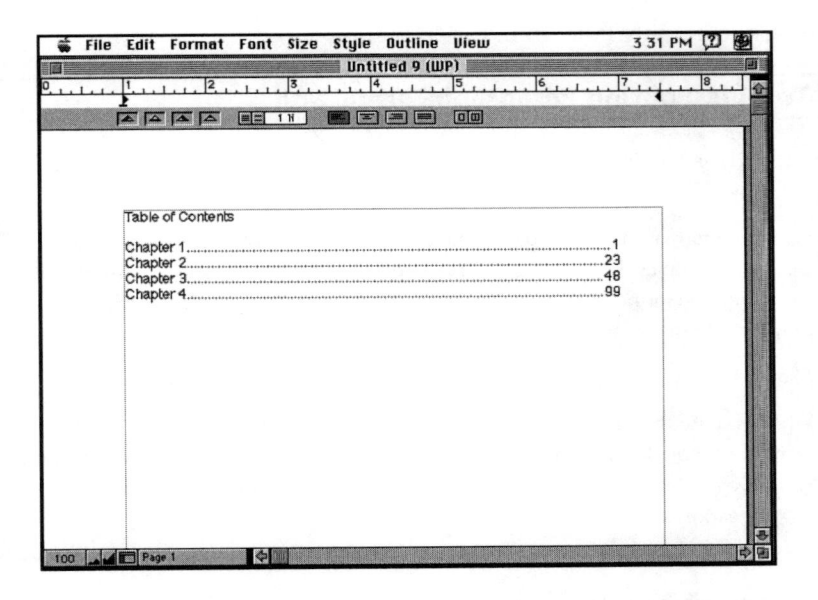

Figure 4.10
This example uses right tabs and a fill character.

Copying Paragraph Formats

As mentioned, the alignment, spacing, and tab settings are applied only to the selected paragraphs—not to the entire document. If you made changes in one paragraph and want to use the same settings in another paragraph, you can copy the formatting. The following paragraph formats can be copied:

- Indents
- Alignment
- Line spacing
- Paragraph spacing
- Tabs

To copy paragraph formatting, follow these steps:

1. Place the insertion point in the paragraph that contains the formats you want to copy.

2. Choose Copy Ruler from the Format menu.

3. Click the paragraph to which you want to copy the formats.

   If you want to copy the formatting to several paragraphs, select them for this step.

4. Choose Apply Ruler from the Format menu.

> **Tip**
> You also can press Shift-⌘-C or click the Copy Ruler button in the Shortcuts palette to choose the Copy Ruler command. Press Shift-⌘-V or click the Paste Ruler button in the Shortcuts palette to choose the Apply Ruler command.

Troubleshooting Paragraph Formatting

I typed a line and then centered it. When I pressed Return, the next line was centered, too. Why?

Paragraph formatting is stored with the paragraph mark. When you press Return, ClarisWorks copies the paragraph formatting to the next paragraph. You must select the paragraph formatting you want for that paragraph. To avert this problem, you may want to make formatting changes after you type the document.

I have trouble setting indents with the ruler. What can I do to make this easier?

When you use the ruler to set indents, you first must click the indent marker you want to change. Initially, the first-line and left indent markers are stacked together. If you have trouble clicking the indent marker you want, try using the Paragraph dialog box instead.

Formatting Pages

Just as you can format the characters and paragraphs in a document, you can set up and format a page the way you want it. Page-formatting options include setting margins and inserting headers and footers.

> **Note**
> This chapter uses a word processing document, but you follow the same steps for other document types—for example, spreadsheet and database documents.

Setting Margins

By default, ClarisWorks uses 1-inch margins on all sides. You can change the margins, if you want. Follow these steps:

1. Choose Document from the Format menu. The Document dialog box appears (see fig. 4.11).

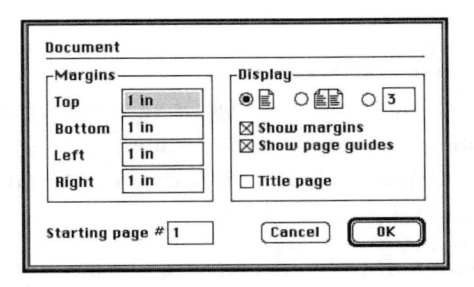

Figure 4.11
Use the Document dialog box to change margins.

2. Click the box for the margin you want to change, delete the current entry, and type the new entry.

3. Choose OK.

You also can use the Document dialog box to change the view of the document. By default, ClarisWorks displays the margins and page guides. You can turn these off by unchecking the Show Margins and Show Page Guides check boxes. Figure 4.12 shows a document with these guides turned off.

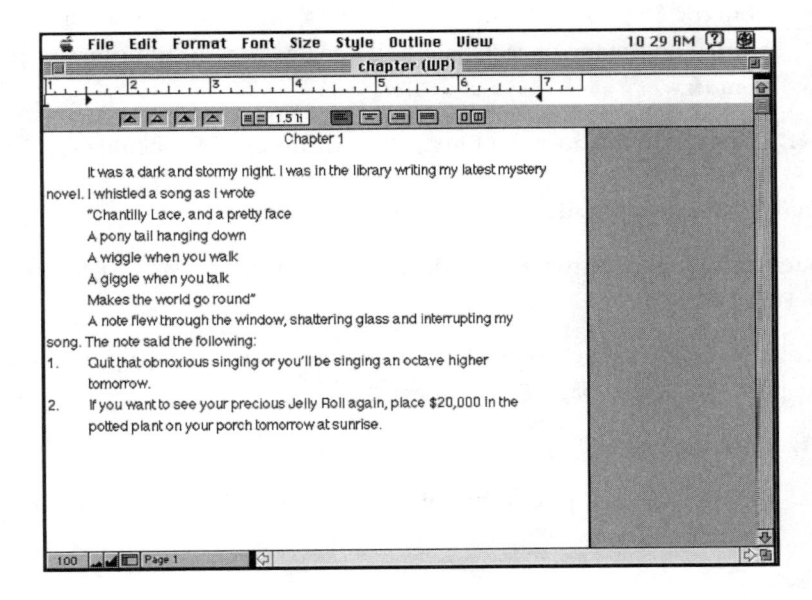

Figure 4.12
In this document, the margins and page guides are turned off.

ClarisWorks also displays the pages one after another. You can use the vertical scroll bars to scroll through the document. If you choose, you can view the pages side by side and scroll through the document by using the horizontal scroll bars (along the bottom of the screen). To view two pages side by side, choose the icon that shows two pages. To view more than two pages, choose the next icon and type the number of pages you want displayed side by side.

Inserting Headers and Footers

If your document is more than a few pages long, you may want to include on each page information that identifies the document. For example, you may want to include the chapter number or report name. Page numbers also are often included on each page.

Information that prints at the top of each page is called a *header*. Information that prints at the bottom of each page is called a *footer*. You can create both headers and footers with ClarisWorks. Follow these steps:

1. Choose Insert Header or Insert Footer from the Format menu. ClarisWorks moves the insertion point to the top (header) or bottom (footer) of the page.

2. Type the text you want to include. You can use any formatting features, such as bold, italic, tabs, and so on.

3. If you want to include the page number, choose Insert Page Number from the Edit menu. ClarisWorks inserts a page number that will be printed on the top of each page and updated to reflect the current page number.

4. To return to the document text, click within the document area.

Figure 4.13 shows a header created for a document.

To remove a header or footer, choose Remove Header or Remove Footer from the Format menu.

If you don't want to include the header or footer on the first page, create a title page for the first page. Follow these steps:

1. Click the page.

2. Choose Document from the Format menu. The Document dialog box appears.

3. Check the Title Page check box.

4. Choose OK.

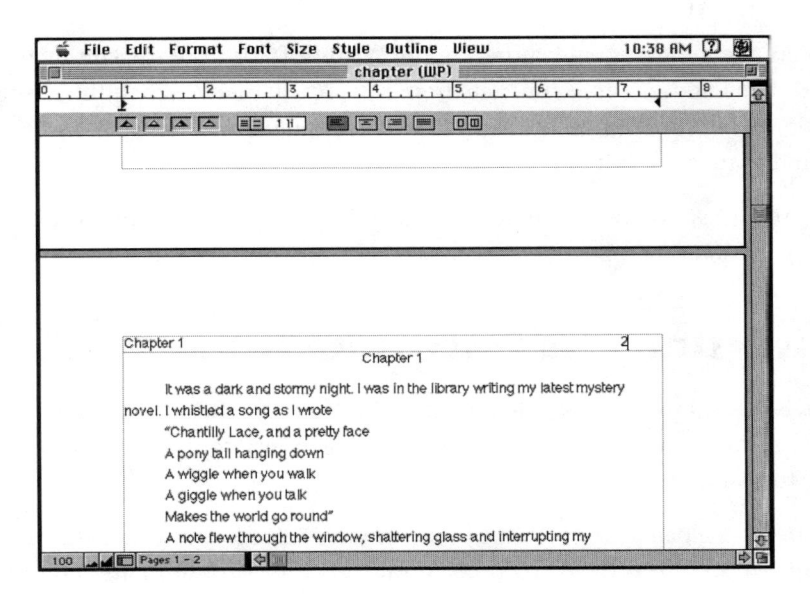

Figure 4.13
Use a header to identify the document name and include pages and numbers.

Adding Page Numbers

You can add page numbers anywhere in the document area, but page numbers are most often included in headers or footers, as described in the preceding section.

To change the starting page number, follow these steps:

1. Choose Document from the Format menu. The Document dialog box appears.

2. In the Starting Page # text box, type the page number you want to start with.

3. Choose OK.

Hyphenating a Document

When you work in a justified document, you may find that the text is too widely spaced within paragraphs. When you work in a multicolumn document, you may have large gaps along the right margin. In either case, you can alleviate the spacing problems by hyphenating the document. ClarisWorks uses its hyphenation dictionary to enter appropriate breaks and hyphens.

To use the hyphenation feature, choose Writing Tools from the Edit menu, and then choose Auto Hyphenate from the pop-up menu. When this feature is on, a checkmark appears next to the command name. Choose the command again to turn it off.

Figure 4.14 shows two documents—one before hyphenation and one after hyphenation.

Inserting the Date and Time

ClarisWorks provides a shortcut method for inserting the current date into a document. If you don't know the current date or just don't want to type it, use this shortcut.

To insert the date, choose Insert Date from the Edit menu. By default, ClarisWorks inserts the date in this format: 2/13/94. For information on changing the date format, see Chapter 20, "Customizing ClarisWorks."

To insert the time, choose Insert Time from the Edit menu. ClarisWorks inserts the time in this format: 12:55 PM. See Chapter 20 for information on changing this format.

Inserting Graphics

The benefit of using an integrated package such as ClarisWorks is that you can easily combine different types of data. For example, you may want to illustrate a word processing document with a drawing or painting that you created, with art from another software program, or with clip art. You can use the following methods to insert a graphic:

- You can use the drawing tools to create a drawing within the document. For information on using these tools, see Chapter 6.

- You can set up frames to contain the drawing or painting. Frames are covered in Chapter 15.

- You can copy the picture from another program to the Clipboard and then paste the picture into the ClarisWorks document.

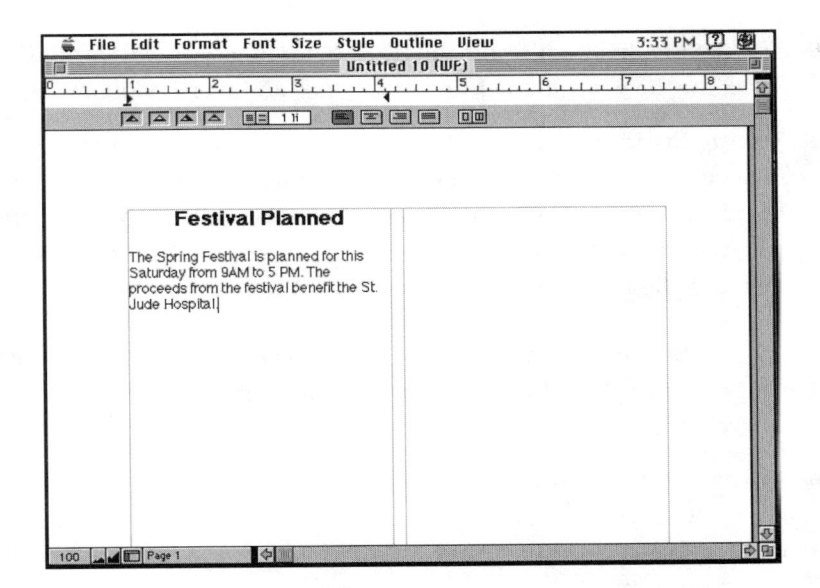

Figure 4.14
Hyphenating a document can help make justified text or multicolumn text align more attractively.

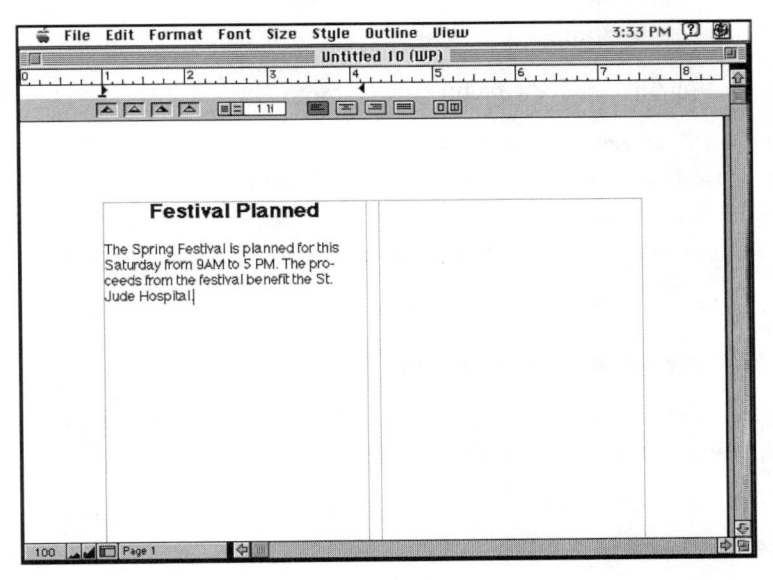

- You can use the Insert command (File Menu) to insert a graphic file. Select the file name in the Insert dialog box, and then choose Insert.

- You can insert a picture as a character. To do so, create the painting or drawing in the paint or draw program, and copy the picture to the Clipboard. In your ClarisWorks document, place the insertion point where you want the picture, and then choose Paste from the Edit menu. You then can align and format the picture as if it were a character.

After the picture is inserted, you can move it, delete it, and control the way text wraps around it. You also can control the way that the text and graphics are arranged on the page (which layer is on top).

Moving and Deleting a Picture

To move a picture, click the picture once to select it. Black selection handles appear around the edges of the object. (An *object* can be a picture, a drawing created with one of the ClarisWorks drawing tools, or a frame.) Then drag the object to a new location.

To delete a picture, click the picture once to select it, and then press Delete.

Wrapping Text around an Object

By default, ClarisWorks does not wrap text around an object; the program moves the text out of the object's way. You can tell ClarisWorks to place an even amount of space around the object or to use an uneven amount.

To control text wrapping, follow these steps:

1. Click the object once to select it.

When an object is selected, the menu bar changes, displaying commands that relate to the selected object.

2. Choose Text Wrap from the Options menu. The Text Wrap dialog box appears (see fig. 4.15).

Figure 4.15
Choose a text-wrapping option in the Text Wrap dialog box.

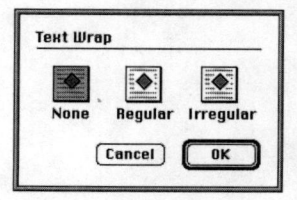

Inserting Graphics   **97**

3. Choose the option you want.

4. Choose OK.

Figure 4.16 shows the three text-wrap options.

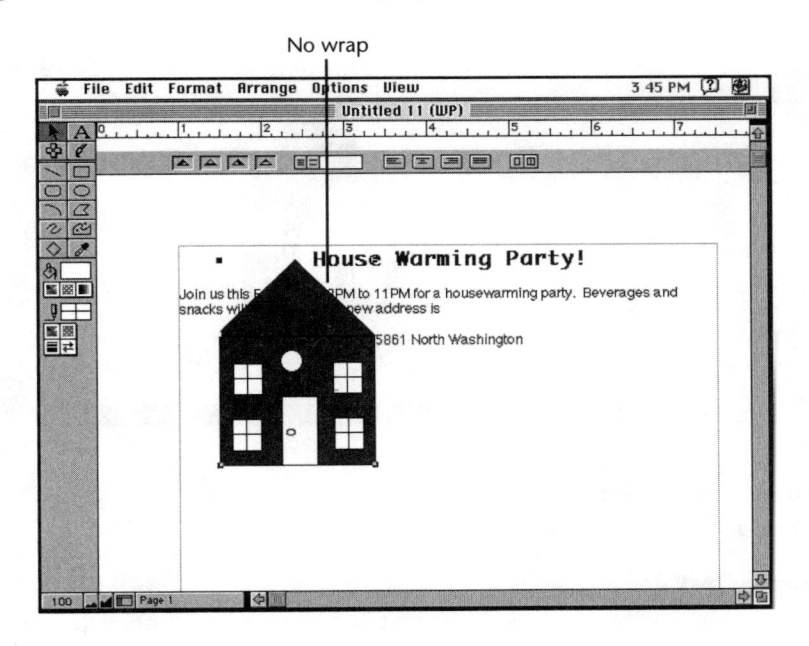

Figure 4.16
You can choose no wrap, a regular wrap, or an irregular wrap.

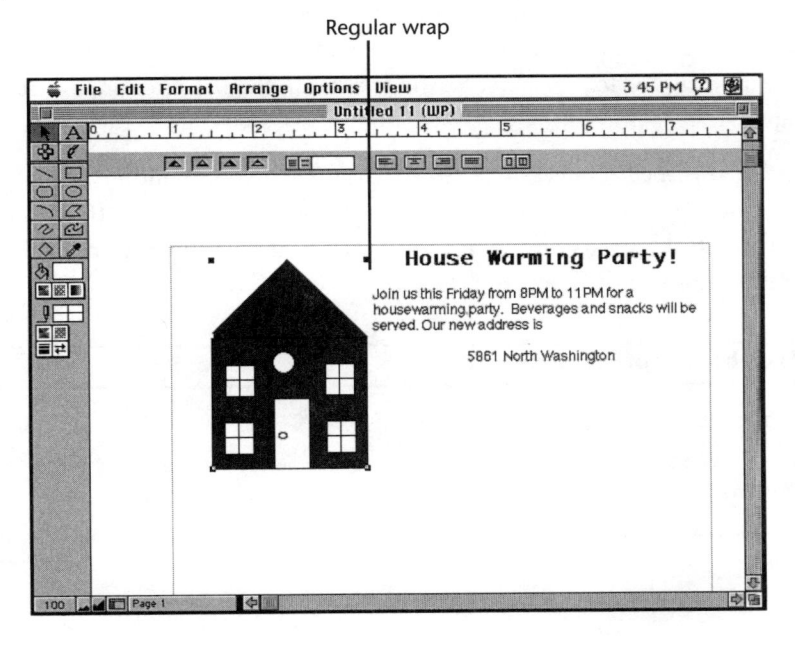

98 Chapter 4—Enhancing Your Text

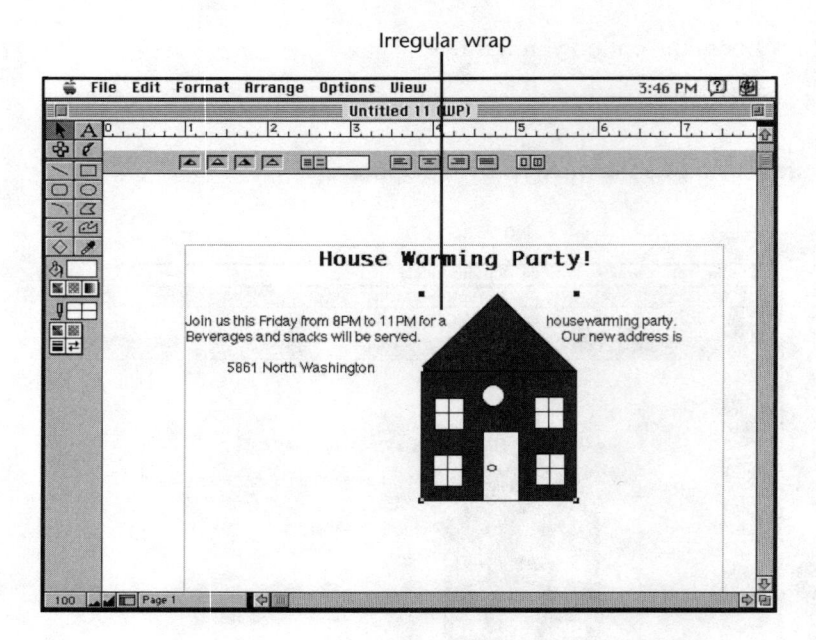

[Figure: Screenshot of a document titled "House Warming Party!" with an arrow pointing to "Irregular wrap" showing text flowing around a house graphic.]

For more information on creating and formatting objects, see Chapter 6, "Drawing."

Layering Text and Graphics

If you choose a text-wrap option, the text and objects do not overlap. If you choose None for the text-wrap option, the object appears on top of the text. You can choose the order in which the text and objects overlap—for example, putting the text on top and the graphic in the background, as shown in figure 4.17.

To create this special effect, make sure that the text-wrap option is set to None. Then, with the object selected, choose Move to Back from the Arrange menu. The text appears on top of the object. For more information on arrange options, see Chapter 6, "Drawing."

Troubleshooting Graphics

I inserted a picture, and now I can't see the text. How do I fix this problem?

If the picture appears over the text, you need to change the wrap option. Choose Text Wrap from the Options menu, and then choose a wrap other than None.

The menus change when I work on a document with graphics. Why?

The menus change depending on where you are working in the document. If the insertion point is inside text, you see word processing commands. If you have a graphic selected, graphic commands appear. If you are working inside a spreadsheet frame, you see spreadsheet commands.

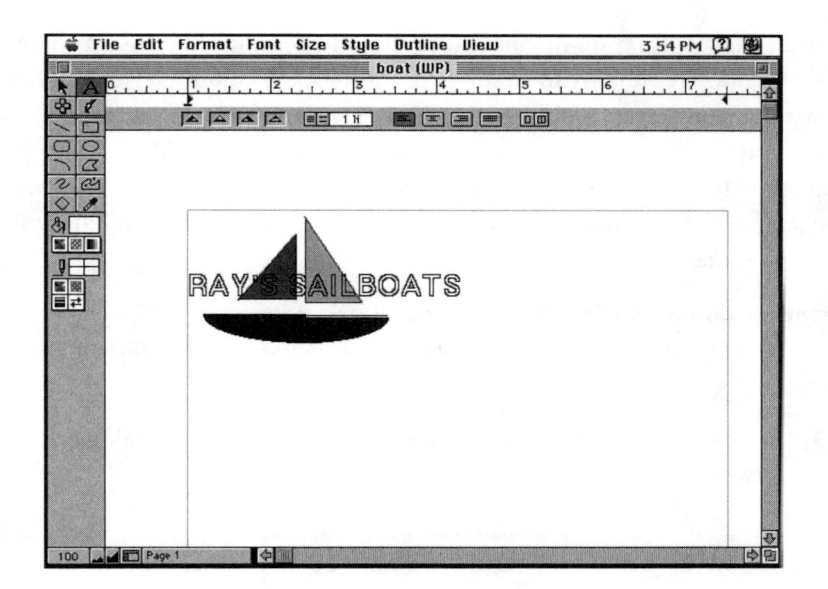

Figure 4.17
When the text-wrap option is None, you can change the order of the text and object.

Working with Columns

Most documents are one-column; the text goes from the left margin all the way to the right margin. For some types of documents, such as newsletters, you may want to use two columns.

> **Note**
>
> You cannot mix column formats—for example, have some text in one column and other text in two columns—without using frames. For details, see Chapter 15, "Creating Integrated Documents."

You can set up columns of equal width or of different widths, using either the ruler or the Columns dialog box.

Creating Columns with the Ruler

When you use the ruler to create columns, all columns are the same size, but you can easily drag a column's guidelines to change its width.

To create columns with the ruler, click the Increase Column icon. Each time you click this icon, another column is added. Click the Decrease Column icon to decrease the number of columns.

On-screen, you see column guides indicating the boundaries of each column. You can drag a boundary to change the width of the column. Press and hold down the Option key, and then click and drag the boundary you want to change. If you want to increase the size of a column, click and drag the right guideline. If you want to change the space between columns, click and drag the left edge of the column. To change two columns, click between the columns and drag.

Creating Columns with the Columns Dialog Box

You also can use the Columns dialog box to create columns. Follow these steps:

1. Choose Columns from the Format menu. The Columns dialog box appears (see fig. 4.18).

Figure 4.18
Use the Columns dialog box to enter the number of columns you want and the space you want between them.

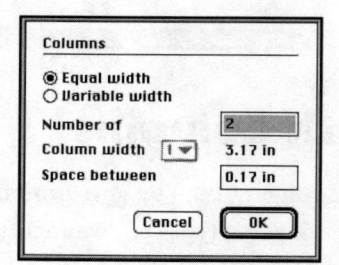

2. In the Number Of text box, type the number of columns you want. (Until you type the number of columns, some dialog-box options are not available.)

3. Click the appropriate radio button to indicate whether you want columns of equal width or of variable width.

4. If you choose Equal Width, enter the amount of space you want between the columns. (This option now is the only one available.)

If you choose Variable Width, click the Column Width box to display the pop-up menu, select the column whose width you want to set, and then enter a width. Repeat this procedure for each column. (The Space Between option is not available.)

5. Choose OK.

Typing in Columns

If you have already typed a document and then formatted it into columns, ClarisWorks will reformat the text into the number of columns you want. Figure 4.19 shows a two-column document.

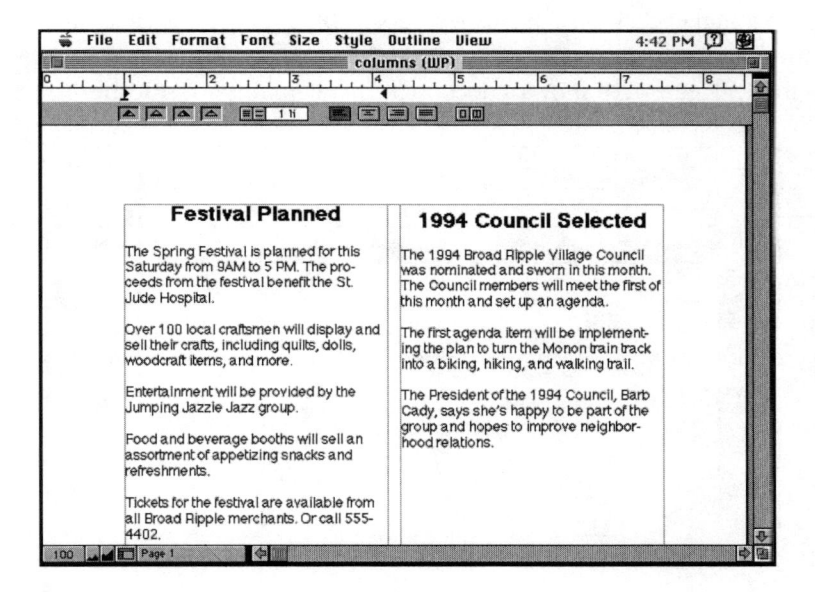

Figure 4.19
Two-column documents are often used in newsletters.

If you format the document into columns before you type the text, the text stays in the first column. When that column fills, the text wraps to the second column, and so on.

To force a column break, place the insertion point where you want the break and then choose Insert Break from the Edit menu.

To edit text, click the spot where you want to make a change, and then use any of the editing techniques covered in Chapter 3, "Working with Text."

Working with Tables

If you need to include a table of information in a document—for example, a a list of projects, project leaders' names, and comments—you can use either of the following methods to create the table:

- Use tabs to set up the table. (For details, refer to "Setting Tabs" earlier in this chapter.)

- Add a spreadsheet frame. (For complete information on frames, see Chapter 15, "Creating Integrated Documents.")

To add a frame, click the Spreadsheet tool in the tool palette, click the place in the document where you want to add the frame, and then drag to draw the frame. Figure 4.20 shows a document that contains a spreadsheet frame.

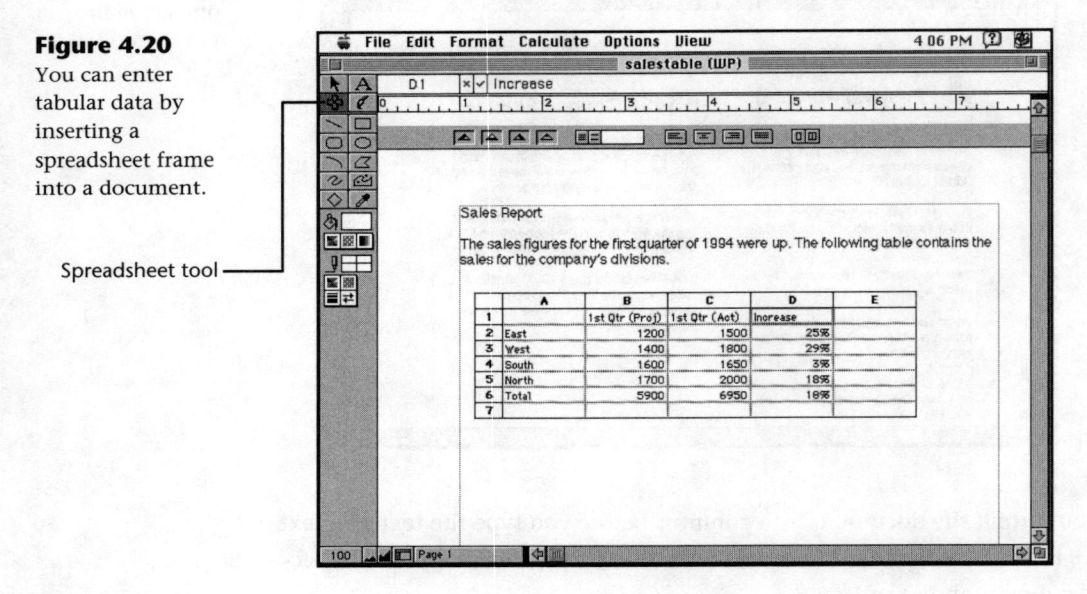

Figure 4.20
You can enter tabular data by inserting a spreadsheet frame into a document.

Spreadsheet tool

To enter text in the spreadsheet, click the cell you want to use and then type the entry. All spreadsheet commands are available when the insertion point is inside a frame, so you can adjust the width of the columns, add or delete columns, and create formulas. For more information on spreadsheets, see Chapter 8, "Spreadsheet Basics."

To return to the document, click the document. To edit the spreadsheet, double-click inside the spreadsheet frame.

A spreadsheet is an object, meaning that you can format and position the frame as you would any other object. To select the spreadsheet, click it once. Black selection handles should appear along the edges of the frame. When the frame is selected, the menu bar displays object-related commands. For example, you can change the way text wraps around the frame. For information on common formatting changes, such as text wrap, refer to "Adding Graphics" earlier in this chapter. See Chapter 6, "Drawing," for more information on all object options.

Adding Footnotes

In scholarly or research documents, you may need to use footnotes to cite sources or references. ClarisWorks makes it easy to enter, format, and number footnotes in a document. This section covers all footnote features.

Inserting a Footnote

To insert a footnote reference, follow these steps:

1. Place the insertion point where you want the footnote number to appear.

    By default, the number appears in superscript. See the following section for details on changing this default.

2. Choose Insert Footnote from the Format menu.

    ClarisWorks inserts a reference number and moves the insertion point to the bottom of the document. A line is inserted as well as the reference number.

    Tip
    You also can press Shift-⌘-F to choose the Insert Footnote command.

3. Type the footnote, and then press Return. The footnote is added, and the insertion point returns to just after the footnote reference number.

> **Caution**
> If you delete the footnote reference number, you also delete the footnote.

104 Chapter 4—Enhancing Your Text

Figure 4.21 shows an example of a footnote.

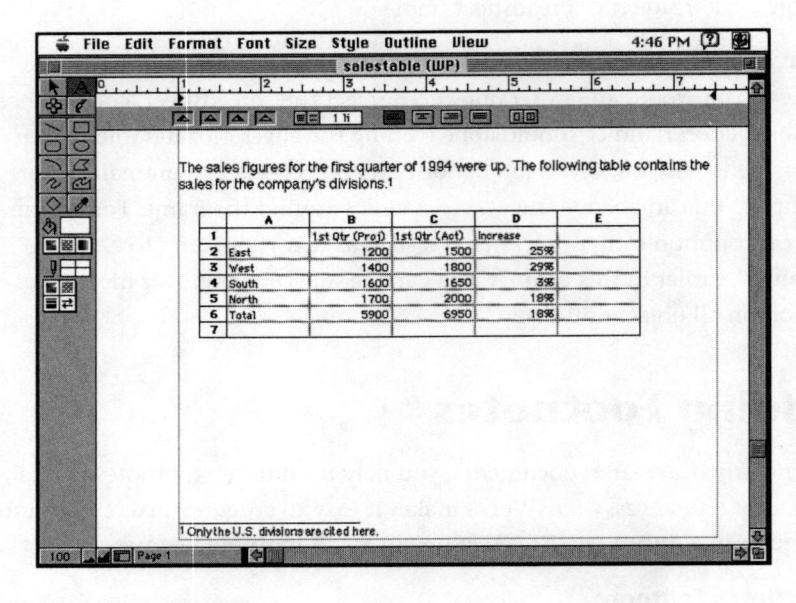

Figure 4.21
The footnote reference number appears in the text. The footnote text appears at the bottom of the document.

Customizing a Footnote

By default, ClarisWorks uses numbers for footnote references, automatically renumbering when you add or delete footnotes. You can use a reference character other than a number, however, and you can specify a different starting number.

To customize a footnote, follow these steps:

1. Choose Preferences from the Edit menu. The Preferences dialog box appears.

2. Click the Text icon. You see the text options, as shown in figure 4.22.

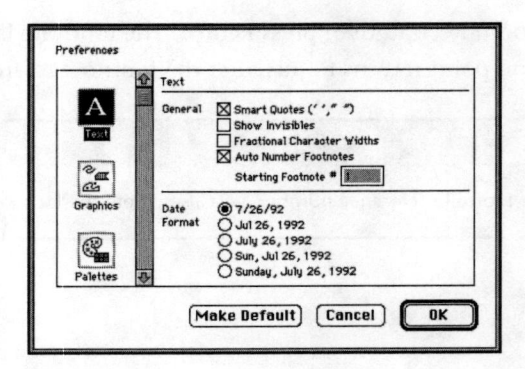

Figure 4.22
Use this dialog box to set footnote preferences.

3. If you want to use a different starting number, type that number in the Starting Footnote text box, and then skip to step 5.

4. If you want to use a different character, uncheck the Auto Number Footnotes check box.

5. Choose OK.

When you turn off Auto Number Footnotes and insert a footnote, a dialog box appears, asking what you want to use to mark the footnote (see fig. 4.23).

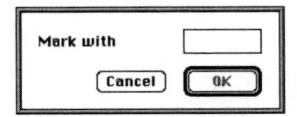

Figure 4.23
You can use a custom footnote character by typing it in this box.

Type the character, and then choose OK.

From Here...

This chapter covers the formatting features you can use to create word processing documents. The following other chapters may be of interest to you:

- If you want to create sophisticated document layouts, see Chapter 15, "Creating Integrated Documents."

- For more information on importing text and graphics, see Chapter 16, "Sharing Data with Other Documents and Applications."

Chapter 5
Working with Outlines

by Shelley O'Hara

Outlines are great ways to organize your thoughts. You can use outlines to plan the organization of a document, such as a report, or a presentation. ClarisWorks provides features that make creating, formatting, and editing outlines easy.

In this chapter, you learn the following:

- How to create an outline
- How to rearrange an outline
- How to change the view of an outline
- How to format an outline

Creating an Outline

You create an outline by turning on the outline feature and typing the outline topics. Follow these steps:

1. Choose Outline View from the Outline menu.

ClarisWorks inserts an outline symbol for the first topic. The default symbol is a small diamond.

2. Type the topic and press Return.

When you press Return, ClarisWorks adds another topic at the level of the first topic.

Tip
You also can press Shift-⌘-I to choose the Outline View command.

3. Type another topic and press Return, or create a subtopic by choosing New Topic Right from the Outline menu. When a topic contains a subtopic, the outline symbol is darkened.

4. Continue typing topics and subtopics until you complete the outline. To move back a level, choose New Topic Left from the Outline menu.

Tip
You also can press ⌘-R to choose the New Topic Right command and ⌘-L to choose the New Topic Left command.

Figure 5.1 shows an outline with several levels.

If you want to type body text (assign no level heading to the text), choose None for the Topic Level.

Figure 5.1
In an outline, you can include up to 16 different levels of topics and subtopics.

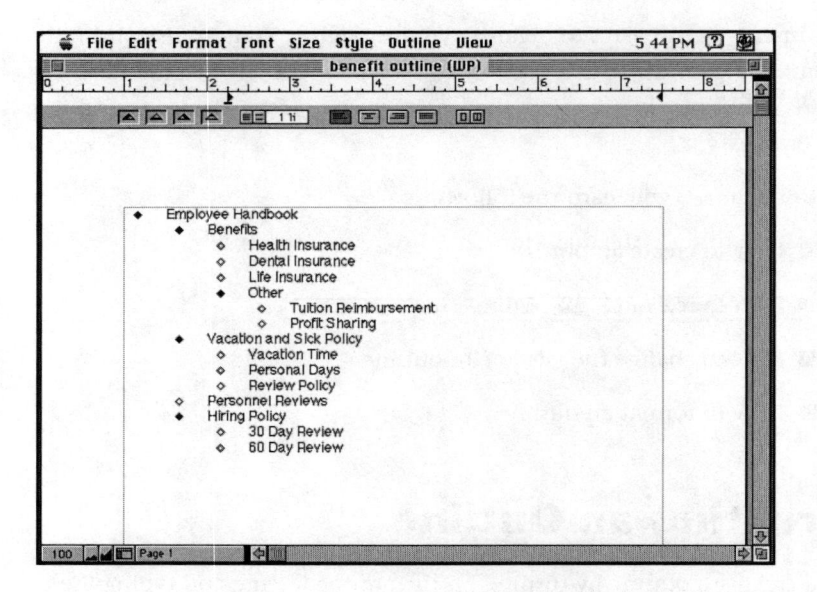

Rearranging an Outline

The outline feature makes rearranging outlines easy. For example, you can change a topic to a subtopic or move another topic up in the outline. The following sections explain how to make both kinds of changes.

Changing the Level of a Topic

You can change the level of a topic by moving it right or left. Moving a topic left makes it a higher-level topic in the outline; moving a topic right makes it a lower-level topic.

To change the level of a topic, follow these steps:

1. Place the insertion point in the topic you want to change.

2. Choose Move Left or Move Right from the Outline menu. ClarisWorks adjusts the outline accordingly.

Another way to move a topic up one level is to place the insertion point in the topic and choose Raise Topic from the Outline menu. There is no shortcut for lowering a topic.

Tip
You also can press Shift-⌘-R to choose the Move Right command and Shift-⌘-L to choose the Move Left command.

Changing the Order of an Outline

When you change the order of the topics in an outline, ClarisWorks moves each topic and its subtopics at the same time. To change the order of an outline, follow these steps:

1. Place the insertion point in the topic you want to move. Remember that ClarisWorks will move this topic and all related subtopics.

   In figure 5.2, the main topic and two subtopics will be moved.

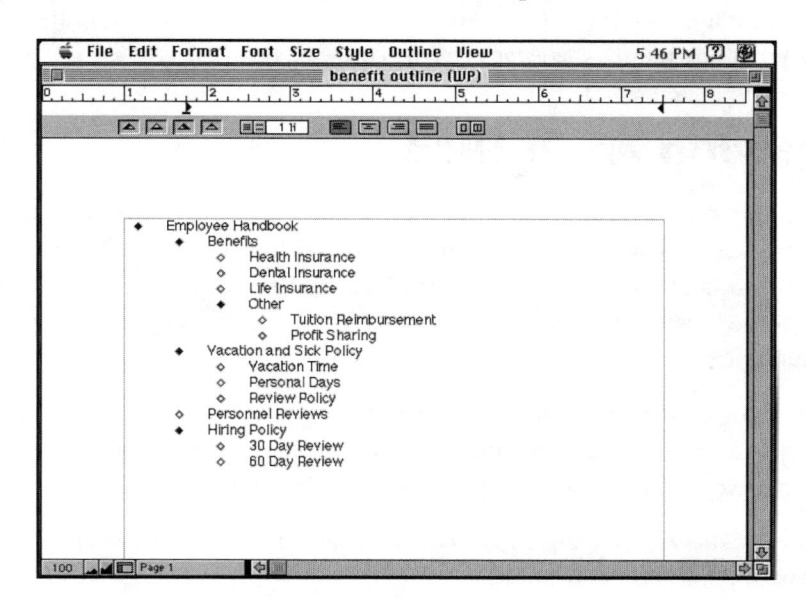

Figure 5.2
In this example, you will move the topic Hiring Policy and its related subtopics to the top of the outline.

2. Choose Move Above or Move Below from the Outline menu. ClarisWorks adjusts the outline (see fig. 5.3).

Figure 5.3
The topic Hiring Policy and related subtopics have been moved to the top of the outline.

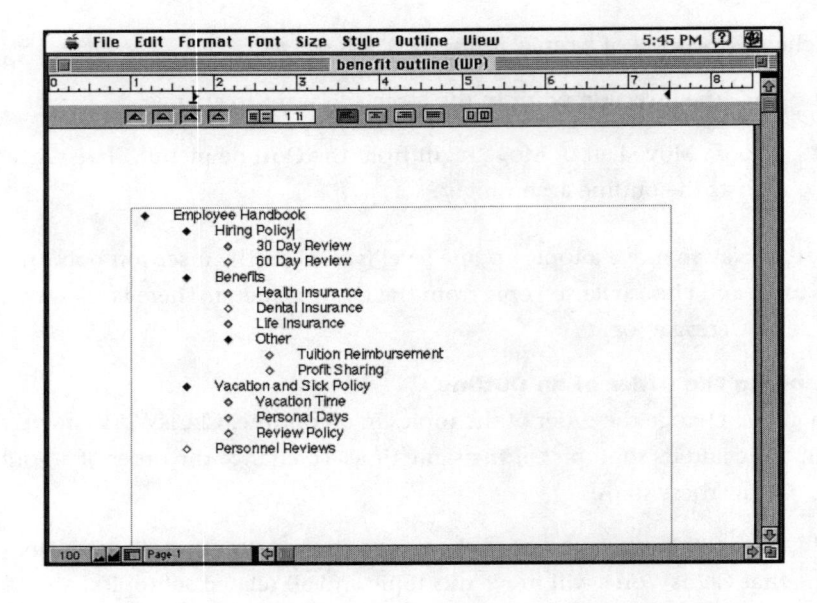

```
                    Employee Handbook
                        Hiring Policy
                            30 Day Review
                            60 Day Review
                        Benefits
                            Health Insurance
                            Dental Insurance
                            Life Insurance
                            Other
                                Tuition Reimbursement
                                Profit Sharing
                        Vacation and Sick Policy
                            Vacation Time
                            Personal Days
                            Review Policy
                    Personnel Reviews
```

Tip
You also can press Shift-⌘-A to choose Move Above and Shift-⌘-B to choose Move Below.

Alternatively, you can select a topic and drag it up or down to rearrange the outline order. Click the outline symbol to select the entire topic, and then drag up or down until the topic is in the correct spot.

Viewing an Outline

By default, ClarisWorks displays all levels of an outline. As you work in an outline, you may want to see only the main-level topics. You can easily collapse or expand the outline to show the level of detail you want. Collapsing an outline hides all subtopics below that level; expanding an outline displays all subtopics.

To collapse a topic, place the insertion point in the topic and then choose Collapse from the Outline menu. To expand a topic, place the insertion point in the topic and then choose Expand from the Outline menu.

Figure 5.4 shows an expanded view of an outline. Figure 5.5 shows the outline with the subtopics collapsed.

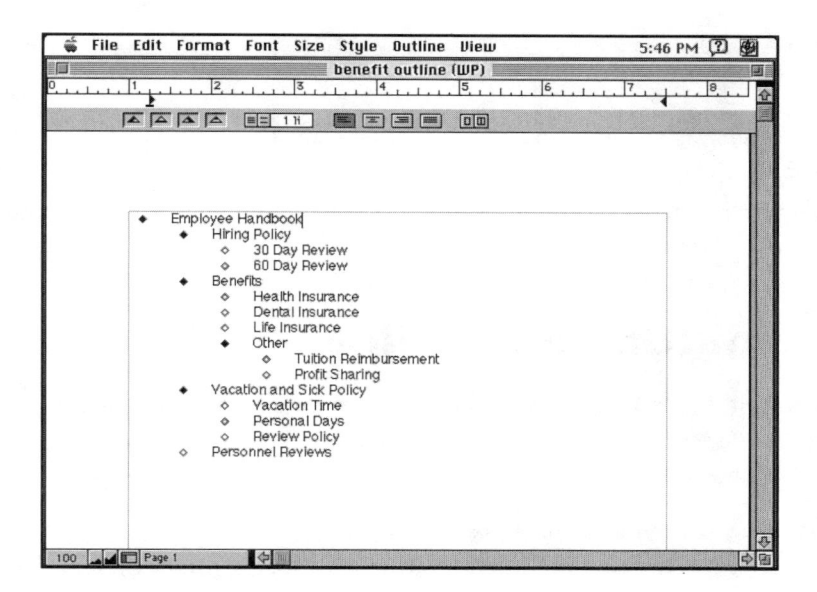

Viewing an Outline 111

Figure 5.4
In an expanded view of an outline, all levels are shown.

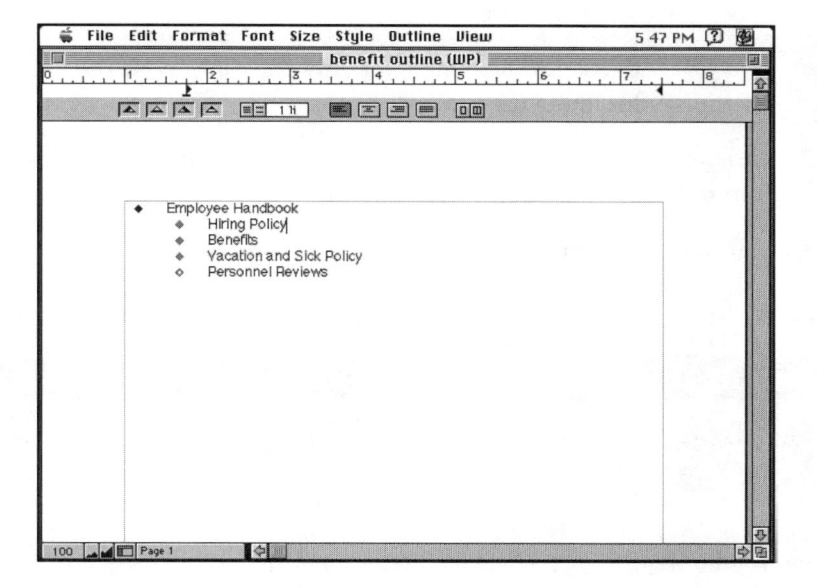

Figure 5.5
In a collapsed view of an outline, only the top-level topics are shown.

To expand the entire outline to a certain level, choose Expand To from the Outline menu. In the dialog box that appears, type the number of levels you want to display (see fig. 5.6), and then choose OK.

Figure 5.6
In this dialog box, you can specify the number of levels to be displayed in your outline.

To return to a normal document view, choose Outline View from the Outline menu.

Formatting an Outline

By default, ClarisWorks uses a diamond to indicate each topic. You can change the symbol that the program uses for a single topic, a set of topics, or all topics. You can even create your own custom outline style.

Changing the Symbol for a Topic

To change the symbol for a single topic or a few topics, follow these steps:

1. Select the topics you want to change.

   If you want to change the symbol for only one topic, place the insertion point in the topic.

2. Choose Topic Label from the Outline menu, and hold down the mouse button to display a submenu of symbols.

3. Choose a new symbol.

Figure 5.7 shows an outline that uses a different symbol for the first section.

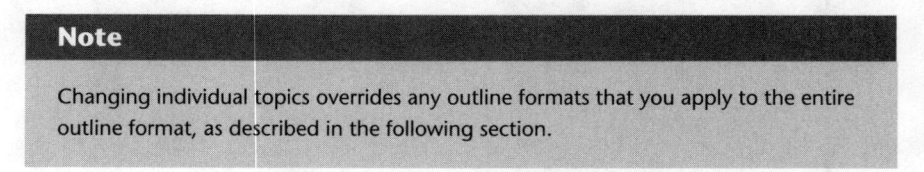

> **Note**
>
> Changing individual topics overrides any outline formats that you apply to the entire outline format, as described in the following section.

If you want to type body text (assign no level heading to the text), choose None for the Topic Level.

Changing the Outline Format

In most cases, you want to use a consistent format for your outline. If you want to apply a formatting change to the entire outline, follow these steps:

Formatting an Outline   113

1. Choose Outline Format from the Outline menu, holding down the mouse button so that you can see the pop-up menu.

2. Choose an outline format.

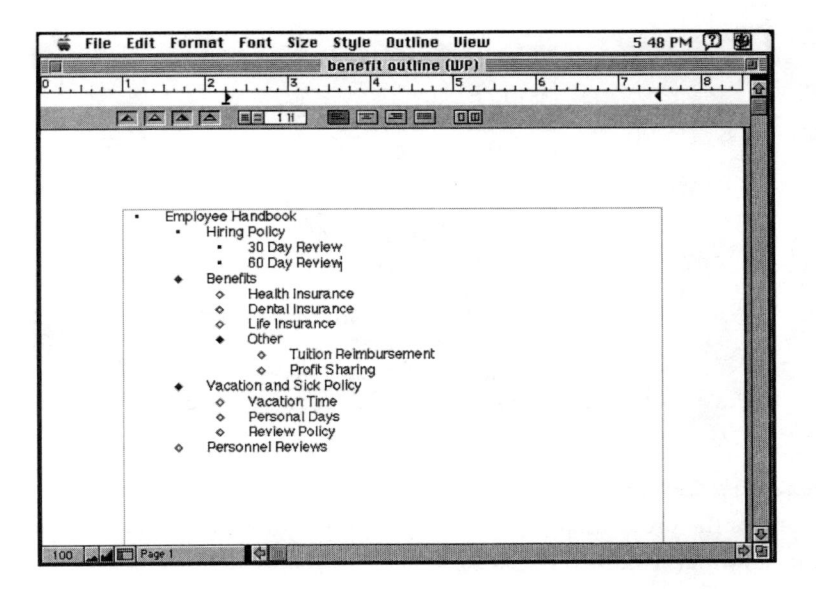

Figure 5.7
In this example, bullets are used as the outline symbol.

Figure 5.8 shows the Numeric format. Figure 5.9 shows the Checklist format.

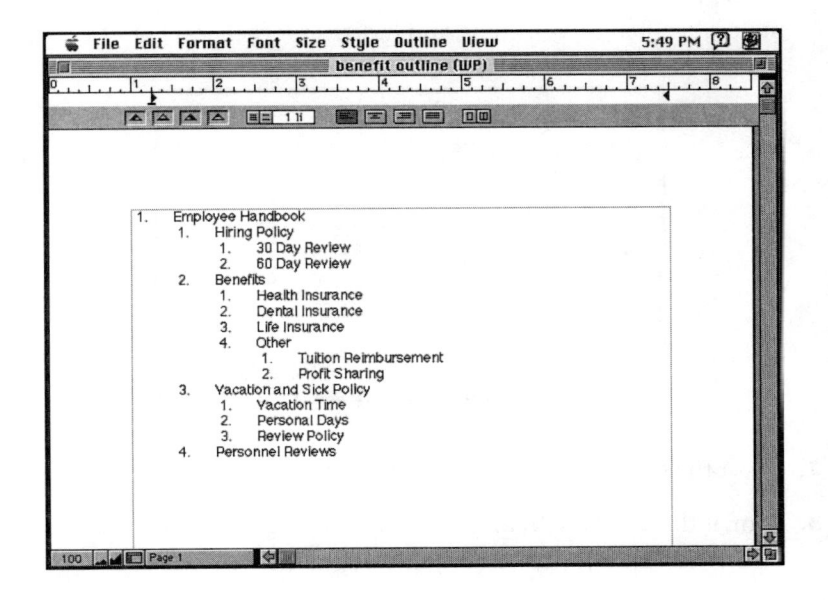

Figure 5.8
The Numeric format uses numbers as the outline symbol.

Figure 5.9
Check boxes are used as the outline symbol in the Checklist format.

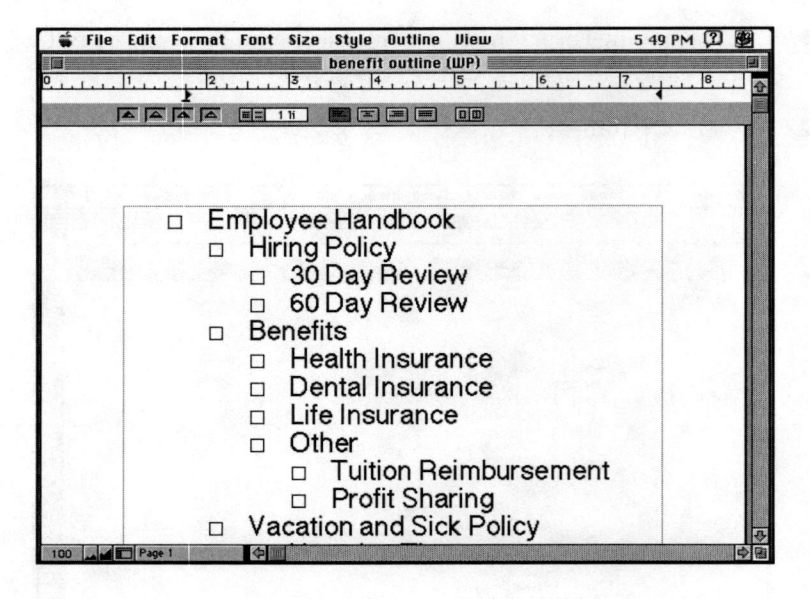

```
☐ Employee Handbook
    ☐ Hiring Policy
        ☐ 30 Day Review
        ☐ 60 Day Review
    ☐ Benefits
        ☐ Health Insurance
        ☐ Dental Insurance
        ☐ Life Insurance
        ☐ Other
            ☐ Tuition Reimbursement
            ☐ Profit Sharing
☐ Vacation and Sick Policy
```

Creating a Custom Outline Format

If none of the predefined outline formats suits your needs, you can create a custom format. Follow these steps:

1. Choose Edit Custom from the Outline menu. The Level Format dialog box appears (see fig. 5.10). In this dialog box, you set the font, size, style, alignment, label, color, and indents for each level of headings.

Figure 5.10
In a custom outline format, you can specify the font, size, style, and more.

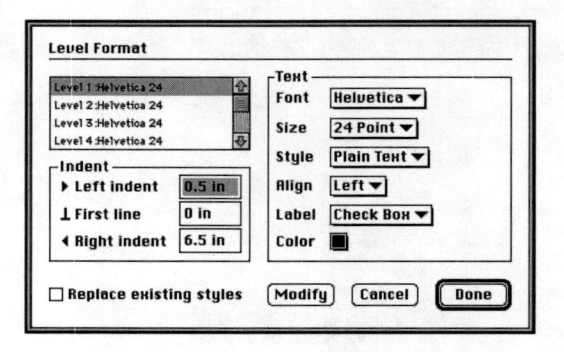

2. Select the level or levels you want to change.

3. Format the text by selecting a new font, point size, style (bold, italic, and so on), label, or color from the drop-down lists.

4. In the Indent text boxes, enter the amount (in inches) for the left, right, and first-line indents.

5. When you finish making changes for that level, click the Modify button.

6. Repeat steps 2 through 5 for each outline level you want to change.

7. When you finish modifying the outline format, choose Done.

Figure 5.11 shows an outline that uses a custom style.

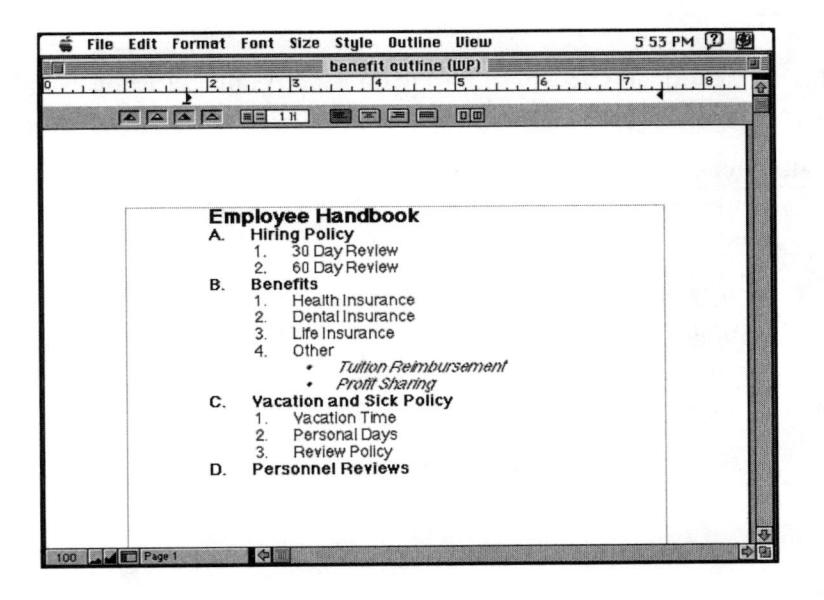

Figure 5.11
In this custom style, level-1 headings are bold 16-point type. Letters are used for the level-2 labels; numbers are used for the level-3 headings. The level-4 headings are italic and use a bullet.

Caution

You can create and use only one custom outline format at a time. If you create another custom format, it replaces the existing custom format.

> **Troubleshooting Outlines**
>
> *How do I get out of an outline?*
>
> To return to the regular view of the document, choose Outline View from the Outline menu.
>
> *I don't like the numbering style used for the outlines. Can I change it?*
>
> You can customize the font, font size, font style, and labels used for the outline. For information, refer to the preceding section, "Creating a Custom Outline Format."

From Here...

This chapter explains how to create and format an outline. The following chapters may also be of interest to you:

- Outlines are good ways to organize a presentation. For information on creating presentations, see Chapter 14, "Enhancing the Presentation of Data."

- For help on editing and formatting text, see Chapter 3, "Working with Text," and Chapter 4, "Enhancing Your Text."

Chapter 6
Drawing

by Catherine Fishel Morris

ClarisWorks 2.1 gives you two options for creating graphics: the drawing module and the painting module. Each module has its special uses, which are described in this chapter and the next.

The tool palette of the ClarisWorks drawing module can appear in the word processing, spreadsheet, and database modules. This palette contains a variety of tools that you can use for many tasks. You can move a drawing; change its size, shape, and color; flip it left or right, or rotate it; and even incorporate text or a spreadsheet into a drawing document.

In this chapter, you learn the following:

- How to use tools to draw objects
- How to draw freehand
- How to edit and move objects
- How to work with colors, patterns, and borders
- How to use frames

Understanding the Drawing Window

To begin a new file, double-click the ClarisWorks folder in the Finder to open it, and then double-click the ClarisWorks program icon to open the program itself. Double-click the button next to Drawing in the New Document dialog box (or click the button and then choose OK) to open a drawing window. Figure 6.1 shows an example of a new drawing document.

118 Chapter 6—Drawing

Figure 6.1
A new drawing document window, with menu and tools.

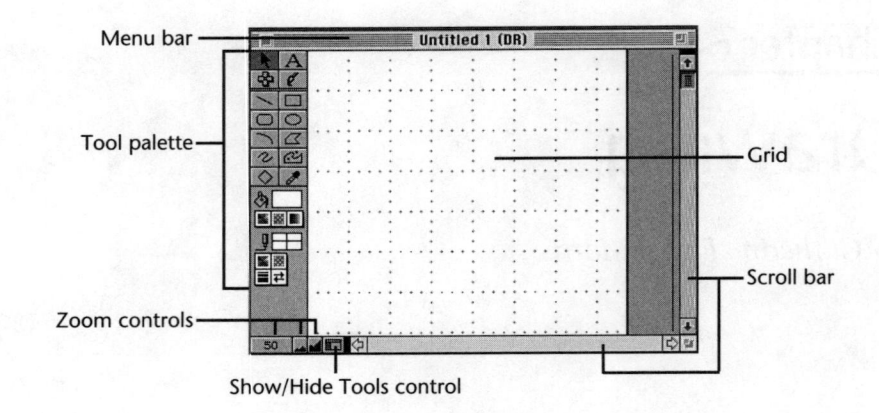

Menu bar — Tool palette — Zoom controls — Show/Hide Tools control — Grid — Scroll bar

ClarisWorks provides a variety of tools for creating and working with graphics. The following table describes the drawing tools.

Table 6.1 Drawing Tools

Icon	Tool Name	Use
	Drawing	Select, move, or resize an object
	Text	Draw text frames and enter text
	Spreadsheet	Create or edit a spreadsheet
	Painting	Draw a painting frame and use the painting tools
	Line	Draw a straight line
	Rectangle	Draw a rectangle (to draw a square, hold down the Shift key while using this tool)
	Rounded Rectangle	Draw a rectangle (or square) with rounded corners
	Oval	Draw an oval (to draw a circle, hold down the Shift key while using this tool)
	Arc	Draw an arc between two points

Understanding the Drawing Window

Icon	Tool Name	Use
	Polygon	Draw a straight-line shape, such as a star or triangle
	Freehand	Draw an irregular shape
	Bezigon	Draw a freehand shape with more control than the Freehand tool provides
	Regular Polygon	Draw a polygon with a specified number of sides
	Eyedropper	"Pick up" any color, pattern, or gradient for use in another object
	Fill palette	Draw or edit a shape with a color (click the first box under the Paint Bucket), pattern (click the second box), or gradient (click the third box)
	Pen palette	Specify line width, color, and pattern; add an arrowhead to a line

The tool palette automatically appears on the left side of the screen when you open a drawing document. To give you more viewing space, you can hide the tool palette by clicking the Show/Hide Tools control at the bottom of the screen. To display the palette again, click the Show/Hide Tools control again. You can also hide or show the tools by choosing Hide Tools or Show Tools from the View menu.

Troubleshooting the Drawing Tools

Sometimes I need to use the same tool to draw several objects. When I finish one object, I try to draw another one, but no matter what I do, the pointer changes back to the arrow pointer. Why?

When you double-click the tool you want to use, that tool remains active, allowing you to draw as many objects as you want with that tool until you click another tool.

(continues)

> (continued)
>
> *If I use the Eyedropper to change the Fill Indicator, it works fine. But I can't get it to change the Pen Indicator. What's wrong?*
>
> If you draw a line, and want to show the color or pattern of that line in the Pen Indicator, hold down the Option key and then click the Eyedropper on the line. The Pen Indicator changes to that color or pattern. You can also use the Option key with the Eyedropper to pick up the color or pattern of a border, but the Fill Indicator will also change to whatever color, pattern, or gradient is in the object that the border surrounds.

Drawing Objects

In the drawing module, it's fun to experiment and see what develops. Experimenting also gives you a good feel for how to use the mouse effectively. The more you use the drawing (and painting) module, the more proficient you will become as a mouse user.

When you place the mouse pointer on any of the drawing tools below the environment tools (the arrow, the *A* , the crossbar, and the paintbrush), the pointer is shaped like an arrow. When you click any of the drawing tools and place the mouse pointer in the grid or working area, the pointer becomes a crosshair pointer. The exception to this rule is the Eyedropper, which remains the same shape as the icon itself. To draw an object, place the crosshair pointer where you want to begin drawing, and then click and drag the mouse until the object is the size and shape you want. (More detailed information about how to use each tool appears later in this chapter.)

Immediately after you draw an object, black squares called *handles* appear around the object. The handles indicate that the object is selected. If an object does not have handles around it, click anywhere within the object to make the handles appear.

> **Note**
>
> You cannot edit an object unless it is selected. For information on what you can do with an object when the handles are present, see "Editing Objects" later in this chapter.

After you create a drawing document, you may want to enlarge it to get a better look at or duplicate a detail. Some documents may require so much room that you will need to use the scroll bars to review all the drawn objects. ClarisWorks provides three controls that enable you to enlarge and decrease a drawing document (see fig. 6.2).

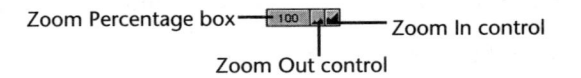

Zoom Percentage box ──── ──── Zoom In control
Zoom Out control

Figure 6.2
The zoom controls.

When you click the first box at the bottom left corner of the screen, a menu appears, showing percentages ranging from 25 to 800. You can select any of the other percentages to get a smaller or larger view of the document. If you select Other, you can type a custom size in a dialog box.

Clicking the second box, which looks like small mountains, enables you to decrease the size of the document. Each time you click the icon, the document size decreases by the percentage in the Zoom Percentage box.

Clicking the third box, which looks like large mountains, enables you to increase the size of a document. Each time you click the icon, the document size increases by the percentage in the Zoom Percentage box.

Drawing a Line, Rectangle, Rounded Rectangle, or Oval

The Line, Rectangle, Rounded Rectangle, and Oval tools create predetermined shapes. You can control the length and width of these shapes, as well as their color or pattern. If you want to draw a mathematically precise square or circle, hold down the Shift key while you use the Rectangle or Oval tool.

To draw one of these shapes, follow these steps:

1. Select the drawing tool you need.

2. Place the crosshair pointer in the work area where you want the object to be. Click and drag to the desired size and shape.

3. If you want the object to be filled, click a color, pattern, or gradient tool in the Fill palette, and hold down the mouse button to display the color, pattern, or gradient palette. Drag the mouse pointer to the choice you want, and then release the mouse button. Your choice appears in the Fill Indicator box. You can make your choice before you begin to draw, or select a drawn object and then make a different choice for the Fill or Pen palettes.

122 Chapter 6—Drawing

4. If you want the object's line or border to be a different color or a different size from the default color and size, click the Pen palette, and do the same as you did in step 3.

As mentioned earlier, with the object selected (handles visible at each corner), you can change the Fill or Pen palette choices. Also, with the object selected, you can soften, or *round*, the corners of objects. Follow these steps:

1. Choose Round Corners from the Options menu (this works with the Rectangle and Oval tools).

2. Click in the circle to select either Radius (enter a number to specify a new radius for the circle that forms the corner curve) or Round (the corners will be semicircles). Figure 6.3 shows the dialog box that appears when you choose the Round option.

Figure 6.3
This dialog box enables you to change default settings for round corners.

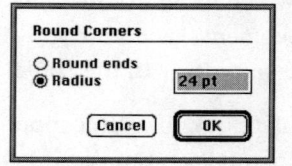

3. Choose OK.

You can make an object larger or smaller by clicking and dragging any of the handles. Alternatively, you can choose Scale Selection from the Options menu to enlarge or decrease the size of an object by a percentage amount. Figure 6.4 shows the Scale Selection dialog box, in which you type new percentages for the dimensions of the object. (Do not go below 25 or above 400.) Then choose OK.

Figure 6.4
The Scale Selection dialog box.

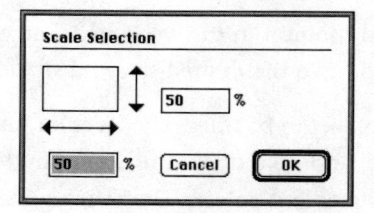

Figure 6.5 gives you examples of the kinds of rectangles, squares, ovals, and circles you can draw. It shows how you can change the width of a border, or

choose to have no border at all on an object. It displays lines of varying widths and lines with arrowheads. There is a variety of possibilities to enhance your drawing documents.

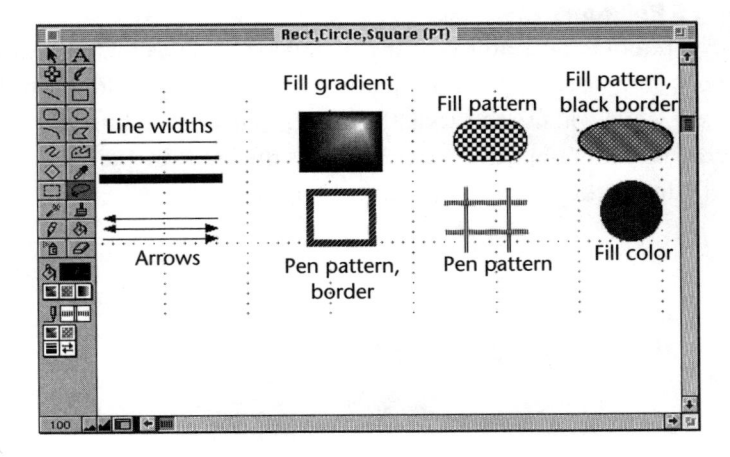

Figure 6.5
Examples of objects created with the Rectangle, Rounded Rectangle, and Oval tools and the Fill and Pen palettes.

Drawing an Arc

To draw an arc shape, choose the Arc tool. Place the crosshair pointer in the work area where you want the arc to be. Click and drag to the desired size and shape. If you drag the mouse to the left, the arc faces left; if you drag the mouse to the right, the arc faces right. You can use the tools in the Fill and Pen palettes to enhance the arc.

You can modify the angle of an arc. You can select the arc and then choose Modify Arc from the Options menu, or you can double-click the arc to access the Modify Arc dialog box (see fig. 6.6). The Start Angle decides the starting point of the arc; the Arc Angle decides the size of the arc.

The blade of the knife shown in figure 6.7 demonstrates one kind of graphic you can make with the Arc tool.

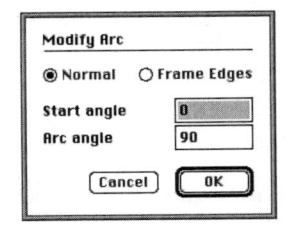

Figure 6.6
The Modify Arc dialog box.

Figure 6.7
The Arc tool was used to draw the knife blade.

Drawing a Polygon

The Polygon tool is a versatile drawing tool, particularly good for creating stars, roofs, and other shapes that involve triangles. If you hold down the Option key while you use this tool, the line can curve, enabling you to draw many other kinds of objects. Figure 6.8 shows the kinds of graphs you can draw with and without the Option key.

Figure 6.8
Examples of objects created with the Polygon tool, with and without the Option key.

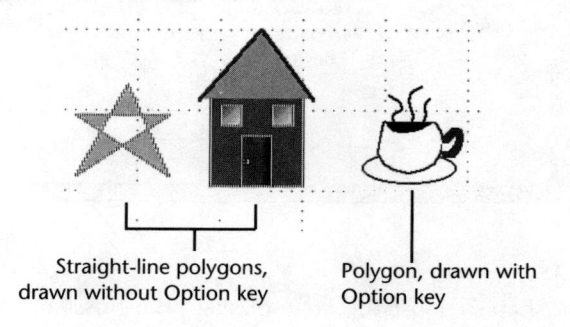

Straight-line polygons, drawn without Option key

Polygon, drawn with Option key

To use the Polygon tool, follow these steps:

1. Select the Polygon tool.

2. Place the crosshair pointer in the work area where you want the object to be. Click and drag the crosshair pointer to draw a line. When the line is the desired length, click again (this ends the first line of a drawing, but allows you to continue making more connecting lines for the object).

3. Draw a second line. Click once to end that line.

4. Continue drawing lines until the drawing is complete. If you want the line to curve, hold down the Option key as you draw.

5. Double-click to end the drawing.

You can create open and closed polygons, as follows:

- For an open polygon (for example, a freehand design), double-click to end the drawing.

- For a closed polygon (for example, stars or triangles), double-click, and ClarisWorks draws the last line for you.

- If you choose Preferences from the Edit menu, you can change the settings for an open or closed polygon. In the Preferences dialog box, click the Graphics icon to see the options available (see fig. 6.9).

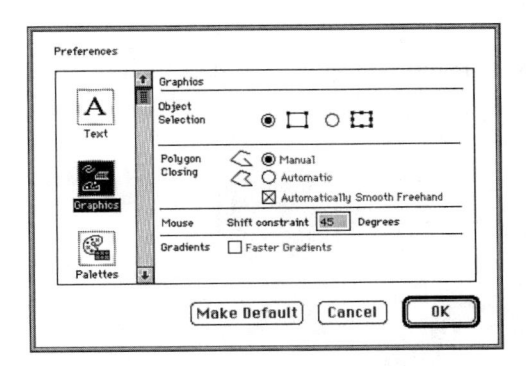

Figure 6.9
The Preferences dialog box, showing the Graphics options.

The Reshape command is helpful after you draw a polygon. You may have a line or part of a line that does not look quite right. Using the Reshape pointer will help fix the situation. When you choose Reshape from the Edit menu, the mouse pointer changes to the Reshape pointer (a small box and crosshair). The Reshape command can be used with the Bezigon, Freehand, and Arc tools as well as the Polygon. Follow these steps:

1. Select the object you want to reshape.

2. Choose Reshape from the Edit menu. Unfilled circles, called *anchor points*, appear at each point you made in the object (you can click anywhere on the line to create more anchor points). The mouse pointer becomes the Reshape pointer.

3. Click any of the object's anchor points, and then drag to create the desired shape.

4. When you finish reshaping the object, select a tool, or choose Reshape from the Edit menu again to get the arrow pointer.

Drawing a Regular Polygon

The Regular Polygon tool enables you to draw a closed polygon with a specific number of sides. The default number of sides is six. To change the number of sides, follow these steps:

1. Select the Regular Polygon tool.
2. Choose Polygon Sides from the Options menu. The Polygon Sides dialog box appears.
3. Change the number of sides to the one you want.
4. Choose OK.

Figure 6.10 shows a regular polygon as well as a many-sided one before and after smoothing.

Figure 6.10
Twelve-sided polygons–regular, reshaped, and smoothed.

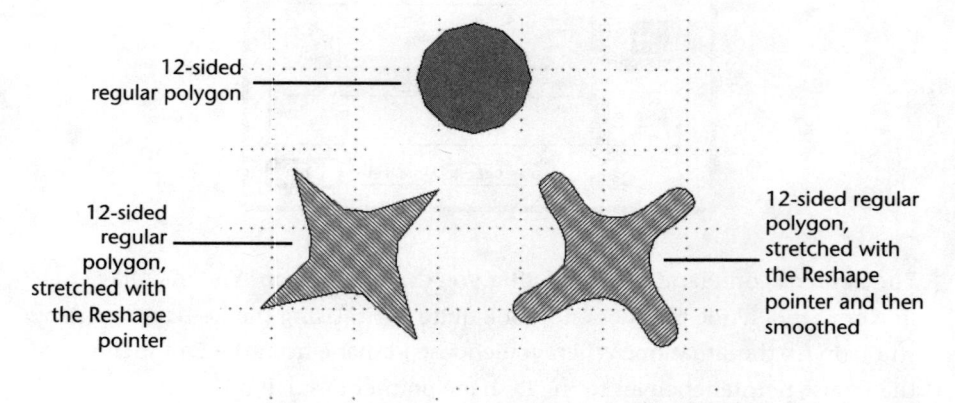

12-sided regular polygon

12-sided regular polygon, stretched with the Reshape pointer

12-sided regular polygon, stretched with the Reshape pointer and then smoothed

You can smooth a polygon or regular polygon by following these steps:

1. Select the drawing.
2. Choose Smooth from the Edit menu. ClarisWorks smoothes out the sharp points in the drawing.

To unsmooth an object, select it and then choose Unsmooth from the Edit menu.

Drawing Freehand

The Freehand tool is for those who have an artistic bent; it is the closest thing to a regular pen or pencil that ClarisWorks offers. You can use this tool to draw shapes that curve or have irregular lines.

After you draw an object with the Freehand tool, it automatically smoothes out. If you want to change this default setting, choose Preferences from the Edit menu. In the Preferences dialog box, select the Graphics icon and then deselect the Automatically Smooth Freehand option.

The Freehand tool was used to draw the tree shown in figure 6.11.

You can use the Reshape pointer on a freehand drawing (see "Drawing a Polygon" earlier in this chapter for directions on using the Reshape pointer). When you click the drawing, many anchor points appear on the freehand figure. You can then proceed to use the Reshape pointer and drag the anchor points to reshape the object. You can also use the Smooth and Unsmooth commands (in the Edit menu) on a selected freehand drawing.

Figure 6.11
An example of what you can do with the Freehand tool.

Drawing with the Bezigon Tool

The Bezigon tool is used to draw Bézier curves. A Bézier curve is an irregular shape between two control handles. You can curve your line to draw objects such as a nautilus shell or spiraling circles with the Bezigon tool.

The Bezigon tool is somewhat more difficult to use than the other drawing tools. To overcome this difficulty, remember to keep the lines short—and to draw many of them to give you better control. Practice using this tool until you get a feel for what it can do; when you learn how to use it, you will see that it is indeed powerful.

To draw with this tool, follow these steps:

1. Select the Bezigon tool.

2. Click and drag to draw a straight or curved line, and click again at the spot where you want the line to end.

3. Draw another line.

4. Continue drawing lines until the drawing is complete. If you end the drawing at the starting point, click that point. If the drawing ends elsewhere, double-click that point.

After you finish drawing with the Bezigon tool, you can use the Reshape, Smooth, and Unsmooth commands to adjust the drawing.

Using the Eyedropper

If you create a drawing with several different colors (or different shades of the same color), patterns, or gradients and then need to use one of those colors, patterns, or gradients a second time, you can use the Eyedropper tool to ease the job. This tool eliminates the need to guess which option to choose from the Fill or Pen palette. The Eyedropper "picks up" a copy of the fill or pen selection from the drawn object and places the object's color, pattern, or gradient in the appropriate indicator. Follow these steps:

1. Select the Eyedropper tool.

2. Using the Eyedropper, click a color, pattern, or gradient in an existing drawing. That color, pattern, or gradient is now displayed in the Fill or Pen (if you hold down the Option key with the Eyedropper) indicator box.

3. You can now select another existing object, and its fill or pen color or pattern will change to what is in the indicators, or you can draw a new object and it will be in the color, pattern, or gradient placed in the indicator box by the Eyedropper.

Editing Objects

You can easily create good-looking graphics with the editing options ClarisWorks provides in the drawing and painting modules. You can select or delete one object, or several at a time. You can move a graphic anywhere on-screen. You can change the size by clicking and dragging any of the handles. Using the Fill and Pen palettes, you can change the color, pattern, gradient, or line width. You can also rotate a graphic, flip it, move it to the background, group it, duplicate it, reshape it, and smooth or unsmooth it.

Before you can edit an object, however, you must select it. The following section explains how to select objects.

Selecting Objects

You can select an object in any of the following ways:

- To select one object, click it.

- To select several objects of the same kind, click the tool that created the shape and then choose Select All from the Edit menu.

- To select several objects of different kinds, click the top left corner of the area containing the objects, and drag the mouse diagonally to the bottom and right until all the objects are enclosed by a flashing rectangle. When all the objects are enclosed, click to select them.

    or

    Holding down the ⌘ key, click and drag the mouse pointer over the objects; then release the mouse button to select them.

    or

    Hold down the Shift key while you click each object individually. Then release the mouse button to select the objects.

To deselect an object or group of objects, click outside the object(s).

Moving Objects

After you select a graphic, you can move it by clicking and dragging it to a new location. A dotted rectangle moves with the mouse pointer. When you release the mouse button, the object takes the place of the dotted rectangle.

If you are moving a polygon, Bézier curve, or freehand shape, a dotted square, larger than the actual object, moves with the mouse pointer. When you release the mouse button, the actual object moves to the new location. To move the object itself, press ⌘ and then click and drag the object; the object becomes dimmed and dotted and moves with the pointer. When you release the mouse button, the actual object takes the place of the dotted one.

If you do not like the new location, you can move the object back to its original position by immediately choosing Undo Move from the Edit menu. You must choose this command before you perform any other action, because Undo reverses only the last action you perform.

Deleting Objects

After you select a graphic, you can delete it in either of the following ways:

- Press the Delete key.

- Choose Clear from the Edit menu.

Rearranging Overlapping Objects

If you create overlapping objects, the normal positioning of those objects depends on the order in which you create them. The first object is in the back, and each new object overlaps the preceding one. ClarisWorks enables you to alter the default positioning of objects by moving any object backward or forward. Figure 6.12 shows different arrangements of three sets of objects.

Figure 6.12
An example of how objects can be rearranged.

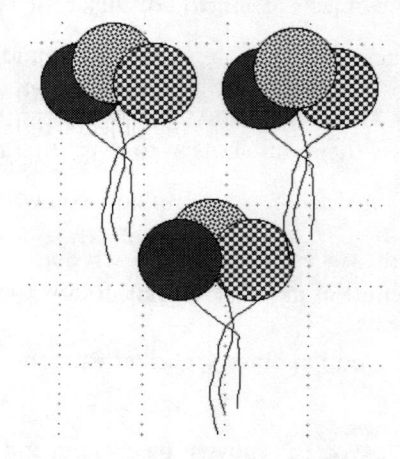

To change the positions of overlapping objects, follow these steps:

1. Select one object.

2. Choose one of the following commands from the Arrange menu:

    - Move Forward moves the object one position forward. (To use this command, you must have at least three objects on-screen.)

    - Move to Front places the object in front of all other objects in the drawing.

    - Move Backward moves the object one position backward. (To use this command, you must have at least three objects on-screen.)

    - Move Back moves the object behind any other objects. You need at least two objects to use this option. With more than two objects, the Move Back command places the selected object behind all others.

Copying Objects

If you need to draw a person's face, it is much easier to draw only one eye and copy it than to draw another eye, as shown in figure 6.13. To accomplish this, you have a choice of the Copy or Duplicate command.

Figure 6.13
An example of using the Copy, Paste, and Duplicate commands.

Choosing the Copy command requires more key work and places the copy of the object wherever you click the screen when you use the Paste command. The Duplicate command places a copy of the object overlapping the original, such as the ice cream cones shown in figure 6.13. It does not replace whatever is being held in the Clipboard. Knowing how you want the document to appear will guide you as to which command suits the purpose best.

To copy and paste an object or group of objects, follow these steps:

1. Select the object(s).
2. Choose Copy from the Edit menu.
3. Click where you want the copy to be pasted.
4. Choose Paste from the Edit menu.

To duplicate an object or group of objects, follow these steps:

1. Select the object(s).
2. Choose Duplicate from the Edit menu.

You can drag the duplicate just as you drag a copy of an object.

Moving Objects

There are additional ways to move or rearrange objects in a document besides selecting and dragging them. You can use the Size palette. Also, Align Objects, Align To Grid (both in the Arrange menu), and Ruler (in the Format menu) give you precise ways of moving and positioning the object(s). Flipping and rotating give additional flexibility to the placement of objects. You can also move one object that overlaps another from a front position to the back, rather like shuffling a couple of cards.

The Size palette lets you change the location of a selected object by designating where it is to appear in relationship to the edges and margins of the page. Figure 6.14 shows how a selected object can be positioned with the Size palette.

Figure 6.14
Using the Size palette to check or edit the location of an object.

Location of the object from:
Top of page — Left edge of page
Bottom of page — Right edge of page

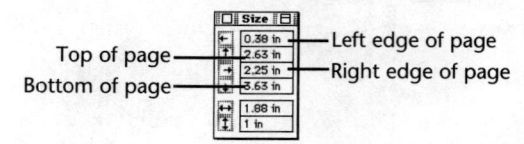

To check the location of an object within a document and, if need be, to change that location, follow these steps:

1. Select the object that you want to move.

2. Choose Object Size from the Options menu. The Size palette appears.

3. Highlight each option and key in the new values. As you key in each value, the object reflects the change.

4. To close the palette, click its close box. The object moves to its final location according to the new value settings.

Tip
To move a selected object one pixel at a time, use the arrow keys.

The grid that you see when you open a document in the drawing module lets you use guidelines to draw precisely measured objects in the drawing environment. The spacing of these guidelines is dependent on how you define the ruler settings. To change the ruler settings, and therefore where the guidelines will be placed, choose Rulers from the Format menu. The Rulers dialog box appears, as shown in figure 6.15.

Figure 6.15
The Rulers dialog box with Show Graphics Ruler selected.

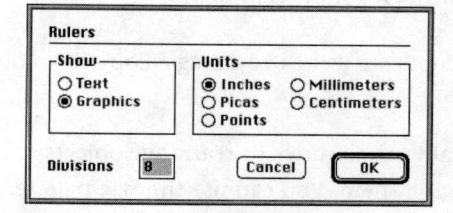

Keying in a smaller or larger number than 8 in Divisions will change column size and number of columns. Clicking the button before the word Text, then clicking OK, adds a ruler near the top of the screen with all the properties of a text ruler. Clicking the button before Graphics, then clicking OK, gives you horizontal and vertical rulers to help you size and place graphics. Choosing any other unit of measure than Inches produces a ruler based on those units.

Editing Objects **133**

The grid is always present in the drawing module unless you decide to hide it by choosing Hide Graphics Grid from the Options menu. To make the grid appear again, choose Show Graphics Grid from the Options menu.

The Autogrid is not something you see, but you know that it defaults to being active. When you move an object to a new location, you may not be able to position it exactly where you want. No matter how many times you try, the computer places the object just to the left or right, up or down of where you want it to be. Actually, that is the Autogrid at work.

Not only can you align objects to the Autogrid when it is active, you can arrange objects in relationship to each other (see fig. 6.16).

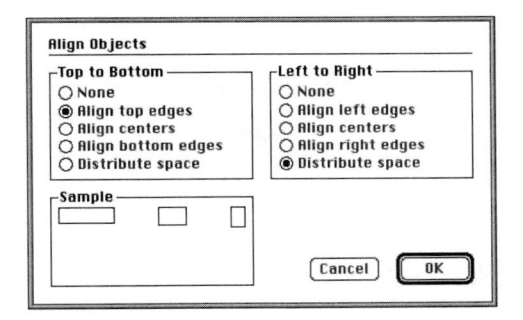

Figure 6.16
The Align Objects dialog box.

Follow these steps to align objects or arrange objects in relation to one another:

1. Select the objects you want to align.
2. Choose Align Objects from the Arrange menu.
3. Click one Top to Bottom option (choosing None leaves the objects as they are).
4. Click one Left to Right option (choosing None leaves the objects as they are).
5. Click OK.

The Autogrid is set to whatever the graphic rulers measure (either default or customized by you). If the Autogrid is interfering with the placement of your objects, you can override the default setting by choosing Turn Autogrid Off from the Options menu. Nothing changes on-screen, but now you can move objects around without their "snapping" to a preset position. To turn on the Autogrid again, choose Turn Autogrid On from the Options menu.

Flipping and rotating objects is not only fun to do, it is a time-saver. You can create one object that faces left, copy or duplicate it, and flip it to the right. Now you have two identical objects turned in opposite directions.

One of the faces in figure 6.17 is flipped horizontally.

Figure 6.17
The bottom face in the figure was rotated until it was upside down.

To flip an object, follow these steps:

1. Select the object to flip.

2. Choose Flip Horizontal or Flip Vertical from the Arrange menu.

To rotate an object, follow these steps:

1. Select the object to rotate.

2. Choose Rotate from the Arrange menu.

Grouping Objects

As stated before, in the drawing environment of ClarisWorks, each object is considered a separate entity. If you use a variety of tools to create a drawing, it may be easier to draw the individual parts, assemble them, and finally group them to make one whole graphic. That is how the man's face was put together in figure 6.18.

The following steps explain how to take several objects and use the Group command to make them one object:

1. Select the objects that are to be grouped by holding down the Shift key and then clicking each item. Handles appear on all objects.

Changing Colors, Patterns, and Borders   **135**

2. Choose Group from the Arrange menu. You now have a total of four corner handles on the object, outlining the object.

To disassemble the group object and return it to its original number of objects, follow these steps:

1. Select the grouped object.

2. Choose Ungroup from the Arrange menu. You now have four corner handles showing on each object once again.

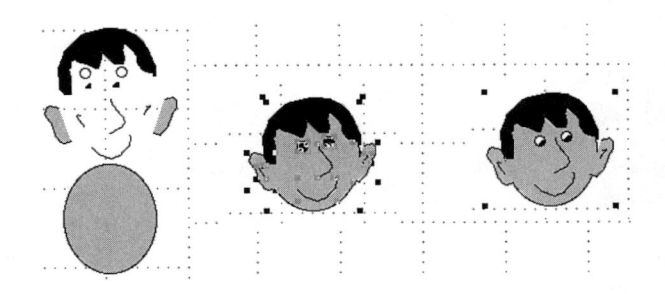

Figure 6.18
Grouping individual objects to make one object.

Changing Colors, Patterns, and Borders

The ease with which you can change the color of an object, the pattern, or the gradient, and the variety of choices available, make this portion of ClarisWorks really enjoyable. The possibilities seem almost endless. You can select any of 81 shades of colors. There are 62 patterns. You can count 32 fills of gradients.

Take some time to experiment. See what combinations of objects and fills you can get. It is easy to get carried away, so remember to keep your documents simple, effective, and eye-appealing.

The Color Editor

You can change colors or mix your own and then display them on the color palette. Hue, saturation, and brightness are the elements that go into making different shades of red, blue, and green. By changing these elements, you create new colors. The following steps show you how to customize your color palette:

1. Choose Preferences from the Edit menu. The Preferences dialog box appears.

Tip
Click the Option key and then the Eyedropper to change the color or patterns of lines and borders in the Pen Indicator easily.

2. Click the Palettes icon.

3. Click in the circle Editable 256 Color Palette.

4. Click Load Palette. A dialog box appears.

5. Double-click Colors and Gradients.

6. Double-click the set of colors you want.

7. Choose OK.

To edit a color in the new color palette, follow these steps:

1. Tear off the color palette icon and place it so it will be convenient to use.

2. Double-click the color you want to edit. A dialog box appears with many choices:

    - The numbers in the boxes (Hue, Saturation, Brightness, Red, Green, Blue) reflect the selected color.

    - The sample box is split in half with the original color on the bottom and the new color on top.

    - You can alter the brightness of the colors by using the scroll bar to the right of the color wheel. The numbers in the boxes at the right will reflect any changes.

    - You can get more precise color shadings by keying a number into any of the boxes (Hue, Saturation, Brightness, Red, Green, Blue) or by clicking the up and down arrows.

3. Click the wheel to select a color. You can use the scroll bar to change the lightness or darkness of the colors in the entire wheel.

4. If you like the color replacement, choose OK. If you do not like the replacement, click Cancel and the color palette remains the same.

5. If you want to save the palette for future use, choose Preferences from the Edit menu and then click Palettes. Choose Editable 256 Save Palette. Give the file a new name and click Save.

The Pattern Editor

The Pattern Editor allows you to replace a default pattern with one you create or to customize one of the existing patterns. (If you customize, be sure to

Changing Colors, Patterns, and Borders **137**

choose a pattern you do not want to use in the document.) You will be surprised by how many variations you can come up with in the small amount of space you have to create a new pattern. An example of a customized pattern that will replace one of the default patterns is shown in figure 6.19.

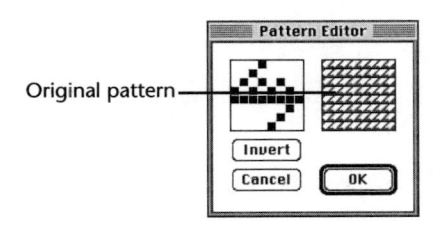

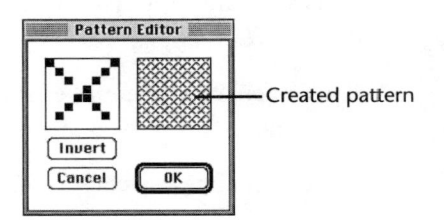

Figure 6.19
An example of a customized pattern in the Pattern Editor dialog box.

The following steps explain how to access the Pattern Editor and customize a pattern:

1. You can select a pattern or double-click the pattern if the palette is already open in the document.

2. Choose Patterns from the Options menu to open the Pattern Editor.

3. In the box showing large individual pixels, click to add or delete pixels to create a new pattern.

4. To reverse the pattern's black and white, click Invert.

5. Any changes you make to a color palette are changes that occur in the present document only. Choose OK if you like the changes. If you do not like the changes and want to return to the original pattern, click Cancel.

The Gradient Editor

Choosing a gradient fill for an object lets the colors gradually blend from one to another. With three types of gradients—directional, circular, and shape burst—you can use up to four colors in each gradient. Using a gradient fill lends depth and shading, creating an eye-catching sweep of color to an object.

You can edit a gradient in the following ways:

- You can select a gradient or double-click the gradient if the palette is already open in the document.

- You can choose Gradients from the Options menu.

You can make changes in the Gradient Editor in the following ways:

- Which gradient you select in the palette determines the type of sweep (directional, circular, or shape burst) in the dialog box.

- You can change the type of sweep by clicking the down triangle on the dialog box.

- You can change the number of colors in the gradient by clicking the Colors box.

- You can change any color by clicking the box of the color you want to alter.

If you are not happy with the changes, click Revert to bring the gradient back to the original or Cancel to go back to the document with no changes to the gradient palette. Any changes you make to a gradient palette are changes that occur in the present document only. Choose OK if you like the changes.

You can also set the angle and focus of the gradient. Figure 6.20 shows the dialog box that allows you to set the direction of the gradient.

Figure 6.20
Gradient Editor dialog box, showing a directional sweep.

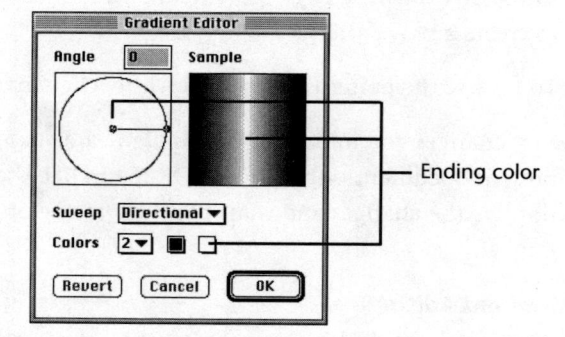

Follow these steps to change the direction of a gradient:

1. Enter a new number in the highlighted Angle box, or click the black-filled circle and drag it to a new point on the outside of the circle.

2. Drag the unfilled circle along the radius to change the position of the focus.

Figure 6.21 shows the dialog box that allows you to set the direction of the circular sweep.

Changing Colors, Patterns, and Borders **139**

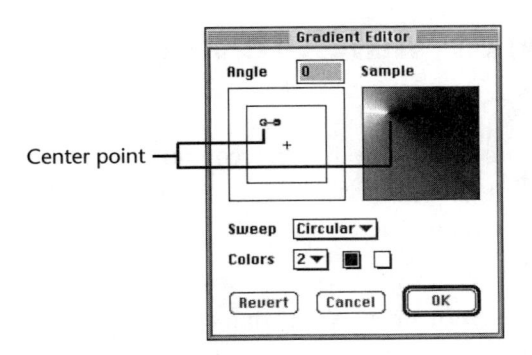

Figure 6.21
Gradient Editor dialog box, showing a Circular sweep.

Follow these steps to change the circular sweep of a gradient:

1. Enter a new number in the highlighted Angle box, or click the black-filled circle and drag it to a new position.

2. Drag the unfilled circle to a new position in the square to change the focus.

Figure 6.22 shows the dialog box that allows you to set the direction of the shape burst.

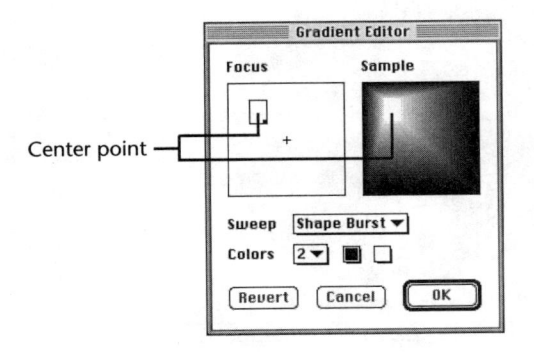

Figure 6.22
Gradient Editor dialog box showing a Shape Burst sweep.

Follow these steps to change where the shape burst is positioned in a gradient:

1. Drag the focus box to change the center point of the sweep.

2. Drag the handle on the bottom right side to change the size of the focus area.

Tip
You can tear off the 81-color palette, but you cannot double-click any color for the color wheel.

Working with Multiple-Page Drawings

There may be an occasion when your drawing requires more than one page. If you want to create something that is poster size, four pages will be required. A brochure may require several pages. That is difficult to do if you can only view one page at a time.

ClarisWorks provides you with a means of seeing and working with several pictures within one screen. You can draw objects that cross pages as well as take an object from one page and place it on another. It makes it possible to use any of the frames—text, spreadsheet, and paint—and span them from one page to the next. Figure 6.23 shows how a four-page document looks on-screen.

Figure 6.23
A multiple-page view of a drawing document.

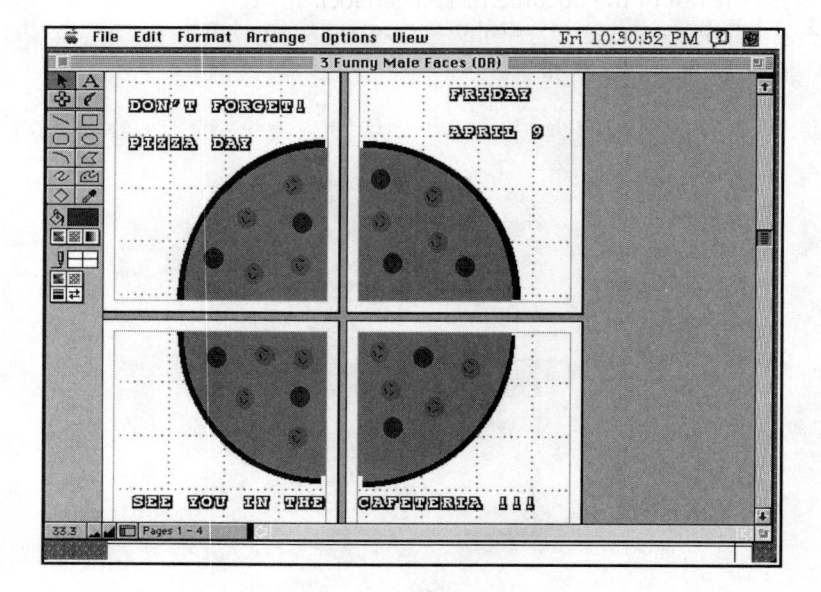

To create a screen of multiple-page drawings, follow these steps:

1. Choose Document from the Format menu.

2. Key in the number of pages you want across and/or down.

3. You can click in the box to deselect Show Margins and/or Show Page Guides.

4. Click OK after you make all your selections.

5. Choose Page View from the View menu. You can make any necessary changes in this view also.

6. Use the icon or number zoom control at the bottom of the screen to decrease the size of the document. That way, you will be able to see the entire document.

It is important to save your document frequently as you are working on it. Waiting until you complete a drawing to save it can cause heartbreak should something happen—hitting the wrong key, an unexpected error message—and you lose all your work. Give your new document a file name right away, using Save As in the File menu, and then save (Save in the File menu) every time you create an object that you want to keep. In addition to that, you may have an object you want to protect from inadvertently changing while you work on the rest of the document. You can lock any object you want (this does not apply to frames), as well as unlock them when they no longer need this special protection. Follow these steps to lock an object:

1. Select the object you want to protect.
2. Choose Lock from the Arrange menu. Now no changes can be made to this object.

You may need to unlock the object to make changes to a specific part. Follow these steps to unlock an object:

1. Select the object you want to unprotect.
2. Choose Unlock from the Arrange menu. Changes now may be made to the object.

From Here...

This chapter explains and illustrates the kinds of objects you can create in the drawing module. It takes you from learning how to use each of the available tools to learning how to customize color, pattern, and gradient palettes for your special needs. For related information regarding the drawing module and graphics, the following chapters will be of interest to you:

- Chapter 2, "Learning the Essentials." This chapter discusses generally how to access and use the drawing tools in a word processing, spreadsheet, or database document.

- Chapter 7, "Painting." This chapter covers the second graphics module available in ClarisWorks.

- Chapter 15, "Creating Integrated Documents." This chapter discusses the use of frames in the drawing module.

Chapter 7
Painting

by Catherine Fishel Morris

Painting is the second of two graphics modules discussed in this book. Just as the drawing application has its unique features (see Chapter 6, "Drawing"), so does painting. The two operations do utilize some of the same tools to create graphics documents. Also, both are set to use editable color, pattern, and gradient palettes. Yet the painting module includes a larger variety of tools. Most important, the manner in which you deal with all these tools in the painting module is quite different from how you use them in the drawing module.

Each item you create in the painting module is an *image*. This image consists of individual pixels. When you use the zoom icon at the bottom menu bar of the document to enlarge the painting, you can see that each pixel looks like a small square. You can edit a painting by removing or adding one pixel at a time. Editing one pixel at a time allows for precision and control over exactly how the picture is to look. Painting is the preferred environment for composing pictures and designs. If you dislike a portion of the image, you can erase that portion only and change it to suit the rest of the picture.

In this chapter, you learn the following:

- How to use the painting tools
- How to apply special effects
- How to edit images

Opening a Painting Document

To open a new painting document, double-click the ClarisWorks folder in the Finder to open it. Double-click the ClarisWorks program icon to open the program itself. In the New Document dialog box, double-click the Painting button, or click the button next to Painting and choose OK (when a command outlined as the OK button is in the New Document box, it indicates that you can choose it either by clicking on it with the mouse pointer or by pressing the Return key on the keyboard).

When you open a painting document, you may see the message `The document size has been reduced to fit the available memory`. If this happens, choose OK. The document screen will be smaller, but all the painting tools and menus will be available, and you can still use the zoom controls to see an enlarged view. If you need a larger working area, you can close other documents or programs to make more memory available. Also, if you have sufficient RAM or memory installed in your system, you can allocate more to ClarisWorks. In most ClarisWorks modules, 1M of memory is sufficient, but for the painting module, a minimum of 3M is recommended.

Tip
To allocate more of the available memory to ClarisWorks, quit the program and highlight the ClarisWorks icon. From the File menu, choose Get Info, and enter a larger number in the Preferred Size box.

A new painting document offers the same menu choices at the top of the document as are available in the drawing module. The tools appear at the left of the document, and scroll bars are at the right and bottom. The four button icons at the bottom of the window are for increasing and decreasing the size of the document, as well as the Show/Hide Tools control.

Using the Tools

As mentioned earlier in this chapter, some tools are specific to a painting document. These tools are shown in figure 7.1. The following paragraphs explain how you use each of these tools.

Use the *Selection Rectangle* to drag the arrow cursor over the entire image or a portion of the image to select a rectangular size to move or edit.

Use the *Lasso* to drag the arrow cursor over a portion or all of the image to select just the image itself with no "empty space."

With the *Magic Wand,* you can "pick up" a color, pattern, or part of a gradient and move it to any other place in the document.

Use the *Brush* to paint brush strokes of various widths and shapes.

Use the *Pencil* to paint thin, pencil-like lines.

Use the *Paint Bucket* to flood an enclosed shape area with a choice of color, pattern, or gradient.

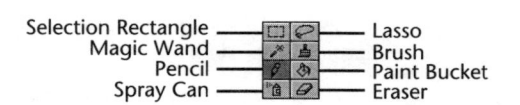

Figure 7.1
Tools found only in painting documents.

Selection Rectangle, Magic Wand, Pencil, Spray Can, Lasso, Brush, Paint Bucket, Eraser

Use the *Spray Can* to give an airbrushed or sprayed look to a painting or part of a painting.

Use the *Eraser* to erase all or part of a painting.

Painting a Picture

When you open a document in painting, the Pencil is the active tool (the default). The default color is black. You can choose whatever tool you need by clicking a tool icon.

Figure 7.2 shows the two palettes, Fill and Pen, available to you in the painting module.

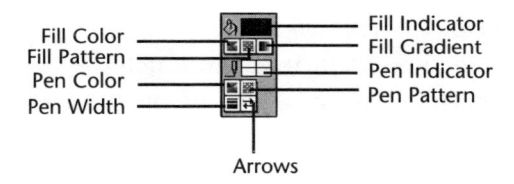

Fill Color, Fill Pattern, Pen Color, Pen Width, Fill Indicator, Fill Gradient, Pen Indicator, Pen Pattern, Arrows

Figure 7.2
The Fill and Pen palettes.

The Fill palette lets you choose a color, pattern, or gradient to fill an image you create. Whatever color, pattern, or gradient you choose (by clicking one of the icons and dragging the mouse pointer to the one you want) is shown in the fill indicator. The Pen palette lets you choose a color or pattern to use with lines and borders. It also lets you change the width of a line or border and add arrow heads at the beginning or end of a line. Just as with the Fill Indicator, whatever color or pattern you choose in the Pen palette is shown in the Pen Indicator box.

When you create an image, it defaults to being opaque. In other words, the image is solid and if one image overlaps another, the image underneath is partially hidden. You can change the default setting to transparent so you can "see through" one image overlapping another. The opaque and transparent icons are located in both the Fill and Pen palettes as shown in figure 7.3. Click the pattern icon in either palette to select the transparent or opaque icon, depending on how you want your images to look.

Figure 7.3
Open Fill palette showing default color, pattern, and gradient choices.

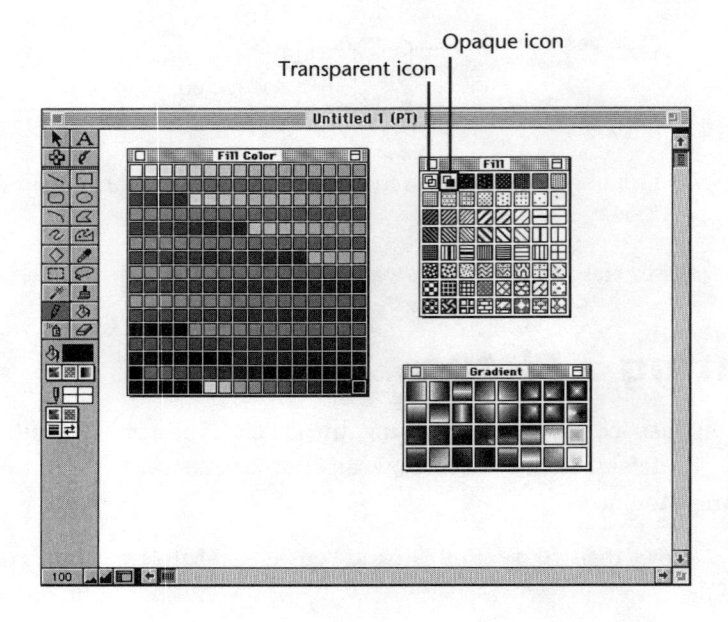

Using the Fill Indicator Palette

You can use the Fill Indicator palette to enhance an image by filling it with colors, patterns, or gradients. You use the Fill palettes on enclosed images (rectangles, ovals, irregular shapes, and so on) with all the tools available in the painting module except the Pencil.

> **Note**
>
> You cannot use a gradient fill with the Brush or the Spray Can. The Spray Can functions when you choose the Patterns palette, but no definite pattern is discernible.

Tip
Remember, in order to change from a pattern to a solid color or gradient, click the transparent or opaque square in the pattern fill.

Choosing the paint settings is easiest before you paint the image. To change the color, pattern, or gradient of an image after you've drawn it, you can use one of two methods. Follow these steps to use the first method:

1. Choose the Eraser and erase each pixel inside the borders of the image. If necessary, use the zoom icon to enlarge the image.

2. Choose the desired fill.

3. Select the Paint Bucket to flood the image with the new fill.

The second method of changing the fill is good to use if the part of the image you want to modify is well defined. Follow these steps when you want a different pattern color than what already exists:

1. Use the Lasso or Selection Rectangle tool to select all or part of the image.

2. Choose the new fill.

3. Choose Fill from the Transform menu. The selected part is filled with the new color, pattern, or gradient.

4. Click anywhere outside the selected area or choose another tool to continue.

Using the Pen Indicator Palette

The Pen Indicator palette changes the width, color, or pattern of the Line and Brush tools and the borders of an image. When you need to edit images you created with the Pencil, Line, or Brush tool, you use this palette. Keep in mind that if you change the width of a line, you also change the width of any border you may draw. If you choose to have no border at all, the next time you try to use the Line tool it will not show any line. To restore a visible line, click the Pen Line icon and choose a width that is either the hairline or one of the point sizes. Here are some ideas that will help you when you need to use the Pen palette:

Tip
To change the fill in a portion of an image, draw a temporary line with the Pencil tool to close the area. After you change the fill, remove the line.

- Try to choose the pen settings you want before you paint the image.

- To change a border color, choose a color from the Fill Indicator, select the Paint Bucket tool, and click the border. If you have a thin line border, enlarge the document before you use the Paint Bucket tool.

- Holding down the Option key and clicking (with the Eyedropper tool) a color you want to duplicate changes the Pen Indicator box so you can use the Line, Pencil, or Brush in that new color.

Painting Images

Within the painting module, you can create or edit painting images. After you paint an image, you can select it with one of three selection tools (the Selection Rectangle, Lasso, or Magic Wand) to make changes or impose some interesting visual effects. If you are familiar with the drawing environment of ClarisWorks but new to painting, you may feel some initial frustration in

Chapter 7—Painting

learning the new system. You don't use the two modules the same way. The following list discusses some features of which you should be aware in the painting module:

- Whatever shape you create is not an object; it is an image that you can enlarge to look at and edit, pixel by pixel.

- If you make an overlapping shape that requires changes, you cannot click handles on it and drag it to another part of the document for editing. If you select the overlapping shape and move it, you also move a portion of the underlying shape. To edit the overlapping shape, you must enlarge the document, focus in on the top shape, and make changes by the pixel.

- Always remember to select the Fill and Pen palette options before you begin to paint with a tool.

- The tool you select remains the active tool until you select another tool.

When you work in the painting environment, you are likely to use the Zoom In or Zoom Out control, or the Zoom Percentage box more frequently than any of the other icon buttons. As shown in figure 7.4, these options simplify the task of editing the small details of an image by enabling you to work on an enlarged view of the image.

Figure 7.4
The zoom controls and the Show/Hide Tools control.

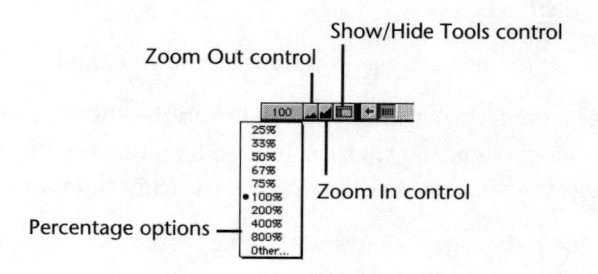

These icons affect the size of the images in a document. The place that you last clicked with the mouse is the work area you see after clicking the Zoom In icon. You may not need to work in that area, however, and when your document is 400 percent of the actual size, using the scroll bars to move to another location in the document can take a long time. You can do one of the following to zoom in to exactly that area in which you need to edit:

- Click either the Selection Rectangle or the Lasso tool and select the whole image or any part of it.

- Click the image with whatever tool you are using or in an area where you want to begin an image or place an image.

You can use the Number icon and select a given percentage to zoom in or zoom out of the document. You can key in an unlisted size by selecting Other.

The approaches to creating a graphic in the painting rather than the drawing module may take some rethinking, but the finished product is worth the effort. The painting module offers ways of working with shapes that are not possible anywhere else. Learning to use the painting tools is the next step in developing your abilities in the area of graphics.

Using the Painting Tools

The painting module uses all the tools that appear in the drawing module as well as eight additional tools. You use some of the additional tools to create images and others to select and edit images. Experiment with the tools to see their versatility.

The Pencil

Using the Pencil tool is similar to using a simple No. 2 lead pencil. When you open a painting document, the Pencil is the selected tool. The Pencil can create a thin black line. To use this tool if another tool is active, click the Pencil tool. You can use the Pencil in several ways:

- Click the Pencil once in a document to make a single pixel. Click and drag the tool to create a line.

- You can change the color of the Pencil line by using the Pen indicators and palettes. You cannot change the line thickness.

- By holding down the Shift key and dragging the Pencil tool, you can create perfectly straight, horizontal, and vertical lines. This feature is especially helpful for editing.

- You use the Pencil tool most frequently when you need to edit individual pixels. Click a black pixel, and it becomes white. Click a white pixel (what looks like unused space in the document), and it becomes black or any other color you choose from the Pen indicator and palettes.

The Brush

Use the Brush to create brush strokes. The default Brush color is black, and the default width size is 1 point. You can change the color and pattern by selecting any of the Fill and Pen palettes. You cannot use the gradients with the Brush tool. The outline of the three mountains in figure 7.5 was created with the Brush tool.

Figure 7.5
An example of an image created with the Brush tool.

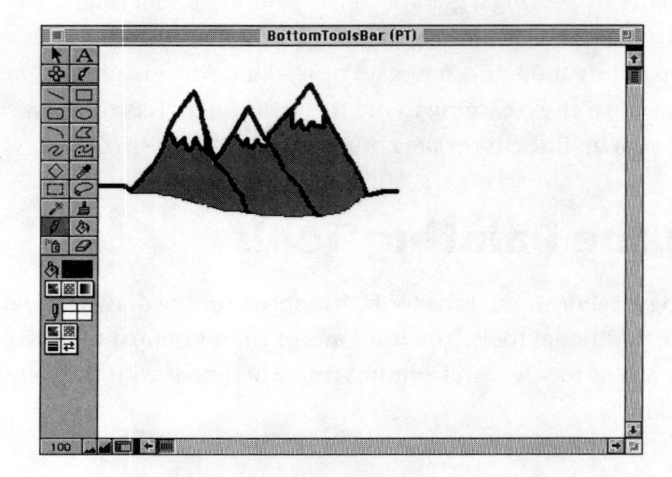

You can change the shape and size of the Brush stroke. Follow these steps to choose a new Brush shape and/or size:

1. Choose Brush Shape from the Options menu (or double-click the Brush tool). The Brush Shape dialog box, shown in figure 7.6, appears. In this dialog box, the current Brush shape is outlined in a box.

Figure 7.6
The Brush Shape dialog box, with the default shape selected.

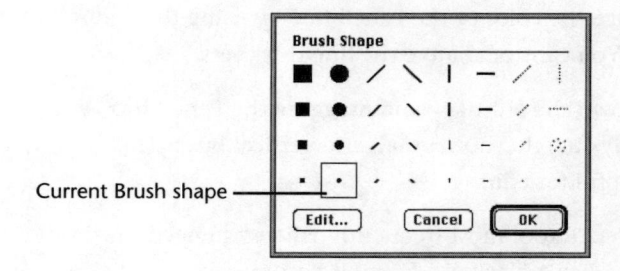

Current Brush shape

2. Click a Brush shape to select it.
3. Choose OK.

Using the Painting Tools   **151**

You also can customize the Brush shape, by following these steps:

1. Choose Brush Shape from the Options menu (or double-click the Brush tool). The Brush Editor dialog box, as shown in figure 7.7, appears.

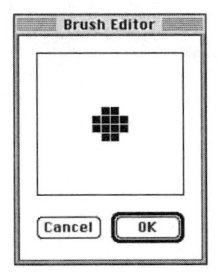

Figure 7.7
The Brush Editor dialog box.

2. In the dialog box, click Edit.

3. You can click each individual pixel or drag the mouse across the pixels to create a new Brush shape. Each click of the mouse produces a pixel.

4. Click OK to accept the new shape. Clicking Cancel deletes the shape.

5. Click OK to return to the document.

The Spray Can

You can change the color (patterns and gradients do not work) of the Spray Can using the Fill indicators and palettes. You can spray with one click at a time—to create the look of falling snow, for example—or with a drag-and-click movement to give a softer look to a picture, as seen in the mountain scene of figure 7.8. The following steps show you how to use the Spray Can tool.

1. Select the fill color you want. It appears in the Fill indicator.

2. Select the Spray Can tool.

3. Click once to apply a single spray, or click and drag to apply a series of sprays.

The density of the Spray Can paint depends on how long you hold the mouse button in one place. The width of the spray and how much area it covers depends on the spray dot size and flow speed. Follow these steps to change both of these settings:

1. Choose Spray Can from the Options menu or double-click the Spray Can tool. The dialog box shown in figure 7.9 appears.

Figure 7.8
An example of using the Spray Can tool.

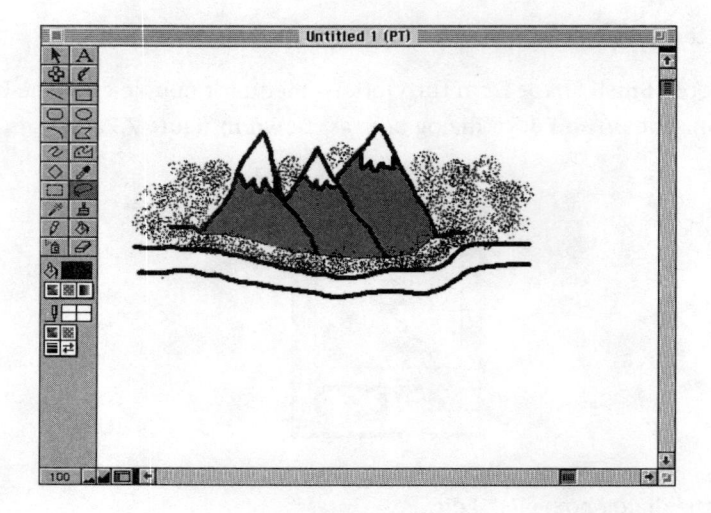

Figure 7.9
The Edit Spray Can dialog box.

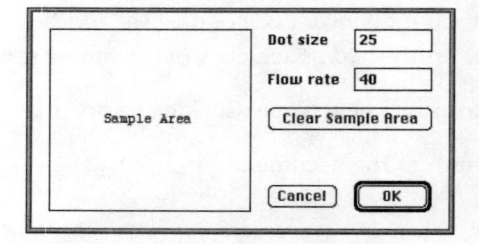

2. Increase or decrease the size of the spray by keying in a number from 1 to 72 in the Dot Size box (the higher the number, the larger the diameter of the spray).

3. Change the speed of the spray by keying in a number from 1 to 100 in the Flow Rate box (the higher the number, the faster the flow of spray).

4. Test the new settings in the Sample Area box. You can click the Clear Sample Area button to get rid of any test spray.

5. Click OK.

The Paint Bucket

You can use the Paint Bucket tool to fill an enclosed image with a color, pattern, or gradient. The flowers in figure 7.10 show how an image looks before and after you use the Paint Bucket.

Figure 7.10
Using the Paint Bucket tool with different fills.

Unfilled — Variety of fills

Carefully plan your use of this tool, because editing a filled image requires some skill (this process was discussed in "Painting Images" earlier in this chapter). You also want to ensure that the image to be filled is completely enclosed. If just one pixel is missing from the border, the paint will "leak" into the adjoining area of your image; in fact, the paint may fill the entire document. If you experience a paint leak, you can use the Edit menu's Undo command to undo the Paint Bucket command.

The Paint Bucket fill is the color, pattern, or gradient you see in the Fill Indicator. You can create your own fill (see the "Changing Color, Patterns, and Borders" section of Chapter 6, "Drawing," for directions). To use the Paint Bucket on an enclosed image or part of an image, follow these steps:

1. Select the color, pattern, or gradient you want to use. The Fill Indicator displays your choice.

2. Choose the Paint Bucket tool.

3. Position the Paint Bucket tool so that the black tip of the paint coming from the Paint Bucket is on the area you want to fill. Click. The enclosed area fills.

4. If you are unhappy with the way the fill looks in your image, or if the fill leaked, immediately choose Undo from the Edit menu. To stop the leak, use the Zoom In control to find the opening in the image. Use the Pencil tool to add pixels and close up the image. Retry the Paint Bucket.

5. If you want to change the fill of an image that already has a pattern or gradient fill, be sure to select the image first and then choose Fill from the Transform menu. The Paint Bucket does not change a whole pattern or gradient. It can only change one color at a time.

Editing an Image with the Painting Tools

The painting module provides four tools that make editing images possible. Before you begin editing an image, you must select it. Once an image is selected, you can move it or change its appearance. Three of the tools—the Selection Rectangle, Lasso, and Magic Wand—allow you to select all or part of an image, each in a different way. The fourth tool, the Eraser, lets you edit by erasing one or more pixels. You do not have to select anything in the document to use the Eraser.

The Selection Rectangle

Use the Selection Rectangle tool to select an image or area that is rectangular. Although this tool is easy to use, you need to enclose the image with the Selection Rectangle's dotted square as closely as you can. Any white space included in the selection moves with the image itself. The following steps show you how to select an image so it can be moved or edited:

1. Choose the Selection Rectangle tool.

2. Place the tool at the upper-left corner of the image; click and hold the mouse button down while you drag diagonally to the lower-right corner.

3. Release the mouse button. A flashing rectangle appears around the image. Edit the image by moving, deleting, or changing the fill (Transform menu), or by using the special effects on the selected image.

There are other ways to use the Selection Rectangle tool. The following list describes additional command keys you can use in conjunction with this tool and what that accomplishes:

- To select only the image, with no extra white space, hold down the ⌘ key as you drag the Selection Rectangle tool across the image.

- To select the entire picture, including the white area, double-click the Selection Rectangle tool. This action selects the entire painting area. With everything selected, press the Delete key to get rid of all the images quickly.

- To select all the images exclusive of the white space, hold down the ⌘ key and double-click either the Selection Rectangle or the Lasso tool.

> **Caution**
>
> Depending on the amount of memory available in your computer and allotted to ClarisWorks, when you double-click the selection tools, you may get the following message: `There is not enough memory to complete this operation`. In that case, use the tools themselves to select.

The Lasso

Initially, you may have more difficulty maneuvering the Lasso than you have maneuvering the Selection Rectangle. You need to master the Lasso, however, because you can use it to go into tight spaces or to select odd shapes. The Lasso selects just the area you encircle, with no white spaces. Sometimes you may need to zoom in on the area first, and then use the Lasso to select it. When you enlarge the document, the Lasso lines also enlarge. Even if you encircle more than one image with the Lasso, each image is treated as an individual selection.

To use the Lasso tool, follow these steps:

1. Choose the Lasso tool.

2. Place the tool next to the image you want to select. Click and drag in a circular motion around the image.

3. Release the mouse button. If you do not complete the circle, the last part automatically fills in so the shape is totally enclosed. If the image is not selected to your satisfaction, click anywhere outside the image and try again.

The Magic Wand

With the Magic Wand, you can "pick up" a color, pattern, or portion of a gradient and move it wherever you like within the document. Clicking the Magic Wand on a color, pattern, or part of a gradient does not copy, or duplicate; it takes the color, pattern, or portion of gradient away from the original location, and allows you to place it somewhere else in the document. The following steps explain how to use the Magic Wand tool:

1. Choose the Magic Wand tool.

2. Place the Magic Wand on the fill you want to move, then click. The selected area "flashes."

3. The Magic Wand pointer changes to the arrow pointer. Use this pointer to move the fill, or while still selected, use one of the Transform menu options such as Perspective, Scale Selection, Free Rotate, and so forth.

The Eraser

The Eraser is a powerful tool in that it deletes whatever crosses its path. You need to use it carefully and with thought. To use the Eraser, follow these steps:

1. Choose the Eraser tool.

2. Place the Eraser over the area you want to delete. Click to erase four pixels (at 100 percent document size), or click and drag the eraser over an area to erase many pixels with one drag.

> **Tip**
> After you select an image with the Selection Rectangle, Lasso, or Magic Wand, you can use the arrow keys to move it pixel by pixel.

There are other ways to use the Eraser tool. The following list describes additional ways to use this tool:

- To force the Eraser to go horizontally or vertically, hold down the Shift key and then drag the Eraser in either of those directions.

- To erase a whole document quickly, double-click the Eraser icon. Choose Undo from the Edit menu if you change your mind.

- Use the Zoom In icon to resize the document to 400 percent or higher so you can use the Eraser in small spaces.

In most cases, erase small amounts and release the mouse button frequently. That way, if you check what you do and find it is not to your liking, you can immediately go to the Undo command and put the last erased part back into the picture.

> **Tip**
> If the Eraser is too large, use the Pencil to delete individual pixels.

The Eyedropper

The Eyedropper tool helps you find a fill or pen choice you used previously in your picture, so you can repeat it without having to search through the palettes. With the Eyedropper, the color you click in an image becomes active and appears in the Fill or Pen indicator. If you use several shades of a color and want to copy a specific one for the next image, drag the Eyedropper across the image (watch the indicator change as you go from one shade to another) and click when the Eyedropper is on the correct shade. The following steps show you how to use the Eyedropper tool:

1. Choose the Eyedropper.

2. Position the Eyedropper on an image's fill and click. The Fill Indicator changes to that color, pattern, or part of the gradient.

   or

   Position the Eyedropper on an image border or line and click. The Fill Indicator changes to that color or pattern. By holding down the Option key and clicking the Eyedropper once on a line, border, or fill, the Pen Indicator color changes to what the border, line, or fill is.

Creating Special Effects

In the painting module, you have the tools to change an ordinary image by giving it perspective, rotating it, resizing it, distorting it, shearing it, or flipping it. Figure 7.11 illustrates some of the interesting results you can achieve with these special effects.

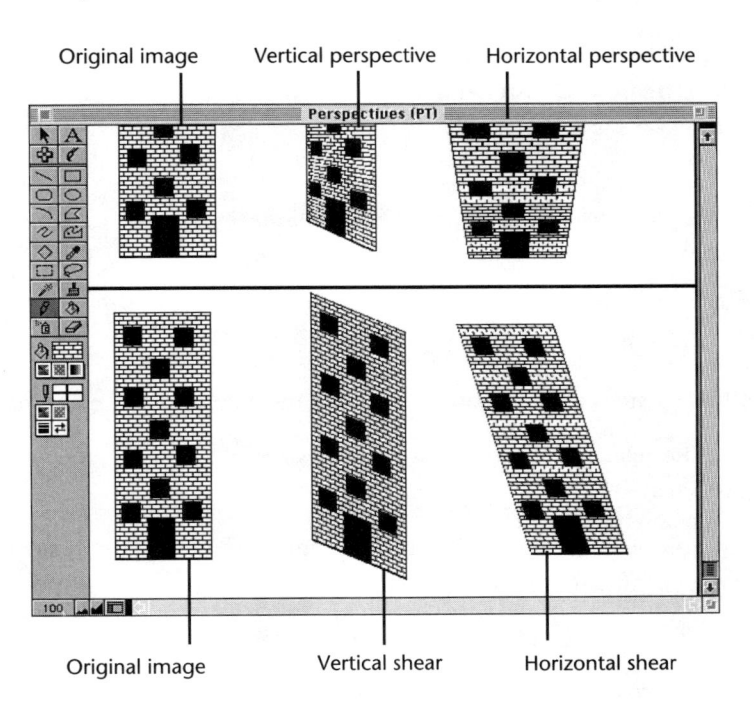

Tip
Press the Tab key to toggle quickly between the last active tool and the Eyedropper.

Figure 7.11
An example of how applying the Shear command affects an image.

Chapter 7—Painting

Tip
If you have room, make a copy of the image and use the copy when applying a special effect. That way, no matter what you do, you still have the original.

To *shear* an image means to slant it horizontally or vertically. Follow these steps to shear an image:

1. Use the Selection Rectangle or Lasso to select the image you want to shear.

2. Choose Shear from the Transform menu. Handles appear at each corner of the image.

3. To slant the image vertically, drag any one of the handles up or down. To slant the image horizontally, drag any one of the handles right or left.

   To remove the shearing effect, choose Undo Shear from the Edit menu while the image is still selected. The image returns to its original state.

4. When the shear is as you want it, click outside the image to remove the handles, then click again to deselect the image.

You can use Distort to stretch an image in any direction. The distorted umbrella in figure 7.12 looks as if a truck ran over it.

Figure 7.12
An example of how applying the Distort command affects an image.

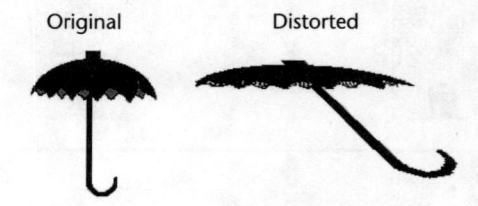

The following steps explain how to use the Distort command on an image:

1. Use the Selection Rectangle or Lasso to select the image you want to distort.

2. Choose Distort from the Transform menu. Handles appear at each corner of the image.

3. Drag on any one of the handles to create the look you want.

   To remove the changes, choose Undo Distort from the Edit menu while the image is still selected. The image returns to its original state.

4. When your image is as you want it, click outside the image to remove the handles, then click again to deselect the image.

When you use Perspective on an image, two sides of the image move simultaneously when you drag one handle. This effect gives depth and a sense of distance to the image, as you can see in the building shown in figure 7.13.

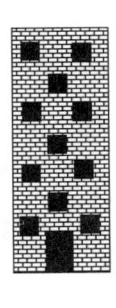

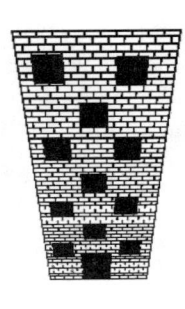

Figure 7.13
An example of how applying the Perspective command affects an image.

Original image   Vertical perspective   Horizontal perspective

The following steps explain how to use the Perspective command on an image:

1. Use the Selection Rectangle or Lasso to select the image to which you want to add perspective.

2. Choose Perspective from the Transform menu. Handles appear at each corner of the image.

3. To add vertical perspective, drag any one of the handles left or right. To add horizontal perspective, drag any one of the handles up or down.

   To remove the perspective effect, choose Undo Perspective from the Edit menu while the image is still selected.

4. When the perspective is as you want it, click outside the image to remove the handles, then click again to deselect the image.

You can use Free Rotate to turn a selected image a small degree around its center each time you drag on a handle. The following steps explain how to use the Free Rotate command on an image:

1. Use the Selection Rectangle or Lasso to select the image you want to rotate.

2. Choose Free Rotate from the Transform menu. Handles appear at each corner of the image.

160   Chapter 7—Painting

3. Drag on any one of the handles to rotate it to the desired angle.

   To remove changes, choose Undo Rotate from the Edit menu while the image is still selected.

4. When the rotation is as you want it, click outside the image to remove the handles, then click again to deselect the image.

If you choose Rotate from the Transform menu, the dialog box shown in figure 7.14 appears. In this dialog box, you can key in a specific degree of rotation.

Figure 7.14
The Rotate dialog box.

The Rotate option was used for the umbrella shown in figure 7.15. Setting the rotate at 90 degrees in the dialog box, you can make it look like a strong gust of wind is going to blow the umbrella away.

Figure 7.15
An example of how applying the Rotate command affects an image.

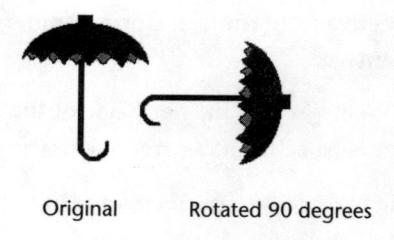

Original   Rotated 90 degrees

> **Note**
>
> Being able to deselect the handles, but have the image still selected, allows you to try different special effects without having to reselect the image.

The Resize option enables you to make an image larger or smaller. You can drag the selected image to the desired size or scale the image to a percentage of its former self. The smaller and larger umbrellas in figure 7.16 show approximately how large and small you can make an image without distorting it.

Creating Special Effects **161**

Figure 7.16
An example of how applying the Resize command affects an image.

Follow these steps to use the Resize option:

1. Use the Selection Rectangle or Lasso to select the image you want to resize.

2. Choose Resize from the Transform menu.

3. Drag any one of the handles that surround the image, to make the image larger or smaller (drag up or down), narrower or wider (drag left or right).

4. Double-click to accept the change(s).

Follow these steps to use the Scale Selection option:

1. Select the object.

2. Choose Scale Selection from the Transform menu.

3. Key in the percentage amount you want to enlarge or reduce the image in the horizontal box, the vertical box, or both boxes (it defaults to 50 percent in the horizontal box which means the image will be reduced horizontally by 50 percent of the original size).

4. If you do not like how the image looks with the resized effect, while it is still selected, choose Undo Scale from the Edit menu. The image will return to its original state.

   If you like the new look of your image and you resized manually, click outside the image to remove the handles; click again to deselect the image. If you used the Scale Selection, click anywhere outside the image to deselect it.

Use Flip to turn a selected image left or right, or even upside down. The picture frame shown in figure 7.17 was created using all three special effects.

Figure 7.17
An example of how applying the Flip commands affect an image.

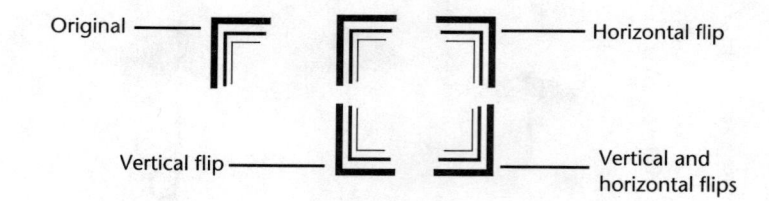

Original — Horizontal flip

Vertical flip — Vertical and horizontal flips

Follow these steps to use the Flip Horizontal and Flip Vertical options:

1. Use the Selection Rectangle or Lasso to select the image you want to flip.

2. Choose Flip Horizontal or Flip Vertical from the Transform menu.

   To remove the flipped effect, choose Undo Flip from the Edit menu while the image is still selected.

   To get a mirrored effect of an image, as shown in figure 7.18 with the mountain reflection in the water, you need to copy the original (be sure to use the Lasso to select), paste it, and flip vertically. Choose Lighter from the Transform menu. Repeat, choosing the Lighter command until the copy of the image is as light as you want.

Figure 7.18
Copied image that is lightened and then flipped to look like a reflection.

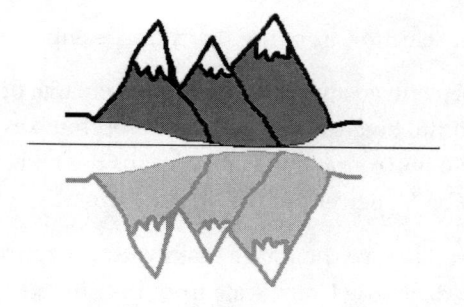

3. If you like the new look of your image, click outside the image to deselect.

Painting also offers additional special effects. These effects are located in the Transform menu, and they all require that you select all or part of an image. Subsequently, when you choose one of these effects, it performs its "magic" on the selected image. The following list explains these options:

■ The Fill command adds a color, pattern, or gradient to a selected part of an image or the entire image. Unlike the Paint Bucket tool, it can fill a pattern with a different color (you cannot change the pattern, only the color of the existing pattern). Enlarge the document first when you want to select an area to fill a specific portion of the image. Enlarging makes selection of the portion easier.

- The Pick Up command lets you transfer the same colors, patterns, or gradients from one image to a selected image. You select an image and place it on top of an image whose colors or patterns you want to duplicate. Select the Pick Up command from the Transform menu, and the colors or patterns fill the top image. While still selected, you can move the top image anywhere within the document. This is especially useful if you create a unique pattern for one part of your picture and decide to repeat the pattern elsewhere. For example, your picture may contain a table covered with a cloth. Repeating the design of the cloth on the curtains will be easier when using the Pick Up command.

- The Invert command lets you reverse the colors of an image. The effect is similar to a photo negative. This is a useful technique to apply when creating your own patterns for borders on the top, bottom, or all around a document, as shown in figure 7.19.

Figure 7.19
Using the Invert command to create a border.

- The Blend command adds a third color between two other selected colors. It gives a softened look to the border where one color overlaps another. The Blend command affects the selected area only once. It does not reach out any farther into the second image regardless of how many times you position the arrow pointer on Blend.

- The Tint command shades a selected image with the color that is current in the Fill indicator. You can draw your image in one color, choose a different fill, select the image or a part of the image, and tint the image with the new fill.

- The Lighter and Darker commands let you lighten or darken a selected image to create a desired effect. The example of the reflected mountains, in this chapter, shows one way to use the Lighter feature.

Changing the Size of a Painting Document

The painting module, similar to other ClarisWorks modules, has certain defaults. Such defaults as the size of the document, its depth and resolution, and the available menu bars, give the format of the painting aspect of this software.

The size of a painting document is 468 pixels by 648 pixels, or to put it in inches, 6.5 inches by 9 inches. The margins are 1 inch, all around. As mentioned earlier in this chapter, if you have another document already open, or want to open a second painting file, the document size is smaller. If you open a third painting file, the size of the document is smaller still. The only way to prevent the document size from "shrinking" is to allocate more memory (anywhere from 2500K to 4000K) to the ClarisWorks program. See the ClarisWorks *User's Guide* for directions.

You can change the size of the document as well as the size of the margins within the document by following these steps:

1. Choose Document from the Format menu. The Document dialog box appears (see fig. 7.20).

Figure 7.20
The Document dialog box.

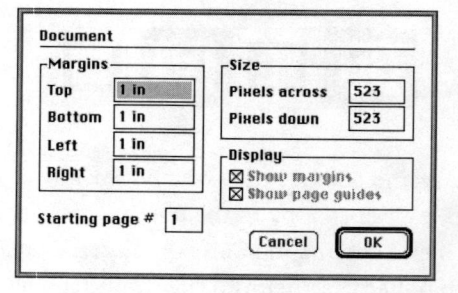

2. Key in the number of pixels you want down and across in the Size boxes. There are 72 pixels to an inch.

3. Change any or all of the margins. Use decimal point 5 (.5) if you want half an inch. Use the Tab key to go from one box to another to change margins.

4. Click OK. This size will affect all new documents you open until you set the size to something else.

Changing the Resolution in a Painting Document

Dots per inch, or *dpi*, is important information to know and understand. The term relates to the number of dots that form one square inch of the screen and print areas. The more dots per inch your printer or monitor allows, the better the resolution of the document you look at or print out. The Macintosh screen has a resolution of 72 dpi, but many printers have a much higher dpi. The Apple ImageWriter has a maximum of 144 dpi, the Apple LaserWriters have 300 dpi, and the Apple StyleWriter boasts 360 dpi. Hewlett-Packard has recently put a 600 dpi printer for less than $2,000 on the market.

Your computer system comes set to certain resolution defaults. In the Resolution and Depth dialog box that appears when you choose Resolution and Depth from the Format menu (this option appears in every module of ClarisWorks except word processing and communications), the resolution is set to 72 and the depth at 256. You can customize the resolution and depth, so that printouts are more in tune to what your printer can handle. Changing these defaults causes your document to get smaller. To overcome this, choose Document from the Format menu. You can increase the number of pixels in the Document dialog box.

Follow these steps to change the default resolution and depth settings:

1. Select the Format menu and position the mouse pointer at Resolution and Depth. The Resolution and Depth dialog box appears (see fig. 7.21).

    If you select a painting frame before opening the dialog box, the position of that frame appears in the dialog box.

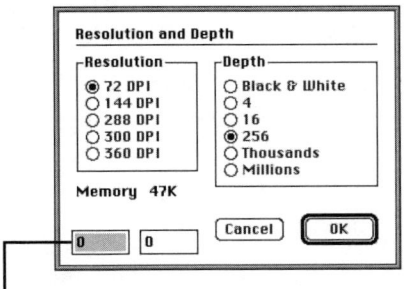

Figure 7.21
The Resolution and Depth dialog box.

Shows the position of the painting frame

2. Click the button in front of the resolution you want.

166 Chapter 7—Painting

3. Click the button in front of the depth (number of colors) you want. The Memory number displays the amount of memory you need for each setting.

4. If you select a paint frame rather than a paint document, you can (but do not have to) set the upper-left corner of the frame by keying a number into the Origin box. If you select linked paint frames (see Chapter 15, "Creating Integrated Documents"), you can select several frames and show the same image or a part of the same image.

> **Caution**
>
> Changing the resolution or depth uses a great deal of memory. Check your Macintosh manual to make sure you have the necessary memory or to learn how to allocate more memory.

Displaying Overlapping Graphics

In the painting module, you can display overlapping graphics in any of three modes (see fig. 7.22).

Figure 7.22
Overlapping images using the Opaque, Transparent, and Tint options.

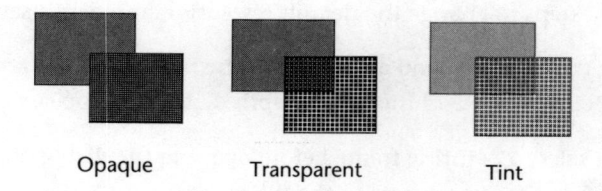

Opaque Transparent Tint

- *Opaque* (the default) shows the overlapping portion of the top image, blocking out that part of the underlying image.

- *Transparent* lets the color, pattern, or gradient of the bottom image come through any white pixels of the overlapping image.

- *Tint* lets the selected color of the overlapping image tint the underlying colors.

Tip
The Transparent mode works best when you use one pattern over another.

Follow these steps to choose a painting mode for your images:

1. Choose Paint Mode from the Options menu. The Painting Mode dialog box appears (see fig. 7.23).

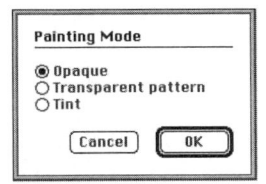

Figure 7.23
The Painting Mode dialog box.

2. Click one of the buttons to choose a different paint mode. That chosen mode remains in effect for any other overlapping images you draw until you return to the Painting Mode dialog box and select another mode.

3. Click OK.

> **Troubleshooting Special Effects**
>
> *Does the Eyedropper tool work with the Pen Indicator to change colors so a different Pencil or Line color can be used quickly?*
>
> Try holding down the Option key and then clicking the Eyedropper icon on the color you want. The Pen Indicator will show the new color.
>
> *Will the Fill command in the Transform menu change a pattern in an existing, selected image?*
>
> The Fill command can change the *color* of a pattern on a selected image, but it cannot change the actual pattern. The only way to change the pattern of an image is to zoom in and use the Eraser and the Pencil (if necessary) to delete the pattern you do not want.

From Here...

In this chapter, you learned to use a different approach to making graphics than in the drawing module. You were introduced to eight new tools and learned how to use them in creating your painting images. For related information regarding the painting module, the following chapters will be of interest to you.

- Chapter 2, "Learning the Essentials." This chapter covers how to access painting tools in word processing, spreadsheet, and database documents.

- Chapter 6, "Drawing." This chapter covers the other graphic module ClarisWorks provides.

- Chapter 15, "Creating Integrated Documents." This chapter discusses how to create painting frames and linked painting frames.

Chapter 8
Spreadsheet Basics

by Shelley O'Hara

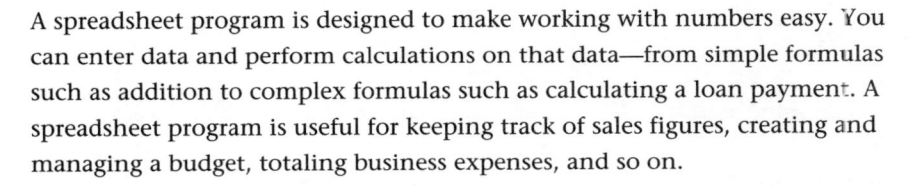

A spreadsheet program is designed to make working with numbers easy. You can enter data and perform calculations on that data—from simple formulas such as addition to complex formulas such as calculating a loan payment. A spreadsheet program is useful for keeping track of sales figures, creating and managing a budget, totaling business expenses, and so on.

This chapter covers spreadsheet basics. You learn the following:

- How to understand the screen display
- How to enter data and formulas
- How to edit data
- How to edit the worksheet layout
- How to sort the worksheet data

Understanding the Screen and Tools

When you create a spreadsheet document, called a *worksheet*, you see a grid of columns and rows. This area is where you enter worksheet data. Figure 8.1 shows the key worksheet screen items.

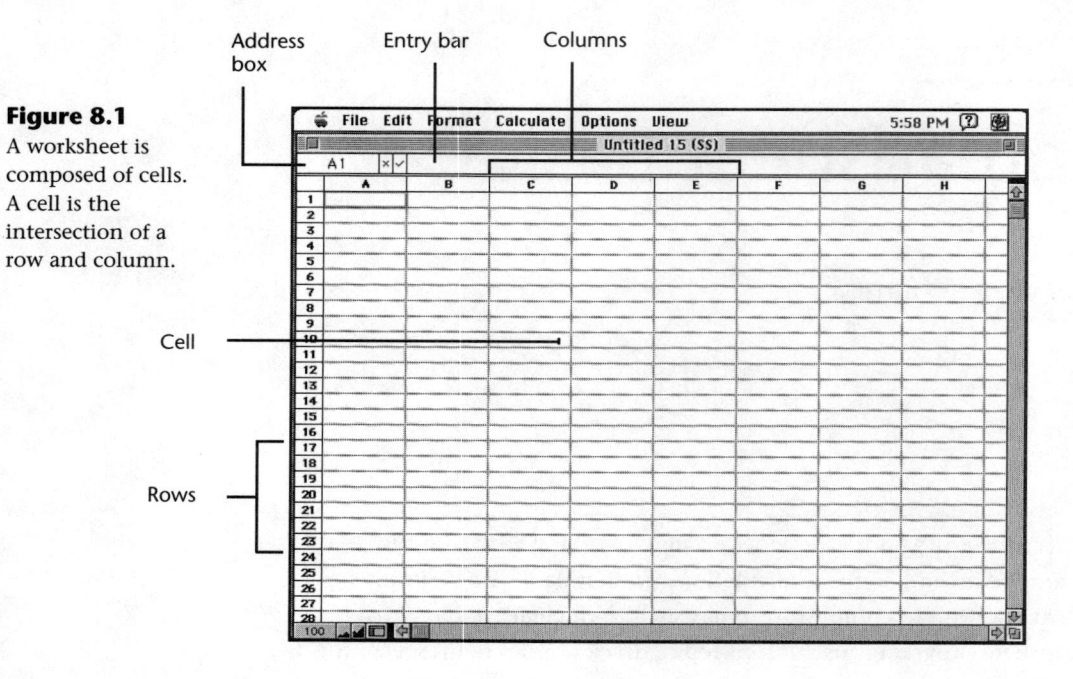

Figure 8.1
A worksheet is composed of cells. A cell is the intersection of a row and column.

Labels on figure: Address box, Entry bar, Columns, Cell, Rows

Columns, rows, and cells are explained in the next section.

Tip
For information on changing the view of the document, refer to Chapter 2, "Learning the Essentials."

The entry bar appears below the title bar. As you type an entry in a cell, the entry appears in this bar. When you edit a cell, you edit it in the entry bar. Next to the entry bar are an X icon and a checkmark icon. You can cancel an entry by clicking the X icon (the Cancel button). You can confirm an entry by clicking the checkmark icon (the Accept button) or by pressing Return.

Understanding Cells, Columns, and Rows

Columns are lettered A, B, C, and so on. Rows are numbered 1, 2, 3, and so on. The intersection of a column and row is called a *cell*. To enter data in a worksheet, you select a cell and then type the data. Only one cell can be active at a time. The active (or current) cell is indicated by a dark or colored border.

A cell is referenced by its column letter and row number. For example, the first cell in a worksheet is A1, which means column A, row 1. The cell address appears next to the entry bar.

For some operations, you can select more than one cell. A group of selected cells is called a *range* and is indicated by notation such as A1..A3. The first cell named is the top left cell in the range; the second cell named is the bottom right cell. Two periods separate the addresses. (For more information, see "Selecting a Range" later in this chapter.)

Using the Shortcuts Palette

As you work on your spreadsheet document, you can display a shortcut palette with buttons applicable to spreadsheet tasks. To display the palette, choose Shortcuts from the File menu, and then choose Show Shortcuts from the submenu. You can add or delete buttons (see Chapter 20 on customizing). To close the palette, click the close box. To move the palette, click and drag it to the location you want.

Table 8.1 lists the shortcut buttons.

Tip
By default, a worksheet contains 40 columns and 500 rows. If you want to change the size of the worksheet (maximum size is 256 columns by 16,384 rows), choose Document from the Format menu to open the Document dialog box. In the Size boxes, type the number of columns and rows required; then choose OK.

Table 8.1 Spreadsheet Shortcut Buttons

Button	Description
	Open
	Save
	Print
	Undo
	Cut
	Copy
	Paste
	Bold
	Italic
	Underline
	Align Left
	Align Center
	Align Right
	Sort Ascending
	Sort Descending
	AutoSum
	Currency Format

(continues)

Table 8.1 Continued

Button	Description
	Percent Format
	Commas Format
	Outline Border
	Right Border
	Bottom Border
	Show/Hide Formulas
	Align Wrap
	Insert Cells
	Delete Cells
	Bar Chart
	Pie Chart
	Area Chart
	Line Chart

Troubleshooting the Display

The columns and rows in my worksheet are smaller than the ones shown in this chapter. Why?

You can change the row height and column width to make the worksheet easier to read. The worksheets in this chapter use a different row height and font so that the worksheets are easy to read.

I don't see the Shortcuts palette. Why not?

The Shortcuts palette does not appear by default. To display this palette of icons, choose Shortcuts from the File menu, and then choose Show Shortcuts from the submenu.

Entering Data

Your worksheet can be composed of different types of data, including the following:

- *Text.* Text entries are useful for column and row headings. Also, some of the data in your worksheet may be text—for example, product names and projects.

- *Numbers* (positive and negative). If you type only numbers, ClarisWorks treats the entry as a numeric entry, meaning that you can perform calculations on the entry.

- *Dates and times.* ClarisWorks stores dates and times in a special format so that you can use them in calculations. Dates are stored as a serial number representing the number of days that have passed since January 1, 1904. Times are stored as a decimal fraction of a day. You can perform date and time calculations—for example, subtract one date from another to see how many days have passed.

- *Formulas.* Formulas perform calculations on entries in the worksheet.

The following sections explain how to enter text, numbers, dates and times, and formulas.

Entering Text, Numbers, and Dates

Follow these steps to enter data:

1. Select the cell you want to use.

   You can use the arrow keys to move to the cell, or place the mouse pointer on the cell you want and click. The current cell is indicated by a dark or colored border.

2. Type the data.

   To enter text, just type the entry. You can type up to 255 characters in a cell. Text entries are left-aligned by default.

   To enter a number, type the number. If you want to enter a negative number, type a minus sign before the number. Numbers are right-aligned and displayed without any numeric formatting. (You can change the alignment and use a different numeric format. For information, see Chapter 9, "Enhancing a Worksheet.")

To enter a date, type it, using this format:

2/13/94

> **Note**
>
> You can change the way the date is formatted. For information, see Chapter 9, "Enhancing a Worksheet."

To enter a time, type it in any of these formats:

4:40 PM

4:40:45 PM

16:40

16:40:45

3. To complete the entry, do one of the following things:

- Press Return to confirm the entry and move to the next cell down.

- Press Tab to confirm the entry and move one cell right.

- Click the Accept button and keep the same cell active.

- Click the Cancel button to cancel the entry.

Tip
To ensure that the entries in your worksheet are spelled correctly, use the Spell Checker. Choose Writing Tools from the Edit menu and then Check Document Spelling from the pop-up menu. For more information on checking spelling, refer to Chapter 4, "Enhancing Your Text."

If a text entry is too long to fit in the cell, the entry spills over to the next cell(s). If the next cell contains data, you see only part of the entry. The entire entry is still there; you just cannot see it all.

If a numeric entry is too long to fit in a cell, you see the number in scientific notation, or you see number signs (###) in the cell. In both cases, you need to widen the column. This topic is covered in Chapter 9, "Enhancing a Worksheet."

Saving Your Worksheet

Keep in mind that the data you enter is stored only temporarily—in the computer's memory. To store the data on disk, you need to save the document by choosing Save from the File menu. You should save the document periodically as you work on it. Saving a document is covered in Chapter 2, "Learning the Essentials."

> **Troubleshooting Data Entry**
>
> *I selected the wrong cell and started typing. I don't want to overwrite the entry. What can I do?*
>
> If you have pressed Return, choose Undo from the Edit menu. If you haven't pressed Return, click the Cancel button to cancel the entry.
>
> *I see the number in a weird format (1.20912e+17). Why?*
>
> When you enter a number that is too long to display in a cell, ClarisWorks displays the number in Scientific format. You can change the format and widen the column. For help on these tasks, see Chapter 9, "Enhancing a Worksheet."
>
> *Part of one of my text entries has disappeared. How do I fix it?*
>
> When a text entry is too long, it spills into the next cell. If that cell contains an entry, ClarisWorks truncates the entry. The cell still contains the entire entry; you just cannot see it all. Widen the column, as described in the next chapter.

Entering Formulas

The backbone of a spreadsheet program is its formula capabilities. A formula enables you to perform calculations on the data you have entered. You can create the formula yourself or use one of ClarisWorks' built-in formulas, called *functions*.

Understanding the Parts of a Formula

A formula is made up of these parts: an equal sign, values or cell references, and operators.

To start a formula, you type an equal sign (=). This sign tells ClarisWorks that you are creating a formula.

You can type *values* (the actual numbers) directly in the formula, as in =6+72, but when you use constant values, the formula always returns the same result. Usually, you *reference* cells in the formula—for example, =B1+B2. If B1 contains 6 and B2 contains 72, the formula returns 78 (the same as the first formula). But if you change B1 so that it contains 8, ClarisWorks recalculates the formula and displays the new result. Using cell references makes it easy to make changes in the data and see how the changes affect the formulas.

Operators represent the mathematical calculations you want to perform. You can use *mathematical operators* (+, –, and so on) and *relational operators* (operators that compare entries). Following are the operators you can use:

Operator	Description
+	Addition
-	Subtraction
*	Multiplication
/	Division
^	Exponentiation
&	Used in text equations to join the text. If cell A1 contained Darlene and cell A2 contained Gerdt, you could use this formula to join the two entries: =A1&A2.
=	Equal to. Used in *relational formulas,* which compare two values. ClarisWorks evaluates the formula and returns TRUE or FALSE.
>	Greater than. Used in relational formulas. If cell A1 contained 50 and cell A2 contained 100, the formula =A1>A2 would return FALSE.
	Greater than or equal to. Used in relational formulas.
<	Less than. Used in relational formulas.
	Less than or equal to. Used in relational formulas.
<>	Not equal to. Used in relational formulas.

Entering a Formula

To enter a formula, follow these steps:

1. Select the cell that will contain the formula.

2. Type an equal sign (=) to indicate that the entry is a formula.

3. Click or type the first cell reference. The cell reference appears in the entry bar.

4. Type the operator.

5. Continue entering cell references and operators until the formula is complete.

6. Press Enter.

In the cell, you see the result of the formula. In the entry bar, you see the formula as you entered it.

Figure 8.2 shows some examples of formulas.

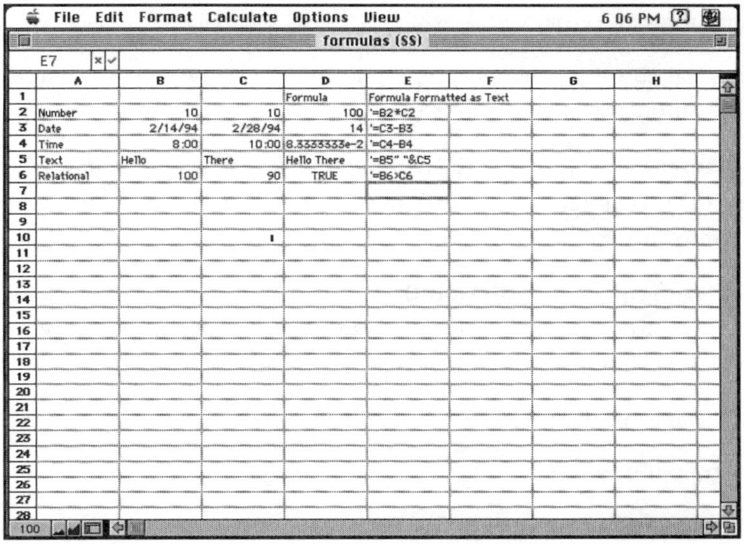

Figure 8.2
Here are examples of numerical, text, and relational formulas.

Understanding Cell References

In a formula, you can use three types of cell references: relative, absolute, and mixed.

Relative References. Relative references track a cell by its position relative to the current cell. As an example, think about how you might tell someone to find your house, relative to that person's location. You might say, "Go three blocks east, turn left, and it's the third house on the right." Relative references work similarly. The formula =A1+A2, entered in A3, can be translated as "Take the value two cells to the left and add it to the value one cell to the left."

Relative references are useful because they adjust when you move or copy them. If you had entries in B1 and B2 and wanted to use the same formula, you could copy the formula. The formula in B3 would still work, because it takes the value two cells to the left (B1) and adds it to the value one cell to the left (B2).

Absolute References. Absolute references refer to a cell exactly. For example, you might tell a friend you live at 5301 North Capitol. That's an exact address. Absolute references are not updated when you move or copy them, which is what you want in some cases.

Suppose that you are calculating a car loan, varying the term but keeping the interest rate the same. If you enter the interest rate in a cell, you want all formulas to refer to that cell.

Tip
If you want to specify an absolute reference while building a formula, hold down the ⌘ and Option keys, and click the cell.

To create an absolute reference, type a dollar sign ($) before the column letter and row number—for example, A1.

Mixed References. A mixed reference contains one absolute and one relative reference. You can tell ClarisWorks to vary the column but freeze the row (A$1), or to vary the row but freeze the column ($A1).

Understanding the Calculation Order

ClarisWorks uses a preset order, called *precedence*, to calculate formulas with many parts. Following is the order that ClarisWorks follows:

- Division by 100 (%)
- Exponentiation (^)
- Sign (+ and –)
- Multiplication and division (* and /)
- Addition and subtraction (+ and –)
- Text operator (&)
- Relational operators (=, <, <–, >, >–, <>)

To change this order, use parentheses. For example, compare the following formulas:

Formula	Result
=50+2*100	250
=(50+2)*100	5200

Changing the precedence, as you can see, can greatly affect the result of the formula.

Calculating the Worksheet

If you make a change in a cell that is referenced in a formula, ClarisWorks calculates the formula again. You can change this setting so that ClarisWorks calculates the formula only when you give the command.

To change the calculation method, choose Auto Calc from the Calculate menu (a checkmark should not appear next to the command). To recalculate the worksheet, choose Calculate Now from the Calculate menu.

> **Tip**
> You also can press Shift-⌘-= to choose the Calculate Now command.

> **Caution**
> If you use manual calculations, keep in mind that nothing appears on-screen to indicate that your worksheet needs to be recalculated. Be sure to recalculate so that any formulas are updated.

Understanding the Parts of a Function

A *function* is a prebuilt formula that performs simple to complex calculations on worksheet data. Rather than create the formulas manually, you can use the function to perform the calculation. For example, you could average a column of numbers by totaling them and then dividing by the number of entries. Or you could use the AVERAGE function, which creates the equation automatically.

Following is an example function:

    =SUM(A1..A3)

This function sums the values in the range A1..A3.

A function is made up of these parts:

- An equal sign, indicating a formula.
- The function name, which usually is a name or an abbreviation— for example, SUM or PMT (payment).
- Parentheses, which are used to surround the arguments.
- *Arguments*, which are the values you want to use in the calculation. Arguments can be single cells, constant values, or ranges.

Chapter 10, "Using Spreadsheet Functions," lists all the functions in the appropriate format. In this chapter, you learn how to enter a function.

Entering a Function

To enter a function, follow these steps:

1. Select the cell that you want to contain the function.
2. Choose Paste Function from the Edit menu. The Paste Function dialog box appears (see fig. 8.3).

180 Chapter 8—Spreadsheet Basics

Figure 8.3
In this dialog box, you select the function you want to use. You may have to scroll the list to find the function you want.

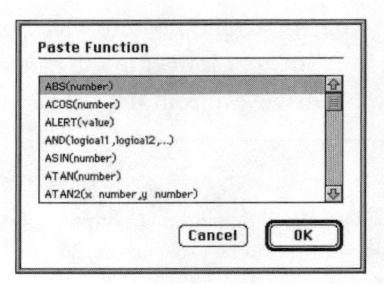

3. Click the function and then choose OK. ClarisWorks enters the function in the entry bar with blank arguments. The first argument is highlighted so that you can replace it with the real argument (see fig. 8.4).

Figure 8.4
Replace the selected argument with the argument you want to use.

Pasted function

Tip
To scroll quickly through the list, type the first letter of the function. ClarisWorks jumps to the first function that starts with that letter.

4. Enter the first argument.

   Arguments can be singular cell references, constant values, or ranges. You can type the argument or point to it in the worksheet.

5. Click the formula bar and select the next argument.

   Some functions include only one argument, in which case you can skip to step 8. Other functions contain multiple arguments. Some arguments are required; others are optional. For information on which arguments you need to enter, see Chapter 10, "Using Spreadsheet Functions."

6. Enter the next argument. If you want to delete the argument, press Delete.

7. Repeat this step for each argument in the function.

8. Press Return. You see the result of the formula in the worksheet; the entry bar displays the function (see fig. 8.5).

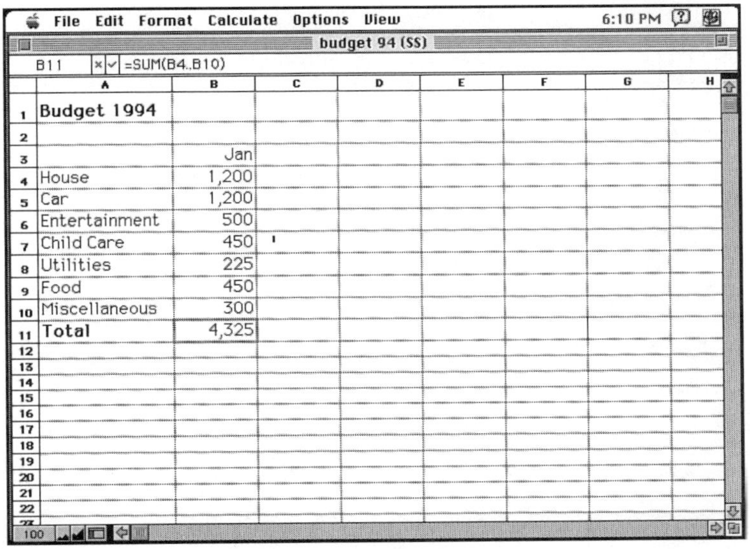

Figure 8.5
The completed function sums the numbers in the column and returns the result.

If you see the error message Bad Formula, check to be sure that you typed the entry in the correct format (see Chapter 10).

If you prefer, you can type the function manually. Select the cell; type an equal sign, the function name, and the arguments; and press Return.

Understanding Error Messages

If you make a mistake in entering a formula or function, you may see an error message. Table 8.2 lists spreadsheet error messages and their meanings.

Tip
To create a SUM function quickly, select the range you want to sum and a blank cell that will contain the formula, and then click the AutoSum button in the Shortcuts palette.

Table 8.2 Error Messages

Error	Description
#N/A!	One of the cells referenced is not available
#DIV/0!	The formula is attempting to divide by zero

(continues)

Table 8.2 Continued

#VALUE!	The formula or function is using mixed values (for example, text and numbers)
#NUM!	An invalid number is used or referenced in the formula
#REF!	The formula refers to a cell that does not exist
#ARG!	The wrong number of arguments or incorrect arguments have been entered
#USER!	User-defined error
#DATE!	Invalid date
#TIME!	Invalid time
#ERROR!	A general error message

Troubleshooting Formulas

My formula doesn't calculate as I wanted. Why?

ClarisWorks uses a preset calculation order. To change the order, use parentheses in the formula.

I get an error message when I enter a function or formula. What's my mistake?

To create and use formulas and functions, you must follow the proper format. If you don't, ClarisWorks flags the formula or function and displays an error message. For more information, see the preceding section ("Understanding Error Messages").

Editing Data

You can easily change the contents of your worksheet. You may want to change the values you entered, or you may want to copy or move data. This section explains those tasks.

Note

To find and change data in a worksheet, choose Find/Change from the Edit menu to display the Find/Change dialog box. Type what you want to find and what you want to change the found text to; then choose Find Next. For more information on finding and changing text, refer for Chapter 3, "Working with Text."

Editing a Cell

When you want to change a cell, you can do one of the following things:

- If the entry is entirely new, click the cell, type the new entry, and press Return. The new entry overwrites the existing entry.

- If you want to edit the existing entry, click the cell; then click the entry bar at the spot where you want to make the change. Delete, add, or edit the entry as needed, and then press Return.

> **Tip**
> You can drag across the entry in the entry bar to select it. You then can quickly delete or replace the selected characters.

To cancel the entry, press Esc or click the Cancel button in the entry bar.

Moving to a Cell

If your worksheet is large, moving to a cell by scrolling through the worksheet may be time-consuming. Instead, you can use the Go To command. Follow these steps:

1. Choose Go To Cell from the Options menu. The Go To Cell dialog box appears.

2. Type the cell address (for example, A1, F35, and so on).

3. Choose OK.

> **Tip**
> You also can press ⌘-G to choose the Go To Cell command.

Selecting a Range

When you want to work on more than one cell at a time, you can select a range of cells. Selecting a range is useful in the following cases:

- When you are entering arguments for a function—for example, summing a range.

- When you want to move or copy the range.

- When you want to format the range. (Formatting is covered in Chapter 9, "Enhancing a Worksheet.")

To select a range, follow these steps:

1. Click the first cell in the range.

2. Hold down the mouse button and drag across the cells you want to select.

3. Release the mouse button.

184 Chapter 8—Spreadsheet Basics

Figure 8.6 shows a selected range. Notice that the first cell has a dotted line around it and isn't highlighted. This is the active cell in the current selection.

Figure 8.6
The selected range is B3..B11.

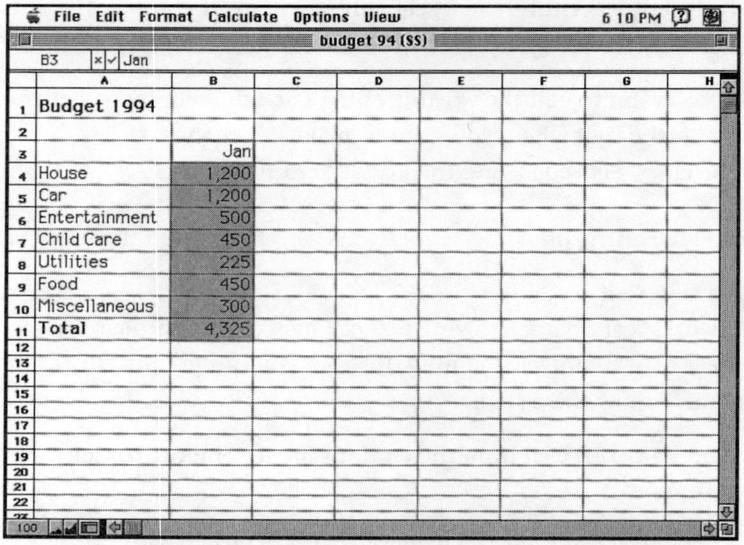

Tip
You also can click the first cell of the range and then Shift-click the last cell. All cells within that rectangular area are selected.

In some cases, you may want to select an entire row or column, or the entire worksheet. Use these shortcuts:

To Select This	Do This
An entire row	Click the row number.
An entire column	Click the column letter.
Several rows	Click the first row; then Shift-click the last row. All rows in between are selected.
Several columns	Click the first column; then Shift-click the last column. All columns in between are selected.
Entire worksheet	Click the small box above the row numbers and to the left of the column letters.
All cells that contain entries	Hold down the Option key and click the small box above the row numbers and to the left of the column letters.

Deleting Cell Contents

You can delete worksheet data that you no longer need, and ClarisWorks will update all cells that reference the deleted cells. If you delete a cell entry that is required in a formula, you may see the error message (#REF!). This error message means that the formula references a cell that no longer exists.

To delete cell contents, follow these steps:

1. Select the cell or range you want to delete.
2. Press Delete.

> **Note**
>
> When you delete cell contents, any cell formats remain. (Formatting is covered in Chapter 9, "Enhancing a Worksheet.") If you want to clear both the entries and the formats, select the range and then choose Clear from the Edit menu.

Moving Cell Contents

You can move a cell or a range of cells to another location in the worksheet or to another worksheet. If you move a formula, ClarisWorks adjusts the relative references, as needed.

To move a cell or range of cells, follow these steps:

1. Select the cell or range you want to move.
2. Choose Cut from the Edit menu.
3. Select the cell where you want to move the cells.

   Be sure to pick a blank area. ClarisWorks pastes the cells you cut over the cells you select as the destination.

4. Choose Paste from the Edit menu. The selected data moves to its new location.

Tip
You can press ⌘-X to choose the Cut command and ⌘-V to choose the Paste command. You also can click the Cut and Paste buttons in the Shortcuts palette.

> **Note**
>
> If you want to move cells and not update cell references within the formulas, select the range and then choose Move from the Calculate menu. Type the cell address of the location of the moved cells, and then choose OK.

Figure 8.7
You can copy this formula to other cells in the row to total the columns.

Copying Cell Contents

Copying data, especially formulas, is a quick way to complete a worksheet. Suppose that you want to total the contents of a series of columns. Rather than enter the formula each time, enter it once and then copy it to the other cells in the row.

Figure 8.7 shows a formula that you can copy to other cells in the row.

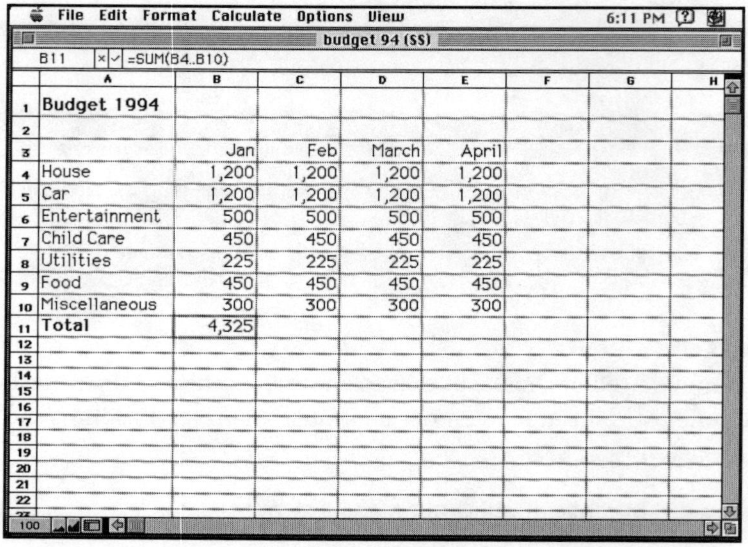

[Screenshot of ClarisWorks spreadsheet "budget 94 (SS)" showing cell B11 with formula =SUM(B4..B10). Columns: Jan, Feb, March, April with values for House 1,200; Car 1,200; Entertainment 500; Child Care 450; Utilities 225; Food 450; Miscellaneous 300; Total 4,325 in Jan column.]

To copy cell contents, follow these steps:

1. Select the cell or range that you want to copy. (If you need help, refer to "Selecting a Range" earlier in this chapter.)

Tip
You can press ⌘-C to choose the Copy command and ⌘-V to choose the Paste command. You also can click the Copy and Paste buttons in the Shortcuts palette.

2. Choose Copy from the Edit menu.

3. Select the cell or range where you want to place the copy.

Be sure to pick a blank area. ClarisWorks pastes the copy over the cells you select for the destination.

4. Choose Paste from the Edit menu. A copy of the selected data appears in the destination cell or range.

Notice that if you copy a formula, ClarisWorks adjusts the references (see fig. 8.8).

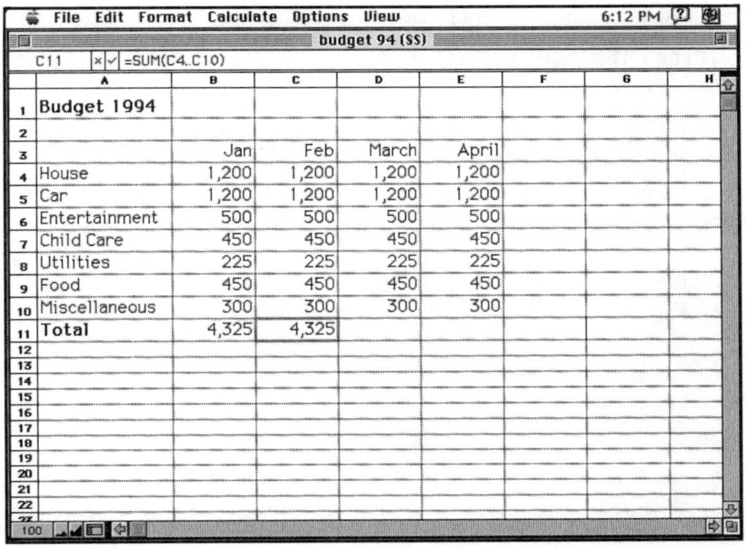

Editing Data **187**

Figure 8.8
The copied formula is adjusted to refer to the current column.

Filling a Range

A variation of copying is filling a range. You can fill a range with the entries in the rows above or the columns to the left. Follow these steps:

1. Select the cells that contain the entries and the range you want filled.

These two groups of cells have to be next to each other. In figure 8.9, for example, you can copy the entries in column B to columns C, D, and E.

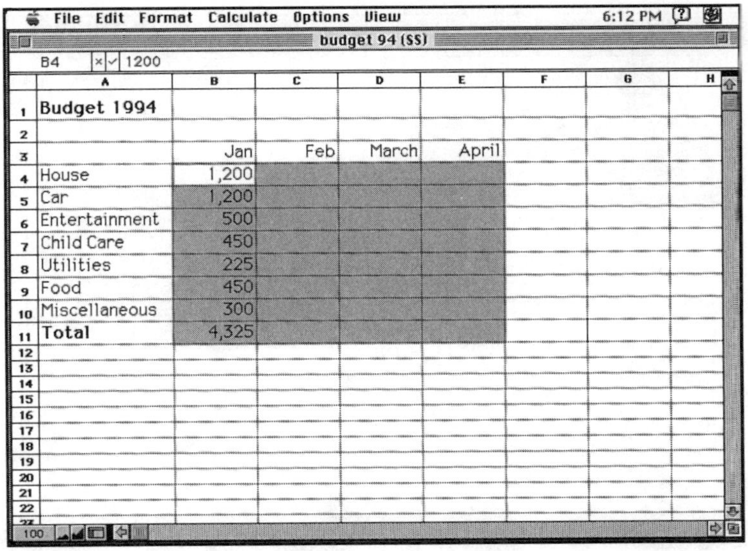

Figure 8.9
Filling a range is a quick way to enter data.

2. Choose Fill Right or Fill Down from the Calculate menu. ClarisWorks fills the range (see fig. 8.10).

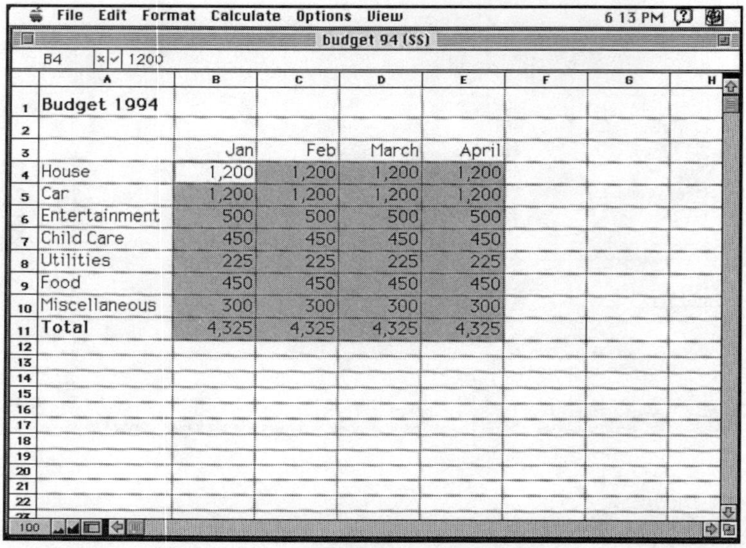

Fig. 8.10
Columns C, D, and E are filled with the values in column B.

Tip
You also can press ⌘-R to choose the Fill Right command and ⌘-D to choose the Fill Down command.

Transposing a Range

If you decide that your worksheet would work better with the rows as columns and the columns as rows, you can transpose the data. Figure 8.11 shows a worksheet before transposing.

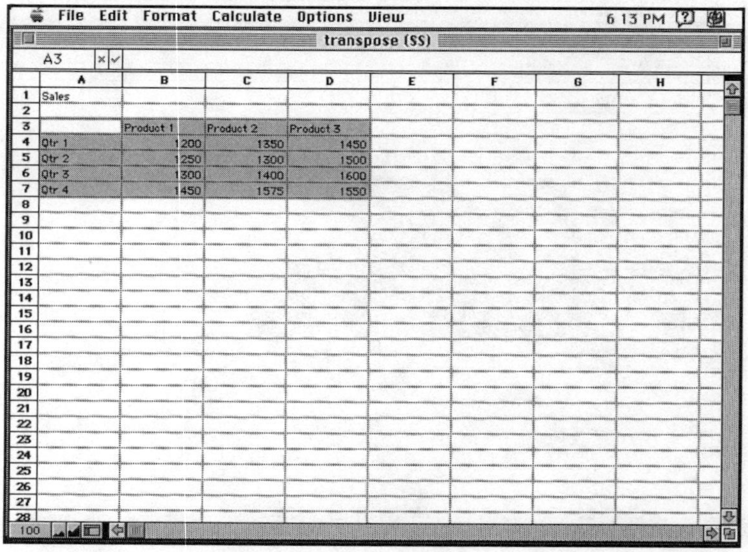

Figure 8.11
In this worksheet, the rows contain quarterly sales information, and the columns contain product information.

To transpose a range, follow these steps:

1. Select the range you want to transpose.

2. Choose Cut from the Edit menu.

3. Choose Paste Special from the Edit menu. The Paste Special dialog box appears (see fig. 8.12).

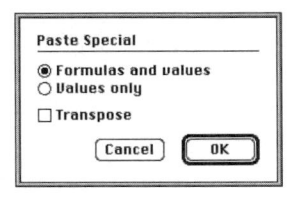

Figure 8.12
Check the Transpose check box to transpose the range.

4. Click the Transpose check box.

5. Choose OK. ClarisWorks transposes the range, as shown in figure 8.13.

Figure 8.13
Now the columns contain quarterly sales information, and the rows contain product information.

Freezing Values

As mentioned, ClarisWorks updates your formulas each time you change cells that are referenced in those formulas. At times, however, you want to *freeze* the values—change the formulas into the results they return. For example, if a cell contains the formula A1+A2 and returns 32, you can take the formula (A1+A2) and convert it to the result (32). If you make any changes in A1 or A2, the formula will not be updated.

To freeze a value, follow these steps:

1. Select the range.

2. Choose Cut from the Edit menu.

3. Choose Paste Special from the Edit menu to display the Paste Special dialog box.

4. Click the Values Only radio button.

5. Choose OK.

Protecting Cells

You can change—edit, delete, or overwrite—any cell in a worksheet. If you want, you can protect cells against certain changes so that they cannot be edited or deleted.

To protect a cell or range, select the cell or range, and then choose Protect Cells from the Options menu. Thereafter, when you try to delete or edit a protected cell, you see the error message Some cells are locked. To remove the error message, choose OK.

Tip
You also can press ⌘-H to choose the Protect Cells command and Shift-⌘-H to choose the Unprotect Cells command.

To unprotect a cell or range, select it and then choose the Unprotect Cells command from the Options menu.

Troubleshooting Data Editing

I accidentally deleted cells that I need. How can I get them back?

If you delete cells by accident, immediately choose Undo from the Edit menu to undo the deletion.

I copied a formula, but it doesn't return the answer I intended. What might be wrong?

Most of the time, you want the references in a formula to be adjusted when you move or copy the formula. For some formulas, though, you may need to refer to one cell specifically. Suppose that you have an interest rate in a cell that is used in a formula. Before you copy this formula, adjust the reference to that cell to make it absolute. For more information, refer to "Understanding Cell References" earlier in this chapter.

Editing the Worksheet Layout

One of the best things about working with data electronically is that you can easily insert something you forgot or delete something you don't need. For example, you can insert a row or column, or delete the information in a column or row. This section explains how to edit your worksheet layout.

Inserting Cells, Rows, and Columns

On paper, if you want to add something, you have to erase something to make room, write in the new information, and then reenter all the information you need. With ClarisWorks, inserting a cell, row, or column is easy. Follow these steps:

1. Select rows or columns to indicate what you want to insert.

    If you want to insert a row, click a row number to select an entire row. ClarisWorks will insert the new row above the selected row. If you want to insert several rows, select the number you want to insert.

    If you want to insert a column, click a column letter to select an entire column. ClarisWorks will insert the new column to the left of the selected column. If you want to insert several columns, select the number you want to insert.

    If you want to insert a range, select an existing range the size of the range you want to insert. ClarisWorks will insert the new range above or to the left of the selected range.

    Tip
    You can press Shift-⌘-I to choose the Insert Cells command. You also can click the Insert Cells button in the Shortcuts palette.

2. Choose Insert Cells from the Calculate menu.

    If you selected entire rows or columns, ClarisWorks inserts the rows or columns. If you selected a range, the Insert Cells dialog box appears (see fig. 8.14).

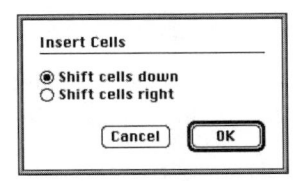

Figure 8.14
You can move existing cells down or right to make room for the new cells.

3. Choose Shift Cells Down or Shift Cells Right.

4. Choose OK.

Deleting Cells, Rows, and Columns

If you want to remove cells, rows, or columns from a worksheet, you can do so. ClarisWorks moves existing cells, rows, or columns to fill in the spot.

> **Note**
>
> Remember that there's a difference between deleting the contents of a cell and deleting or removing the cell itself from the worksheet. Deleting cell contents (covered in "Deleting Cell Contents" earlier in this chapter) leaves blank cells in the worksheet. Deleting or removing cells (covered in this section) results in the movement of existing worksheet data to fill the space left by the deleted cells.

Tip
You can press Shift-⌘-K to choose the Delete Cells command. You also can click the Delete Cells button in the Shortcuts palette.

To delete cells, columns, or rows, follow these steps:

1. Select the range, rows, or columns you want to delete.

2. Choose Delete Cells from the Calculate menu.

    If you selected entire rows or columns, ClarisWorks deletes the rows or columns. If you selected a range, the Delete Cells dialog box appears (see fig. 8.15).

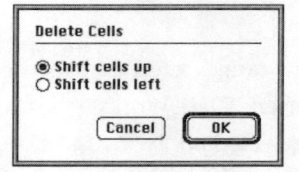

Figure 8.15
You can move existing cells up or left to fill in the space left by the deleted cells.

3. Choose Shift Cells Up or Shift Cells Left.

4. Choose OK.

Setting Display Options

You can control which items are displayed on-screen. If you don't want to see the column or row headings, for example, you can turn them off.

To make changes in the display options, follow these steps:

1. Choose Display from the Options menu. The Display dialog box appears (see fig. 8.16).

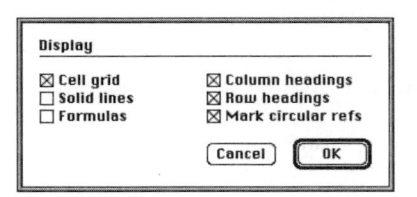

Figure 8.16
Check items that you want to display; uncheck items that you don't want to display.

2. Check and uncheck the options in the dialog box, as needed (see the following mini-table).

Option	Description
Cell Grid	If you don't want the grid displayed, uncheck this option, which is checked by default.
Solid Lines	If you prefer solid lines to dashed lines for the grid, check this option.
Formulas	ClarisWorks displays the result of a formula in the cell and the actual formula in the entry bar. If you want to see the formulas in the cell, check this option. This feature is useful for checking your formulas.
Column Headings	Uncheck this option if you don't want column headings (A, B, C) displayed.
Row Headings	Uncheck this option if you don't want row headings (1, 2, 3) displayed.
Mark Circular Refs	A *circular reference* is a formula that refers to itself. Usually, this type of reference is a mistake, and ClarisWorks flags the reference by placing bullets before and after the formula. If you prefer not to mark the references, uncheck this option.

Tip
You can click the Display Formulas button in the Shortcuts palette to change from displaying results to displaying formulas.

3. Choose OK.

Locking Row and Column Titles On-Screen

In large worksheets, you may be unable to see the column and row headings as you enter data. You can lock the titles on-screen so that they remain in view.

Follow these steps:

1. Select the columns or rows you want to lock in place.

2. Choose Lock Title Position from the Options menu.

When this option is activated, a checkmark appears next to its name in the Options menu. To turn the option off, select it again.

Sorting Worksheet Data

If you want to arrange your worksheet data in alphabetical or numerical order, you can use the Sort command. You can sort by columns or rows and in ascending or descending order. You also can sort on more than one column or row. When you perform a sort, you define a *sort key*—that is, you tell ClarisWorks which column you want to sort on.

To sort worksheet data, follow these steps:

1. Select the range you want to sort.

    In figure 8.17, the range will be sorted first by the entries in column A and then by the entries in column C.

Figure 8.17
You can sort the project names alphabetically and then by project priority.

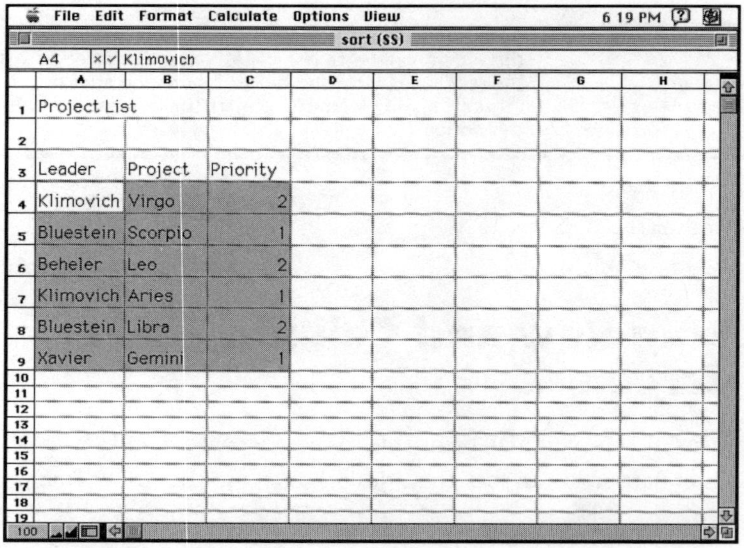

Sorting Worksheet Data **195**

2. Choose Sort from the Calculate menu. The Sort dialog box appears (see fig. 8.18).

3. If you want to sort by columns, choose Vertical in the Direction area. If you want to sort by rows, choose Horizontal in the Direction area.

Tip
You also can press ⌘-J to choose the Sort command.

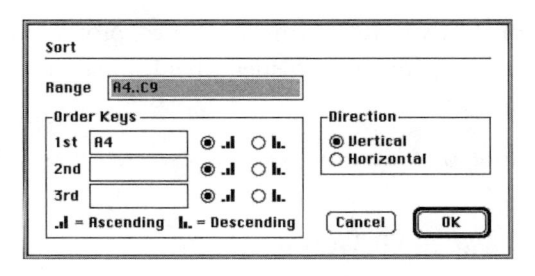

Figure 8.18
In the Sort dialog box, you can select which column or row you want to sort on and the sort order.

4. Type a cell address in the column or row that you want to use as the first sort. ClarisWorks will sort the entries in this column or row first.

5. Choose Ascending or Descending sort order.

6. If you want to use a second sort key, type a cell address for the column or row for this key, and then choose Ascending or Descending.

7. If you want to use a third sort key, type a cell address for column or row for the key, and then choose a sort order.

8. Choose OK. ClarisWorks sorts the worksheet data (see fig. 8.19).

Tip
You also can click the Sort Ascending and Sort Descending buttons in the Shortcuts palette.

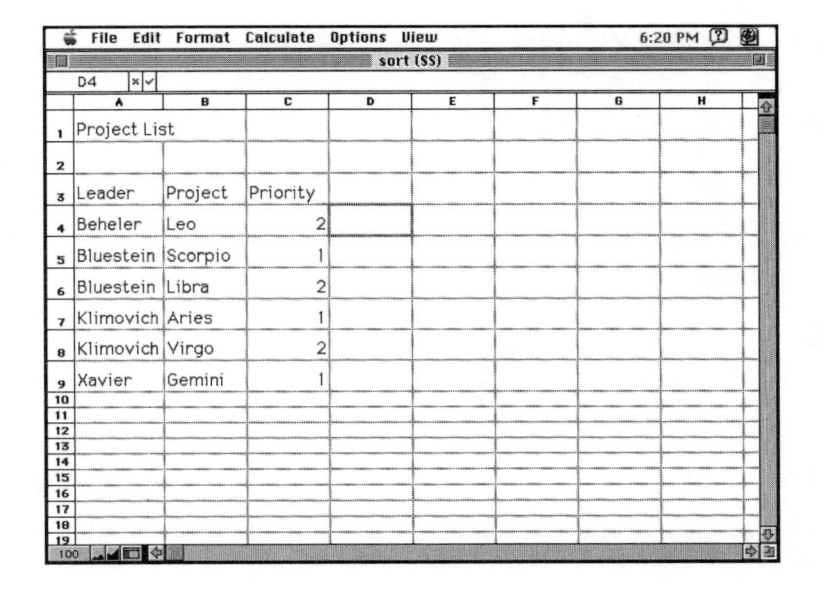

Figure 8.19
The worksheet is sorted first by leader name and then by priority.

If the sort doesn't go as you planned, immediately choose Undo Sort from the Edit menu.

From Here...

Entering data is the first step in creating a polished, professional worksheet. ClarisWorks' spreadsheet module provides other features, as described in the following chapters:

- For information on formatting a worksheet, see Chapter 9, "Enhancing a Worksheet."

- If you want to present the data graphically in a chart, see Chapter 11, "Creating Charts," which covers all the charting features.

- If you want more information on available functions, see Chapter 10, "Using Spreadsheet Functions."

Chapter 9
Enhancing a Worksheet

by Shelley O'Hara

The data you enter in a spreadsheet document has much more impact if you take the time to format it appropriately. Without formatting, a worksheet is just a jumble of numbers and results. With formatting, a worksheet can contain appropriate numeric formats, boldface entries, a border, and more.

This chapter covers formatting options. In this chapter, you learn the following:

- How to change the number format
- How to change the font, type size, style, and color of cell entries
- How to change the alignment of data
- How to change the column width and row height
- How to print the worksheet

Changing the Number Format

The number format can change the meaning of a cell entry. For example, the entry **1000** can be formatted several ways:

1000%

1,000

$1,000.00

You can use an appropriate number format to tell your readers what the values represent.

To apply a number format, follow these steps:

> **Tip**
> You can press Shift-⌘-N to choose the Number command. You also can double-click a single cell to display the Numeric dialog box and change the format of the cell.

1. Select the cell or range you want to change.

2. Choose Number from the Format menu. The Numeric dialog box appears (see fig. 9.1).

3. If you are formatting a number, select the number style you want (General, Currency, Percent, Scientific, or Fixed). If you want to use commas, check the Commas check box. If you want to display negative numbers in parentheses, check the Negatives in () check box. In the Precision text box, type the number of decimal places you want to display.

   If you are formatting a date, select a date format.

   If you are formatting a time, select a time format.

Figure 9.1
In the Numeric dialog box, you can select a number, date, and time format.

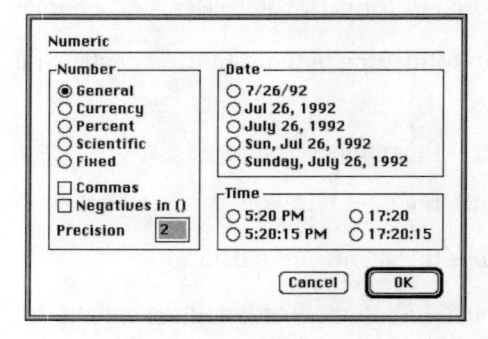

4. Choose OK.

Figure 9.2 shows different number, date, and time formats.

> **Note**
> Sometimes changing the format of a number makes the number too large to display. If you see number signs (###) in the cell or range, you need to widen the column. For directions, see "Changing the Column Width" later in this chapter.

You also can use the number-formatting buttons in the Shortcuts palette (see next page). For information on displaying and using this palette, refer to Chapter 8, "Spreadsheet Basics."

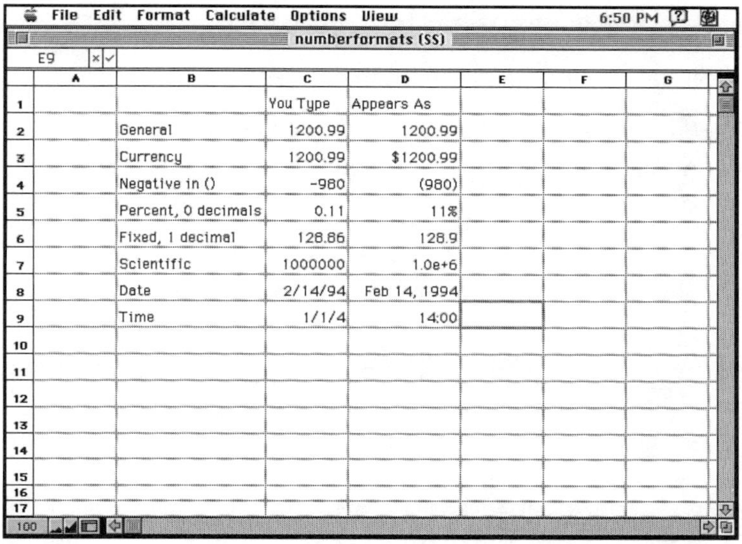

Changing Fonts, Type Size, Style, and Color   **199**

Figure 9.2
Here are examples of number, date, and time formats.

Button	Description
 🖬	Currency format
 %	Percent format
 0,0	Commas format

Changing Fonts, Type Size, Style, and Color

You can make entries stand out by changing the font, type size, style, or color.

You may want to make your headings bold so that they are easy to see, or you could use a larger type size for the worksheet title. If you are printing on a color printer or planning to display the document on-screen, you may want to change the color of the entries. This section covers those tasks.

Changing Fonts

The default font used for spreadsheet documents is 9-point Geneva. You can change the font for the entire document, part of the document, or all new documents.

Chapter 9—Enhancing a Worksheet

To change the font in a worksheet, follow these steps:

1. Select the cell or range you want to change.

2. Choose Font from the Format menu, and hold down the mouse button so you can see the Font pop-up menu.

3. Choose the font you want.

Figure 9.3 shows a worksheet formatted with the New York font.

Figure 9.3
In this worksheet, the font has been changed to New York.

To change the default font used for a worksheet, follow these steps:

1. Choose Default Font from the Options menu. The Default Font dialog box appears (see fig. 9.4).

Figure 9.4
You can specify the font and type size to be used for the entire worksheet.

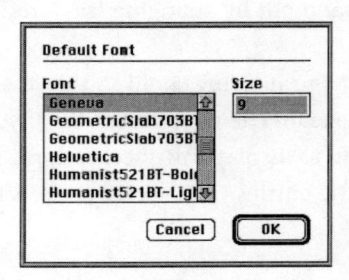

2. In the Font list, select the font you want to use.

3. In the Size text box, enter the type size you want to use.

4. Choose OK.

Adjusting Type Size

The default 9-point type size is pretty small. You may want to use a different type size.

To change the size of the entries in a worksheet, follow these steps:

1. Select the cell or range you want to change.

2. Choose Size from the Format menu, and hold down the mouse button so you can see the Size submenu.

3. Choose the size you want.

If you use a larger type size, you may have to adjust the row height; ClarisWorks does not adjust the height automatically to fit the new size. (For directions, see "Changing the Row Height" later in this chapter.)

In figure 9.5, the worksheet title has been changed to 24-point type, and all row heights have been adjusted.

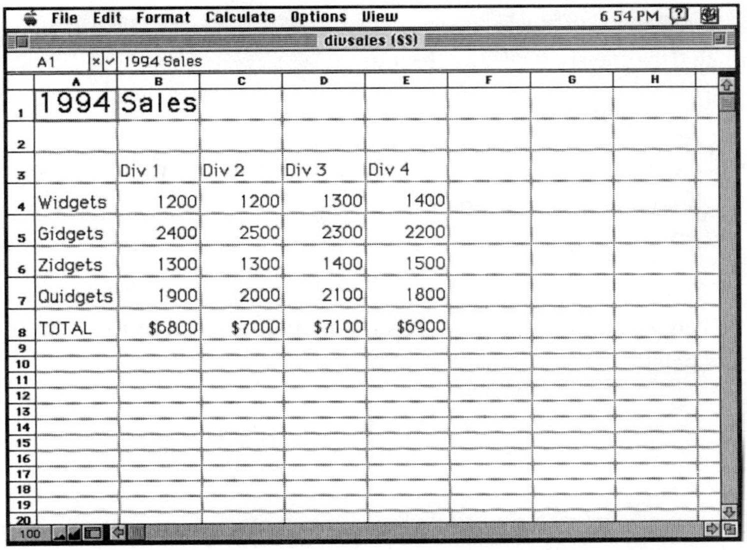

Figure 9.5
Larger type sizes are useful for making the title of a worksheet stand out.

Using Type Styles

In addition to changing the font and type, you can use different styles for the entries in a worksheet. Figure 9.6 shows each of the available styles. (Notice that the grid lines have been turned off for this worksheet so you can see the styles better. For information on turning off the grid lines, refer to Chapter 8, "Spreadsheet Basics.")

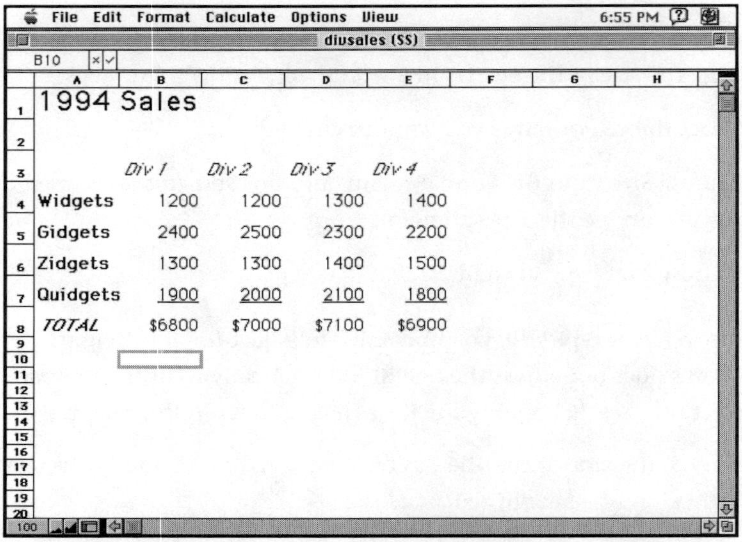

Figure 9.6
Examples of the bold, italic, and underline type styles.

To change the type style, follow these steps:

1. Select the cell or range you want to change.

2. Choose Style from the Format menu, and hold down the mouse button so you can see the Style submenu.

3. Choose the style you want.

You also can use the following shortcut keys and shortcut buttons (in the Shortcuts palette):

Tip
You can define and save styles and then apply them to other cells in the worksheet. See Chapter 20, "Customizing ClarisWorks," for information on custom styles.

Changing Fonts, Type Size, Style, and Color

Option	Shortcut Key	Shortcut Button
Bold	⌘-B	**B**
Italic	⌘-I	*I*
Underline	⌘-I	U

Adding Color

If you plan to print a worksheet on a color printer, or if you are using the document in an on-screen display, you can jazz up the colors—for example, display all negative numbers in red.

To change the text color, follow these steps:

1. Select the cell or range you want to change.

2. Choose Text Color from the Format menu, and hold down the mouse button so you can see the color palette.

3. Choose the color you want.

Troubleshooting Number Formats and Fonts

When I change the number format, I see ### in the cell. How do I fix this?

Some number formats take more space than the original. In this case, you see pound signs. To correct this problem, widen the column.

I don't like the number format I used. How do I go back to the original?

By default, all entries are formatted as General. You can choose Undo from the Edit menu to undo the formatting, or display the Numeric dialog box and choose General and OK.

When I change the font, the text overlaps the row borders. How do I fix this?

ClarisWorks does not adjust the row height automatically when you make the font larger; you need to adjust the row height yourself. For instructions, see "Changing Column Width and Row Height" later in this chapter.

Adding Borders

Another way to add emphasis to your worksheet data is to add a border.

To add a border, click the border buttons in the Shortcuts palette, or follow these steps:

1. Select the cell or range you want to change.

2. Choose Borders from the Format menu. The Borders dialog box appears (see fig. 9.7).

Figure 9.7
In this dialog box, choose the sides to which you want to add borders.

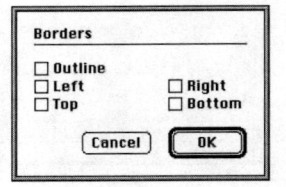

3. If you want to outline the cell or range, check the Outline check box. If you want to add borders only to certain sides, check the appropriate check boxes (Left, Right, Top, or Bottom).

4. Choose OK. ClarisWorks adds the borders to the cell or range.

Figure 9.8 shows a document in which the totals are outlined.

Figure 9.8
In this worksheet, an outline was added to the Total row.

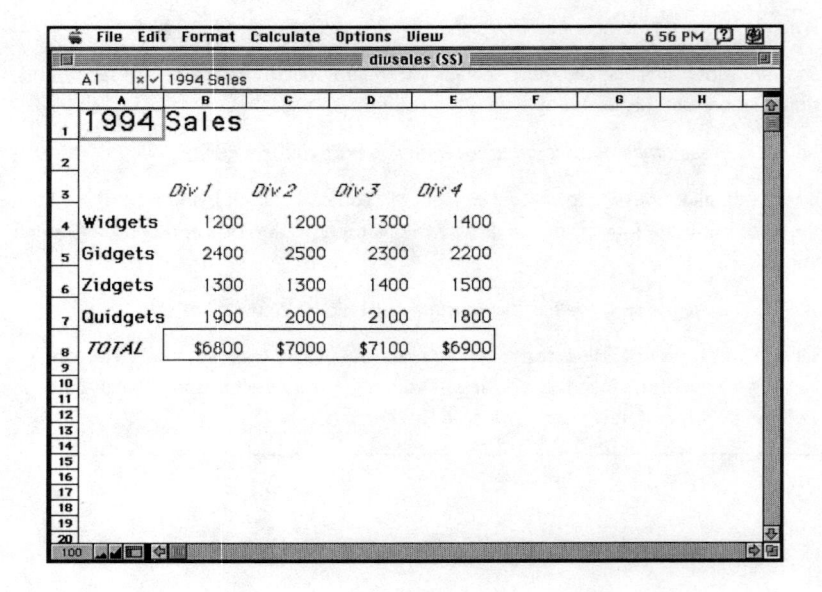

Aligning Data

By default, ClarisWorks aligns numbers right and text left. Under this alignment scheme, however, numbers and text may not line up (see fig. 9.9). You can fix this problem by using a different alignment.

To align data, follow these steps:

1. Select the cell or range you want to change.

2. Choose Alignment from the Format menu, and hold down the mouse button so you can see the Alignment submenu.

3. Select the alignment you want (General, Left, Right, or Center).

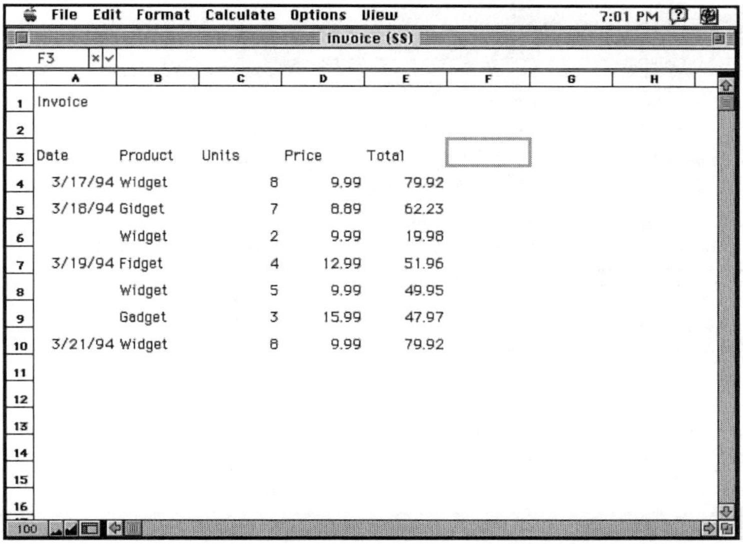

Figure 9.9
In this worksheet, grid lines have been turned off so you can see the alignment of the data better.

Figure 9.10 shows different types of alignments.

Figure 9.10
Here you see examples of left, right, and center alignment.

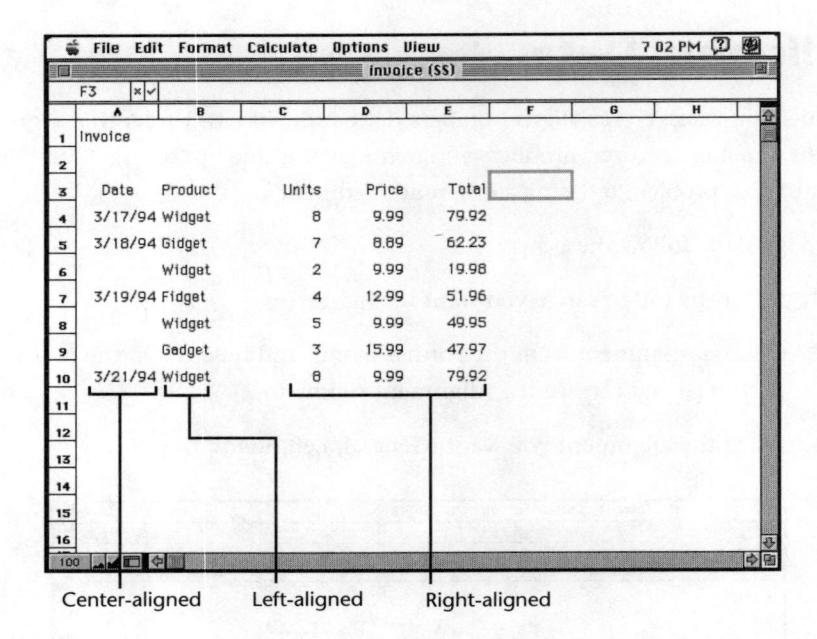

```
                                    Invoice (SS)
  F3
        A        B         C        D        E        F        G        H
1  Invoice
2
3       Date     Product            Units    Price    Total
4       3/17/94  Widget             8        9.99     79.92
5       3/18/94  Gidget             7        8.89     62.23
6                Widget             2        9.99     19.98
7       3/19/94  Fidget             4        12.99    51.96
8                Widget             5        9.99     49.95
9                Gadget             3        15.99    47.97
10      3/21/94  Widget             8        9.99     79.92
```

Center-aligned   Left-aligned   Right-aligned

You also can use the following shortcut keys and Shortcuts-palette buttons:

Option	Shortcut Key	Shortcut Button
Left	⌘-[	
Center	⌘-\	
Right	⌘-]	

On some occasions, you may enter a paragraph of text into the worksheet, and you may want to wrap the text in the cell. To do this, type the text in one cell and then choose Alignment Wrap from the Format menu. You also may have to adjust the row height to see the entire entry. You can use any alignment with the Wrap feature.

Figure 9.11 shows an example of wrapped text.

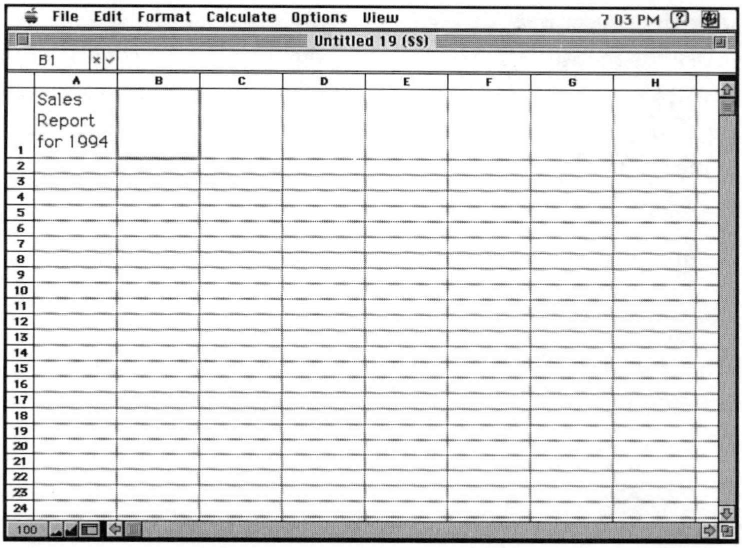

Figure 9.11
In this worksheet, the text is wrapped, and the row height is adjusted.

Copying Formatting

If you get the formats just right for one cell and want to use the same formats in another cell or range, you can copy the formatting from one cell to another. Follow these steps:

1. Select the cell that contains the formatting you want to copy.

2. Choose Copy Format from the Edit menu.

3. Select the cell or range you want to format.

4. Choose Paste Format from the Edit menu.

Tip
You also can press Shift-⌘-C to choose the Copy Format command and Shift-⌘-V to choose the Paste Format command.

Changing Column Width and Row Height

If your entries spill over into the next cell, if your entry is truncated, or if you see ### or scientific notation in a cell, you have to widen the column. When you change the type size, you may have to adjust the row height. This section explains how to make both changes.

Changing the Column Width

You can use the mouse or a menu command to change the column. To use the mouse, place the pointer on the right border of the column header you want to change, next to the column letter. The pointer should change to a vertical line with arrows on either side. Drag the column border left to decrease or right to increase the width of the column.

To use a command to change the column width, follow these steps:

1. Select the column or columns you want to change.

   If you are changing only one column, you can select any cell in that column. If you are changing multiple columns, select a range that spans the columns you want to change.

2. Choose Column Width from the Format menu. The Column Width dialog box appears (see fig. 9.12). The preset width is 72 points, or 1 inch.

Figure 9.12
Enter the width of the column in this dialog box.

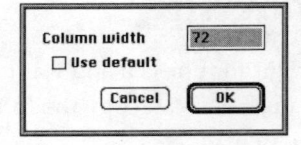

3. Type the number of points you want to use. (Remember that 72 points equals 1 inch.)

4. Choose OK.

To return to the default width, select the column, choose the Column Width command, choose Use Default in the dialog box, and then choose OK.

Changing the Row Height

Tip
To hide a column, drag the column border to the left until it passes the left border. To unhide a column, drag the hidden column to the right.

Unfortunately, ClarisWorks does not adjust the row height automatically when you make font and type-size changes. You must adjust the height, using the mouse or a command.

To use the mouse, place the pointer on the bottom edge of the row, below the row number. The mouse pointer changes to a horizontal line with two arrows. Drag the border down to increase the size; drag up to decrease the size.

To change the row height with a menu command, follow these steps:

1. Select the row or rows you want to change.

    If you are changing only one row, you can select any cell in that row. If you are changing multiple rows, select a range that spans the rows you want to change.

2. Choose Row Height from the Format menu. The Row Height dialog box appears (see fig. 9.13). The preset height is 14 points.

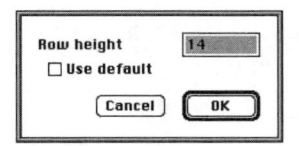

Figure 9.13
Enter the height of the row in this dialog box.

3. Type the number of points you want to use. (Remember that 72 points equals 1 inch.)

4. Choose OK.

To return to the default height, select the row, choose Row Height from the Format menu, choose Use Default in the dialog box, and then choose OK.

Troubleshooting Column Width and Row Height
When I try to drag a column border, I resize the wrong column. Why?
When you want to resize a column, place the mouse pointer on the right border of the column you want to change. If you are pointing to the left border, you will resize the column to the left.
I want to resize all the columns. Can I do this?
To resize all columns, click the Select All area of the worksheet (above the row numbers and to the left of the column letters), and then drag one of the columns. All columns will be adjusted.

Tip
To hide a row, drag the row border up past the top border. To unhide a row, drag the row border down.

Adding Graphics

You can add a graphic to your worksheet with the paint or draw tools. To display the tools, choose Show Tools from the View menu. For information on using these tools, refer to chapters 6 and 7. You can also cut and paste clip art, and insert a frame to add a graphic. For details on frames, see Chapter 15, "Creating Integrated Documents."

Figure 9.14 shows an example of a simple graphic added to a worksheet.

Figure 9.14
A graphic has been added to the worksheet.

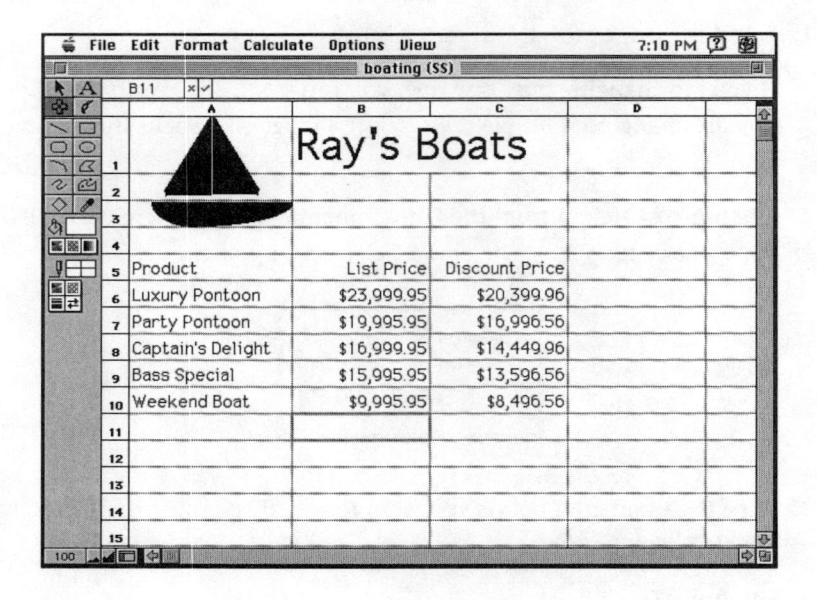

Printing the Worksheet

The result of all your data entry and formatting probably will be a printed copy of the information. You control what part of the worksheet is printed and where page breaks occur.

> **Note**
>
> For information on changing margins, adding headers or footers, and adding page numbers, see Chapter 4, "Enhancing Your Text."

Entering a Page Break

ClarisWorks enters page breaks as required. If you want to enter a break manually, you can do so. Follow these steps:

1. Select the cell where you want the page break to occur.

    If you select a row, ClarisWorks breaks the page below the selected cell. If you select a column, ClarisWorks breaks the page to the right of the column. If you select a cell, ClarisWorks breaks the page below and to the right of the selected cell.

2. Choose Add Page Break from the Options menu. ClarisWorks adds the break.

To delete a page break, select the cell in which you entered the page break and then choose Remove Page Break from the Options menu. To delete all manual page breaks, choose Remove All Breaks from the Options menu; you need not select the entire worksheet first.

Setting the Print Range

You can control how much of a worksheet is printed by setting the print range. You can print all cells that contain data or only one range. Follow these steps:

1. Choose Print Range from the Options menu. The Print Range dialog box appears (see fig. 9.15).

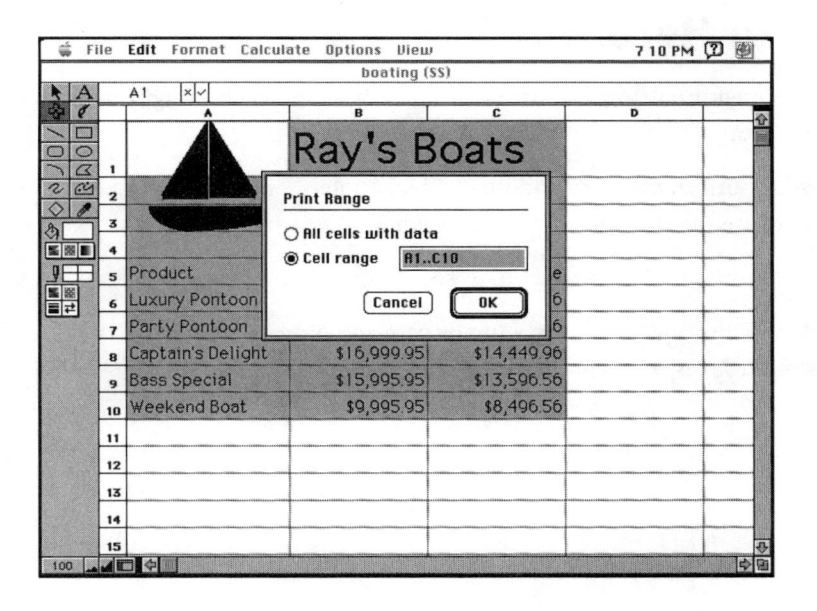

Figure 9.15
You can tell ClarisWorks to print all cells that contain data or just the range you enter.

2. To print all cells that contain data, choose the All Cells with Data radio button. To print a cell range, choose the Cell Range radio button; then enter the range you want to print.

3. Choose OK.

> **Troubleshooting Printing**
>
> *Something unexpected prints at the top and bottom of every page. How do I get rid of this?*
>
> You can create headers that print at the top and footers that print at the bottom of each page. For more information on headers and footers, refer to Chapter 4, "Enhancing Your Text."
>
> *How do I fit my worksheet on one page?*
>
> To print a worksheet on one page, try the following:
>
> - Use a smaller type size.
> - Change the page margins (see Chapter 4).
> - Change the page orientation (see Chapter 2).

From Here...

As you are formatting your worksheet, these chapters also might be of interest to you:

- For information on adding headers, footers, and page numbers and on changing the margins, see Chapter 4, "Enhancing Your Text."

- If you want to create a chart, see Chapter 11, "Creating Charts."

- For information on drawing or painting objects, see Chapters 6 and 7, respectively.

Chapter 10

Using Spreadsheet Functions

by Cyndie Shaffstall-Klopfenstein

As you learned in the two preceding chapters, spreadsheets are mathematical representations of data. They might include dates, payment tables, or even projections. This chapter works with formulas and functions to show how they can be used to influence the data.

A *formula* performs a calculation, using cell references, numbers, operators, and functions. A *function* is a built-in formula provided by ClarisWorks. You can easily place a function in a cell by selecting the cell and choosing Paste Function from the Edit menu. The function that you select is pasted in the cell in the proper format, or *syntax*, and the first segment that requires your data is highlighted.

Functions contain *arguments*, which are numbers, cell references, or other values to be acted on by ClarisWorks. Parentheses enclose the arguments, which are separated by commas. In the example =ROUND(*number,number of digits*), *number* and *number of digits* are the arguments, and ROUND is the name of the function.

In this chapter, you learn the following:

- How to use date and statistical functions

- How to use logical or test functions

- How to set up worksheets to compare loan repayments and investments

- How to use lookup functions

Expanding Basic Skills

One of the most popular types of spreadsheet applications is a home budget. This is a great learning example because it contains many of the simpler functions. Understanding these functions will prepare you for much more complex tasks.

You can create a sample budget worksheet, using your own monthly expenditures and ideas from figure 10.1 on how to lay out the columns. In figure 10.1, the month names run across the top row. The types of expenditures run down the first column. Your expenses might be different from those used in the figure. Use commands in the Format menu to change the style, font, and size of the text, if you want.

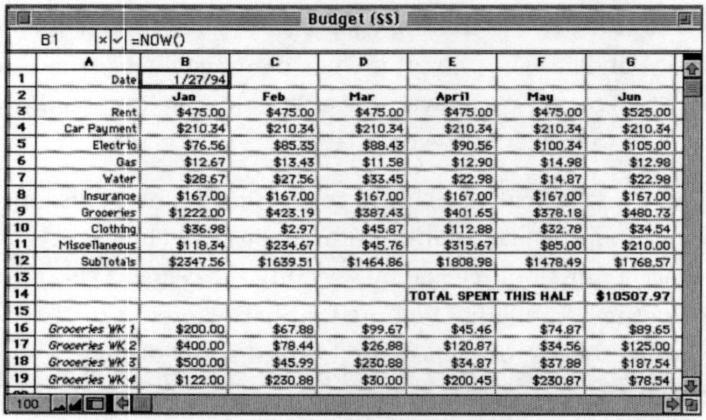

Budget (SS)

B1 =NOW()

	A	B	C	D	E	F	G
1	Date	1/27/94					
2		Jan	Feb	Mar	April	May	Jun
3	Rent	$475.00	$475.00	$475.00	$475.00	$475.00	$525.00
4	Car Payment	$210.34	$210.34	$210.34	$210.34	$210.34	$210.34
5	Electric	$76.56	$85.35	$88.43	$90.56	$100.34	$105.00
6	Gas	$12.67	$13.43	$11.58	$12.90	$14.98	$12.98
7	Water	$28.67	$27.56	$33.45	$22.98	$14.87	$22.98
8	Insurance	$167.00	$167.00	$167.00	$167.00	$167.00	$167.00
9	Groceries	$1222.00	$423.19	$387.43	$401.65	$378.18	$480.73
10	Clothing	$36.98	$2.97	$45.87	$112.88	$32.78	$34.54
11	Miscellaneous	$118.34	$234.67	$45.76	$315.67	$85.00	$210.00
12	SubTotals	$2347.56	$1639.51	$1464.86	$1808.98	$1478.49	$1768.57
13							
14					TOTAL SPENT THIS HALF		$10507.97
15							
16	*Groceries WK 1*	$200.00	$67.88	$99.67	$45.46	$74.87	$89.65
17	*Groceries WK 2*	$400.00	$78.44	$26.88	$120.87	$34.56	$125.00
18	*Groceries WK 3*	$500.00	$45.99	$230.88	$34.87	$37.88	$187.54
19	*Groceries WK 4*	$122.00	$230.88	$30.00	$200.45	$230.87	$78.54

Figure 10.1
This figure shows a completed budget with a subset for groceries.

Figure 10.1 contains a subsection for groceries so that as grocery purchases are made each week, they can be added in separately. This example demonstrates that you don't always have to use the SUM function at the bottom of columns. Cell B9 in the figure contains the following function:

=SUM(B16..B19)

You might choose to subtotal other types of expenses instead (or also). Perhaps your car makes regular visits to the repair shop. This would be a handy way of tracking that expense, however discouraging.

This type of worksheet has several different subtotals and a grand total. It can be affected each month by unexpected expenditures. (What a surprise!) There is a row of text cells for adding in miscellaneous expenses. You might want to list them individually below the groceries section.

Using Date Functions

There is a date in cell B1 of the budget worksheet that was entered by using a date function. Arguments in date functions must be serial numbers. A serial number is calculated as the distance (in number of days) that a date is from January 1, 1904. If you choose the date December 24, 1994, for example, ClarisWorks will recognize this date as 33,230 because it is 33,230 days after January 1, 1904.

Date functions are most useful for performing calculations such as the number of days' interest charged on a past-due payment. The number of days past due is simply one serial number subtracted from another; ClarisWorks does not need to factor in which months have 28, 30, or 31 days.

Cell B1 contains the NOW function, which displays the date the function was entered, as recorded by your Macintosh's internal clock. The syntax of the NOW function is:

=NOW( )

No arguments are used in this function. When you press Enter (in the numeric keypad), the date appears as a serial number in the cell and can then be formatted with any of the five date formats available in the Format Number dialog box.

> **Note**
> The date provided by NOW will not automatically update if you open and save the worksheet on another day. The NOW function updates only if you choose Calculate Now from the Calculate menu each time you work with the file.

To make your own date cell, follow these steps:

1. Select the cell to house the date.
2. Choose Paste Function from the Edit menu. The Paste Function dialog box appears (see fig. 10.2).
3. Select NOW. That function appears in the data entry line.
4. Press Enter. The date appears as a serial number in the designated cell of the worksheet.

Tip
If you want the date in a worksheet to change to today's date each time you work with it, add a date in the header or footer. For details on adding dates to headers and footers, see Chapter 4, "Enhancing Your Text."

Figure 10.2
The Paste Function dialog box.

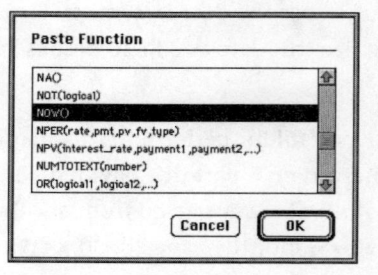

5. Select the cell containing the date, and then choose Number from the Format menu. The Number Format dialog box appears.

6. Select a date format, and then choose OK.

> **Note**
>
> If you try to use the NOW function and the date is incorrect, go to the Macintosh Control Panel and reset the clock to the correct date.

The DATETOTEXT function formats a date serial number. Following is the syntax of the function:

=DATETOTEXT(*serial number,format number*)

This function enables you to display dates as text even when they are part of a calculation. You can create a DATETOTEXT cell in the same manner as you did for NOW. Follow the same steps, but choose DATETOTEXT from the Paste Function dialog box rather than NOW.

You can use the following table to determine the format in which you want your date to appear. If you don't include a *format number* argument, ClarisWorks uses the default format, which is the first one in the following table.

Number	Format
0	12/24/94
1	Dec 24, 1994
2	December 24, 1994
3	Sat, Dec 24, 1994

Number	Format
4	Saturday, December 24, 1994

Using Statistical Functions

A number of statistical functions are available in ClarisWorks. One that is particularly useful is AVERAGE. You can use this function to average speeds, times, numbers, and even grades. The syntax of the AVERAGE function is:

=AVERAGE(*number 1*,*number 2*,...)

Figure 10.3 shows the result of a simple AVERAGE formula that averaged test grades per student and per class.

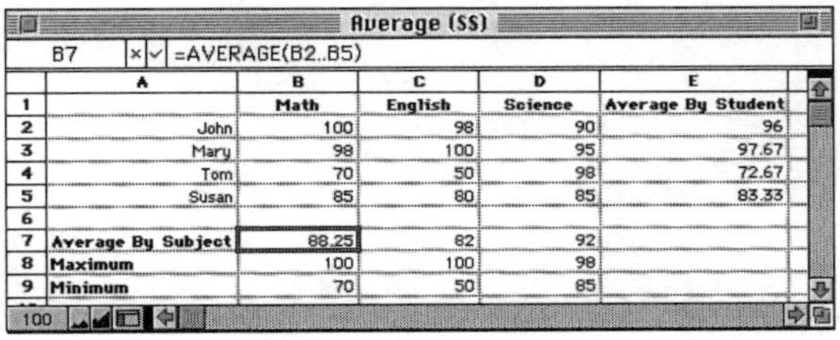

	A	B	C	D	E
1		Math	English	Science	Average By Student
2	John	100	98	90	96
3	Mary	98	100	95	97.67
4	Tom	70	50	98	72.67
5	Susan	85	80	85	83.33
6					
7	Average By Subject	88.25	82	92	
8	Maximum	100	100	98	
9	Minimum	70	50	85	

Figure 10.3
An average, maximum, and minimum is shown for each column of test scores.

This example shows that the same cell can be used in more than one formula. To use a particular cell multiple times, follow these steps:

1. Click the cell in which you want the average of a cell range to appear.
2. Choose Paste Function from the Edit menu. The Paste Function dialog box appears.
3. Select AVERAGE. That function appears in the entry bar.
4. Select the text within the parentheses. Then, while this text is highlighted, select the cell range that you want to average.
5. Press Enter.

Two other simple functions are MAXIMUM and MINIMUM. These two functions perform exactly the operations that their names imply. Each function searches a range of cells for the highest (maximum) or the lowest (minimum) value. If you were a teacher with many grades recorded, these functions would provide a simple method for returning the lowest and the highest grades.

Chapter 10—Using Spreadsheet Functions

To create your own Maximum or Minimum cell, refer to the AVERAGE example (see fig. 10.3), and notice the last two rows of column A. After you select a cell in your worksheet to house the Maximum or Minimum data, choose one of these two functions from the Paste Function dialog box, and follow the steps given for AVERAGE.

Calculating and Auto Calc

Just to watch the recalculation process, try changing one of the variables in the grades. Notice that ClarisWorks recalculates the averages in both directions (see fig. 10.4). This recalculation happens only when Auto Calc is selected in the Calculate menu.

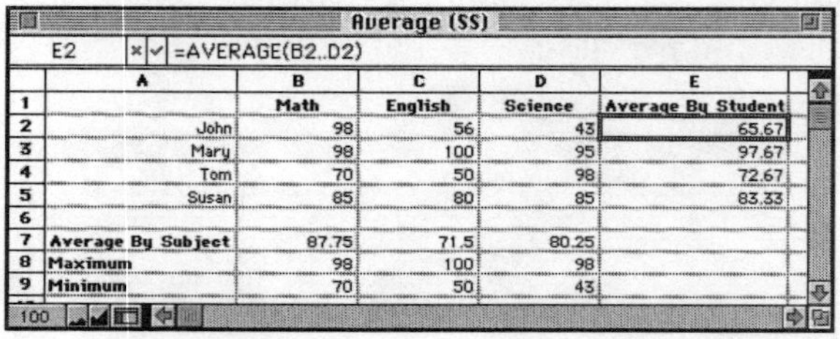

Figure 10.4
John's grades were changed, and averages in both directions reflect this change.

You may not want to use Auto Calc in a large worksheet. Auto Calc forces ClarisWorks to perform a calculation each time you enter data or edit a formula cell. In a large worksheet, this process can make data entry very slow. If there is a checkmark next to Auto Calc in the Calculate menu, choose Auto Calc, and the checkmark will disappear. Later, when you want ClarisWorks to calculate the functions, choose Calculate Now from the Calculate menu.

> **Caution**
>
> If you turn Auto Calc off, don't forget to turn it back on or to use Calculate Now before printing the worksheet. Otherwise, the totals for the formulas will not reflect any new changes.

Tip
You can press Shift-equal sign (=) to calculate on demand.

> **Troubleshooting Functions**
>
> *Why do I get a gray outline, not highlighting, when I click a cell?*
>
> You are still in an active formula. Make sure that you apply the formula by pressing Enter or clicking the checkmark icon in the entry bar. You also can press Esc to move out of an active formula.

Why do I see a Bad Formula dialog box each time I press Enter?

Look over the formula very carefully. Formulas are constructed like sentences. Make sure that your formula reads correctly, and that it starts with an equal sign and is enclosed in parentheses.

When I used a date function, the date displayed in an incorrect format. Why?

Check the function. The number after the comma (0 through 5) dictates the format.

Using Logical Functions

Some spreadsheet functions are used to test or confirm conditions. This means that a function in one cell is set up to look at the contents of another cell and verify that it contains specific data. The function then returns either a statement or a number, depending on which function was used.

The checkbook worksheet in figure 10.5 is an example of the IF function. Notice the formula in the entry bar:

```
=IF(H10<=0,"NO MONEY")
```

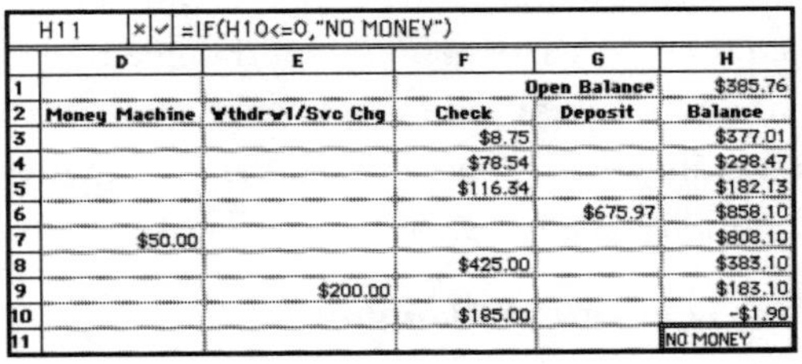

H11 =IF(H10<=0,"NO MONEY")

	D	E	F	G	H
1				Open Balance	$385.76
2	Money Machine	Wthdrwl/Svc Chg	Check	Deposit	Balance
3			$8.75		$377.01
4			$78.54		$298.47
5			$116.34		$182.13
6				$675.97	$858.10
7	$50.00				$808.10
8			$425.00		$383.10
9		$200.00			$183.10
10			$185.00		-$1.90
11					NO MONEY

Figure 10.5
The cell is warning you that there is `NO MONEY`.

The formula sentence can be read this way: "If cell H10 is equal to or less than zero dollars, print `NO MONEY` in cell H12." This is a logical function.

This cell will return the `NO MONEY` text each time you make an adjustment in the worksheet that takes the balance to equal or less than zero. `NO MONEY` will appear in cell H12, because that is the cell you selected. It will not affect the information or the formula in H10. If H10 equals more than zero, H12 will display the message `FALSE`, because the answer is no longer true.

If you want to hear a warning beep, use the same formula, but instead of typing **NO MONEY**, type **BEEP**. Use the double parentheses and closing parentheses after the word, as follows:

=IF (H10<0,BEEP( ))

Now when the balance is less than zero, ClarisWorks will beep and display 0. You can use this warning in all different types of scenarios. Try it in other worksheets.

> **Note**
> All arguments must be contained within parentheses, and all formulas must begin with an equal sign. If you see the Bad Formula dialog box, check your formula carefully for the error.

Using Financial Functions

Spreadsheet programs are used because of their mathematical strengths. This might be especially true for people who aren't as adept at number crunching as CPAs are. A spreadsheet program can simplify a difficult financial table or perform complex computations, depending on the needs of the user. Some common uses for financial functions are figuring payments on a loan or calculating how much money will grow during a defined savings period. The following sections give you a glimpse of the power of spreadsheets.

Using Functions for Investment Planning

Another use for spreadsheets is investment planning. Suppose that your child wants to go to a college where tuition is $40,000. If you want to save a certain amount of money every year, at 5 percent interest, toward your child's tuition, you can use a spreadsheet function to calculate how long you will have to save. You don't have to use a huge worksheet; sometimes all the information you need is contained in a single cell, as shown in figure 10.6.

Figure 10.6 uses the Future Value (FV) function to calculate, at the current rate of interest, how much money you will have in 21 years if you save $75 each month. Following is the syntax of the FV function:

=FV(*rate,nper,pmt,pv,type*)

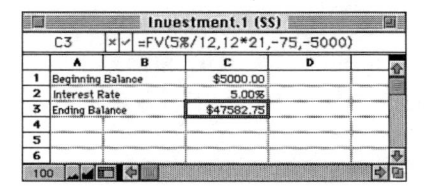

Figure 10.6
An investment-planning worksheet.

When you paste the FV function into a cell, the first value is highlighted. That value, *rate*, is the interest rate. Click the cell that contains your rate or type this value. Notice in the figure that this rate is divided by 12 (/12). (The slash is used as the divide symbol.) This is because there are 12 months to each year. The percentage rate is annual, and because you are making a monthly payment, the interest must be divided by how many payments will be made annually.

The next portion of the function is *nper*, or the number of periods—in other words, for how many of these periods (years) you will be adding deposits. The correct data here is 12 payments per year for 21 years, or 12*21. (The asterisk is used as the multiplication symbol.)

Now you must tell the function what the payment is. This example uses $75. Highlight *pmt* in the formula and replace it with the amount of payment. Notice that this entry is in negative form because it is cash paid out.

The *pv* argument is the present value (current value) of the investment. This value is optional; if you omit *pv*, the present value is assumed to be zero. The present value in the example is $5,000. Here again, the entry is a negative value because it is cash paid out.

The *type* argument, which also is optional, is not used in this example. The only options are 1 and 0. Use 1 for payments at the start of the period and 0 for payments at the end of the period.

After you enter all the arguments, press Enter. The Ending Balance cell (C3) now reflects the total accumulated monies, including 5 percent interest.

Even though the interest rate and the beginning balance could have been entered as typed numbers, you might choose to find a cell for them on the page so you can click the cell to add the numbers to the formula rather than type them. Also, if you print the worksheet, it is handy to have all variables in front of you and labeled. You might forget which variables you used to arrive at the total and inadvertently put away less than necessary. Imagine your surprise in 21 years when the totals don't match!

Several other functions work with investment planning, including IRR (internal rate of return) and MIRR (modified internal rate of return). With the help of these functions, you can watch investments grow and estimate when the cash flow will equal the value of the initial return. For more information on how to use these functions, see Appendix A, "Functions."

Using Functions to Compare Loan Payments

Comparing loan payments is another type of financial spreadsheet application. You could create a worksheet like the one shown in figure 10.7 to help identify the amount of time you will need to pay off a loan in order to stay within your budget.

Figure 10.7 This worksheet compares loan payments and how they fluctuate depending on the length of the loan and the interest rate at which you borrow.

Interest Loan.1 (SS)

C5 =PMT(B1/12,C$4,-$B$2)

	A	B	C	D	E	F	G	H	I
1	Interest Rate	4.25%							
2	Loan Amount	$11000.00							
3									
4	Months of Loan	12	18	24	30	36	42	48	54
5	Monthly Charge	$937.91	$631.88	$478.90	$387.14	$325.99	$282.33	$249.60	$224.16
6	Total Amount	$11254.87	$11373.81	$11493.58	$11614.17	$11735.59	$11857.83	$11980.90	$12104.79
7									
8		4.25%	4.50%	4.75%	5.00%	5.25%	5.50%	5.75%	6.00%
9	12	$937.91	$939.16	$940.42	$941.68	$942.94	$944.20	$945.47	$946.73
10	18	$631.88	$633.11	$634.35	$635.59	$636.82	$638.06	$639.31	$640.55
11	24	$478.90	$480.13	$481.35	$482.59	$483.82	$485.05	$486.29	$487.53
12	30	$387.14	$388.36	$389.59	$390.82	$392.06	$393.29	$394.53	$395.77
13	36	$325.99	$327.22	$328.45	$329.68	$330.92	$332.15	$333.40	$334.64
14	42	$282.33	$283.56	$284.80	$286.03	$287.27	$288.52	$289.77	$291.02
15	48	$249.60	$250.84	$252.08	$253.32	$254.57	$255.82	$257.08	$258.34
16	54	$224.16	$225.40	$226.65	$227.90	$229.16	$230.41	$231.68	$232.95
17	60	$203.83	$205.07	$206.33	$207.58	$208.85	$210.11	$211.38	$212.66
18									
19									

100

The top section is where you can record the interest rate and the loan amount. Below this section is a table that provides a breakdown of the top area. This area includes the months in which to pay the loan off (Months of Loan), the monthly payment (Monthly Charge), and the total amount you pay, including interest, if you pay the loan off in the selected number of months (Total Amount).

The top table assumes that the interest rate is 4.25 percent and indicates the total amount paid out at the end of the loan term. The bottom table is a sliding scale that reports what the monthly payment will be at each of the different interest rates; it does not show the total paid out. Each type of table has its uses. Both of these tables use the PMT function. Following is the syntax of this function:

=PMT(*rate,nper,pv,{fv},{type}*)

To set up a table with the PMT function, follow these steps:

1. Select the cell where you want to calculate the payment, and then choose Paste Function from the Edit menu. The Paste Function dialog box appears.

2. Select PMT. This function now appears in the entry bar, with the first value (*rate*) highlighted.

3. Replace the *rate* argument by clicking the cell that contains the rate (in fig. 10.7, this is cell B1).

> **Note**
>
> Because you are figuring an annual rate, you must divide this rate by 12 (months to a year).

4. Add dollar signs before the B and the 1. This will instruct ClarisWorks that this cell location is *absolute*, meaning that no matter where the formula is pasted, it will always return to column B and row 1 for this piece of data. As you fill this formula to the right, the B1 will remain constant.

5. Highlight the next value (*nper*), and click the cell that contains the number of periods (in this example, cell B4).

6. Add a dollar sign in front of the 4, but not in front of the B. The dollar sign makes this an absolute reference. (The keyboard shortcut for absolute value is ⌘+Option+click cell.) It means that when the formula is filled to the right, it will always return to row 4 to find the number of months, but the columns will move to the right with your fill. They are a relative reference. Hence, the formula in C5 will read 18 months instead of 12 months because that is the value in C4.

7. Select the next value (*pv*), and replace it with the present value (the loan amount). For this example, click B2.

8. Add dollar signs in front of the B and the 2 to keep them both absolute values when you fill to the right.

9. Highlight and delete the *{,fv}* and *{,type}* values. Because they are enclosed in braces ({}), they are optional, and you won't be needing them for this worksheet.

> **Note**
>
> Type a minus sign (–) if you want the payment amounts to be represented by a positive number. Having a positive number in the formula will create a negative number in the table. Technically, a payment would be subtracted from your budget.

10. Press Enter. Cell B5 should contain $937.91 if you used the data shown in figure 10.7 and typed the formula correctly.

11. Fill the formula to the right by clicking cell B5 and dragging to J5, and then choosing Fill Right from the Calculate menu. All Monthly Charge values should appear.

The table at the bottom of figure 10.7 is a more detailed way of showing payments due. Like the table at the top, it refers to cell B2 for the amount borrowed, but it uses cells B8 through M8 for the interest rate and cells A9 through A17 for the term of the loan. All formulas in cells B9 through M17 were filled from the formula in B9. Remember that the dollar sign will make a row or column absolute. To create this type of formula, follow these steps:

1. Click cell B9, and then choose Paste Function from the Edit menu. When the Paste Function dialog box appears, paste the PMT function into the selected cell.

2. Replace *rate* with **B$8/12** (the row of interest rates divided by 12 months).

3. Replace *nper* with **$A9** (the column of terms).

4. Replace *pv* with **B2** (the loan amount).

5. Press Enter.

6. Fill to right and fill down. Notice the use of absolute values in the cells and how those values instruct ClarisWorks which row or column to return to each time.

Your payments should match those shown in figure 10.7 if you used the same values. Try changing the value of one of the interest rates, and watch the changes in the payment table. The table will recalculate only if you have chosen Auto Calc or Calculate Now from the Calculate menu.

Using Lookup Functions

Figure 10.8 introduces the lookup functions. These functions go to other places in a worksheet, look up information, and report it.

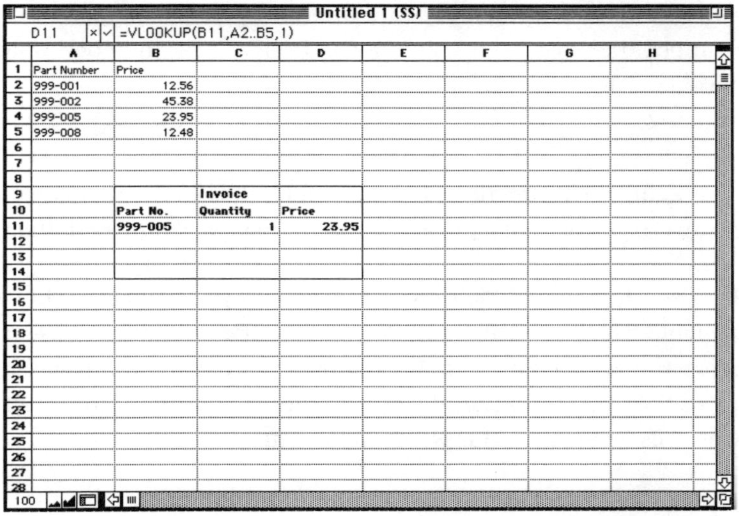

Figure 10.8
This invoice automatically looks up the price of part numbers in the table.

In this example, the table at the top contains part numbers and prices. In the invoice below, the VLOOKUP function is used to find the price for a particular part number. This example uses the VLOOKUP function because it is reading the table vertically—that is, the part numbers are listed in order and in a vertical column. The VLOOKUP function contains the following arguments:

=VLOOKUP(*lookup value,compare range,index*)

To use the VLOOKUP function, follow these steps:

1. Select the cell where you want the information to appear, and then choose Paste Function from the Edit menu. The Paste Function dialog box appears.

2. Select VLOOKUP. The function appears in the entry bar with the first argument, *lookup value*, highlighted. This is the cell or number that you want ClarisWorks to match.

3. Enter the number or click the appropriate cell. In figure 10.8, this is cell B11, which contains part number 999-005.

4. Highlight the *compare range* argument, and then select that range in the worksheet. In this example, the range is A2..B5, where ClarisWorks will look for the part number and its corresponding price.

5. Highlight the *index* argument. The index is the number of rows you want ClarisWorks to move to find the value you're looking for. In this example, the price is one column over from the part numbers that are looked up.

6. Enter the index number.

7. Press Return. The function "looks up" the value. In the example, it returns the value $23.95, which is the price of part number 999-005.

Tip
To make the lookup function provide an extended price, add *C11 (see fig. 10.8) at the end of the function. This will instruct ClarisWorks to multiply the lookup amount by the amount in cell C11.

The HLOOKUP function works exactly the same way for data listed horizontally in a table. The LOOKUP function is a little different in that it uses a result range rather than an index. It looks up a value in the compare range and returns the value it finds in the corresponding position of the result range (the cells where the value will be returned).

From Here...

Although you might not have use for them every day, spreadsheet functions certainly make short work of the tasks that you assign to them. Functions are simple to use, whether you're counting, averaging, borrowing, or balancing. For more information on this topic, refer to the following chapters:

- Chapter 8, "Spreadsheet Basics." Return to this chapter if you are having difficulty understanding how rows, columns, and cells relate to one another.

- Chapter 9, "Enhancing a Worksheet." In this chapter, you'll find information on how to change the typeface and size of cell contents, as well as the alignment of the cells.

- Chapter 19, "Automating Your Work." Macros are handy even inside a worksheet. Look ahead to this chapter for information on automating spreadsheet processes.

- Appendix A, "Functions." The appendix lists all the functions available in ClarisWorks, with brief explanations and examples.

Chapter 11
Creating Charts

by Shelley O'Hara

The numbers and data in your spreadsheet documents don't always tell the entire story. A visual presentation of the data—a chart—can show trends, spikes, and other information you might not see when you look at the data. Charts are useful in slide shows and at any time you want to present information visually.

In this chapter, you learn the following:

- How to create a chart
- How to pick an appropriate chart type
- How to edit a chart
- How to format a chart

Creating a Chart

To create a chart, you start by selecting the data you want to chart. For the worksheet shown in figure 11.1, for example, you may want to chart divisional sales.

You don't include the totals in the range to be charted. If you do, the chart will not be correct.

After you create a chart, you can make editing and formatting changes as needed. To create a chart, follow these steps:

1. Select the range you want to chart. ClarisWorks creates a data series for each column or row you select.

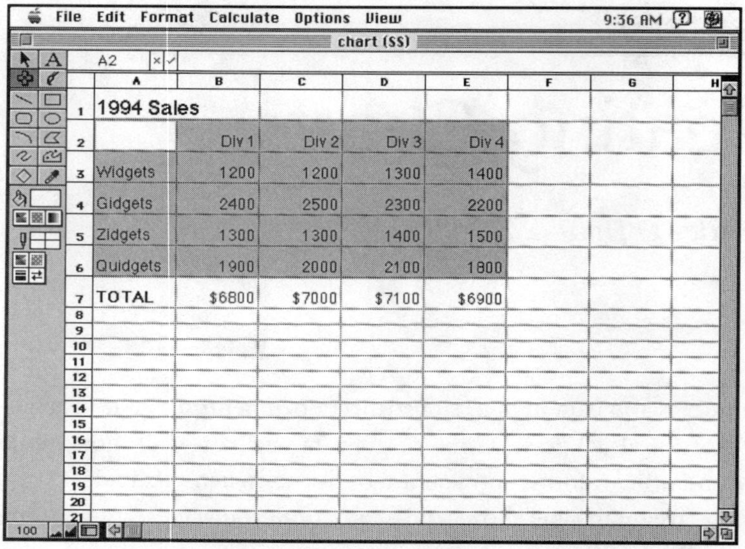

228 Chapter 11—Creating Charts

Figure 11.1
A worksheet containing sales data you can chart.

Tip
You also can press ⌘-M to choose the Make Chart command.

Tip
As an alternative to steps 2 through 5, click one of the chart-type buttons in the Shortcuts palette. (For information on specific buttons, see "Understanding Chart Types" later in this chapter.) If the button you want doesn't appear in the Shortcuts palette, see the "Setting Palette Preferences" section of Chapter 20, "Customizing ClarisWorks."

2. Choose Make Chart from the Options menu. The Chart Options dialog box appears (see fig. 11.2).

3. Select a chart type. The default chart type is bar. The following section explains each chart type.

   Depending on the chart type you select, you see different check boxes in the dialog box. (Table 11.1, following these steps, summarizes the options.)

4. Choose the options you want to use.

5. Choose OK. The chart appears over the worksheet (see fig. 11.3).

Table 11.1 Chart Type Options

Option	Description	Available For
Color	Creates a color chart	All chart types
Horizontal	Creates a horizontal rather than vertical chart	Bar, area, line, scatter, pie, pictogram, stacked bar, stacked area, high-low, stacked pictogram
Shadow	Creates a shadow effect for the chart series	All chart types

Creating a Chart   **229**

Option	Description	Available For
3-Dimensional	Creates a 3-D chart	Bar, pictogram, stacked bar, stacked pictogram
Scale Multiple	Creates pie charts of different sizes, representing the size of the value	Pie
Tilt	Tilts the chart	Pie
Square Grid	Uses a square grid	x-y line, x-y scatter

Tip
You also can click the Axis, Series, Labels, and General command buttons to format the chart. For information, see "Formatting a Chart" later in this chapter.

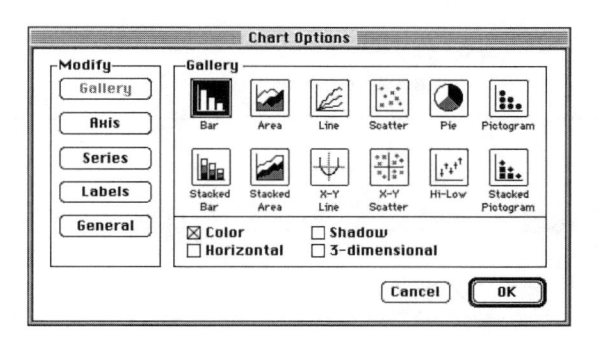

Figure 11.2
In this dialog box, choose the type of chart you want.

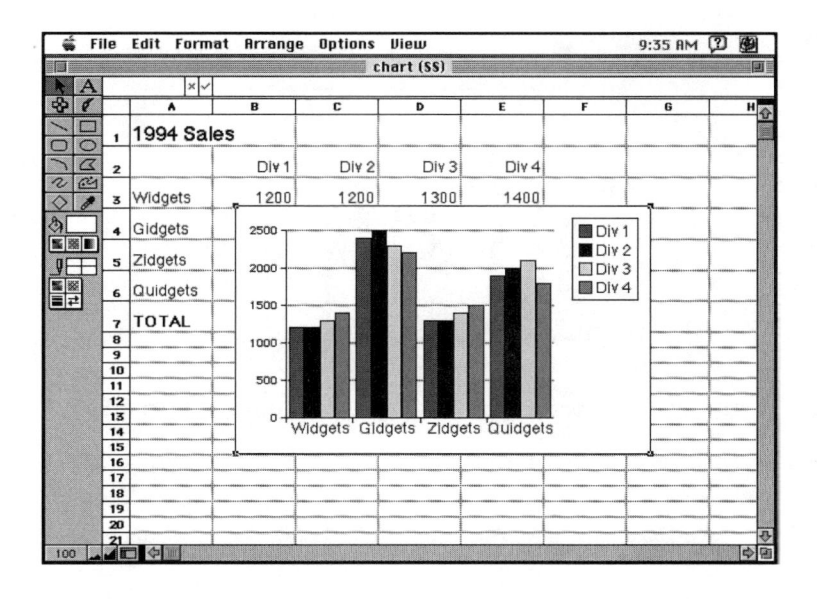

Figure 11.3
The chart is created and placed on top of the worksheet.

Chapter 11—Creating Charts

> **Note**
> The chart and chart data are linked. If you make a change in the chart data, ClarisWorks updates the chart to reflect the change.

Troubleshooting Chart Creation

If I picked the wrong chart type, do I have to start over?

You can easily change the chart type after you create a chart; you don't have to start over. Double-click the chart, and then select another chart type from the gallery.

How do I delete a chart?

To delete a chart, click once to select it, and then press Delete.

Understanding Chart Types

Your choice of chart type depends on the message you want the chart to convey. The following chart types are available:

Bar. This chart type is useful when you want to compare items. You can plot

Figure 11.4
A bar chart is useful for comparing data.

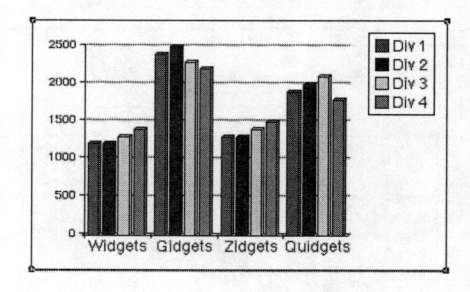

the values horizontally or vertically. Figure 11.4 shows a 3-D bar chart.

Stacked bar. A variation on the bar chart, a stacked bar chart stacks values on top of one another to show a cumulative value. You can see how much one value contributes to the whole.

Area chart. Use this type of chart when you want to show change in volume or magnitude over time. Figure 11.5 shows a black-and-white area chart.

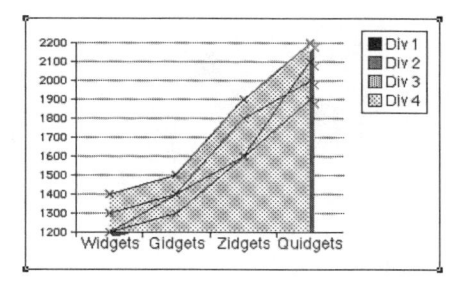

Understanding Chart Types   **231**

Figure 11.5
An area chart is a variation on a line chart. The area below the line is shaded.

Stacked area chart. A variation on the area chart, a stacked area chart adds the values to show the cumulative value (see fig. 11.6).

Figure 11.6
A stacked area chart stacks the areas on top of each other.

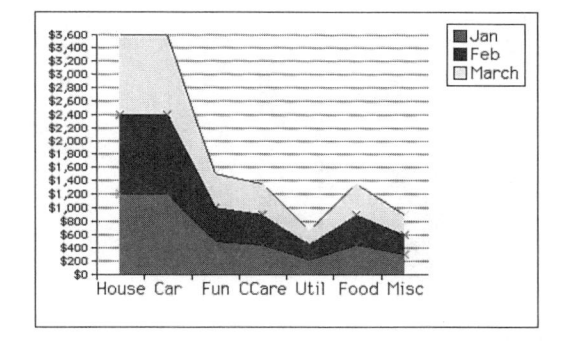

Line chart. Use this chart type when you want to show trends or to emphasize change over time. Line charts are similar to area charts, but an area chart emphasizes the amount of change, whereas a line chart emphasizes the rate of change. Figure 11.7 shows a line chart.

Figure 11.7
A line chart is useful for showing trends.

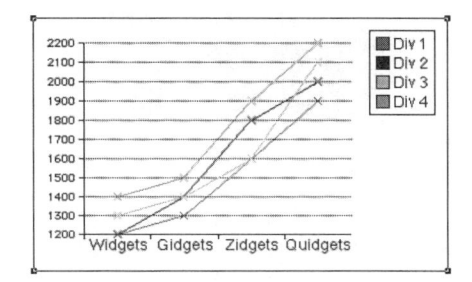

Pie chart. Use this type of chart when you want to show the relationship of each individual value to the whole. You can chart multiple data series in a pie chart. Figure 11.8 shows a pie chart.

232 Chapter 11—Creating Charts

Figure 11.8
Pie charts are useful for showing the relationships of the values to the whole.

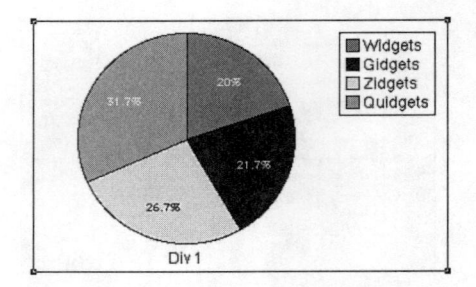

Pictogram. This type of bar chart uses pictures to represent the values. Figure 11.9 shows a pictogram.

Figure 11.9
A pictogram uses a picture and a bar to represent the values in the chart.

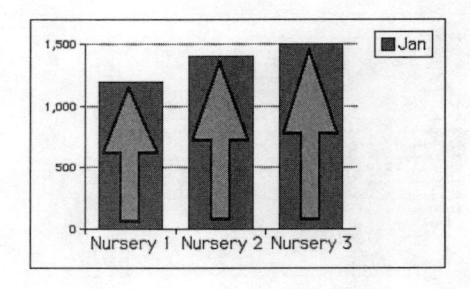

Stacked pictogram. In a stacked pictogram, the values are stacked on top of one another to show the cumulative total. Figure 11.10 shows a stacked pictogram.

Figure 11.10
A stacked pictogram stacks the values on top of each other.

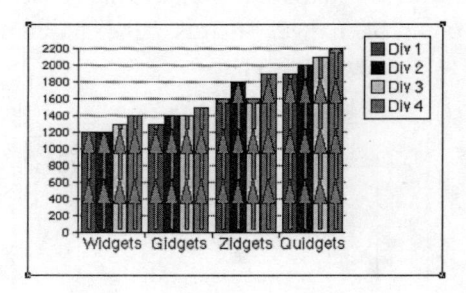

Scatter. In this chart type, the values are plotted as points on the chart. Each point is represented by a symbol. This chart type is useful for charting scientific data.

x-y line. Use this chart type to show the relationship of a pair of values to other sets of values. You select two columns of data. Data in the first column is plotted along the x-axis; values in the second column are plotted along the y-axis. The symbols are connected by a line.

x-y scatter. This type of chart is similar to an x-y line chart, except that the data points are not connected by a line.

High-low. This chart type is useful for charting the high and low prices of stocks. Figure 11.11 shows a high-low chart.

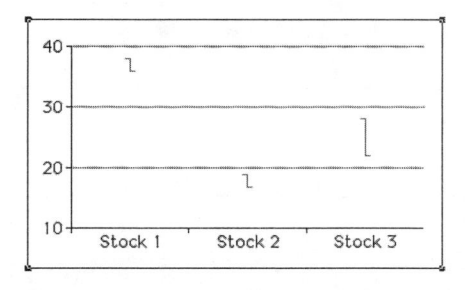

Figure 11.11
This high-low chart shows the high and low stock prices.

Editing a Chart

If the chart doesn't appear in the spot you want, you can move it. You also can resize or delete the chart, as described in this section.

Moving a Chart

The chart is an object placed on top of the worksheet. You can easily move the object to a different place. First, click the chart once to select it. Black selection handles appear along the edges, indicating that the chart is selected (see fig. 11.12).

To move the chart, click the chart and drag it to a new location. Be sure not to click the selection handles. Clicking and dragging the handles resizes the chart.

Resizing a Chart

If you want to make the chart bigger or smaller, you can resize it. First, select the chart; black selection handles appear along the edges of the chart. Then click one of the handles and drag to resize the chart.

Tip
To move a chart to another document, select the chart, choose Copy from the Edit menu, open the document in which you want to place the chart, and then choose Paste from the Edit menu.

Figure 11.12
The black selection handles indicate that the chart object is selected.

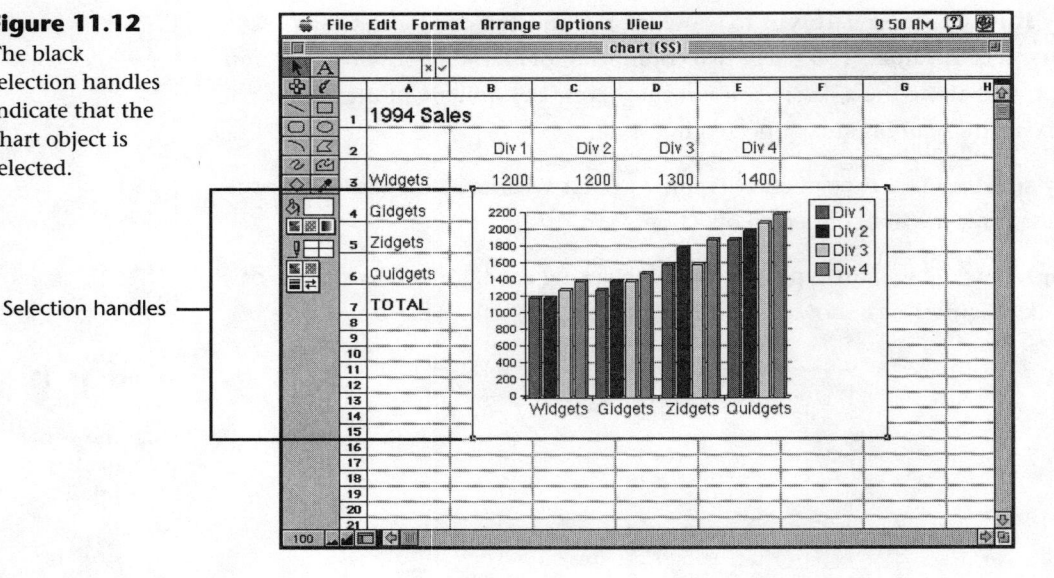

Selection handles

> **Note**
> If you make the chart too small, you see the message Frame too small to draw chart. Make the chart bigger.

Deleting a Chart

To delete a chart, click it once to select it, and then press Delete. To undo the deletion, immediately choose Undo from the Edit menu or press F1.

Formatting a Chart

When you create your chart, you may not know what options you want to use or how you want certain chart elements to appear. You can easily format the chart after you create it—for example, change the chart type, add a chart title, and change the legend.

Tip
You also can use menu commands for objects to format a chart object. For more information, refer to Chapter 6, "Drawing," and Chapter 7, "Painting."

Changing the Chart Type

If you decide that another chart type would work better, you can easily change the chart type. Follow these steps:

1. Select the chart.

2. Choose Modify Chart from the Options menu. The Chart Options dialog box appears.

3. Choose the chart type and any chart options you want.

4. Choose OK. ClarisWorks changes the chart type to the one you chose.

Tip
As a shortcut, you can double-click the chart, or click the chart once and then press Shift-⌘-I.

Changing the Formatting of Chart Data

You can chart data by rows or by columns. ClarisWorks makes a choice based on the number of rows and columns and on the chart type. You can change the orientation of the charted data. Follow these steps:

1. Double-click the chart to display the Chart Options dialog box.

2. Click the General command button. The General dialog box appears (see fig. 11.13).

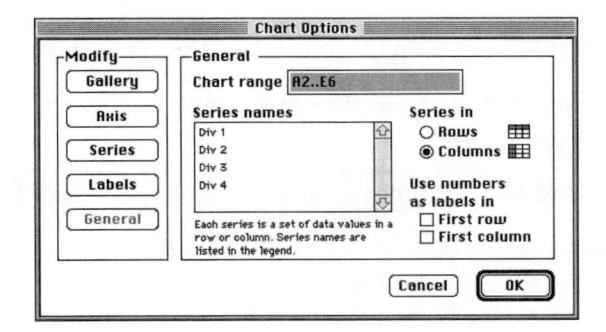

Figure 11.13
In this dialog box, you can change the range that is charted or change the orientation of data.

3. If you want to use a different chart range, type it in the Chart Range text box.

4. If you want to change the orientation of the data series, choose Rows or Columns.

5. If your first row or column contains data that should be used as labels, click the First Row or First Column check box; the data is listed in the Series Names list box.

6. Choose OK.

Formatting the Chart Series

The chart series is the set of values plotted in the chart. You can add a label to the chart series and change the chart type for the individual series. To format the chart series, follow these steps:

1. Double-click the chart to display the Chart Options dialog box.

Figure 11.14
Select the series you want to edit. Then choose options to determine how the series is charted and whether a label is added.

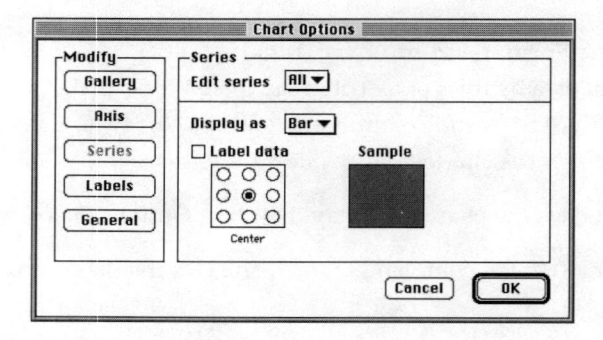

Tip
You can create a combination chart—for example, chart one series as a line and the rest as bars—by changing how the series is displayed.

2. Click the Series command button. The Series dialog box appears (see fig. 11.14).

3. In the Edit Series pop-up list, select the series you want to edit.

4. If you want to change how the series is plotted, open the Display As pop-up list and select an option.

5. Choose any other options you want to use.

   Depending on how the series is displayed, the options may vary. For line charts, for example, you can choose the symbol that is used and enter a size for the symbol.

   For pie charts, you can enter labels and then choose where the percentage appears (in the legend, in the slice, or both places). You also can choose to explode a pie slice.

   For pictogram charts, you can select the picture you want to use. Select the sample box, and then paste in a different symbol from the Clipboard. By default, ClarisWorks stretches the picture. If you'd rather repeat the image, check the Repeat check box and enter any overlap you want to use.

6. To display the numeric values for each point, check the Label Data check box, and then choose a placement for the labels.

7. Choose OK.

Figure 11.15 shows a stacked bar chart that displays data labels.

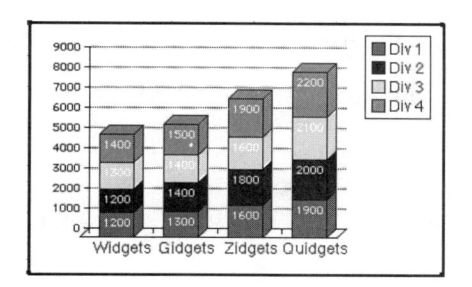

Formatting a Chart   **237**

Figure 11.15
A stacked bar chart that displays data labels for the data series.

Changing the Chart Colors

If you don't like the chart colors, you can use different ones. Color charts are useful for slide shows or for color printers. If you don't have a color printer and aren't going to display the chart on-screen, you may want to create a black-and-white chart. To do so, uncheck the color option in the Chart Options dialog box. (You still can change the chart patterns.)

To change the chart colors, you select the appropriate *legend*—the key to the charted values—and then use the drawing tools shown in figure 11.16. Click and hold down the mouse button on the tool you want to use. A palette appears. Click the color, pattern, or style you want.

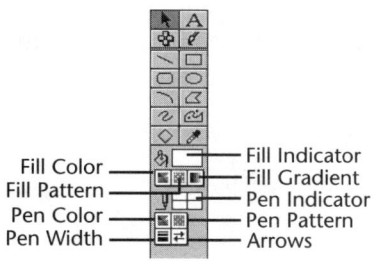

Tip
The palette you see is a *tear-off palette*, which means you can drag the palette to keep it displayed on-screen.

Figure 11.16
Use the fill and pen tools to change the colors, patterns, and style of the fill or line.

Fill Color
Fill Pattern
Pen Color
Pen Width
Fill Indicator
Fill Gradient
Pen Indicator
Pen Pattern
Arrows

> **Note**
> For complete information on all drawing tools, refer to Chapter 6.

To change the chart colors, follow these steps:

1. In the legend, select the data series you want to change. A small dot appears in the center of the legend.

2. Display the drawing tools (if they aren't already displayed) by choosing Show Tools from the View menu.

Tip
If you want to keep any of the palettes displayed, click to display the palette and then drag it. The tear-off palette remains on-screen.

Tip
For a gradient effect, display the Fill Gradient palette and then choose a gradient.

3. Display the Fill Color palette and choose another color.

4. To change the pattern, display the Fill Pattern palette and display another pattern.

5. To change the line style, color, or width, choose the Pen Width, Pen Color, Pen Pattern, or Arrow tool. Then choose the style, color, or thickness you want.

Figure 11.17 shows a black-and-white chart that uses different patterns.

Figure 11.17
You can choose colors, patterns, and line styles for each data series.

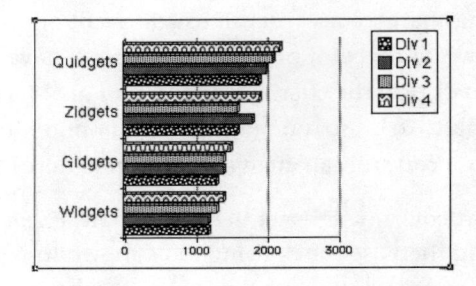

Formatting the Chart Title

By default, ClarisWorks uses the text in the top-left corner of the chart range as the title. If you did not select the title and want to add one later, or if you want to format the chart title, you can do so by following these steps:

1. Double-click the chart to display the Chart Options dialog box.

2. Click the Labels command button. The Labels dialog box appears (see fig. 11.18).

Figure 11.18
Enter the chart title, and then choose a placement.

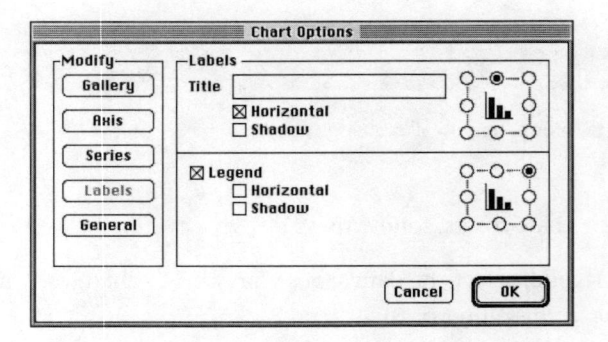

3. To add a title, type it in the Title text box.

4. If you want the title to appear vertically, uncheck the Horizontal check box.

5. If you want to use a shadow for the title, check the Shadow check box.

6. Choose a placement for the title.

7. Choose OK.

Figure 11.19 shows a chart title in a shadow box.

Tip
To format the title text, click the text box to select it; choose Font, Size, or Style from the Format menu; and then choose the font, size, or style you want.

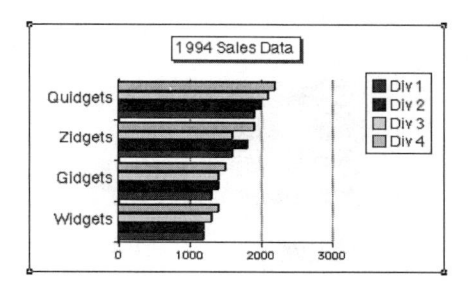

Figure 11.19
You can add a title to your chart.

Formatting the Chart Legend

ClarisWorks automatically adds a legend to your chart. You can change the placement and orientation of the legend. If you don't want to use a legend, you can turn it off. Follow these steps:

1. Double-click the chart to display the Chart Options dialog box.

2. Click the Labels command button. The Labels dialog box appears (see fig. 11.20).

Tip
You also can double-click the legend to display the Labels dialog box.

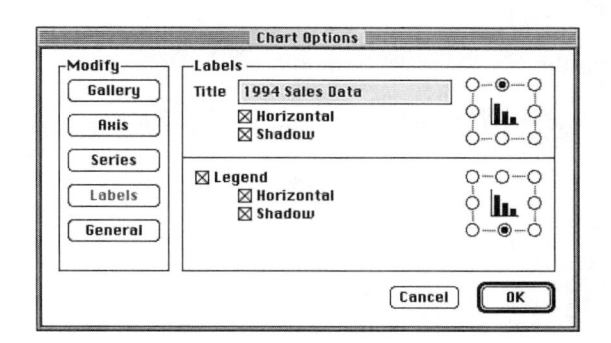

Figure 11.20
In the Labels dialog box, select the title and title placement and the legend placement.

240 Chapter 11—Creating Charts

3. If you want the title to appear horizontally, check the Horizontal check box.

4. If you want to use a shadow for the title, check the Shadow check box.

5. Choose a placement for the legend.

6. Choose OK.

Figure 11.21 shows a horizontal legend placed at the bottom of the chart.

Figure 11.21
You can change the placement of the legend.

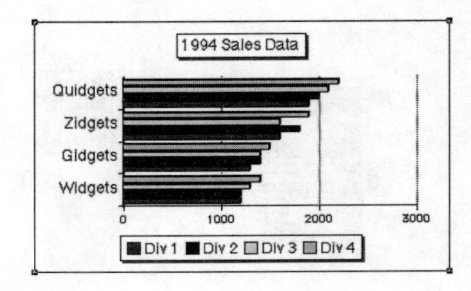

Formatting the Chart Axes

The *x-axis* is the horizontal axis; the *y-axis* is the vertical axis. You can change the appearance of the axes: add a label; change the placement of the tick marks; turn off grid lines; or enter minimum, maximum, and step values for the axis. Follow these steps:

Tip
You also can double-click an axis to display the Axis dialog box.

1. Double-click the chart to display the Chart Options dialog box.

2. Click the Axis command button. The Axis dialog box appears (see fig. 11.22).

3. Choose the axis you want to modify.

Figure 11.22
In the Axis dialog box, chose the axis you want to format and then make the changes.

4. If you want a label to appear along the axis, type it in the Axis Label text box.

5. If you want to change the placement of the tick marks, display the Tick Marks pop-up menu and select a placement.

6. If you want to turn off the grid lines, uncheck the Grid Lines check box.

7. If you want to use different maximum or minimum values, type them in the Minimum and Maximum text boxes.

8. If you want to change the increment used for the axis, type the increment in the Step Size text box.

9. To use a logarithm scale, check the Log check box and enter the log base in the text box.

10. Choose OK.

Figure 11.23 shows a chart with the grid lines turned off, a different placement for the tick marks, and a label added.

Troubleshooting Chart Formatting

The labels on the x-axis overwrite one another. How do I fix this problem?

The x-axis labels are created from the column or row labels in the worksheet. If the labels are too long, shorten the text by editing the text entries in the worksheet.

How do I add a chart title?

To add a chart title, double-click the chart and then click the Labels button. Enter a title in the Titles text box.

How do I change the chart colors?

You use the drawing tools to change a chart color. First, click the series you want to change; then click the appropriate fill or pen tool and make a selection.

When I print the chart, some of the data series look the same. How can I make them look different?

Unless you have a color printer, the chart colors will print in shades of gray and black. Some colors may print the same in black and white. In this case, change the chart to a black-and-white chart, and use patterns instead of colors to distinguish the data series.

Figure 11.23
The y-axis is formatted to include a label. The tick marks are displayed inside the axis. The grid lines are not displayed.

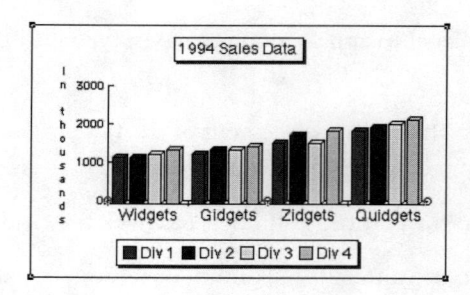

From Here...

If you want to use charts in other documents, the following chapter will be of interest to you:

- See Chapter 15, "Creating Integrated Documents," for information on working with frames.

- Also see Chapter 15 for information on creating slide shows.

Part III

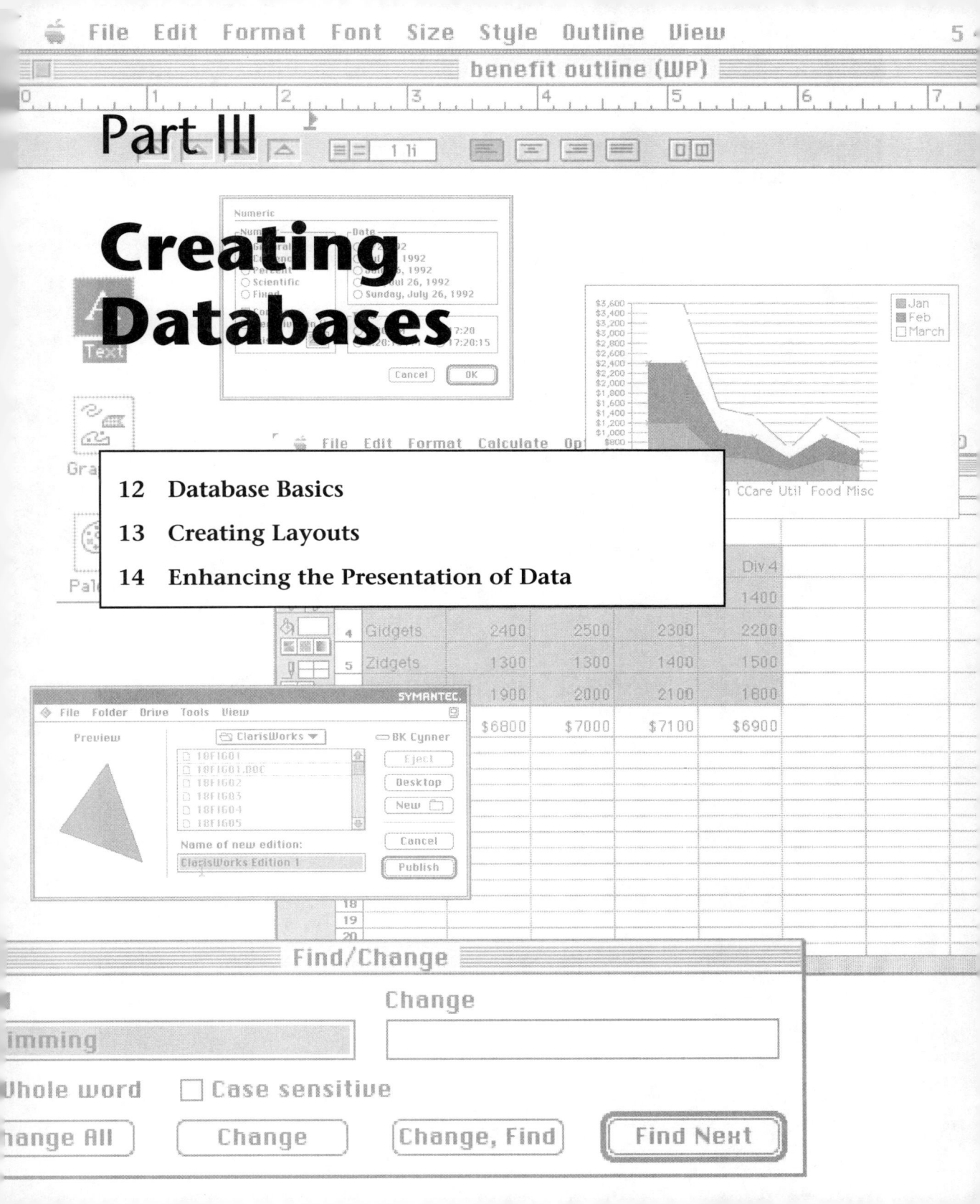

Creating Databases

- 12 Database Basics
- 13 Creating Layouts
- 14 Enhancing the Presentation of Data

File Edit Format Font Size Style Outline View

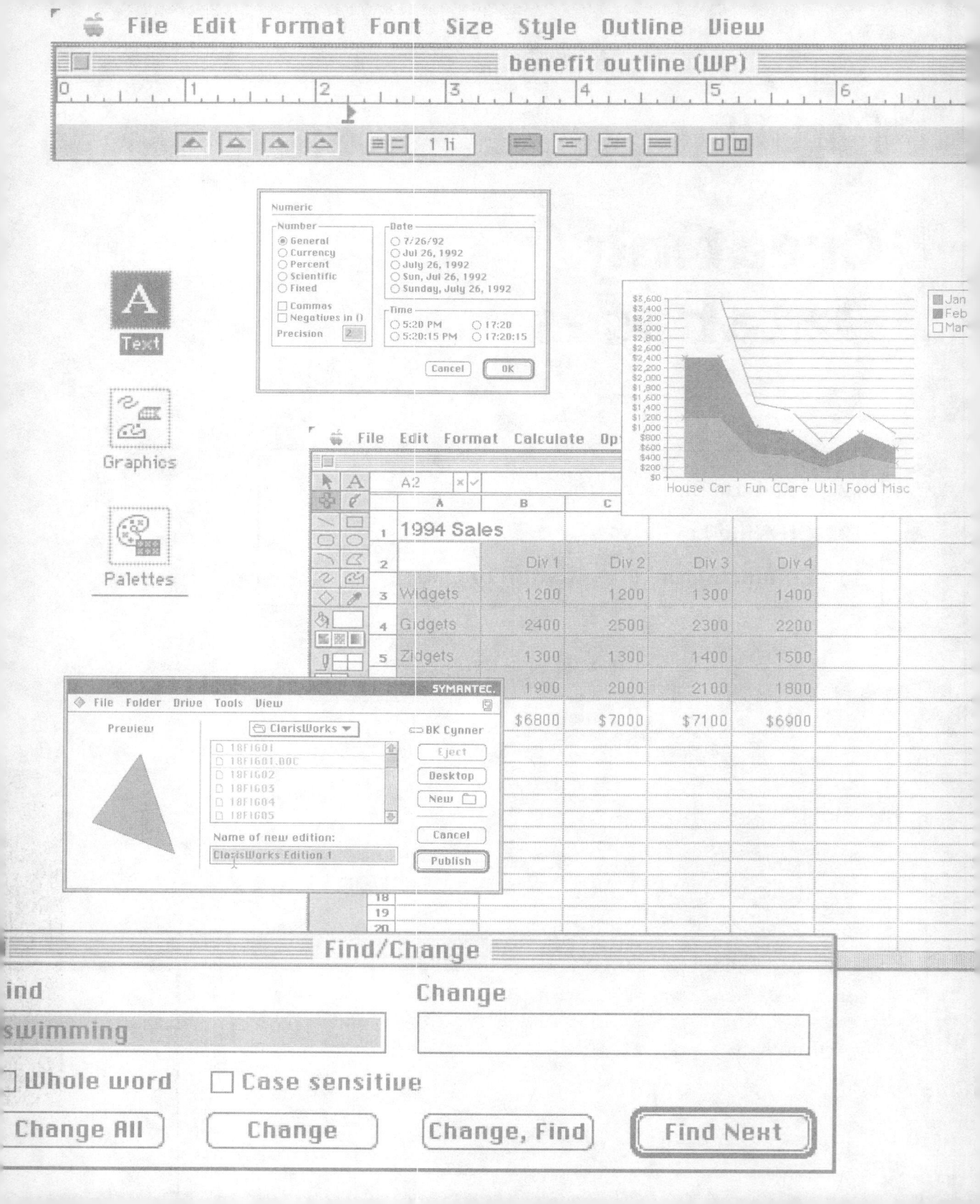

benefit outline (WP)

| 0 | 1 | 2 | 3 | 4 | 5 | 6 |

1 li

Numeric

Number
- ● General
- ○ Currency
- ○ Percent
- ○ Scientific
- ○ Fixed

☐ Commas
☐ Negatives in ()
Precision 2

Date
- ○ 7/26/92
- ○ Jul 26, 1992
- ○ July 26, 1992
- ○ Sun, Jul 26, 1992
- ○ Sunday, July 26, 1992

Time
- ○ 5:20 PM   ○ 17:20
- ○ 5:20:15 PM   ○ 17:20:15

[Cancel] [OK]

Text

Graphics

Palettes

$3,600
$3,400
$3,200
$3,000
$2,800
$2,600
$2,400
$2,200
$2,000
$1,800
$1,600
$1,400
$1,200
$1,000
$800
$600
$400
$200
$0

House Car Fun CCare Util Food Misc

■ Jan
■ Feb
☐ Mar

File Edit Format Calculate Op...

A2

	A	B	C	
1	1994 Sales			
2		Div 1	Div 2	Div 3	Div 4
3	Widgets	1200	1200	1300	1400
4	Gidgets	2400	2500	2300	2200
5	Zidgets	1300	1300	1400	1500
		1900	2000	2100	1800
		$6800	$7000	$7100	$6900

SYMANTEC.

File Folder Drive Tools View

Preview

📁 ClarisWorks ▼   ⇦ BK Cynner

- 18FIG01
- 18FIG01.DOC
- 18FIG02
- 18FIG03
- 18FIG04
- 18FIG05

[Eject]
[Desktop]
[New 📁]

Name of new edition:
ClarisWorks Edition 1

[Cancel]
[Publish]

18
19
20

Find/Change

Find
swimming

Change

☐ Whole word   ☐ Case sensitive

[Change All]   [Change]   [Change, Find]   [**Find Next**]

Chapter 12
Database Basics

by Shelley O'Hara

If you keep track of information on paper—for example, invoices—you know that quickly finding the information you need isn't easy. You have to manually sort through the filing system to find information. If someone else happens to have the information or if someone didn't put the information in the correct spot, you may never find what you need.

An electronic database is different. Using this type of database, you can easily enter, sort, and find the information you need. Databases are appropriate for keeping track of any type of data—names and addresses, sales transactions, inventory, and more.

In this chapter, you learn the following:

- How a database is set up
- How to create and edit a database
- How to enter and work with database records
- How to find and sort database records

Understanding Database Concepts

Before you begin creating a database document, you should understand the terms and concepts associated with a database.

A *database* is a collection of related information. For example, you may have a database to store your clients' names and addresses. You can create and use more than one database. In ClarisWorks, the database is stored as a document on disk.

Each database contains a set of records. A *record* is a set of information about one individual, event, or transaction—for example, the name, address, and phone number of one person could be a record in a client database.

Each piece of information in a record is contained in a *field*. In a client database, for example, you might have a field called Last Name. You choose the fields that you want to include in the database.

Planning a Database

Before you create a database, it's a good idea to sketch out the database on paper. You can modify the database after you create it, but it's best to start with a solid plan and get the database pretty close to final form before you start entering records. Ask yourself the following questions:

- What information do you need to keep track of?
- What types of information will you enter?
- What information should come first in the database?
- How much information do you need to keep track of?

Think about how you track and enter data on paper, and then use this method to help plan the database. If you already have a form you use to track data, use this form to help design the database. Write down all the fields you will need.

You probably will want to keep each piece of information in a separate field. You could enter both the first and last name of a client in one name field, but if you do, sorting the database by client name will be difficult.

When you have a solid plan, you can create the database.

Creating a Database

To create a database, choose New from the File menu, and then choose Database as the document type. ClarisWorks automatically displays the Define Fields dialog box (see fig. 12.1). In this dialog box, you can select the types of fields you want to add. The following section describes each of the field types.

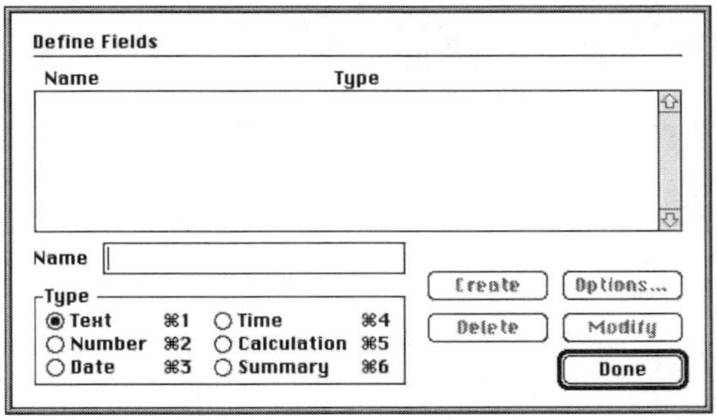

Creating a Database 247

Figure 12.1
In the Define Fields dialog box, you name the field and select a field type.

> **Note**
>
> For information on creating and saving documents, refer to Chapter 2, "Learning the Essentials."

Understanding Field Types

In your database, you most likely will keep track of different types of information. You might keep track of a client's name (text), a sales amount (number), and a sales date (date). You assign an appropriate field type to each field. Table 12.1 describes the different field types.

Table 12.1 Field Types

Field Type	Description
Text	Text fields are the most common type. This type of field can contain up to 500 characters. In a client database, the last name, first name, address, city, state, and ZIP code would all be stored in text fields.
Number	Number fields contain numbers and can be used in calculations. A number field can contain 254 characters, all of which must be on one line. You might use a number field for the cost of a service.
Date	Date fields contain dates and must be on one line. You might use dates to track the transaction date, the payment date, or the start and end dates of a project. If you want to perform date calculations, you must define the field as a date field. You cannot enter a date in a text field and then use the date in calculations. The same is true for time, the next field type.

(continues)

248 Chapter 12—Database Basics

Table 12.1 Continued	
Field Type	**Description**
Time	Time fields contain times and must be on one line. If you have a database that tracks hours of service, you might enter the start and end time in separate fields.
Calculation	You can create a calculation field that displays the result of a formula or function. You can use the other fields in the database in the calculation formula. For example, you might have a Total field that multiples the amount of hours by the hourly fee. (For more information, see "Defining a Calculation Field" later in this chapter.)
Summary	You can create a summary field that summarizes a field in several records. Summary fields are used when you create different layouts. (For information on using summary fields, see Chapter 14, "Enhancing the Presentation of Data.")

Defining Fields

To define a field, follow these steps:

1. Open the Define Fields dialog box, and type a field name in the Name text box.

   > **Note**
   >
   > You can use up to 63 characters in a field name, including spaces.

2. In the Type area, choose a field type by clicking the appropriate radio button or by pressing the following shortcut keys:

Text	⌘-1
Number	⌘-2
Date	⌘-3
Time	⌘-4
Calculation	⌘-5
Summary	⌘-6

3. Click the Create button. You see the name and type listed in the list box.

4. Repeat steps 1 through 3 to add all the fields you want. (For information on adding a calculation field, see the following section. For information on adding a summary field, see Chapter 14, "Enhancing the Presentation of Data.")

5. When you finish, choose Done. ClarisWorks displays a blank record in the standard layout, which you can change (see Chapter 13, "Creating Layouts"). You can also change the format of the data.

Tip
You can change the view of the database. For information on changing views, refer to Chapter 2, "Learning the Essentials."

Defining a Calculation Field

If your database contains numbers and you need to calculate those numbers, you can create a calculation field. If you have a billing database, for example, and enter the project, hourly fee, and total hours, you can calculate the project fee by multiplying the hourly fee by the total hours.

Follow these steps to define a calculation field:

1. Type the field name.

2. Choose Calculation as the field type.

3. Click the Create command button. The Enter Formula dialog box appears (see fig. 12.2).

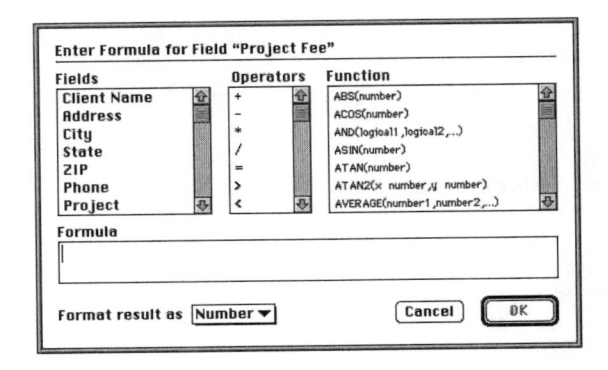

Figure 12.2
In the Enter Formula dialog box, you create the formula for the calculation field.

4. In the Fields list, select the field you want to use in the calculation. When you click the field, the field name appears in the Formula box.

5. In the Operators list, select the operator you want.

6. Continue selecting fields and operators until the formula is complete.

7. In the Format Result As pop-up menu, select the format you want to use: Number, Date, Time, or Text.

Tip
You can use functions in your database. For more information on functions, see Chapter 10, "Using Spreadsheet Functions."

8. When you finish, choose OK. You return to the Define Fields dialog box, where you can add more fields or choose Done to complete the database definition.

Figure 12.3 shows a formula that multiplies the hourly rate by the project hours to come up with the project fee.

Figure 12.3
This formula multiplies the hourly rate by the project hours.

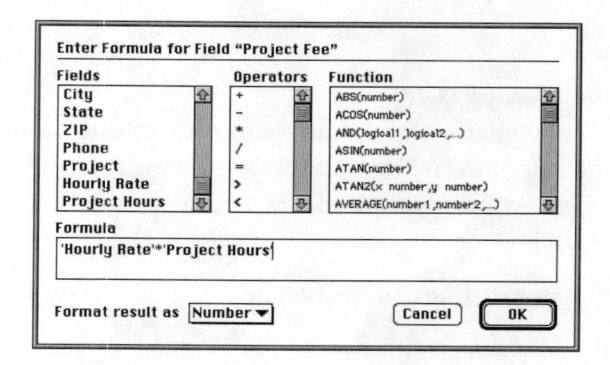

Customizing Fields

To make data entry quicker or more accurate, you can customize the data fields. You can have ClarisWorks make an entry automatically, check an entry for accuracy, or display a list from which you can choose entries. This section explains how to customize a data field.

Entering Data Automatically. You can enter the following information in a record automatically:

- The date or time when a record was created
- The date or time when a record was changed
- The person who created or modified the record
- A serial number
- Any data you specify

> **Note**
> You cannot enter data automatically in a calculation or summary field. ClarisWorks calculates those values.

Creating a Database 251

To enter data in a field automatically, follow these steps:

1. In the Define Fields dialog box, click the field you want to customize.

   If you customize the database as you create fields, this dialog box is still open. If you have already created the fields and now want to customize them, you must choose Define Fields from the Layout menu to display this dialog box.

2. Click the Options button. The Entry Options dialog box appears (see fig. 12.4).

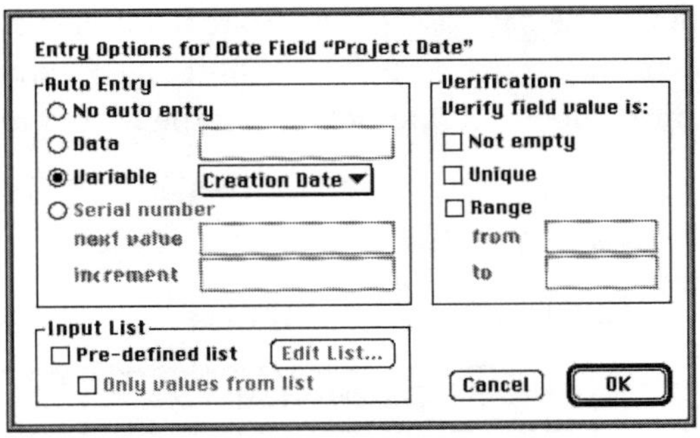

Figure 12.4
In the Entry Options dialog box, you can specify what entry you want ClarisWorks to enter in the database field automatically. You also can choose verification options and create an input list.

3. Select the entry you want to enter automatically:

Entry	Description
Data	Type the data you want entered automatically. Keep in mind that this data will be entered in the field in every record in the database. The data you type must match the field type. If you are customizing a date field, for example, you must type a date here.
Variable	Display the Variable pop-up menu, and select the variable you want to enter. Again, the data you select must match the field type. Therefore, if you are customizing a date field, only Creation Date and Modified Date are available.
Serial number	Type the first value to use and the increment to use. For example, if you want to start with 100 and number by 10s (100, 110, 120), type **100** in the Next Value text box and **10** in the Increment text box.

4. Choose OK. You return to the Define Fields dialog box. If you are finished with the database definition, choose Done.

III

Creating Databases

Checking the Entry. Another way to customize a data field is to check it for accuracy. You can check the following things:

- Whether the field contains data
- Whether the field contains a unique value
- Whether the entry is within a certain range

To check an entry, follow these steps:

1. In the Define Fields dialog box, click the field you want to check.

   If you customize the database as you create fields, this dialog box is still open. If you have already created the fields and now want to customize them, you must choose Define Fields from the Layout menu to display this dialog box.

2. Click the Options button. The Entry Options dialog box appears.

3. Select the verification option you want to use:

Option	Description
Not Empty	Check this box if you want ClarisWorks to ensure that the field always contains an entry.
Unique	Check this box if you want ClarisWorks to accept only unique entries in the field.
Range	Check this box, and then enter an acceptable range in the From and To text boxes if you want ClarisWorks to ensure that the entry is within the required range.

4. Choose OK. You return to the Define Fields dialog box. If you are finished with the database definition, choose Done.

The settings shown in figure 12.5 check the hourly rate to make sure it is within the range 50 to 150.

Creating a Database   253

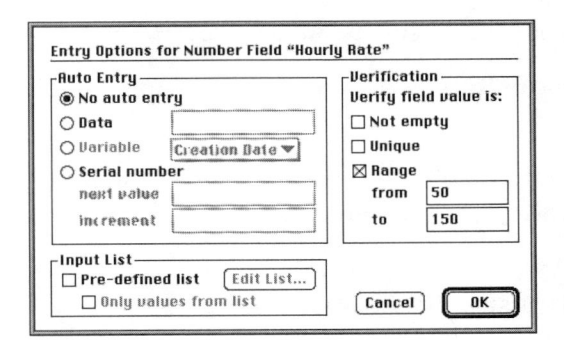

Figure 12.5
In this example, ClarisWorks will check the hourly rate to ensure that it is within the range entered.

Creating a List of Entries. If you want to be able to choose field entries from a list, you can define an input list. If you offer five services that you track in the database, for example, you can enter those services in an input list. The person entering the records for each service then can select the appropriate service from the list.

To create an input list, follow these steps:

1. In the Define Fields dialog box, click the field you want to customize.

    If you customize the database as you create records, this dialog box is still open. If you have already created the fields and now want to customize them, you must choose Define Fields from the Layout menu to display this dialog box.

2. Click the Options button. The Entry Options dialog box appears.

3. Check the Pre-defined List check box. The Values dialog box appears (see fig. 12.6).

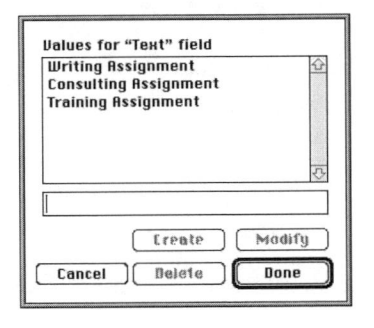

Figure 12.6
In the Values dialog box, type the input values you want to display in the list.

Tip
To change an item in the input list, click it, type the change, and then click the Modify button. To delete a list item, click it and then click the Delete button.

4. Type the input-list items, pressing Return after each one.

5. When you finish, choose Done. You return to the Entry Options dialog box.

6. If you want to be able to enter only the values in the input list, and no others, check the Only Values from List check box.

7. Choose OK. You return to the Define Fields dialog box. If you are finished with the database definition, choose Done.

Saving the Database

After you finish defining the database, you should save the document. (Chapter 2, "Learning the Essentials," covers saving, opening, and working with documents.) You also should save the document periodically as you enter and edit the records in the database.

Troubleshooting Database Creation

More than one person is going to enter data in the database, and I want to make sure that entries are within a certain range. Is there a way to check this?

To ensure that data entries fall within a range, set the database options to verify the entry. For more information, refer to "Checking the Entry" earlier in this chapter.

I set up my database, but now I need to add fields. Can I do so?

You can add fields to a database after you create it. The new fields will be blank in all existing records. For more information, see "Adding Fields" later in this chapter.

Editing the Database

It's best to make any changes in the database definition *before* you begin adding records. If you change the definition after you enter records, the following problems may occur:

- If you add a new field, that field will be blank in all records you have entered so far. Automatic-entry fields also will be blank.

- If you delete a field, all information in all records in that field will be deleted.

- If you change the field type, ClarisWorks may be able to convert some information to the new field type. If not, you lose all the information in the affected field.

Changing Field Definitions

To change a field definition, follow these steps:

1. Choose Define Fields from the Layout menu. The Define Fields dialog box appears.

2. Click the name of the field you want to change. (You may need to click the scroll arrows to scroll through the list and find the field you want.)

3. If you want to change the name, type the new name.

4. If you want to change the field type, select the new field type. (For information on field types, refer to "Defining Fields" earlier in this chapter.)

5. Click the Modify button.

6. Continue to modify fields as needed. When you finish, choose Done. You return to the standard layout view of the records.

Tip
You also can press Shift-⌘-D to choose the Define Fields command.

Adding Fields

If you forget a field in the database, you can easily add one. Follow these steps:

1. Choose Define Fields from the Layout menu. The Define Fields dialog box appears.

2. Type the name of the field.

3. Select the field type.

4. Click the Create button.

5. Continue adding fields as needed. When you finish, choose Done. You return to the standard layout view of the records.

Deleting Fields

If you no longer need a field, you can delete it. Keep in mind that deleting a field deletes not only the field but also all data entered in that field in all records.

To delete a field, follow these steps:

1. Choose Define Fields from the Layout menu. The Define Fields dialog box appears.

2. Click the field you want to delete.

3. Click the Delete button. An alert box appears, asking, `Permanently delete this field and ALL of its contents?`

4. Choose OK. You return to the Define Fields dialog box.

5. Choose Done. You return to the standard layout view of the records.

> **Troubleshooting Database Editing**
>
> *I want to keep the information in a field, but the name isn't accurate. Should I delete the field?*
>
> If you delete the field, all data in that field also is deleted. If you want to change only the name, change the field definition.
>
> *I created one type of field when I meant to create another. Can I change the field type?*
>
> You can change the field type, but if the field contains data that is not compatible with the field type, you lose all the data in that field.

Entering Data

When you finish defining the database, you see a blank record in the standard layout view (see fig. 12.7). The fields appear, one on each line, in the order in which you entered them. If you customized any fields so that they contain automatic entries, those entries appear in the fields. Any calculation fields appear as 0.

To enter data in a record, follow these steps:

1. Click the first field in which you want to enter data. A black box surrounds the field to show that it is the active field.

Entering Data **257**

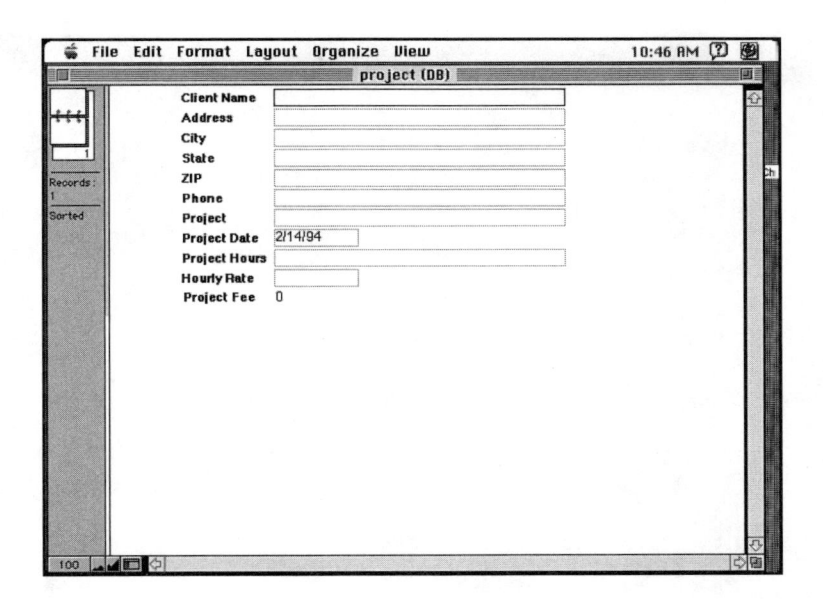

Figure 12.7
Here you see a blank record in standard layout view.

2. Type the entry for this field, keeping in mind these points:

   ■ You can type text or numbers in a text field.

   ■ You can type negative or positive numbers only in a number field.

   ■ Type dates and times in the format you used when you defined the date or time field.

   ■ If the field contains an automatic entry, you can accept the entry or type over it.

   ■ When you select a customized field that has an input list, you see a pop-up list of choices. Click the choice you want.

   ■ If you have customized the field so that it can contain data only within a certain range and you enter a value outside the range, you see an alert box. Accept the value (click OK), or enter a new value (click No and then type a value within the acceptable range).

   ■ You cannot make an entry in a calculation field; entries in calculation fields are computed and entered by ClarisWorks.

3. To move to the next field, press Tab.

Tip
To enter the current date or time in a field, press ⌘-minus sign (–). You can do this only in date or time fields.

258   Chapter 12—Database Basics

> **Note**
>
> By default, ClarisWorks moves to the next field when you press Tab. If you want to change the tab order, choose Tab Order from the Layout menu. The Tab Order dialog box appears. Select the first field you want, and click the Move button. Do this until you add all the fields in the database. Then choose OK.

4. Continue typing entries until you complete the record.

Figure 12.8 shows a completed record in the project database.

Figure 12.8
The database now contains one record.

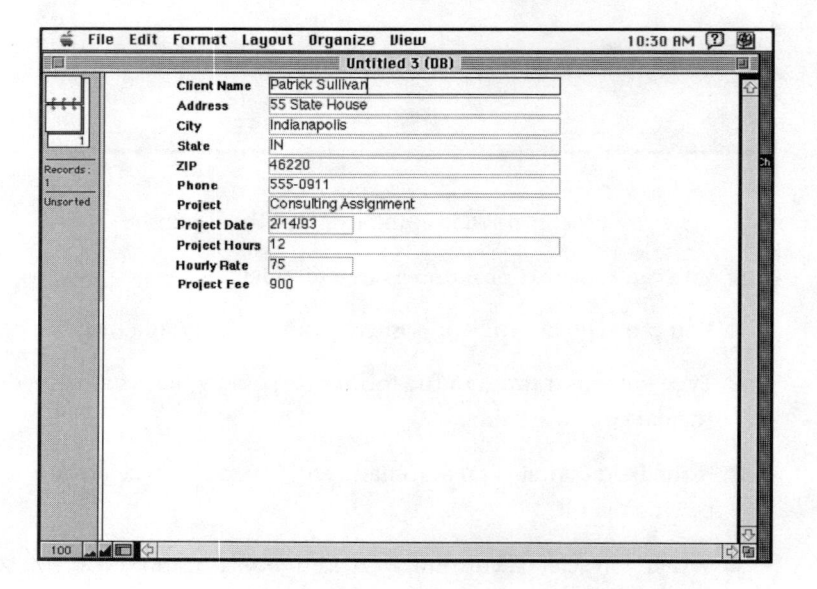

[Screenshot of ClarisWorks database window "Untitled 3 (DB)" showing one record with fields: Client Name: Patrick Sullivan; Address: 55 State House; City: Indianapolis; State: IN; ZIP: 46220; Phone: 555-0911; Project: Consulting Assignment; Project Date: 2/14/93; Project Hours: 12; Hourly Rate: 75; Project Fee: 900]

You can add new records, edit existing records, duplicate records, and perform other tasks, as described in the following section.

Troubleshooting Data Entry

I made a mistake when I entered a record. How do I make a change?

To delete an entry, drag across it and press Delete; then retype the entry. You also can click within the entry to add or change information as needed.

I have information I don't need in the database. How can I delete it?

If you created a field and no longer need the information in the field, delete it. ClarisWorks will delete the field and all the data it contains. For details, refer to

> "Deleting Fields" earlier in this chapter. For information on deleting a record, see "Deleting Records" later in this chapter.

Working with Records

Records are the backbone of your database. Each record contains key information about a person, event, product, place, and so on. ClarisWorks provides many features for working with records so that you can easily add, edit, duplicate, and hide records.

Adding Records

After you type the first record, you can add other records. To add a new record to the database, choose New Record from the Edit menu. A blank record appears below the first record (see fig. 12.9). Type the information for this record.

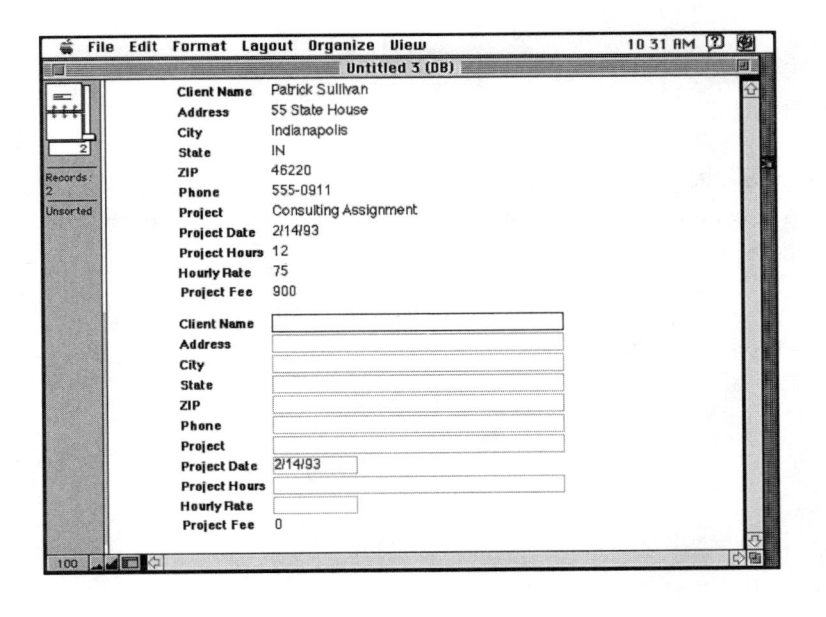

Tip
You also can press ⌘-R to choose the New Record command.

Figure 12.9
Type the information for the next record.

Duplicating a Record

If you are entering similar records in your database, it may be easier to duplicate the first record and then modify the copy. To duplicate the current record, choose Duplicate Record from the Edit menu.

Tip
You also can press ⌘-D to choose the Duplicate Record command.

Scrolling through Records

As you enter records, ClarisWorks keeps track of the number of records in the database. If you want to display a different record, you can do any of the following things:

- To move to the preceding record, click the top page of the book or press ⌘-Shift-Return.

- To move to the following record, click the bottom page of the book or press ⌘-Return.

- To move several records, drag the bookmark (see fig. 12.10). As you drag, the record number is updated to show the current record. When the record number you want is displayed, stop dragging.

Figure 12.10
The bookmark icon enables you to scroll through records quickly.

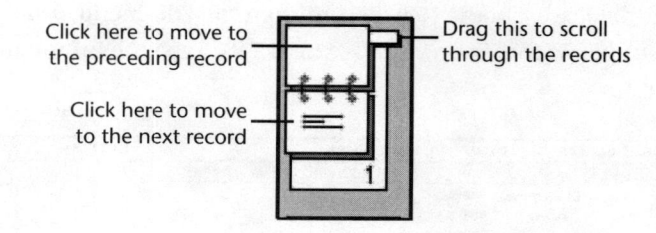

Click here to move to the preceding record
Drag this to scroll through the records
Click here to move to the next record

Going to a Particular Record

If you know the number of the record you want to display, you can use the Go To Record command. Follow these steps:

1. Choose Go To Record from the Organize menu. The Go To dialog box appears (see fig. 12.11).

Figure 12.11
In this dialog box, type the number of the record to which you want to go.

2. Type the record number.

3. Choose OK. ClarisWorks displays the record you want.

Editing a Record

To edit a record, display the record you want to change. You can scroll through the records, as described in the preceding section. If you have trouble finding the record you want, you can search for the record (see "Finding Records" later in this chapter).

With the record displayed, click the field you want to change, type the new entry, and press Tab to move to the next field. Continue making changes as necessary.

To check the spelling of the information in your database, use the Spelling Checker (choose Writing Tools from the Edit menu). The Spelling Checker is covered in Chapter 3, "Working with Text."

Selecting a Record

If you want to work with an entire record—for example, to copy or delete it—you first must select the record. To select a record, click outside the fields somewhere next to the record you want to select. The entire record is highlighted (see fig. 12.12).

To select multiple records, drag across the records you want to select, or click the first record and then Shift-click the last record. All records in between are selected. To select records that aren't next to each other, click the first record and then ⌘-click the next record you want to select.

Tip
You can select text in a field and delete, cut, or copy the text, using the standard editing techniques. You also can use the Find/Change command. Chapter 3, "Working with Text," covers these procedures.

Tip
To select all records, choose Select All from the Edit menu or press ⌘-A.

Figure 12.12
The entire record is selected.

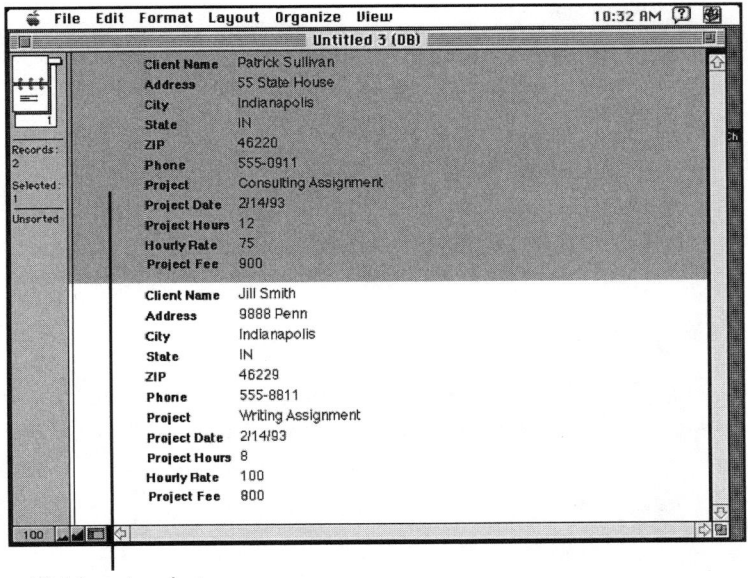

Click here to select the entire record

Hiding Records

If you want to see only certain records, you can hide the records you don't want to work with. For example, you might want to view the records of all clients who live in a particular state or all clients for whom you performed a particular service. To hide records, do one of the following things:

> **Tip**
> You also can press ⌘-(to choose Hide Selected Records, ⌘-) to choose Hide Unselected Records, and ⌘-Shift-A to choose Show All Records.

- Select the records you want to display, and then choose Hide Unselected Records from the Organize menu. ClarisWorks hides all the records that you did not select.

- Select the records you want to hide, and then choose Hide Selected Records from the Organize menu. ClarisWorks hides all the records that you selected.

To review all records, choose Show All Records from the Organize menu.

Deleting Records

To delete a record, select the record and then choose Clear from the Edit menu. ClarisWorks deletes the record from the database.

Troubleshooting Records

How can I find a record quickly?

If you have just a few records, you can scroll through one by one to find the record you want. If you have several records, this method isn't very efficient. Instead, use the Layout command (Find menu) to find the record.

I want to edit a field, but ClarisWorks selects the entire record. How do I select a field?

When you click outside the database fields, ClarisWorks selects the entire record. To select an individual field, click within the field (close to the field names).

Finding Records

When you have only a few records in a database, locating the one you want is easy. When you start entering more and more records, finding the record you want may not be so easy. In such a case, you can search the database to find the records you want.

Searching also is useful when you want to work with a particular set of records—for example, a certain type of service transaction or clients in one region. You can tell ClarisWorks to display only the found records and hide all others, or to show all found records.

Searching the Database

To search a database, you create a find request, telling ClarisWorks which field(s) to search on and what to find.

> **Note**
>
> You can search from different layouts. For more information on using and switching layouts, see Chapter 13. You can also use the Find/Change command (refer to Chapter 3, "Working with Text").

To search a database, follow these steps:

1. Choose Find from the Layout menu. A blank record appears on-screen.

2. Click the field on which you want to search.

3. Type the search criteria by doing one of the following things:

    - To find an exact match, type the value. To find all clients in Indiana, for example, type IN in the State field.

    - To find records within a range, type an operator and the range in the field. You can use the following operators:

>	Greater than (press Option-< to enter this symbol)
<	Less than (press Option-> to enter this symbol)
=	Equal to

    Tip
    You also can press Shift-⌘-F to choose the Find command.

    In figure 12.13, the find request will find all Indiana clients for whom the project fee is greater than $500.

4. If you want to omit records that match the search criteria, check the Omit check box in the status area. All records that match the criteria are *not* displayed.

5. In the status area, click Visible to search only visible records (not hidden ones) or All to search all records. ClarisWorks searches the database and displays the found records (see fig. 12.14). The status area shows the number of records found as well as the total number of records in the database.

You can edit, format, or print the found records.

264 Chapter 12—Database Basics

Figure 12.13
In this find request, ClarisWorks will search all records and display only those in which the state is IN and the project fee is greater than 500.

Status area

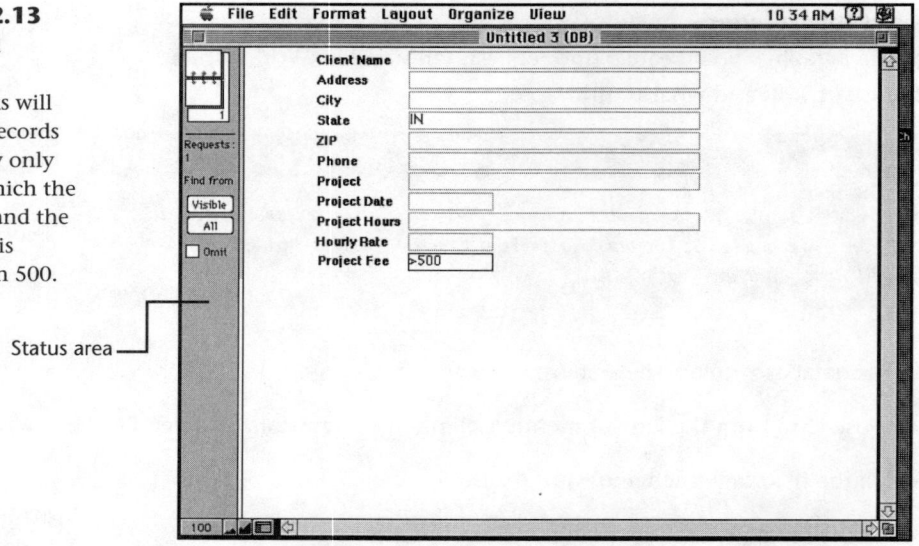

Figure 12.14
All found records are displayed.

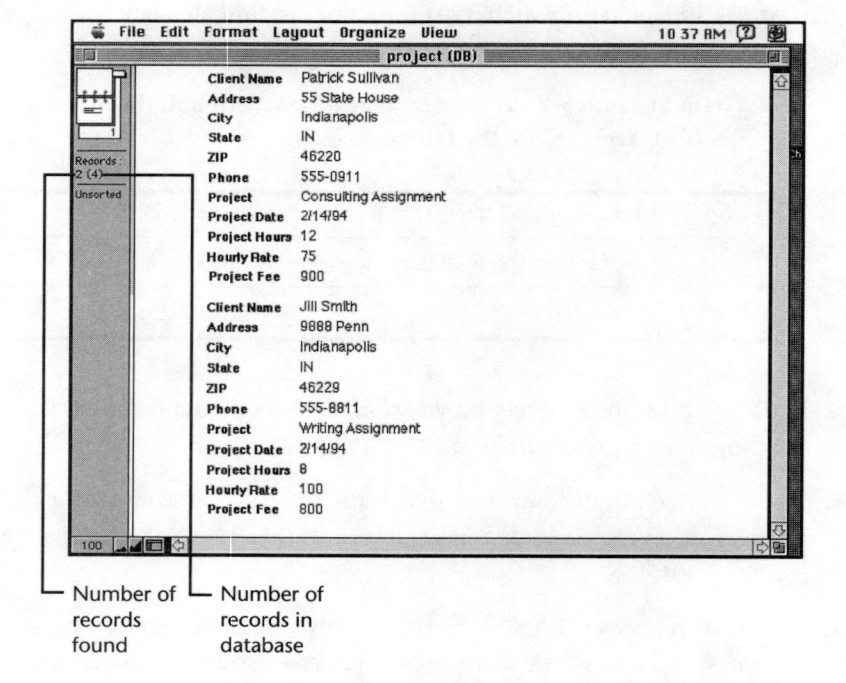

Number of records found

Number of records in database

Using Multiple Find Requests

You can search on more than one field, and ClarisWorks will display only the records that match all the criteria. In some cases, you may need to search for records that meet more than one criterion—for example, all training projects *and* all project fees of more than $250.

To do this, you need to create multiple find requests. Follow these steps:

1. Choose Find from the Layout menu. A blank record appears.
2. Create the first request, as described in the preceding section.
3. Choose New Request from the Edit menu, and then type the criteria for the next request.
4. Repeat step 3 until you have created all the find requests you need.
5. Click Visible or All in the status area to begin the search.

Matching Records

If you need to perform sophisticated searches, you may not want to create multiple find requests. Instead, you can tell ClarisWorks to match the records. When the program finds matching records, it selects all those records.

To match records, follow these steps:

1. Choose Match Records from the Organize menu. The Enter Match Records dialog box appears (see fig. 12.15). Notice that this dialog box is the same one you use to define a calculation field.

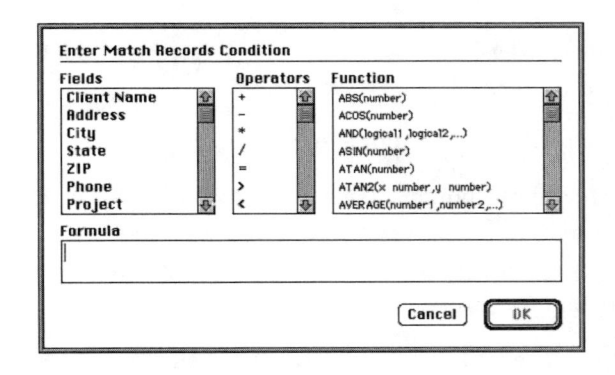

Tip
You also can press ⌘-M to choose the Match Records command.

Figure 12.15
In the Enter Match Records dialog box, create a formula that will match the records you want.

2. Click the field names and operators to create the match formula. (For information on creating formulas, refer to Chapter 8, "Spreadsheet Basics.")

3. When you finish, choose OK. ClarisWorks selects all matching records.

Sorting Records

Records appear in the order in which you enter them. You can sort the records in a different order, if you want. For example, you may want to sort a client database by last name or by ZIP code. You can sort on more than one field.

To sort a database, follow these steps:

1. Choose Sort Records from the Organize menu. The Sort Records dialog box appears (see fig. 12.16).

Figure 12.16
In the Sort Records dialog box, select the field you want to sort on and the sort order.

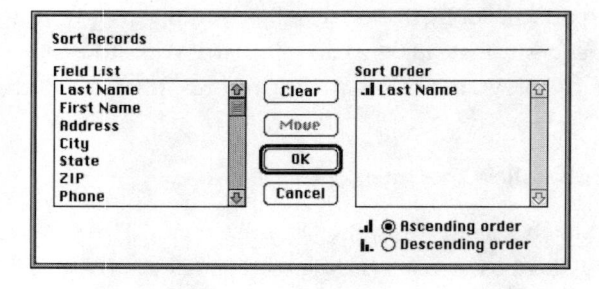

Tip
You also can press ⌘-J to choose the Sort Records command.

2. Click the first field on which you want to sort.

   If you are sorting on more than one field, select the first field on which you want to sort.

3. Choose a sort order: Ascending or Descending.

   If you choose Ascending, ClarisWorks sorts the fields in alphabetical order (A to Z) for text, low to high (1 to 100 or more) for numbers, and early to late (January to December) for dates. If you choose Descending, the program sorts in the opposite order.

4. Click the Move button. ClarisWorks lists the field in the Sort Order list.

Sorting Records   **267**

   5. Repeat steps 2 through 4 to select additional sort orders.

   6. When you finish specifying sort fields, choose OK. ClarisWorks sorts the records in the new order and displays Sorted under the bookmark to remind you that the records have been sorted.

Figure 12.17 shows the project database sorted by project.

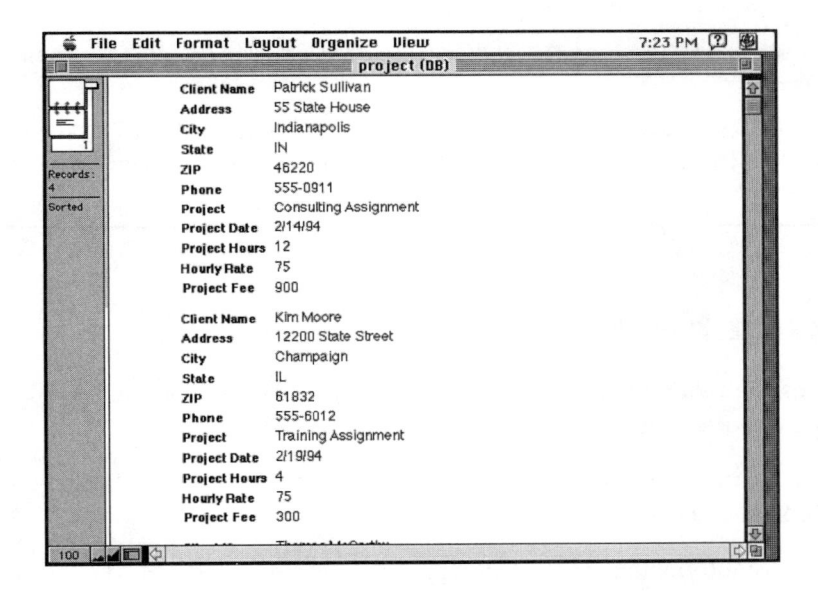

Figure 12.17
The database is sorted by project.

To undo a sort, immediately choose Undo from the Edit menu. ClarisWorks renumbers the records (the book number) to reflect the preceding sort order.

> **Note**
> If you need to keep track of the order in which records are entered, create a Record Number field and have ClarisWorks enter a serial number in that field automatically. For more information, refer to "Entering Data Automatically" earlier in this chapter.

> **Troubleshooting Sorting**
>
> *I want to sort my database, but I also need to keep track of the order in which I entered the records. Is there a way to do this?*
>
> ClarisWorks renumbers the records based on the sort order. If you need to keep track of the order in which records are entered, create a number field, and have ClarisWorks enter a serial number automatically in the field. You then can sort on this field to return to record order.
>
> *When I sort by contact name, ClarisWorks sorts on the first name. How can I sort by last name?*
>
> If you need to sort by last name, you need to define two fields for the name. Create one field for the first name and another for the last name. Then sort on the last-name field.

From Here...

ClarisWorks offers many more database features. For information, investigate the following chapters:

- For information on using functions, refer to Chapter 10, "Using Spreadsheet Functions."

- For information on formatting a database, see Chapter 14, "Enhancing the Presentation of Data."

- For information on creating and working with layouts, see Chapter 13, "Creating Layouts."

Chapter 13
Creating Layouts

by Cyndie Shaffstall-Klopfenstein

One of the most useful features of the ClarisWorks database is the capability it affords you to create custom layouts. Layouts are the way a collection, or list, of data is presented. Layouts also can perform functions such as totaling columns. A carefully planned database layout (see fig. 13.1) can bring efficiency to both complex and simple tasks, such as tracking client names in a card-file format or billing and invoicing.

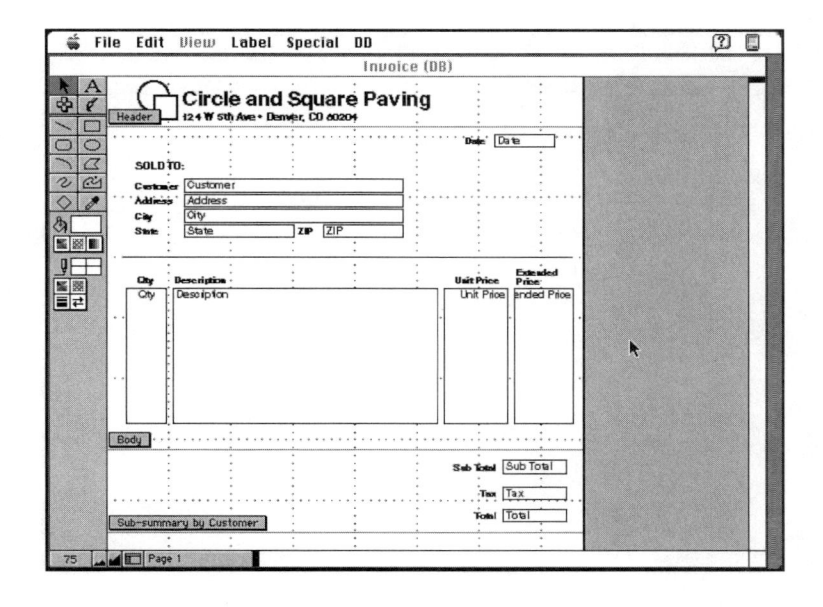

Figure 13.1
Invoices, a popular layout.

Chapter 13—Creating Layouts

In this chapter, you learn the following:

- How to plan a layout
- What information to include in a layout
- How to create a ClarisWorks database layout
- How to change the text attributes of the layout
- How to change the field attributes of the layout
- How to print layouts

Planning a Layout

You probably have layouts around your office or home right now. A recipe card can be a type of layout, as can a mailing list, an address book, or a listing of all your video or audio tapes. Just about anything that you can list and categorize is a perfect candidate for a database and, hence, a layout. A simple layout is shown in figure 13.2.

Figure 13.2
A list of your favorite 8-track tapes, sorted by group, is a perfect example of a database. The layout displays the list in a user-defined fashion.

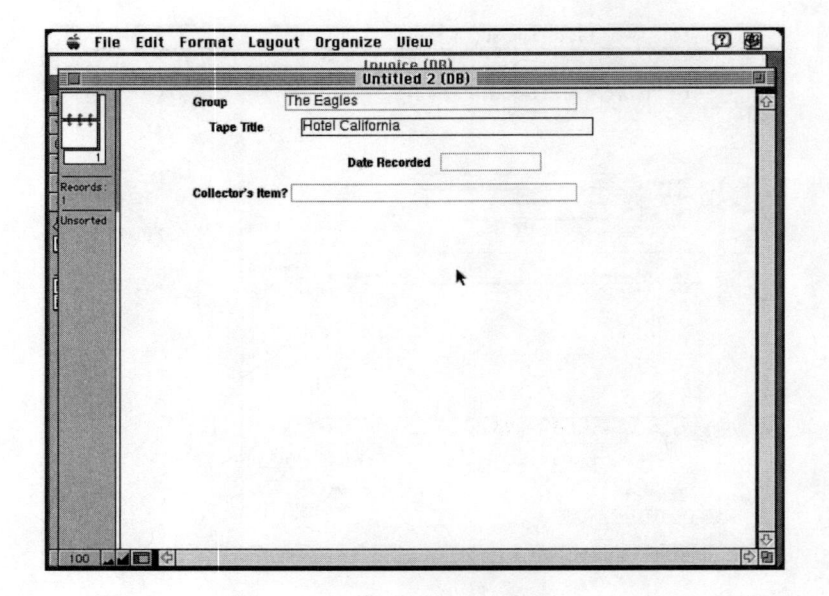

For ideas on how to create an efficient layout, look around you. Database tracking may simplify many of the tasks that you currently perform with pen and paper, or even on your computer. Maintaining a current address book or mailing list is a good example of such a task. The layout shown in figure 13.3 is designed to track a business contact's name. The fields in this layout include those for the Name (First and Last separately, as you learned in Chapter 12, "Database Basics"), Address, City, State, ZIP, Last Contact date, and Further Action.

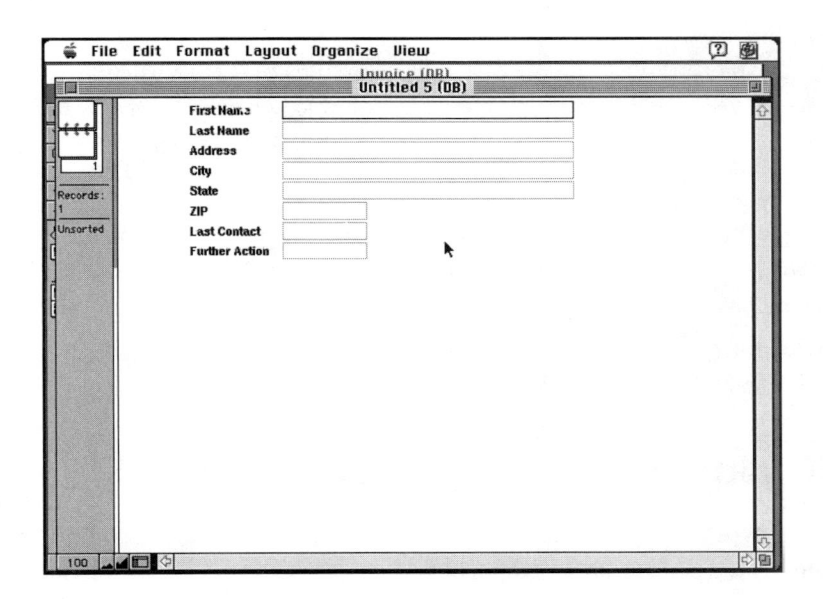

Figure 13.3
This database for tracking names and addresses is shown here in Layout view.

To plan the look of your layout, think about the fields and how you plan to use and retrieve the information in the fields. If you plan to use the layout to track the people you need to contact this week, for example, the information in the Address field may be less important than the information in the Further Action field. Be sure to consider all the options important to efficient retrieval.

Working with Views

Layouts can be viewed in different manners. These manners are referred to as *views*. You can choose the view that best suits the use to which you want to put your layout. Each of the three view types affords certain possibilities, and some limitations. The view choice is selected from the topmost area of the Layout menu.

There is also a View menu. The View menu contains different ways to view the document. It controls the view of the window and the palettes. The Layout views are for looking at the records in different manners.

The Browse View

The Browse view displays records you select from the Organize menu. From Organize, you can select a range of records to be displayed in your view. Though you cannot edit fields in Browse view, this is the only view where records can be edited.

The Find View

You use the Find view when you need to search records for particular matches. You may use the Find view, for example, when you need to find all records within your database that have "Colorado" in the State field.

The Layout View

You use the Layout view when you want to edit the layout, not the fields. In Layout view you can change the field sizes, placement, and even the style of text the fields contain, but not the field contents. For example, you can change the style to bold text, but you cannot change the data (where a name or information appears) in the field.

Working with Layouts

No one type of layout is the best for all tasks. Versatility is one of the most useful features of working with layouts. You even can use several different layouts for the same database. For a general client database, for example, you may use one layout to create statements, another for invoices, another for form letters (mail merge), and still another for the mailing labels.

When you create the layout, you can move, resize, or delete fields so each layout includes only the fields that need to appear in the final page. For example, in a customer database you might have a telephone number field that would be unnecessary when you print mailing labels. It can be deleted from the layout. You also can add text and graphics that aren't contained in the database. The headline and corporate logo in figure 13.4 are examples of such added elements. The layout in this figure is created using the New Layout option of the Layout menu (the New Layout option is described later in this chapter).

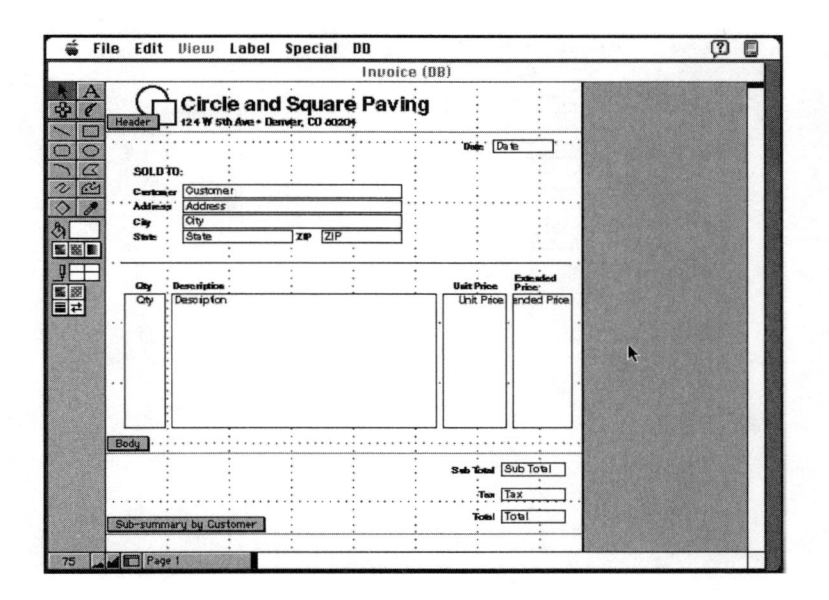

Figure 13.4
This invoice uses a database for the name, address, and so on, but the company name and logo are created in the Layout view with the drawing tools.

As the above sections indicate, you can take advantage of ClarisWorks' flexibility to create a wide variety of layouts. The following sections, however, describe some of the preset layout styles that ClarisWorks provides. After you activate a layout, whether a custom or a preset style, you can select the layout from the bottom of the Layout menu. To see which layout is current, click the Layout menu; a check mark appears next to the active layout.

Using the Standard Layout

The Standard layout (see fig. 13.5) is the default layout style. If you choose Layout from the Layout menu, the Standard layout opens. The Standard layout contains all the fields of the database, stacked vertically in the order of their creation. As you learn later in this chapter, you can make changes to this layout style at any time.

Figure 13.5
A Standard layout.

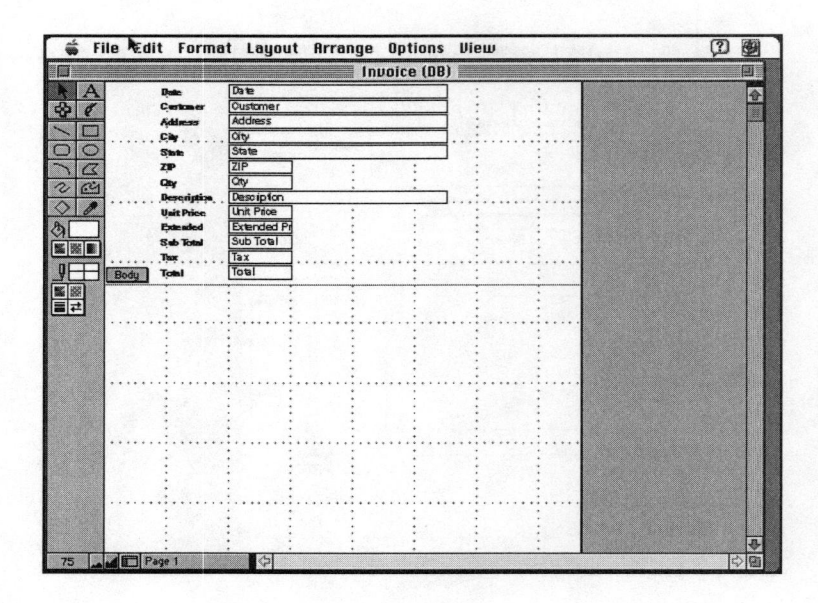

Using Columnar Report Layouts

A Columnar Report layout displays all fields in vertical columns, with the appropriate field name at the top of each column. A Columnar Report layout displays information in a simple and easy-to-read manner.

Creating a Columnar Layout. To create a Columnar Report layout, follow these steps:

1. From the Layout menu, choose New Layout. The New Layout dialog box appears.

2. In the Name text box, type a descriptive name for the layout (something that will remind you of the type of layout) and choose the Columnar Report button in the Type list box. The Set Field Order dialog box appears (see fig. 13.6).

Figure 13.6
When you create a new view you can choose the fields for the view from the Set Field Order dialog box.

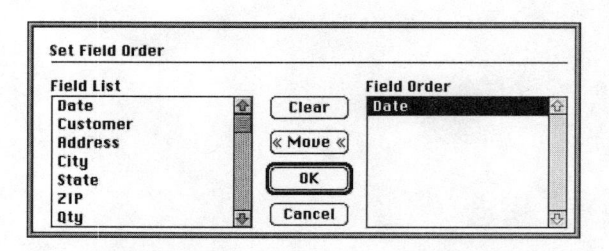

3. From the Field window on the left, choose the first field you want to include in the columnar report by double-clicking the name of the field, or by clicking the name and then clicking >>Move>>. The field name now appears in the window on the right. This is the list of fields that will be column heads in the layout.

4. Continue choosing fields until you have moved all desired fields to the Field Order window.

If you inadvertently move a field that you don't need in your report, click its name in the Field Order window and click <<Move<<. The name moves back to the Field List. Click Clear to remove all the names from the Field Order window. If you change your mind and decide not to create a Columnar Report layout, click Cancel to dismiss the dialog box without creating the report.

If you choose more field names than can fit in the width of the document, the names wrap to the next line (see fig. 13.7).

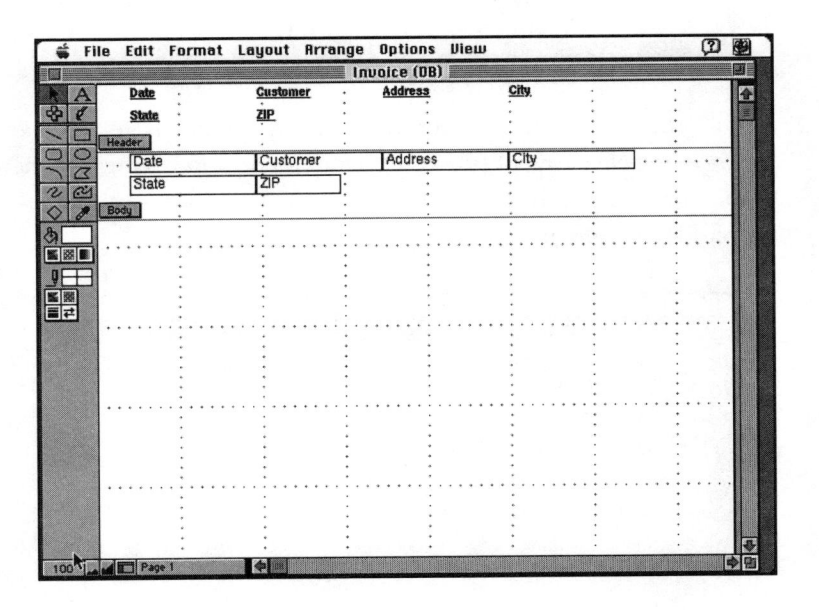

Figure 13.7
A Columnar Report layout with text that has wrapped to a second line.

If you don't want the field names to wrap, use one of the following three methods to avoid wrapping:

- From the File menu, choose Page Setup and click the Landscape page orientation icon (use this fix before you begin the layout).

276 Chapter 13—Creating Layouts

- Edit the field widths to make the fields narrower, as shown in figure 13.8. (See the "Editing Field Shapes, Sizes, and Positions" section later in this chapter for lessons on how to edit the column widths.)

Figure 13.8
The Columnar Report layout with field widths edited.

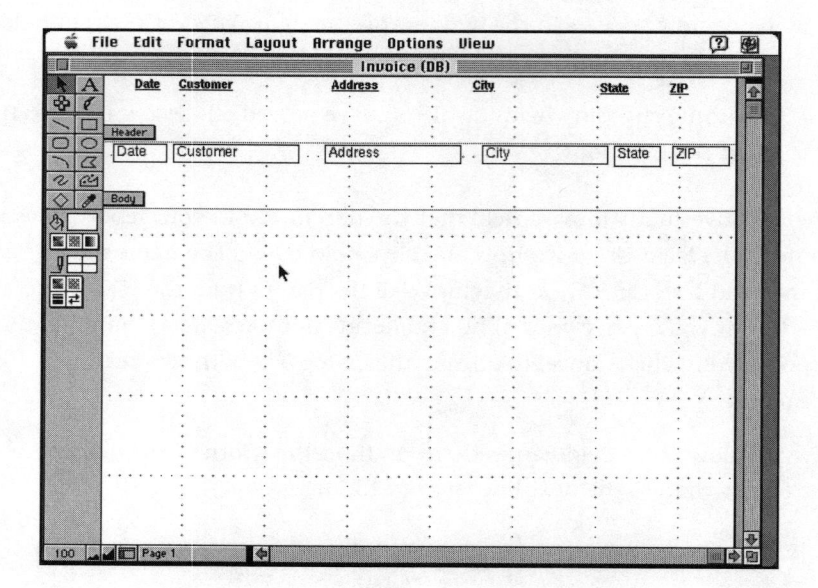

- Reduce the number of fields contained in the Columnar Report layout by choosing New Layout from the Layout menu and beginning a new layout, or by using the Layout view to delete field names from the current layout (see fig. 13.9).

Figure 13.9
From the View menu choose the Page view to display the Columnar Report layout with document margins showing.

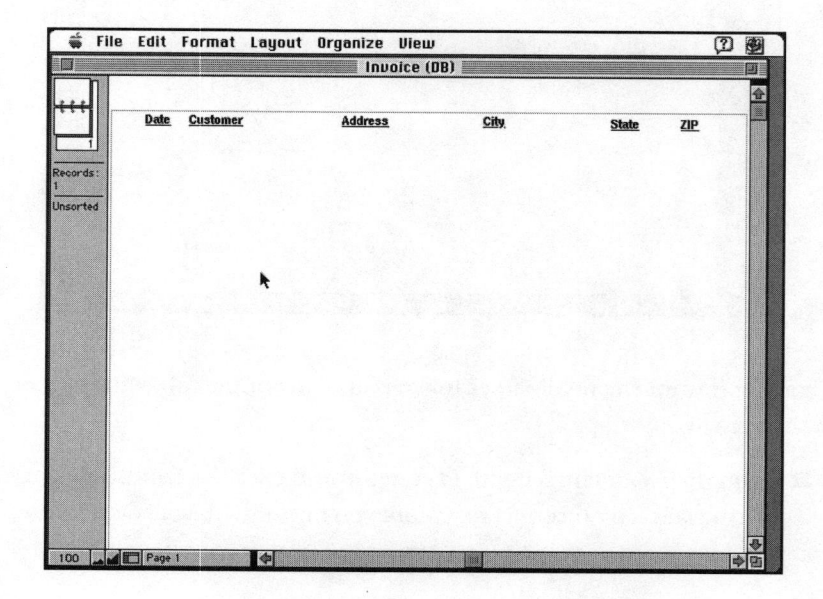

Working with Layouts   **277**

Changing the Fill Order for Columns. You may want to display the records in a Columnar Report layout across, rather than down, the page. In figure 13.10, the sample Columnar Report layout from figure 13.9 has been changed to fill across first. Changing the fill order only has an effect when the Columnar Report contains more than one column.

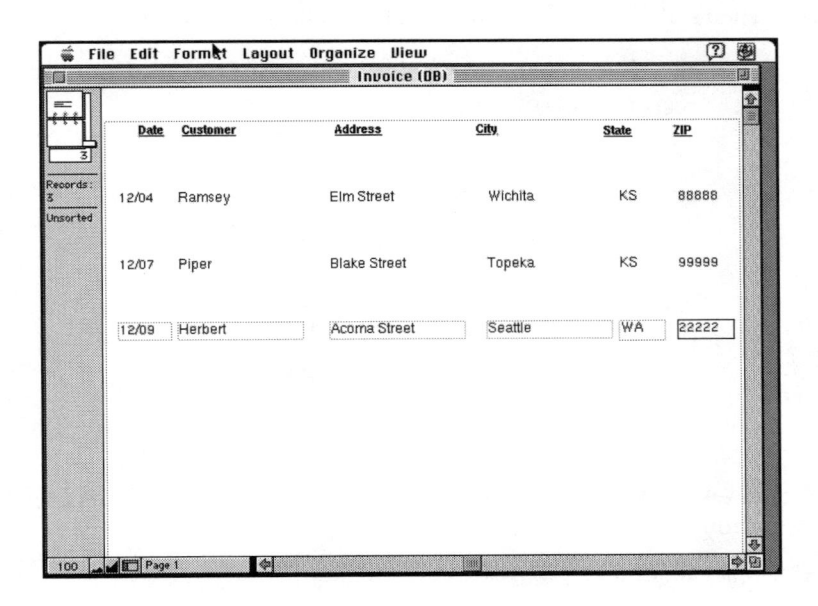

Figure 13.10
The Fill Order is the direction in which data fills fields. You might choose to fill the fields downward first rather than across. Here the data was filled downward.

To change this parameter, place your Columnar Layout in Browse view, then follow these steps:

1. From the Layout menu, choose Layout Info. The Layout Info dialog box appears.

2. If the name of the layout you want to change does not appear in the Name text box, type the name in the text box.

3. In the Columns section of the dialog box, type the Number Of columns across (or down) you want to display, then choose Across First or Down First.

4. Click OK to apply the changes to the Browse view. From the Window menu, you can select Page view to display the document. (You also can select Page view from the Window menu to display the document.)

Creating Label Layouts

Another common use for databases is for creating mailing labels. To print your mailing labels, you can buy precut labels and run them through your desktop laser printer. ClarisWorks includes more than 50 different Avery label layouts. You also can create layouts in ClarisWorks for printing mailing labels on custom label sheets.

Creating Layouts for Avery Mailing Labels. Similar to working with other layouts, you begin with a database when you want to create a layout for labels. Then follow these steps to create the mailing label layout:

1. From the Layout menu, choose New Layout. The New Layout dialog box appears (see fig. 13.11).

Figure 13.11
Use the Labels layout for printing on precut stock labels. When you use Avery labels, you can match the layout number with the label number.

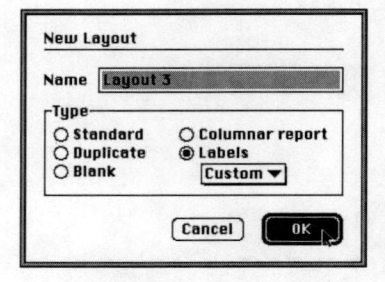

2. Type a name for the layout in the Name text box and click the Labels button in the Type list box.

3. Click and hold Custom. The Custom pop-up list appears.

4. Choose the Avery label that matches the label number you have purchased.

5. Click OK. The Set Field Order dialog box appears.

6. In the Field List window, double-click the name of each field you want printed on the labels or click each field name you want to print, and then click >>Move>>. The field name moves into the Field Order window. Continue until all the fields you want to print on the labels are in the Field Order window.

7. Click OK to create the Label layout.

Creating Layouts for Custom Labels. The New Layout option also enables you to create a layout for printing your mailing list on a custom label sheet. This is helpful if there is not a standard Avery layout for the size you need. To create a custom label layout, follow these steps:

1. From the Layout menu, choose New Layout. The New Layout dialog box appears.

2. Type a name for the layout in the Name text box and choose Labels from the Type list box.

3. Leave the Custom pop-up menu at Custom. (Do not select a standard Avery setup.) The Label Layout dialog box appears.

4. Refer to your label sheet to find the information you need to enter in the Label Layout dialog box. Type in the number of labels that occur across your label sheet, and type in the labels' width and height measurements in the Label Size fields (see the following note).

> **Note**
>
> The label width is the measurement from the left edge of one label to the left edge of the label immediately to the right. The label height is the measurement from the top edge of one label to the top edge of the label directly below it.

5. Click OK to apply the label sizes. The Set Field dialog box appears.

6. In the Field List window, double-click the name of each field you want printed on the labels or click each field name you want to print, and then click >>Move>>. The field name moves into the Field Order window. Continue until all fields you want to print on the labels are in the Field Order window.

7. Click OK to create the Label layout.

In Layout view, you can adjust the sizes and positions of the field names. When those adjustments are complete, you are ready to print the labels (refer to the sections "Printing Labels" and "Removing Space between Fields" later in this chapter for information on setup and printing).

Using Blank Layouts

A Blank layout is an empty document page; it contains no fields. To add fields to a Blank layout, choose the fields you want to use and add them using the drawing module, as described in the "Editing Field Shapes, Sizes, and Positions" section later in this chapter. You can choose this type of layout if you are only using a small number of the fields. It may be easier than deleting a large number of unused fields.

Using Duplicate Layouts

You frequently may create layouts that, with only minor changes, you can use to create different uses for databases. For instance, statements and invoices have many similar fields and might look very much alike. Using the layout for one to create the other may save you time in creating two layouts of the same basic setup. Follow these steps to create a duplicate layout:

1. Type a name for the layout in the Name text box. This is the name of the layout that you want to duplicate.

2. Click the Duplicate button.

3. Click the OK button as shown in figure 13.12 to create the layout.

Figure 13.12
To duplicate a layout, choose Duplicate while in the New Layout dialog box.

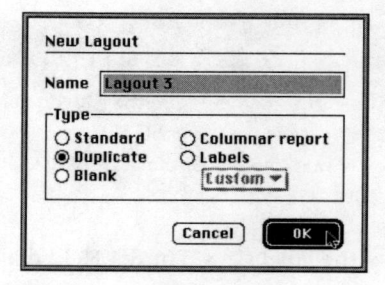

4. From the Layout menu, choose the new layout.

5. Choose Layout View To from the Layout menu to make changes to the new layout.

The new layout is now accessible from the Layout menu. A list of the names of all existing layouts appears at the bottom of the Layout menu. You can choose a layout from this menu. A check mark appears next to the current layout. The open window toggles between layouts as you choose layouts from this menu.

Renaming Layouts

As you use a layout, you may decide that you want to change its name. You can change the layout's name in the Layout Info dialog box, as follows:

1. Choose the layout's current name from the list at the bottom of the Layout menu.

2. Choose Layout Info. The Layout Info dialog box appears (see fig. 13.13).

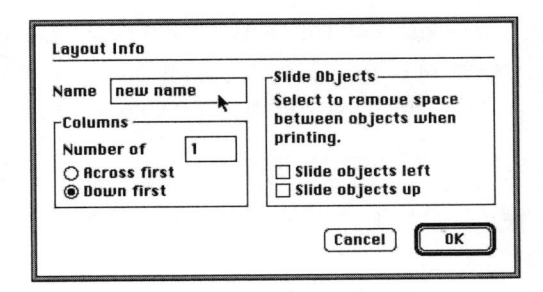

Figure 13.13
Use the Layout Info dialog box to rename a layout.

3. In the Name text box, type the new name.
4. Click OK to apply the new name.

Deleting a Layout

You can remove a layout from the Layout menu list by choosing Delete Layout from the Layout menu. A warning dialog box appears and asks if you want to permanently delete this layout (see fig. 13.14). Click OK to delete. Click Cancel to dismiss the dialog box without deleting the layout.

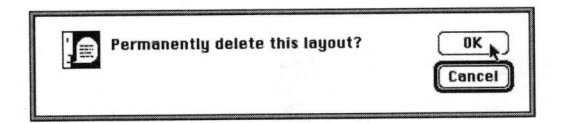

Tip
You needn't use the Delete key to remove the old name from the Name text box. The old name is highlighted when you first choose Name from the menu and the window appears. You can replace it by typing the new name.

Figure 13.14
To remove a layout, choose Delete from the Layout menu and this warning dialog box appears.

Editing a Layout

All layouts are edited in Layout view. Here you can move fields around the page, delete fields, change the text styles, and even add graphics. All of these are examples of editing a layout. Layout view affords many items that help you to create a professional-looking layout; these tools are not available in the other views. The background grid helps to align fields; the tool palette contains tools for editing text style, the fill pattern of the fields, and even the general placement of fields. But sometimes all these tools can crowd your view of the finished layout. For this situation there is Browse view.

Using Browse and Layout Views

You may best understand your database when you look at it in Browse view. With ClarisWorks, you can open two windows at the same time and display a different view of the same database in each window. You can display both windows at the same time, enabling you to see the database in Browse view while you edit it in Layout view. This arrangement is particularly useful for editing on large-screen monitors. If you have a smaller monitor, you may prefer to toggle back and forth between the two views.

To open a second window follow these steps:

1. From the View menu, choose New View. The view of the new window will be the same view as the currently active window.

2. From the Layout menu, choose Layout to change the view.

When you choose New View, you see both documents layered, or *tiled*, on the screen. The new document is in front of the original document. You can make both windows small enough to fit side by side on your screen, or you can toggle back and forth between the windows by clicking on any visible portion of the window. As figure 13.15 illustrates, a large monitor gives you more than enough space to display both windows side by side. The active window, or the window you are currently working in, is the window with horizontal bars across the top. You can also recognize it because the scroll bars are gray.

Figure 13.15
Two database windows, tiled.

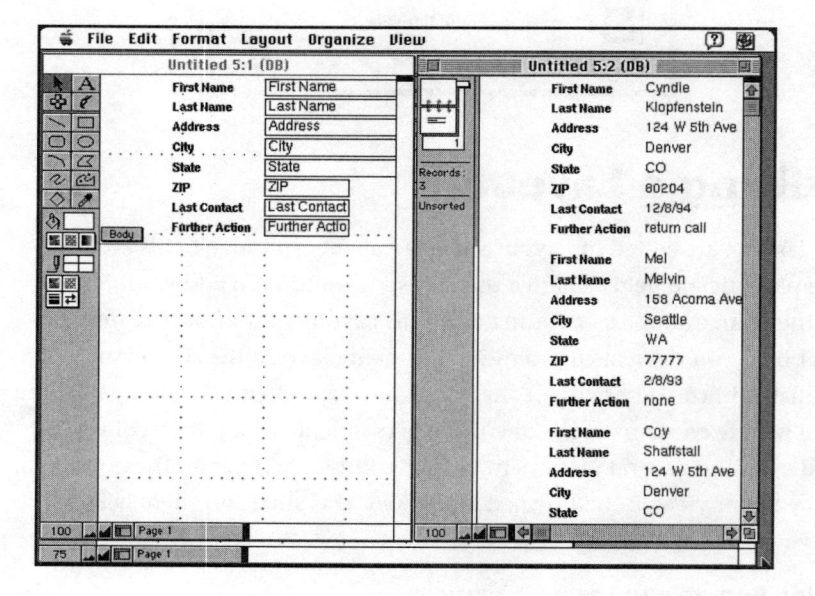

When you work with the Browse and Layout views open side by side, you can click the window of the Layout view to make it the active document. You then can edit the layout and create a super-efficient data card (an

Editing a Layout   **283**

information card on each client). In editing your layout, remember that your goal is to have all of the data displayed in a manner that helps the user find important fields quickly and easily.

> **Note**
>
> You can use either of two methods to make a view the active window (the one in which you can work):
>
> Choose the view from the list of all currently open windows at the bottom of the View menu. A check mark appears to the left of the current view's name.
>
> or
>
> Click any visible part of the window; even clicking an edge that barely shows makes that window active.

When you change to Layout view (see fig. 13.16), your document switches from the ClarisWorks database module to the drawing module. In the drawing module, the fields are considered graphic elements. You can fill or outline the fields just as you do when you work with all other elements in the drawing module. The field names are text blocks and, therefore, you can edit them with the text tool. You use this technique to change the type style or font of the fields and titles.

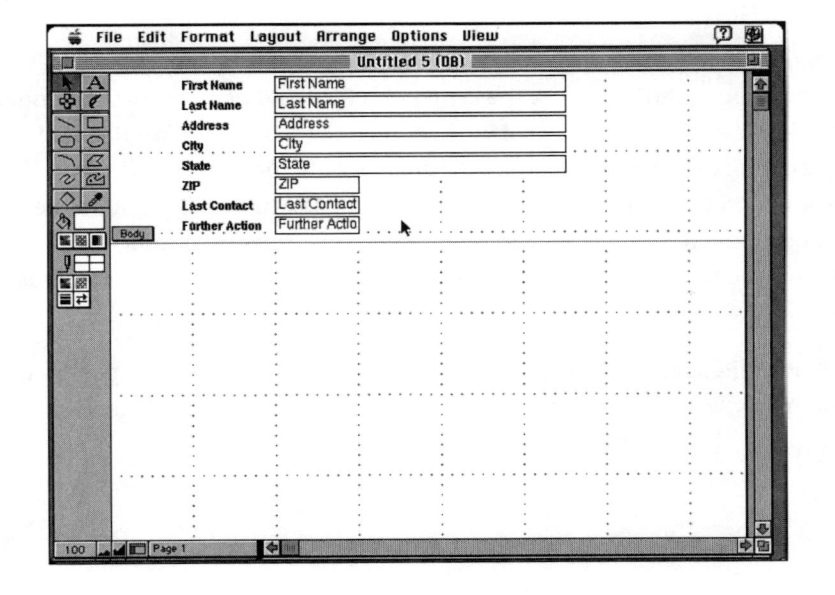

Figure 13.16
The Layout view contains the database fields in a ClarisWorks drawing document. This is recognized by the presence of the drawing tool palette.

Editing Field Shapes, Sizes, and Positions

As mentioned earlier, layout fields are graphic elements. You change the size and placement of fields in exactly the same manner as you change other drawing elements. When you click (make active) a field, handles appear at each corner of the field box. These handles can be pulled to extend the width or height of a particular field. Figure 13.17 shows fields that have been moved.

Figure 13.17
Field titles and fields that have been moved to make a more desirable layout.

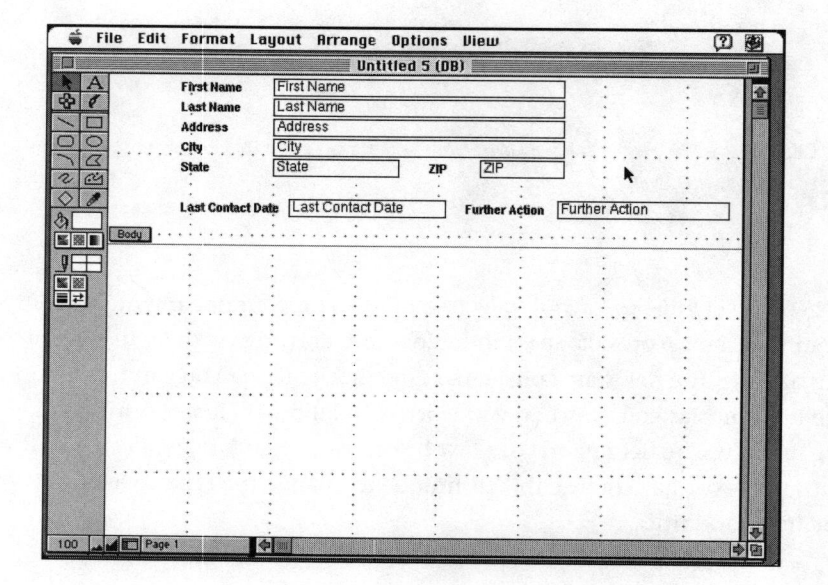

You drag the handles of an active field to change its size (see fig. 13.18). To practice this technique, click the center of a field and pause until the handles appear; next, click and drag a handle. Notice that you can make the field wider and taller at the same time. To change only the height or only the width, hold the Shift key down while you drag the handle. Pulling to the left or right will change the width. Pulling the handles up or down will change the height. A gray outline shows the original size of the field in case you want to match a particular feature of the original.

To move fields and field titles, click and drag them to the desired position. You may choose to place the field name in small type below the field box.

Editing a Layout **285**

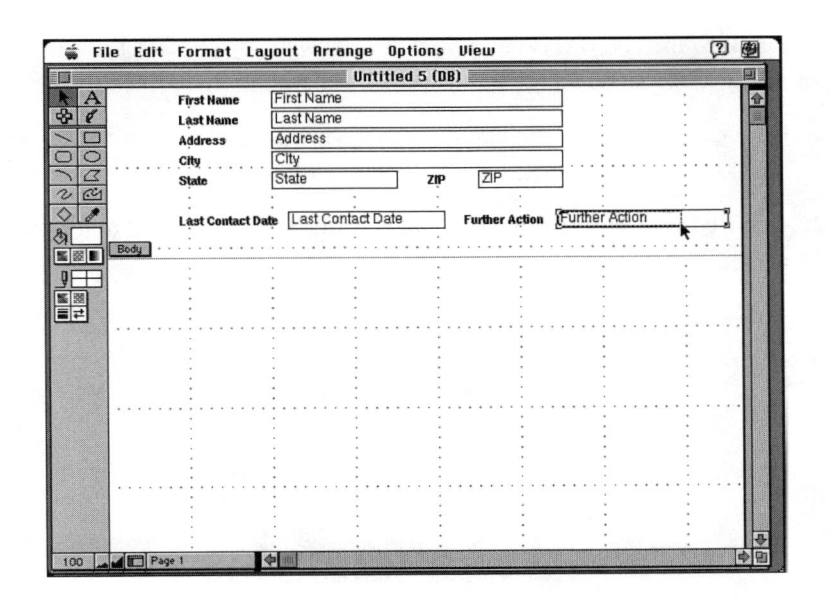

Figure 13.18
To change a field size, click on the field and drag the handles until the field is the correct width or height.

Keep in mind that in Browse view you need to quickly and efficiently find the data most important to you. Sometimes, what looks good in Layout view may not look quite as good in Browse. While you edit in Layout view, therefore, keep an eye on the Browse view display. Refer to Chapter 14, "Enhancing the Presentation of Data," for help with changing the text attributes of your layout.

Deleting Fields
To remove a field, click to make that field active, then press Delete on the keyboard to delete the field. If you change your mind and want to restore the field, you must immediately choose Undo from the Edit menu to reverse the deletion.

Adding Fields to a Layout
From the Layout menu you can add fields. You can only add fields that were either never added to the layout (perhaps you started with a Blank layout and only added some of the fields) or that were deleted from the layout during

Chapter 13—Creating Layouts

an earlier session. You can insert a field in the layout by choosing Insert Field from the Layout menu. To accomplish this task, follow these steps:

1. Choose Layout from the Layout menu. The layout appears in the window. You must be in Layout view to add fields.

2. Choose Insert Field from the Layout menu. The Insert Field dialog box appears (see fig. 13.19).

Figure 13.19
Choose the Insert Field option from the Layout menu to place deleted fields back into the layout.

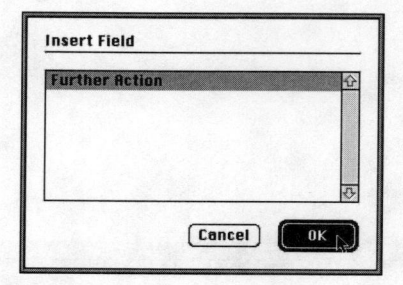

3. In the list in the left portion of the dialog box, double-click the name of the field you want to add. (If the list contains no fields, then all fields from the database are present in the layout.)

4. Click OK to add the field.

Changing the Size of the Record

In Layout view, the horizontal line extending across the document below the fields determines the area the records occupy when in Browse view or when you print the layout. For instance, you might want to print only one record per page even though the actual space the records use is smaller than a full page. You can increase or decrease the size of this area that will be used to display or print a record by clicking and dragging on the line (see fig. 13.20). Release the mouse to assign the new record area.

Editing a Layout **287**

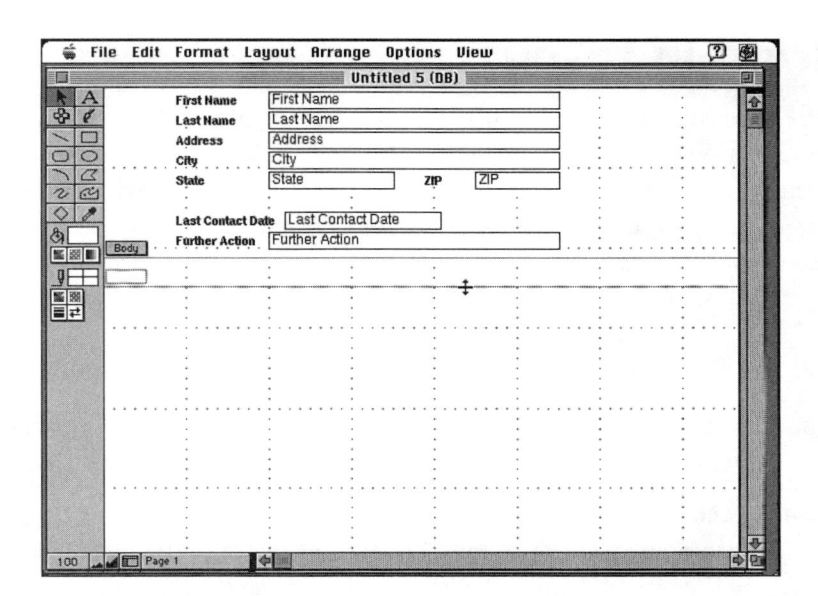

Figure 13.20
The horizontal rule below the record can be dragged downward or upward to change the amount of vertical space the entire record occupies.

Troubleshooting Layouts

I can't edit my layout. Nothing I click and drag will move.

You are not in Layout view. Go to the Layout menu and select Layout.

While in the Columnar Report layout type, my columns wrap to a second line.

The fields you have created are too wide for the document size. Change the page orientation to Landscape, delete fields, or reduce the widths of fields in the Layout view.

I have a layout that's pretty close to a new style that I need, but I don't want to edit the original. Do I need to completely re-create the layout with the minor changes?

Layouts can be duplicated without affecting the original. Choose the layout you want to copy and then choose Duplicate from the Layout menu.

I don't like the way the date is displayed in my layout. Can I change the date display format?

Several different date formats are available. In Layout view, double-click the Date field. In the Date type dialog box, select the style you prefer.

I want to use more vertical space for each record; how can I enlarge this space?

In Layout view, click the horizontal bar that runs across the width of the document and drag the bar down to create more room for each record.

Printing Layouts

Before you print a layout, you may find it useful to put the layout in Page view. This step is not essential, but the Page view gives you the best preview of the way the final printed job will look. You can check the Page view to determine that your database layout looks the way you want it to look. Return to the Layout view to make any last-minute adjustments.

1. Choose Print from the File menu. The Print dialog box appears.

2. Select Current or Visible Records to choose which records to print.

3. Click OK to Print. The database information is sent to the printer and printed.

Printing Labels

Before you can print labels you must create a label layout. After you have edited the label layout, choose Browse or Layout from the Layout menu (you cannot print from the Find view). To begin printing, select Print from the File menu, then click OK. Click Cancel to dismiss the dialog box without printing.

Try printing a few pages of the database to plain paper before loading the labels. If your setup is incorrect, better to waste a sheet of paper than a sheet of labels. Use the page range in the Print dialog box to print only a few pages of the database. For instance, type 1 in the From field and 1 in the To field to print only page 1, as in figure 13.21.

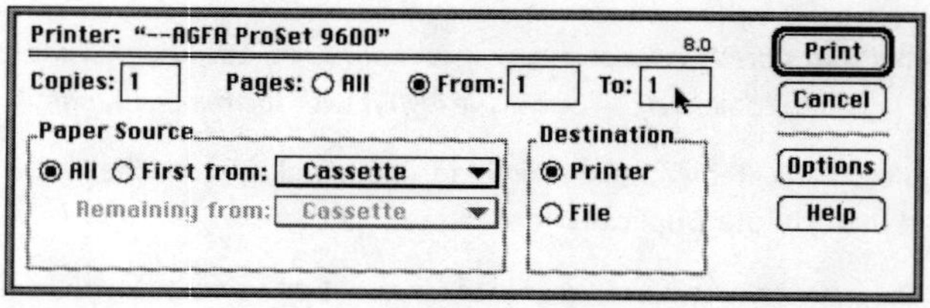

Figure 13.21
Type specific page numbers in the page range area of the Print dialog box to print only selected pages.

Removing Space between Fields

In some circumstances you may have empty fields; for example, if you define a Middle Name field and some records have no middle name. In such circumstances you can remove the space left by an empty field to prevent its appearance in your printed job. To tell ClarisWorks to automatically close up spaces left by empty fields, follow these steps:

1. From the Layout menu, choose Layout Info. The Layout Info dialog box appears, as shown in figure 13.22.

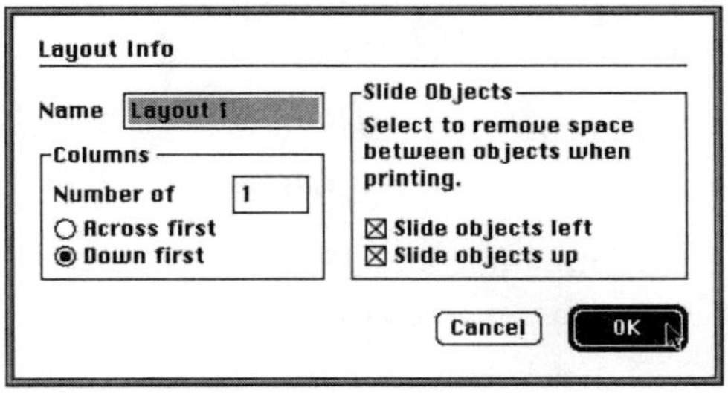

Figure 13.22
To remove spaces left by blank fields, click one or both of the check boxes of the Layout Info dialog box.

2. In the Slide Objects section of this dialog box, choose to Slide Objects Left or to Slide Objects Up, or choose both options.

3. Click OK to apply this format.

Troubleshooting Printing

I have created a custom Label layout and the labels are printing across the seams of the labels on the sheet.

The measurements in the custom Label dialog box are incorrect. Try adjusting these measurements and printing just page 1 until the labels print correctly.

When I print my layout I get several records on each page when I only wanted one per page.

Use the horizontal bar going across the document in Layout view to edit the amount of area each record uses.

From Here...

In this chapter we covered the tasks for creating moderately difficult layouts. You can use the skills discussed in this chapter to create many different types of layouts. In Chapter 14, "Enhancing the Presentation of Data," you learn about more complex types of layouts.

- Chapter 6, "Drawing." Return to this chapter for help with using the drawing tools available when in Layout view.

- Chapter 12, "Database Basics." This chapter will help you to decide what type of data to track and how to track it.

- Chapter 14, "Enhancing the Presentation of Data." Now that you've learned to create layouts, jazz them up with the skills in this chapter.

- Chapter 15, "Creating Integrated Documents." Printing letters to all the people in your database is a great way to simplify the tedious task of addressing letters. Use Chapter 15 for help.

Chapter 14

Enhancing the Presentation of Data

by Cyndie Shaffstall-Klopfenstein

In Chapter 13, "Creating Layouts," you learned how to create simple layouts. In this chapter, you learn how to make a more finished layout. You learn techniques for changing text attributes and changing field colors and borders. You also explore such complex issues as how to make fields work for you. Further, you learn to recognize the parts of a record and how to use those parts to generate finely tuned reports.

> **Note**
>
> You perform most data enhancement in Layout view. Choose this view from the Layout menu before you attempt to change the attributes.

In this chapter, you learn the following:

- How to format fields to perform mathematical functions
- How to format number fields
- How to create record bodies and summaries
- How to format text fields
- How to change the tab order of fields

Formatting Function Fields

Databases can do much more than track data; they also can summarize, group, and print different layout styles of the data. To perform certain functions, you need to "train" some of the fields you use in databases. Changing a field to display a certain style of date, time, currency, or other type could be referred to as training. To begin this training, you first must select the correct field type when you create the new database. You also can change the type of field by choosing Layout Info.

To create a new database with particular field types, click one of the Type buttons as you add a field name. Different fields require different kinds of data. For instance, a name field might be styled for text while a ZIP code field would be styled for numbers. Other types of fields, like subtotals and totals, might contain formulas like SUM.

Figure 14.1
Some buttons, such as Summary, require further action, as shown in figure 14.2.

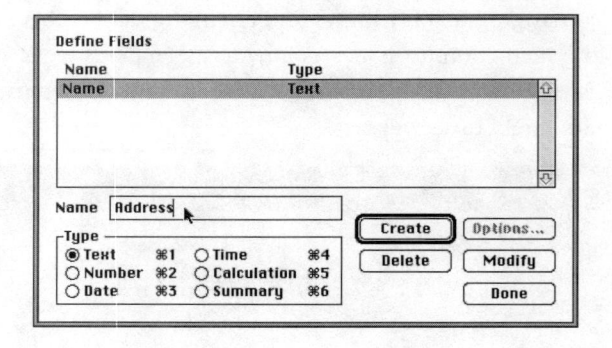

Figure 14.2
Choose the formula from the list on the right. Choose the symbols from the list in the center.

Formatting Numbers

"Training" a field to display the proper number format is very simple. Number formats can be very complex; formats range from General to exponential powers of 10. Table 14.1 lists and illustrates some of the more common number formats.

Table 14.1 Number Formats

Format	Result
General	54 (not 54.00)
Currency	$1.00
Percent	50% (not .5)
Scientific	1.00e+6
Fixed (fixed number of decimal places)	43.67 (not 43.673)
Commas	1,000 (not 1000)
Negatives in ( )	(1,000) (not –1000)

As you begin the database, click Number in the Type section of the dialog box. This will format the field with a number style. The window at the top of the dialog box now displays the name of the field and shows that the type of the field is Number. If you change your mind and wish to change the type of field, highlight it in the window above, click the new type you wish to apply, and click the Modify button.

If you've already created the database you can switch to Layout view and change the type of a field here also. This is done by double-clicking the field box or clicking the box and choosing Define Fields from the Layout menu. When the Define Fields dialog box appears, make your new selection and click the Modify button to apply the new type.

While in Layout view, you can further define the number type by choosing Field Format from the Options menu. This gives the options shown above in Table 14.1. From the buttons, select the format that most closely matches the way you want your numbers to appear in the field. Applying the correct format ensures that the content of the field consistently conforms to the type of numbers you intend to represent in that field—all currency, all commas, and so on. Finally, choose a Precision amount. This action specifies how many digits to the right of the decimal a number will be rounded. For example, the number 1.0005 with a Precision amount of 2 will be displayed as 1.00 in the number field.

When in Layout view you can change the type of number format for a field. Click on the field to change and choose Field Format from the Options menu. The Number Format dialog box appears (see fig. 14.3).

Figure 14.3
Choose Field Format from the Options menu to change a field's number format.

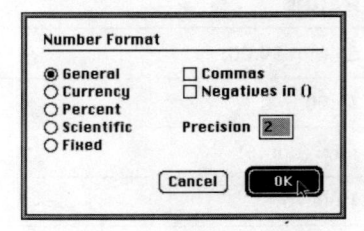

Formatting Dates

When the content of a field will be date text, you might want to specify a date format to ensure that this field always contains text for a date. You can even dictate exactly how the text will display the date. This option does not add the date text for you; it only formats the text you put in the field. (There are formulas that can add the current date to this field. Refer to Chapter 10, "Using Spreadsheet Functions," for more information on this type of formula.)

To apply a date format to a field, click the Date button in the Type area of the Define Fields dialog box when you create a new database. Click the Create button at the lower-right corner of the dialog box and the name of the field and its type will be displayed in the window above. Click Done only when you have finished adding all of the fields you need.

When in Layout view, you can change an existing field's format to date format by using Define Fields in the Layout menu. This will bring up a dialog box exactly like the New Document dialog box. Click on the field whose type you wish to change, click the Type button that you want to change to, and click the Modify button before the Done button to apply style changes to the field.

From Layout view, you also can change the style of the date field by double-clicking on the field. Choose Field Format from the Options menu. The Date Format dialog box appears (see fig. 14.4).

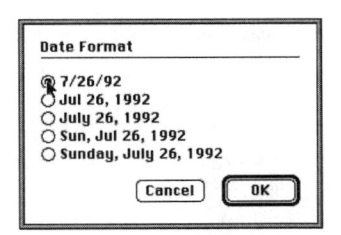

Figure 14.4
Choose Field Format from the Options menu and the Date Format dialog box allows you to change the date format.

There are several different styles for a field that contains a date; choose the style that best suits your needs. Click the button next to the field style you prefer. Click OK to apply this style change.

You can choose from among the following date formats in ClarisWorks:

- 7/26/92 (the default)
- Jul 26, 1992
- July 26, 1992
- Sun, Jul 26, 1992
- Sunday, July 26, 1992

Formatting Times

To create a time field, choose Time in the Type section of the Define Fields dialog box when you begin a new database document. Once you click Create, the field name and type are displayed in the window above.

Once you have created a database, you can change a field type with the Layout menu. To accomplish this task, choose Define Field from the Layout menu. Click on the field to change and click the desired Type button. Click the Modify button after making a type change, then click Done. Click Cancel to dismiss the dialog box without making a type change. Use one of the following formats:

- 5:20 PM
- 5:20:15 PM
- 17:20 PM
- 17:20:15 PM

To format a time field, choose Format Fields from the Options menu or double-click the field containing the time. The Format Fields dialog box appears (see fig. 14.5). Choose a time format and click OK.

Figure 14.5
Use the Time Format dialog box to change the format of the time display.

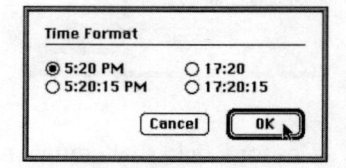

Performing Calculations and Summaries

Certainly the calculation and summary fields are the most proactive of all field definitions. They perform similar functions, but the calculation field type is limited to calculating within a single record, whereas the summary field can perform the same types of functions over many records. Summary and calculation fields can add, average, divide, round off, or calculate square roots, to name a few possibilities. These types of functions also are a part of the spreadsheet module of ClarisWorks. An example of a function is the Total field of an invoice. This type of field, when totaling columns within a single record, is a calculation field.

If this field were a summary field, you would place it in a special area of the record called the sub-summary or grand summary. We'll cover summaries in greater detail later in this chapter. A field in a summary area, such as Add All, will perform a calculation of the total sales entered into a series of invoices or perhaps the average billing for a series of invoices. For a complete listing and definition of the types of summaries refer to Appendix A of the ClarisWorks user's guide.

To create a summary or calculation field, choose the desired button in the Define Fields dialog box when creating a new database. This will bring forward a second dialog box where you will select the type of summary or calculation to be performed.

You also can change the style of a calculation or summary field while in Layout view. Choose Define Fields and make the change. Figure 14.6 shows the dialog box. Don't forget to click Modify to go to the next dialog box, where you will choose the type of summary or calculation before clicking OK. Click Cancel to dismiss the dialog box without changing the style of a field.

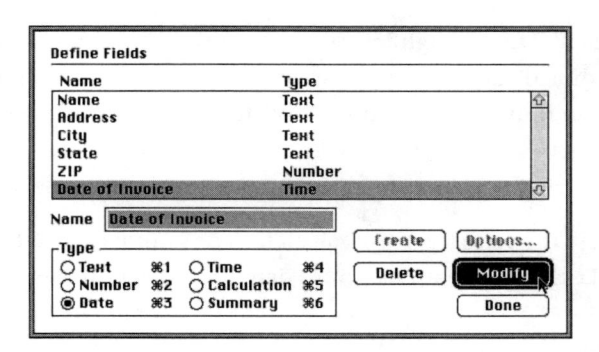

Performing Calculations and Summaries **297**

Figure 14.6
To change the format of a field you created earlier, choose Define Fields from the Layout menu. Click the Modify button to apply the changes.

To create a summary or calculation field in a new database, follow these steps:

1. From the File menu, choose New.

2. Click the database button.

3. Add the fields and field types. When you get to the Total field, type **Total** and select Summary or Calculation from the Type buttons.

4. Click Create. Figure 14.7 shows the dialog box where you will choose the type of summary (or calculation).

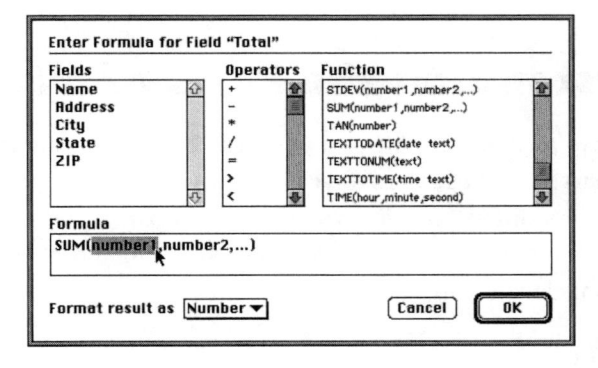

Figure 14.7
When you create a summary field, this dialog box appears. The first part of the formula is replaced with the first field.

5. Choose a function by clicking its name in the Function list on the far right of the dialog box. The function appears in the window at the bottom of the dialog box.

6. In the Formula window, the highlighted (selected) text is ready to be replaced with a field name.

7. While this text is highlighted, click on the field name in the field window directly above that you wish to add to this function. Highlight the next portion of the function (leave the commas in place to separate field names) and replace it with the next field; continue until all fields that you wish to include in the function have been added.

8. Choose the format for the calculation or summary field from the Format Result As pop-up menu. As described earlier in this chapter, each field
is a specific type. It can be a number, time, date, etc.

9. Click OK to save the summary or calculation field.

10. Click Done.

The summary or calculation field you just created does not yet display the result of the formula; you first enter data into the fields that this field summarizes.

The following section discusses the parts of a layout. With a good knowledge of that information, you will be ready to move on to a discussion of how the sub-summary enables the summary fields to display the sums of selected records.

Understanding the Parts of a Layout

Any layout can include four different parts: the header, sub-summary, grand summary, and the footer. You can add these parts as appropriate in your layout. In addition, all layouts include a *body*. The body, as shown in figure 14.8, contains the data portion of each record and, therefore, is not an optional layout part.

Understanding the Parts of a Layout   **299**

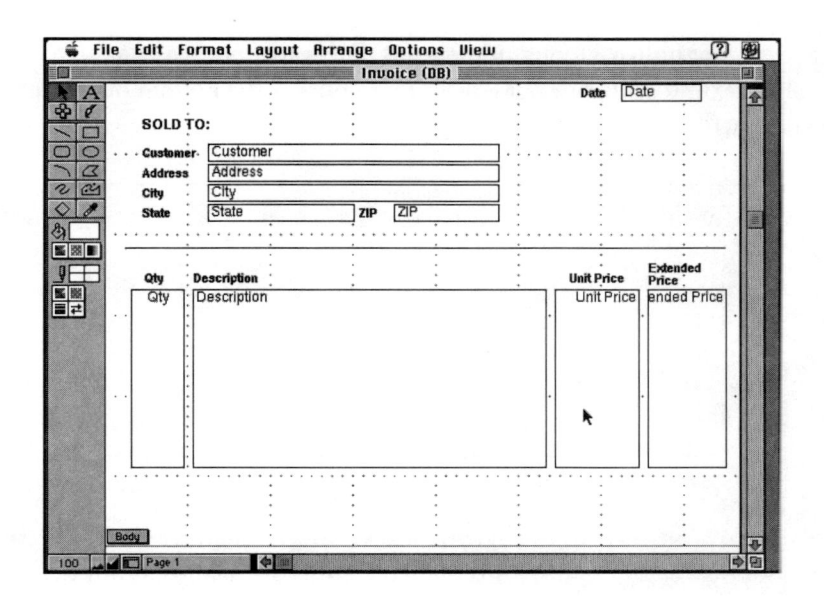

Figure 14.8
All layouts have a body. This is the area above the horizontal line labeled Body.

Adding Headers and Footers

The *header* appears at the top of each page of the layout (see fig. 14.9). On most invoices, the header is the name of the company presenting the invoice; but the header doesn't have to be the company name. You can include in the header anything you want to appear at the top of each page—even a graphic element.

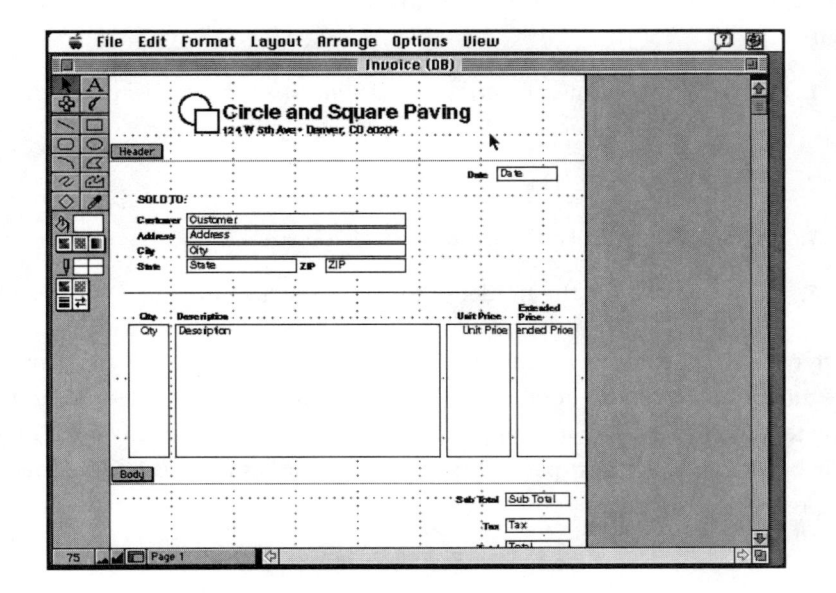

Figure 14.9
A header appears at the top of each page of the layout. It can contain graphics, text, or both.

Creating Databases

The *footer*, not unlike a footer in the word processing module, is an item (graphic, text, or both, but not a field) that prints at the bottom of each page (see fig. 14.10).

Figure 14.10
A footer appears at the bottom of each page of the layout. It can contain graphics, text, or both. It cannot contain a field.

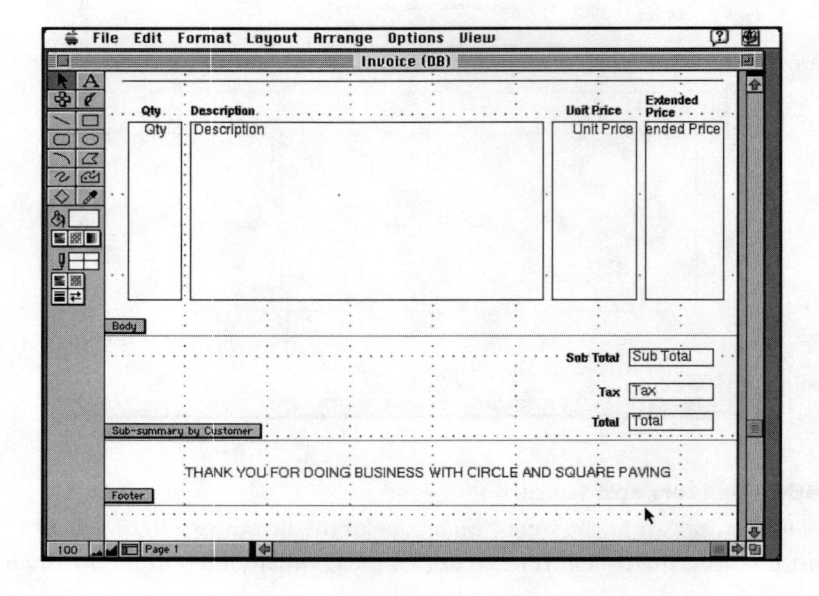

You use the same technique to add either a header or a footer to the layout. You must be in Layout view to add these elements to the layout. When you are in Layout view, follow these steps to add a header or footer to your layout:

1. From the Layout menu, choose the layout to which you want to add the header or footer.

2. Choose Insert Part. The Insert Part dialog box appears.

3. Choose Header or Footer from the dialog box.

4. Click OK to apply the header or footer to the layout.

After placing the header or footer in Layout view (see fig. 14.11), you can begin editing it. Use the tools from the drawing module tool palette to add the text or graphic. Any item appearing above the horizontal line separating the header from the next part prints on each record as the header. Any item appearing in the footer section appears at the bottom of each record.

Understanding the Parts of a Layout 301

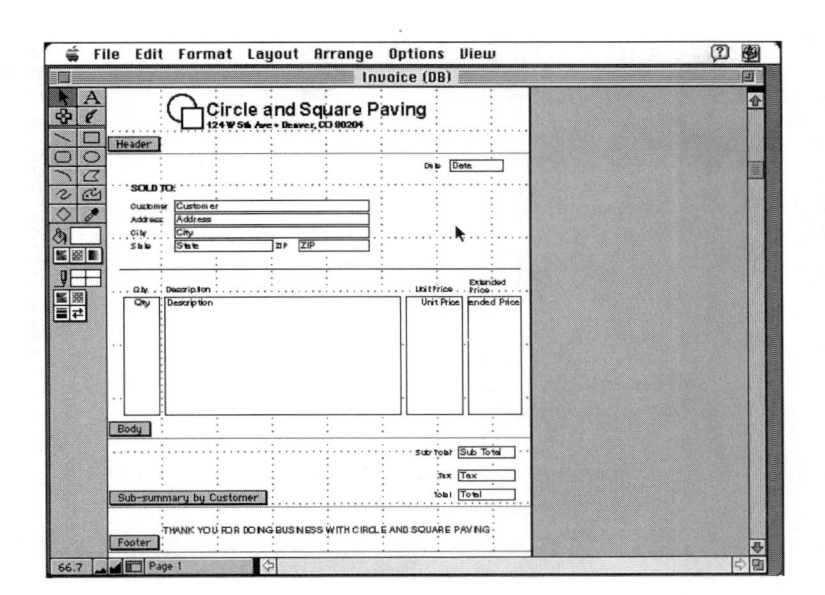

Figure 14.11
This sample layout shows the header and footer parts in Layout view.

Using a Sub-Summary

With a sub-summary you can create a layout in which a particular field of selected records is *summarized*. For instance, you might need to quickly locate the amount of produce received from a database of suppliers or the average sales for all of your employees. You can use the sub-summary part of your layout to display a particular field of information. Sub-summary does not work alone—you must *flag* it to figure this information for you. Figure 14.12 shows an example of a layout that would include a sub-summary. So, with the produce suppliers, you could *sort* by date of delivery, and the sub-summary would *summarize* the contents of a particular field from all the selected records and display this information in the sub-summary area of the layout.

You must include a summary field in your database if you want to add a sub-summary to the layout. You create the summary field when you name and define the fields as you create a new database from the File menu. To define a summary field, click the Summary button in the Type area of the Define Fields dialog box. You can add a summary field to an existing layout by using Define Fields in the Layout menu.

> **Note**
>
> After creating a field, you can change its type by choosing Define Fields from the Layout menu.

302   Chapter 14—Enhancing the Presentation of Data

Figure 14.12
In this example, ClarisWorks calculates a particular field from the records of the database and enters the summary in the sub-summary field.

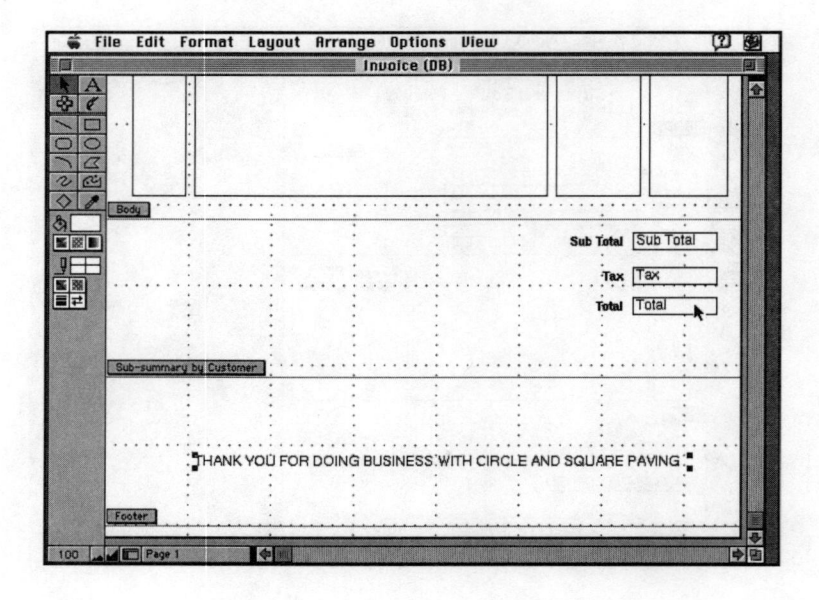

To create a sub-summary part in your layout, follow these steps:

1. From the Layout menu, choose the layout to which you want to add a sub-summary. The layout document will open.

2. From the Layout menu, choose Insert Part. The Insert Part dialog box appears (see fig. 14.13).

Figure 14.13
Choose Sub-Summary and the field name from the dialog box to create the sub-summary part.

3. Choose Sub-Summary When Sorted By.

4. From the window on the right, choose the field which is to trigger the summarization; this field is the flag.

5. Click OK to create the sub-summary part. A message window appears in which you indicate whether the summary is to appear above or below the record it summarizes (see fig. 14.14).

Understanding the Parts of a Layout   **303**

Figure 14.14
You can position the summary above or below the record it summarizes by clicking the appropriate button.

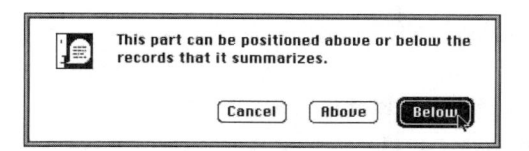

6. Choose Above, Below, or Cancel. According to your indications, a new part is added to the layout. This is the sub-summary part and it is labeled just above the horizontal line separating this part from the others.

7. Now the summary field that you created earlier must be dragged into this sub-summary part. Click the field and drag to the desired location.

After you have added a sub-summary part and moved the summary field to within its area, you can use the Sort command in the Organize menu. Sort by the same field you used in the When Sorted By field. Once you have completed the sort, the formula in the summary field will now display the total, or average, or sum in this field.

The sub-summary *part* and the field(s) it contains are only visible in Layout view as shown in figure 14.15, not Browse or Find; the summarized data appears when you switch to Page view or when you print.

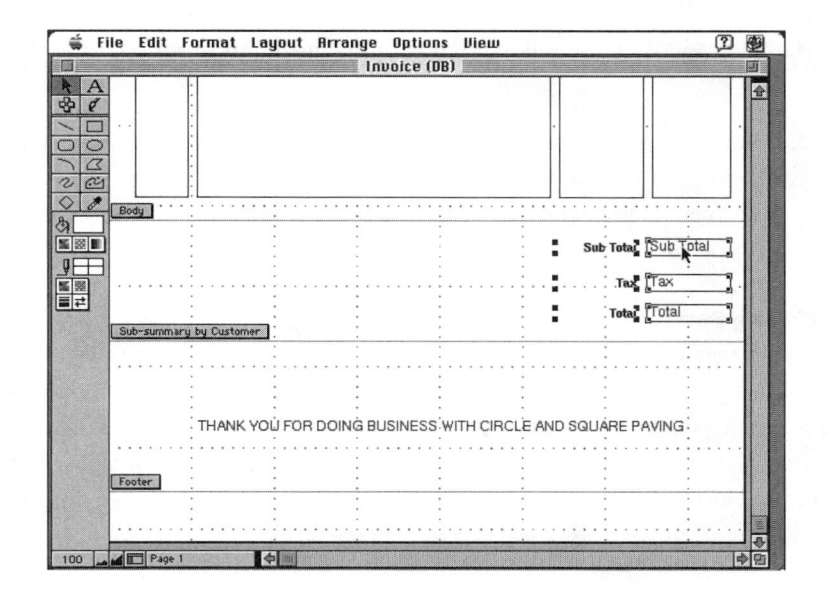

Figure 14.15
This view shows the Subtotal, Tax, and Total fields in between the horizontal rules that divide parts. You can adjust the amount of area allocated for a part.

Using Grand Summary

A grand summary part contains one or more summary fields that calculate all the values of selected fields of the records. You can use a grand summary part, for example, to create a total of all invoices in a database of invoices. To accomplish this task, you choose the fields (which also can be calculation fields) and create a layout for the report that includes the grand summary part to total the fields.

You can use either of two types of grand summary: A *leading* grand summary appears above the information it summarizes; a *trailing* grand summary appears after the information it summarizes.

You must be in Layout view to add a grand summary part to your layout. To add the grand summary, follow these steps:

1. From the Layout menu, choose the layout to which you want to add a grand summary. Make sure you are in Layout view.

2. Choose Insert Part. The Insert Part dialog box appears.

3. Choose Leading Grand Summary or Trailing Grand Summary. This part is now added to the layout in the area that you indicated—either above the body or below.

4. Click and drag the field(s) that contain the grand summary total into the grand summary part.

5. Unlike the sub-summary, you do not need to sort to view the results. Go to Page view in the View menu or print the document. The part is only visible in Layout view. A trailing grand summary is shown in figure 14.16.

Deleting Parts

You can delete any optional part (any part other than the body) from your layout. To delete a part from your layout, delete or move to another part all the layout's fields, field names, graphics, text, and so on, and click the horizontal rule at the bottom of the part. Drag the rule up until it melds into the rule above. This is shown in figure 14.17. Release the mouse to remove the part.

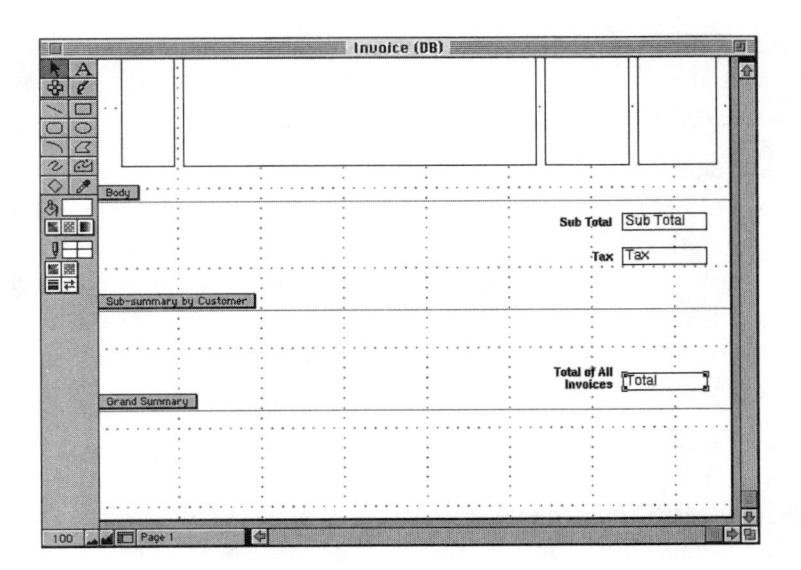

Figure 14.16
The Grand Summary at the bottom of this layout is called a Trailing Grand Summary.

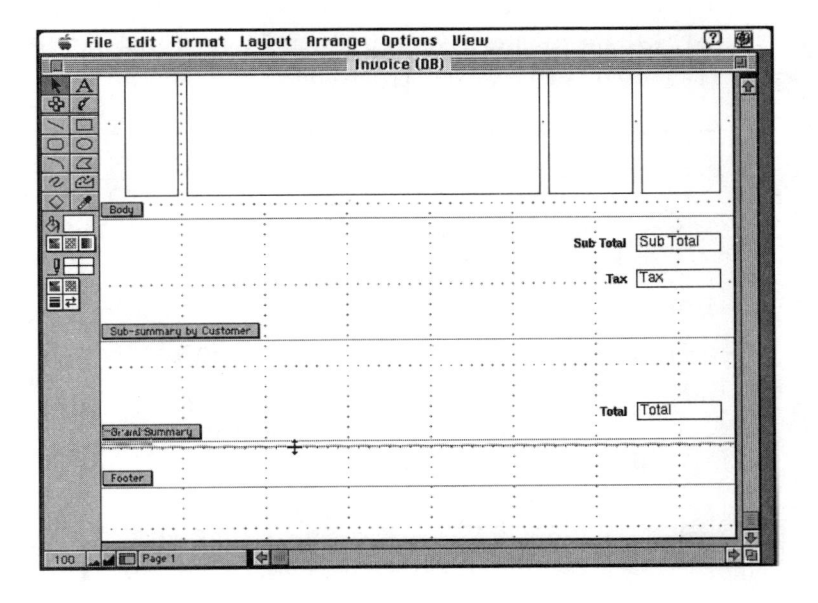

Figure 14.17
Delete all items within a part and move the lower horizontal rule up to remove a part from the layout.

Using the Graphics Tools in a Layout

Because Layout view is in the drawing module of ClarisWorks, you can use the drawing module tools right in your layout. You can add simple text or detailed corporate logos. You can place graphics in any of the parts of a layout and jazz them up with color and fill patterns. Use your imagination and let the graphics speak for you. Add icons to represent totals or shade the field boxes. Creating borders and outlines is simple, too.

Shading Fields

To draw attention to the important fields of a layout, try coloring or giving a fill pattern to the fields. Use the Fill palette to select a pattern or color that suits you. You cannot give a gradient fill to the fields, but you can add a different color or fill to a field. If you have both a Browse and a Layout view open, notice that the Browse view dynamically reflects the changes you make to these fields.

Outlining Fields

You also can color or fill the outline or border of a field. Choose a style from the Pen palette. If you don't like those styles of borders, you can create a border using the other tools of the drawing module. You can use the Line tool, the Rectangle tool, or the Polygon tool to create different types of borders. In figure 14.18 the palettes have been "torn off" and placed near the work area. The Polygon tool is used to create odd-shaped borders.

Figure 14.18
Use the Fill and Pen palettes to create emphasis in fields.

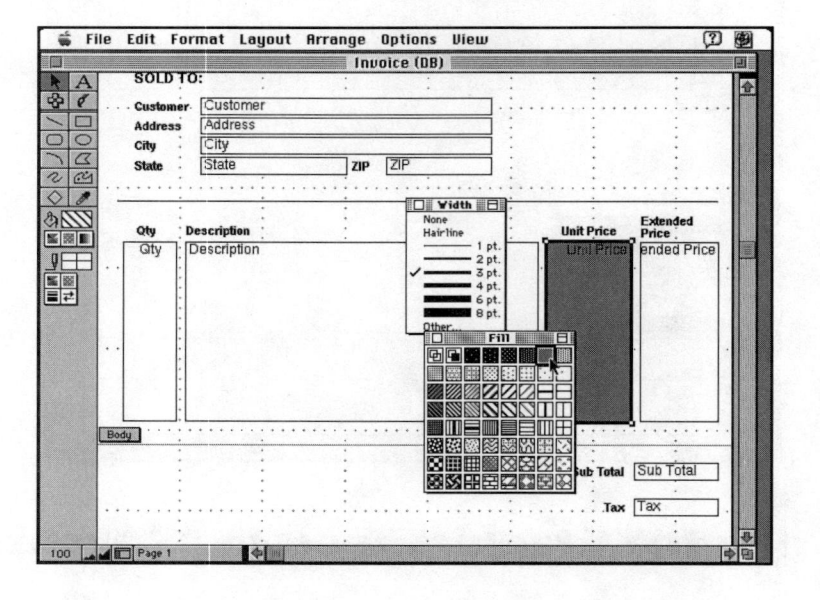

You make changes to the look of the database in Layout view with the drawing module tools. These changes affect all the records of the database. Changes made in the Browse view will only affect the current record on which you are working. Changes include everything from the font of the text to the alignment of the titles of the fields. For more information on editing in the drawing module, see Chapter 6, "Drawing."

Making Changes to Text

Your text's appearance is every bit as important as the graphics to the overall look of your layout. Bold text always draws the reader's eye. Italic adds mild inflection, large type practically jumps off the page, and all-caps text is said to "scream" at the reader. Use the Font, Size, Style, and Text Color menu options of the Format menu to change the attributes of text. If you need help working with text in the drawing module, refer to Chapter 6, "Drawing."

To change text attributes, select the text by clicking on it and go to the Format menu. Select the changes from the pop-up menus. All changes made to the text in Layout view will affect all records. To change the text attributes of only one record at a time, switch to the Browse view and make the changes in the same manner. You cannot change the attributes of the field title in the Browse view, only the data contained within a field.

Changing Text Attributes

When in Layout view, the field names and records are text items, and you edit them in the same manner that you edit any other text items created in the drawing module of ClarisWorks. The following steps detail the process for changing the attributes of the text (for more information on changing text attributes, see Chapter 3, "Working with Text"). Follow these steps to change the text attributes:

1. Choose Layout from the Layout menu if you are not already in Layout view.

2. Click on the field to which you wish to make text style changes. If you want to change more than one field at a time, click on the first field, then hold the Shift key down while clicking one at a time on the other fields to be changed. Selected fields will show small black square handles at each corner of the field box.

3. Go to the Format menu and the Font submenu to select an appropriate typeface (see fig. 14.19). When the menu is released, the new font is applied to the active field(s).

Figure 14.19
Use the Font submenu to change the typeface of selected text.

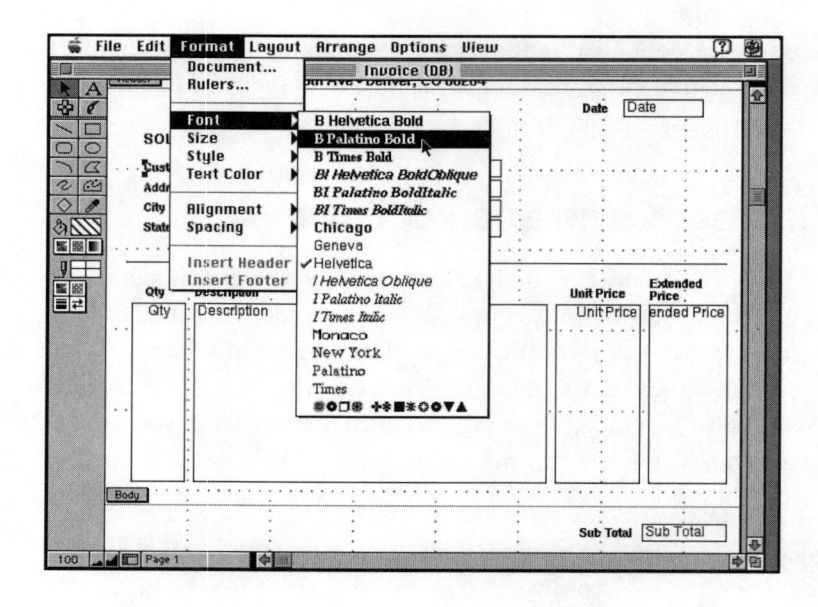

To change the font size, use these steps:

1. Choose Layout from the Layout menu, if you are not already in Layout view.

2. Click on the field to which you wish to make text style changes. If you want to change more than one field at a time, click on the first field, then hold the Shift key down while clicking one at a time on the other fields to be changed. Selected fields will show small black square handles at each corner of the field box.

3. Go to the Format menu and the Size submenu to select an appropriate type size. If the type size you want does not appear on the menu, choose the Other option. A dialog box appears like that shown in figure 14.20. Type in the desired size.

Tip
Use the key equivalent ⌘-Shift-O to quickly bring up the Size dialog box.

4. Click OK to apply the size.

You can choose only whole numbers for the point size. If you make the text larger than the box that contains the field name, you may need to adjust the box to accommodate the larger text.

Making Changes to Text   **309**

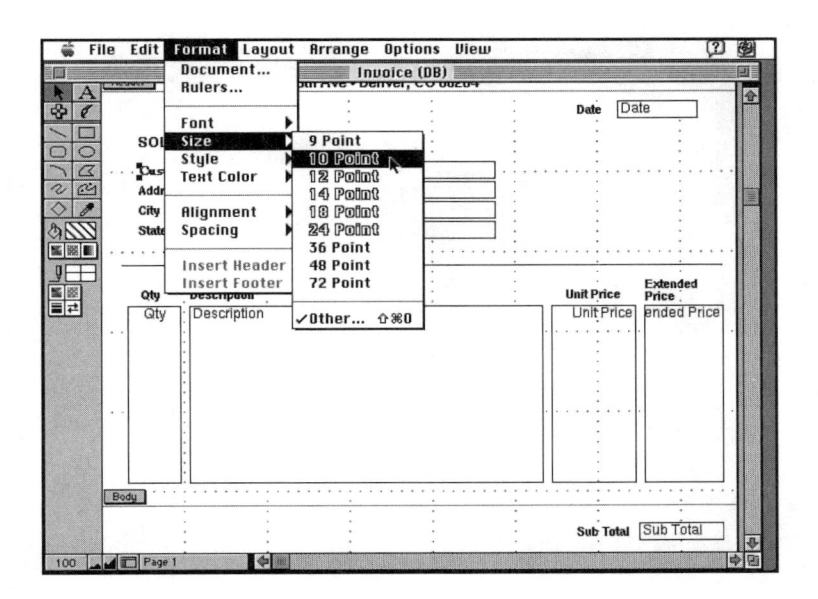

Figure 14.20
Use the Size submenu to change the height of the letters of selected text.

To change the color of the text, return to the Format menu and use the Text Color option. Follow these steps for changing the color of the text within a field or field title:

1. Choose Layout from the Layout menu if you are not already in Layout view.

2. Click on the field to which you wish to make text color changes. If you want to change more than one field at a time, click on the first field, then hold the Shift key down while clicking one at a time on the other fields to be changed. Selected fields will show small black square handles at each corner of the field box.

3. Select the color from the Format menu and the Text Color submenu. If you have a color monitor, you can choose colors from a displayed color palette like the one in figure 14.21. On a monochrome monitor, a short list of eight available colors appears. Either way, choose the color you want from the Text Color pop-up menu.

Use the Format menu to change the alignment and the line spacing of text in the layout. The alignment is to which edge of the field the text flushes. In *right-aligned* text, all text pushes up to the right edge. *Left-aligned* text, the default text alignment, is flush on the left edge. Change the alignment of a field or fields by selecting the fields and choosing Alignment from the Format menu.

Chapter 14—Enhancing the Presentation of Data

Figure 14.21
Use the Text Color menu to change the color of the selected text. This palette shows the colors available to a user on a color monitor.

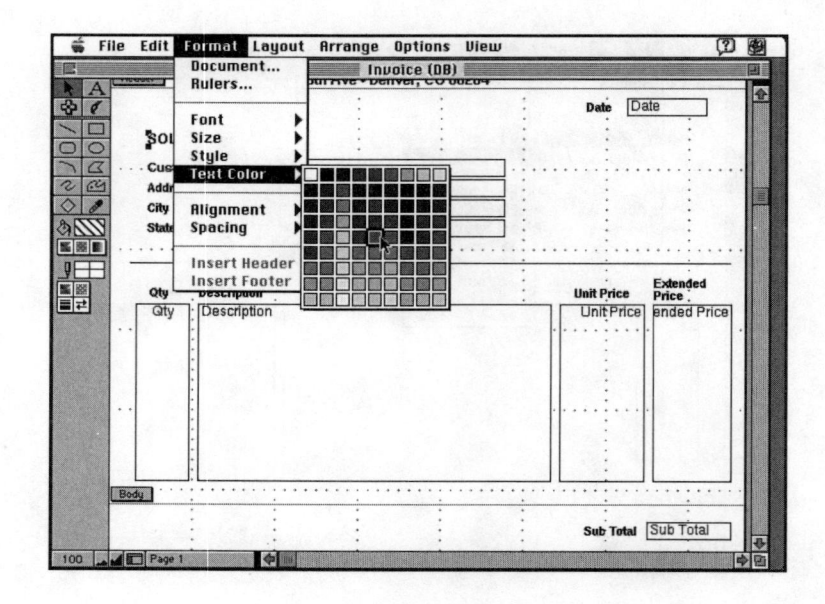

In figure 14.22 the column head Extended Price is two lines. The amount of space between these lines is the line spacing. Widen this space by choosing 1.5 or 2 from the Spacing submenu.

Figure 14.22
Use the Spacing options to change the amount of space between fields that contain two lines.

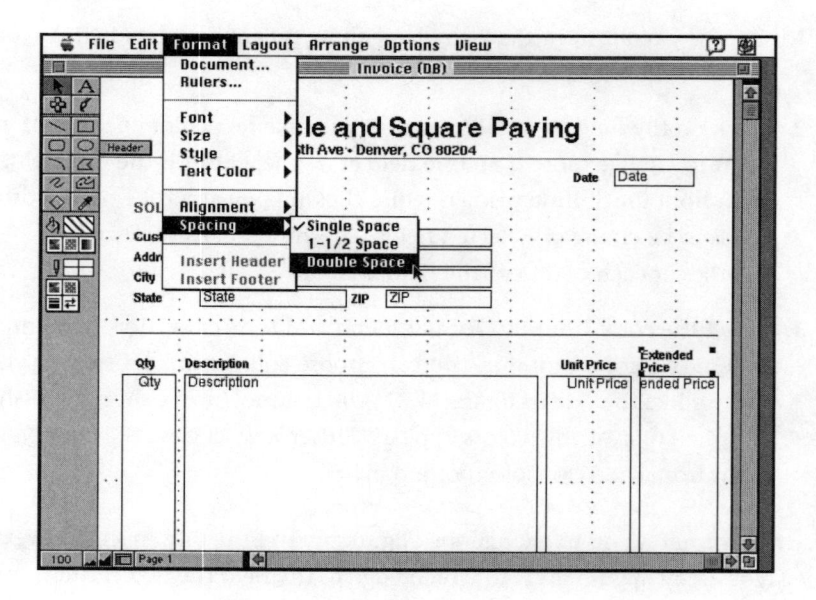

Changing the Tab Order of the Fields

One other method for making the layout somewhat more efficient is to change the tab order of the fields. The tab order determines in what order the cursor jumps from field to field when you press Tab. The default order is the order that the field was added to the new document when you first began. It might be more efficient to be able to tab directly to the most-used fields rather than in the order in which they were added. To change the tab order, follow these steps:

1. Choose Tab Order from the Layout menu. The dialog box that appears should look like the one shown in figure 14.23.

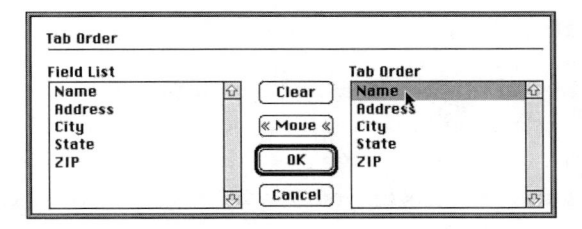

Figure 14.23
Use the Tab Order option to change in what order the Tab key travels the fields.

2. Insert the cursor in the Tab Order window and press Clear.

3. Double-click the field names in the Field List, working in the order you want the tab order to follow.

4. If you make a mistake, select just that field name and click <<Move<<.

5. Click OK to apply the new tab order.

Make sure that you are in Browse view and try inserting the cursor in the field in which you want to start and continue to press the Tab key. Watch which field the cursor jumps to with each tab. Does it follow the path you wanted? If not, go back to Tab Order and make the adjustments.

Troubleshooting Text Attribute Changes

I'd like to format all the field names to look the same. Do I have to do each one separately?

No. To change the text attributes of several fields at once, click the first field, then hold the Shift key down and click each of the other fields to be changed. Choose the attribute changes from the Format menu.

(continues)

> (continued)
>
> *When I make the text size bigger, it no longer fits in the field.*
>
> Click on the field to show the handles. Click and drag a handle to increase the size of the field. Hold the Shift key down to constrain the size change to either taller or wider.
>
> *My color palette doesn't contain all the colors that I see in the figures.*
>
> If you are working with a monochrome monitor, the color palette becomes a pop-up list of eight colors.

From Here...

Chapters 12, 13, and 14 guided you through the processes of creating database layouts. This chapter has introduced you to the more difficult tasks of creating finished layouts with formulas and formatting. You learn these skills best by putting them to work for you. Try different database layouts. You can expect to master the techniques in a very short time.

- Chapter 3, "Working with Text." This chapter will help reacquaint you with formatting text.

- Chapter 6, "Drawing." When working in Layout view, you are actually using the drawing module of ClarisWorks. Return to Chapter 6 for help with these tools.

- Chapter 15, "Creating Integrated Documents." Databases can contain mailing lists that can be merged with form letters and addressed automatically to each record of the database.

- Chapter 19, "Automating Your Work." Macros are a great way of simplifying repetitive tasks like entering data. This chapter will help you determine what can be automated and how to implement the tools.

Part IV

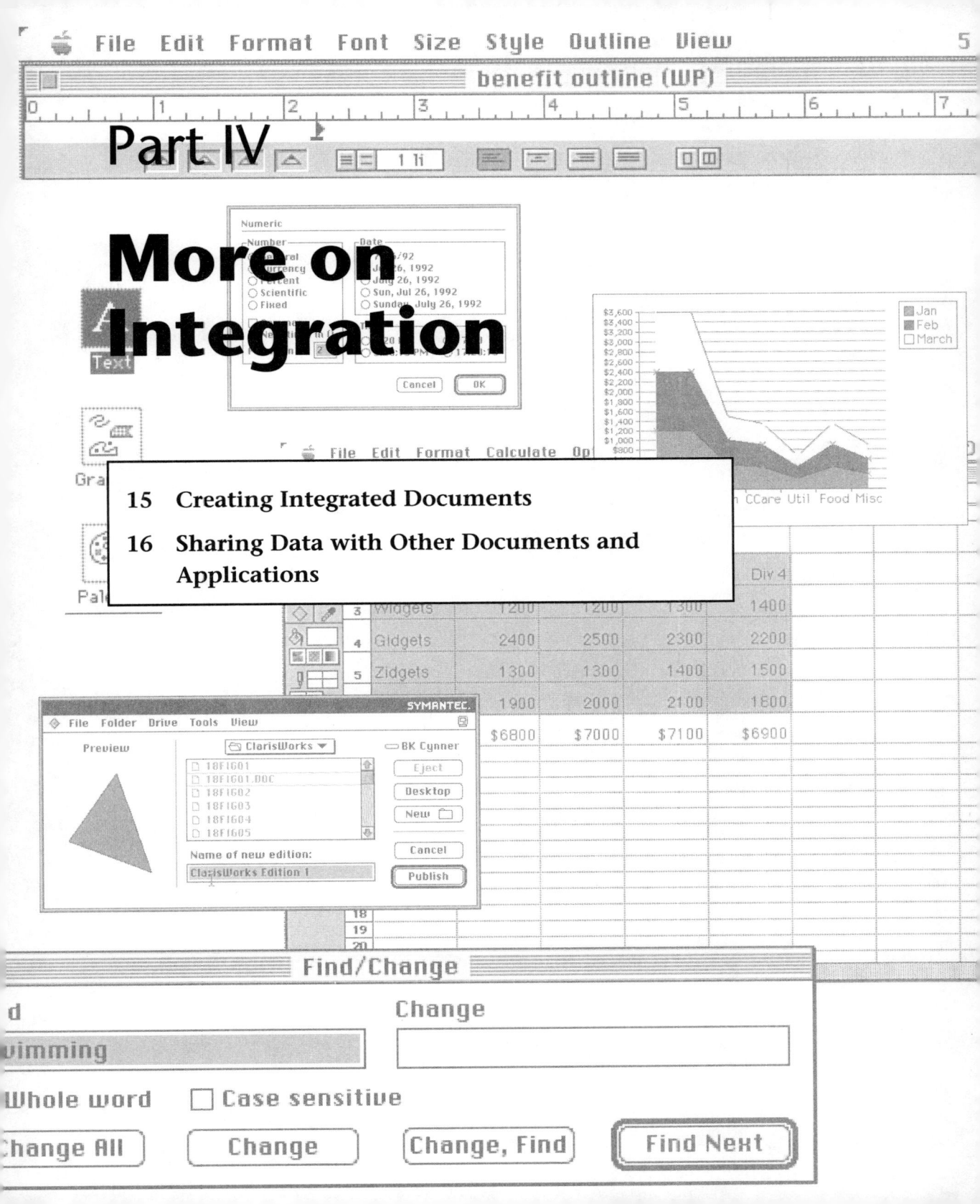

More on Integration

15 Creating Integrated Documents

16 Sharing Data with Other Documents and Applications

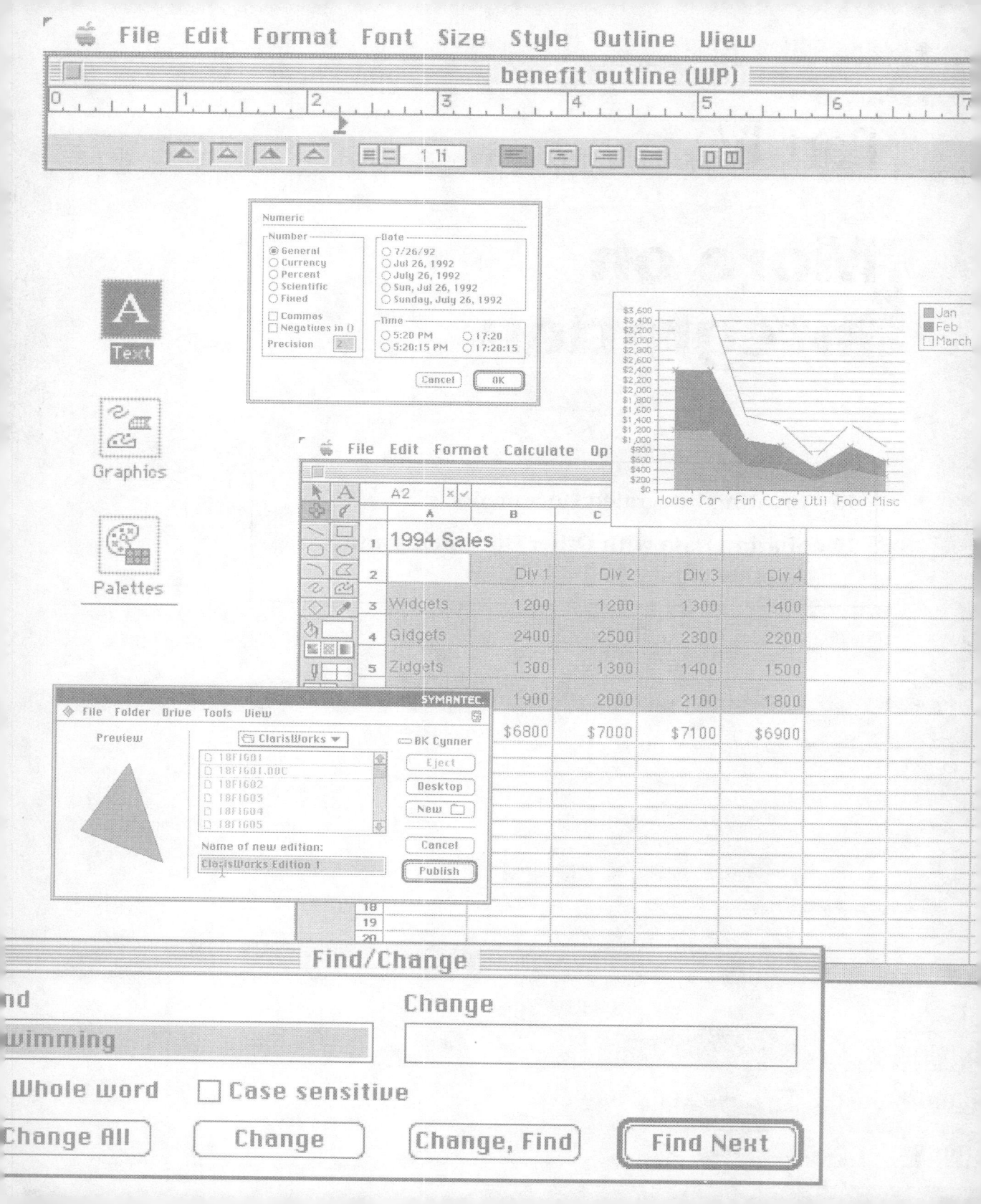

Chapter 15
Creating Integrated Documents

by Catherine Fishel Morris

There are several ways to combine information, or share information from one module to another, in ClarisWorks 2.1. One method is to create frames within a document. Another method is to import an existing file (whole or part) into the active, or current, document. You can also share and update information across several documents and formats using Publish and Subscribe (see Chapter 16, "Sharing Data with Other Documents and Applications").

In this chapter, you learn the following:

- How to create and link frames
- How to create a form letter and save it as Stationery
- How to merge database information with text
- How to import graphics
- How to create a slide presentation

Using Frames in a Document

One of the best features of ClarisWorks 2.1 is the convenience and ease you have placing a frame of one module into another module. This means you can be working in a spreadsheet format, and draw a text frame to comment on the figures or draw attention to a particular aspect of the spreadsheet. You can be in a word processing document and decide to enhance your text by adding a painting frame. You can create a spreadsheet, graph, or painting

Tip
To get handles on a text frame you create in a word processing document, you need to select the drawing tool and click the text, as the frame is hidden.

frame in the word processing module. You can make text, spreadsheet, and painting frames in the drawing module. You can produce text and painting frames in a spreadsheet to go with a graph as well as the data information. You can link text, painting, or spreadsheet frames to spill over from one page to another, and even create a text frame in a text document. Figure 15.1 shows what kinds of frames you can make in the different modules of ClarisWorks.

Figure 15.1
One document with several frames.

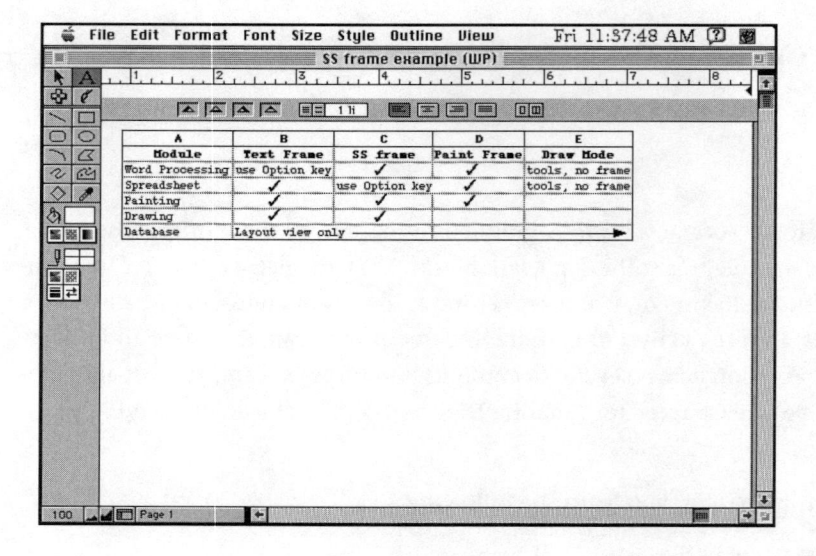

Module	Text Frame	SS frame	Paint Frame	Draw Mode
Word Processing	use Option key	✓	✓	tools, no frame
Spreadsheet	✓		✓	tools, no frame
Painting	✓	use Option key	✓	
Drawing	✓	✓	✓	
Database	Layout view only			

Adding a Frame to a Document

You can add a frame at any time and anywhere within the documents shown in the spreadsheet frame above. Working with a text or spreadsheet frame in the painting module is somewhat different from working with frames in other modules. Creating the frame, and having the painting tools available while working within the frame, is just the same. When you finish a frame in the painting module and click outside the frame, there will be no handles as there are in other modules. That is because once you deselect anything in the painting environment, it becomes an image, rather than an object (see Chapter 7, "Painting," for an explanation of the difference between images and objects). Figure 15.2 shows the environment tools and what kind of frame each can create.

Click this to select frames and drawings   Creates a text frame

Creates a spreadsheet frame   Creates a painting frame

Figure 15.2
The environment tools create or help select and edit frames.

Follow these steps to add a frame:

1. While working in a document, select the appropriate environment tool to create the frame you need.

2. Place the pointer at the upper left corner where you want the frame to begin. Drag the mouse diagonally down and to the right. Let go of the mouse button when the frame is the size you want.

3. With the handles visible, you can resize the frame, move the frame, and copy and paste the frame.

4. The menu (and tool palette, if you create a painting frame) now displays the options available to the frame's environment, and the frame is ready to receive information. Figure 15.3 shows examples of what environment tool is used to create the frame.

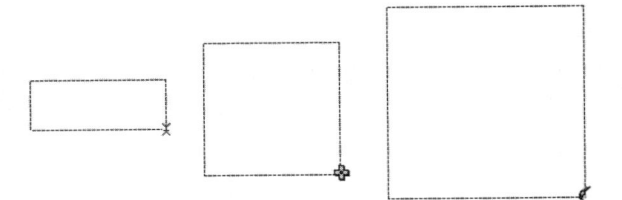

Tip
To create a text frame in a word processing document, hold down the Option key as you drag the text tool to form the frame.

Figure 15.3
Frames created by different environment tools.

Moving between the Frame and Document

If the handles show on the frame, you have the frame's tools available and you can work with and edit within the frame. With a frame present in a document, but no handles showing, you can work in the document's environment and with the main document's tools. Just clicking the mouse switches you from one environment to another.

- To make a frame active in order to resize, move, or copy, click anywhere in the frame.

- To edit within the frame, double-click anywhere in the frame. The pointer changes, as does the menu bar (and the tools, if you have a painting frame).

- To return to the main document, click outside the frame. The pointer and menu (and the painting tools, if a painting document is the main document) change to the main document's environment.

Working with an Open Frame

When you create a painting or spreadsheet frame you see the size you draw. Actually, what you see is only a portion of the available spreadsheet frame. You can see a whole view of a spreadsheet by selecting the frame, then choosing Open Frame from the View menu. This allows you to work in as many columns and rows as you need. It also lets you create a chart within the spreadsheet data frame. It allows you to rearrange the information to fit into linked frames. When you finish, click the spreadsheet's close box. This brings you back to the main document, with the frame at the original size you made. If all the data you entered is not in view, you can resize the spreadsheet (clicking once with the arrow pointer so handles appear), and then size it to accommodate all the information you want to show.

You can view a full window of a painting frame in the same manner. The difference is that when you get the open view, the size of the work space is exactly the same size as the frame you create. You are able to manipulate the picture (copy it and paste it outside the frames) which makes editing possible. To get out of the open view, click the window's close box.

> **Caution**
> You cannot use the Open Frame command when you are working with a text frame.

Creating a Chart from a Spreadsheet Frame

Just as you can make a chart, or graph, from spreadsheet document information, you can also make a chart from spreadsheet frame data within a word processing document. Although you can create a spreadsheet frame, you cannot use that data to make a chart in a painting document.

You can place the chart within the spreadsheet frame, or, as shown in figure 15.4, position it as the separate object it is. You can place the spreadsheet data on top of the chart (select the data, and then choose Move to Front from the Arrange menu). Making a chart from data in a spreadsheet frame is similar to making a chart from document data. Be sure to have the tools available in case you want to edit the chart's color, pattern, or gradient.

Using Frames in a Document   **319**

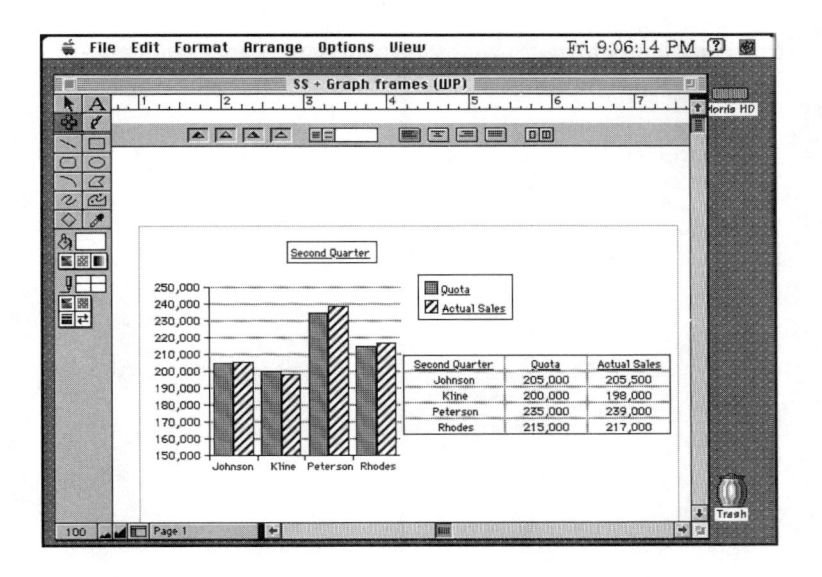

Figure 15.4
Chart created from spreadsheet data.

Follow these steps to create a chart from the data in a spreadsheet frame:

1. Double-click the spreadsheet frame. The pointer becomes the spreadsheet tool icon. (If the frame was already selected when you double-clicked it, you see the Number Format dialog box. Click Cancel to close this dialog box.)

2. If you want the chart to appear inside the spreadsheet, choose Open Frame from the View menu.

3. With the spreadsheet icon, highlight the data to be charted.

4. Choose Make Chart from the Options menu, and select the type of chart, the kinds of labels, and the other options you want in your chart. You can use the shortcut icons (Show Shortcuts submenu) to create bar, pie, area, and line charts.

5. You can change the default colors used in the chart by selecting (one click) any of the Series Name boxes and choosing a different color, pattern, or gradient from the Fill Indicator.

6. Click OK.

You can change the default display choices of a frame, such as showing the grid, headings, and so on, as shown in figure 15.5, the same way you do for a

320 Chapter 15—Creating Integrated Documents

spreadsheet document. Figure 15.6 shows the same data as figure 15.5, but without the grid and headings.

Figure 15.5
Spreadsheet frame with cell grid, column, and row headings visible.

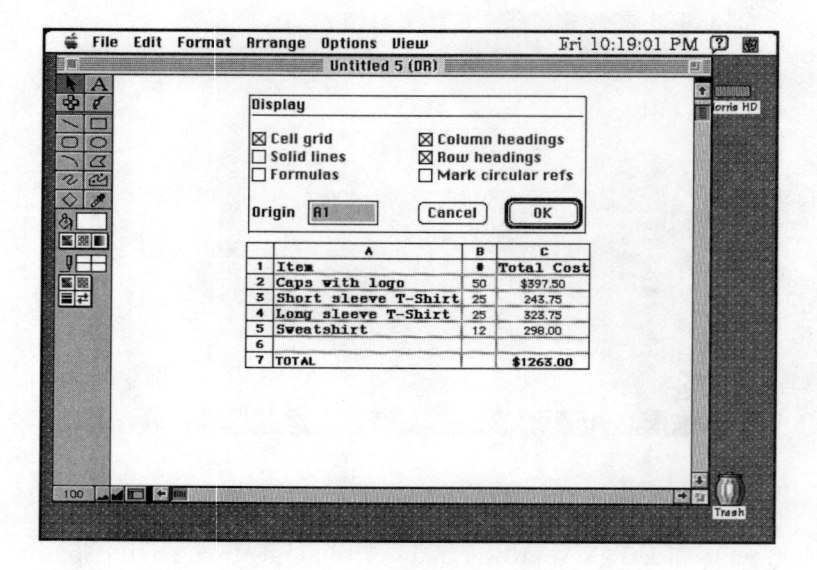

Figure 15.6
Spreadsheet frame with cell grid, column, and row headings removed.

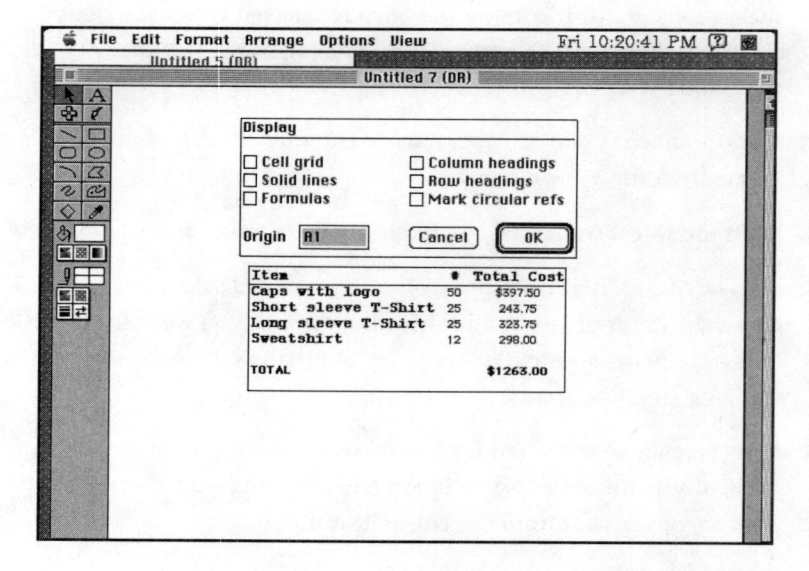

To make changes to how you display the spreadsheet information, follow these steps:

1. If the spreadsheet icon is not the active tool, double-click the frame to make it active.

2. Choose Modify Frame from the Options menu.

3. Make your choices of how you want the frame to appear.

4. Click OK.

Linking Frames

Being able to link pieces of information gives you the control to show parts of your informational data exactly where it will be most effective. For example, you can have a spreadsheet data frame on one page of a word processing document and a chart, giving an interpretation of that data, on another page. Of course, by linking these two spreadsheet parts, the chart reflects immediately any editing changes you make to the spreadsheet data.

The kind of linked frame you make determines how you display the document information. Both spreadsheet and painting frames show portions of the same document, depending on how you size each frame. If your painting document consists of a man looking at a delicious-smelling pie, you can break that into two frames, each having one graphic (see fig. 15.7). Text, on the other hand, "flows" from one frame to another, using as many frames as necessary until there is no more text.

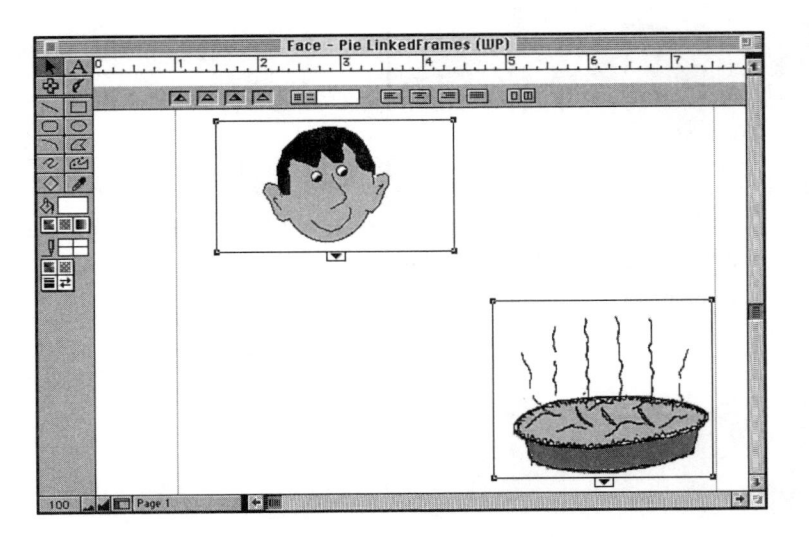

Tip
You can remove the rectangular border from a frame by selecting the frame and choosing the Transparent icon in Fill Patterns, choosing white in the Pen Color box, or choosing None in Line Widths.

Figure 15.7
Linked painting frames.

Tip
When you link painting or spreadsheet frames, it is best if the information in the original frame flows downward rather than across. Frames insert information in a vertical flow.

Linked and unlinked frames can coexist within the same document. You cannot link one existing frame to another. Nor can you link different kinds of information (i.e., text and spreadsheet frames). Once done, you treat a linked frame as an object which you can resize and move around just as you can an individual frame.

Linking Text Frames

Linking large bodies of text in order to create a newsletter, for example, gives you a different flexibility than just using the word processor and setting up page columns. It allows you to determine the heights and widths of individual columns so they can vary from one to another. The lack of standardization allows you a variety of ways to arrange your text as well as any charts or graphics you want to include. Follow these steps:

1. In a new drawing document (or Layout view of a database file), choose Frame Links from the Options menu.

2. Select the text tool. Starting at the top left, drag the tool diagonally and down until the frame reaches the desired size.

3. Click outside the frame. A Top-of-frame indicator, handles at each corner, and a bottom Continue indicator all appear with the frame.

4. Click the Continue indicator and draw another frame. The first frame is now hidden. If you want to see it, press the Shift key and click in the area where the frame is drawn. When more than one frame is showing, the bottom indicator becomes the Link indicator and Top-of-frame indicator on the second frame. Figure 15.8 shows the linked frames, with their handles and indicators.

5. Repeat steps 3 through 5 until you have all the necessary frames.

6. If you need the same frame layout for reuse (i.e., a monthly newsletter format), save the linked, blank frames as a stationery file. (See Chapter 2, "Learning the Essentials," for information on how to set up a stationery document.)

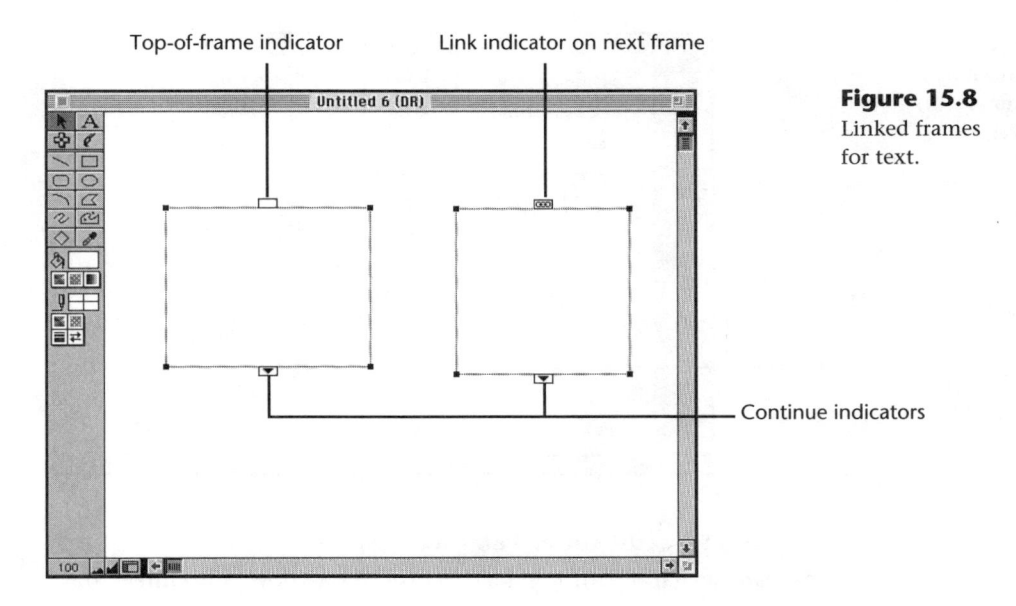

Top-of-frame indicator   Link indicator on next frame

Figure 15.8
Linked frames for text.

Continue indicators

Once you set up the blank, linked frames, you are ready to create the text right in the frame, or bring in a text document. No matter whether you key in the text or bring it in from another file, you must have the text pointer active and the Insert icon flashing where you want the first text to appear in the frame. When the first frame is full, the text automatically goes into the second frame. When that fills up, the text goes into the third frame, and so forth. Figure 15.9 shows there is more text than fits in the available frames.

There are several things you can do if there is more text than frames:

- You can create more linked frames.

- You can change the width of the frames by dragging on a handle, thereby accommodating more text per frame.

- You can make the text font smaller by choosing Select All from the Edit menu. With all your text highlighted, select Size and position the arrow pointer at a point size smaller than what you are using, or choose Other to key in a size option not available.

Figure 15.9
Linked text frames with overflow indicator.

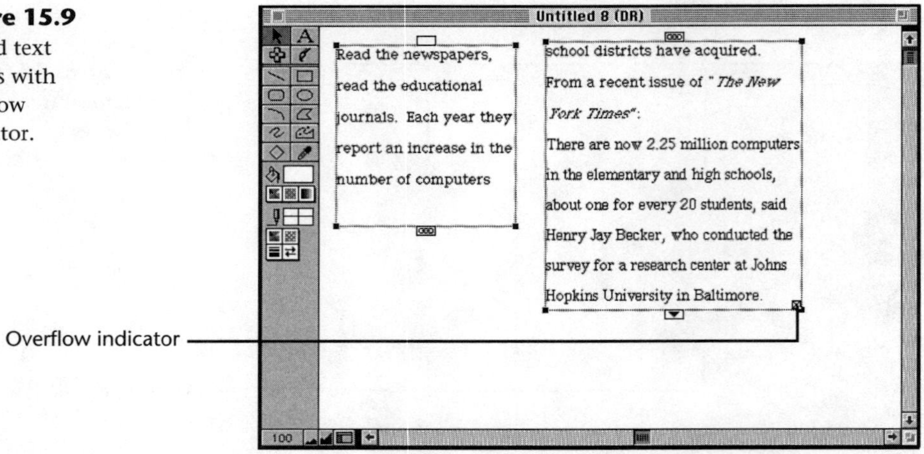

Overflow indicator

Linking Spreadsheet or Painting Frames

Spreadsheet and painting documents do not "flow" into linked frames the way text does. There will be no indicator at the top letting you know a frame is the next frame and no indicator telling you there is more data than fits into the last frame. It may seem as if the spreadsheet or painting frames are not really linked. But indeed they are.

You know a spreadsheet frame is linked if you make changes in the data frame, and changes also occur in the chart frame, regardless of how many pages separate the two frames in the document. Figure 15.10 shows linked painting frames. You can tell they are linked because when the fill was applied on one frame, it affected the two others. The "spill-over" changes (such as changing a color, gradient, or pattern over a large area) that take place in linked painting frames depend on where the enclosed areas are in the original painting.

There is another difference between spreadsheet and painting frames and text frames. With spreadsheet and painting frames, you need to use information which already exists. You cannot create a linked frame and then place data or pictures in it as you can with text. However, you can create a frame and then decide to "subdivide" or link it. Using an open frame, as shown in figure 15.11, is a way to deal with this problem.

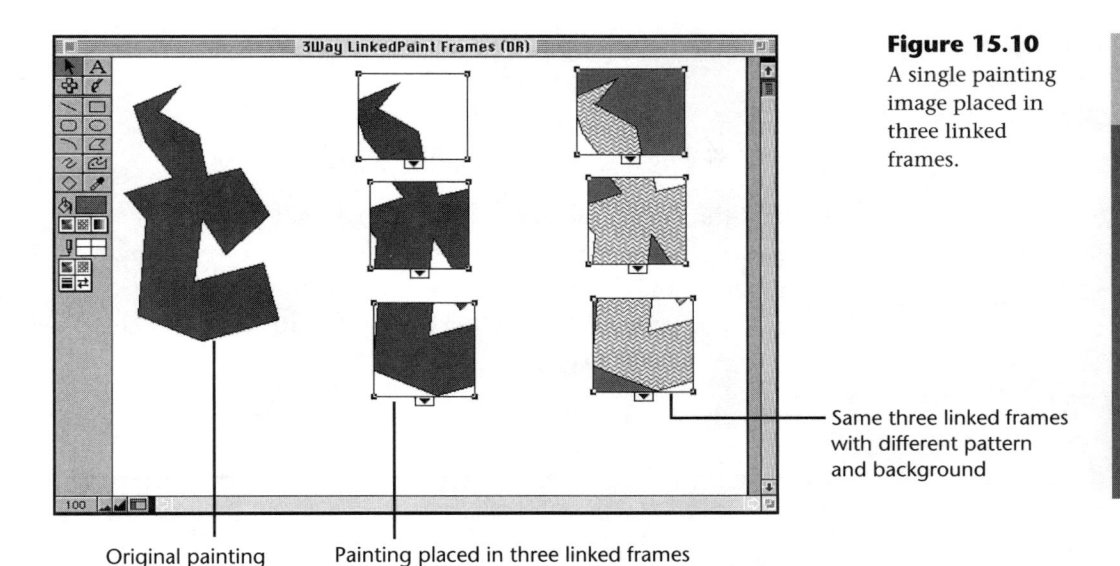

Figure 15.10
A single painting image placed in three linked frames.

Same three linked frames with different pattern and background

Original painting   Painting placed in three linked frames

You can also use the open frame when you want to import data from an existing file and place it into a frame. Follow these steps:

1. If the tools are not visible, click the Show/Hide Tools control at the bottom left of the document or choose Show Tools in the View menu.

2. If you are using a spreadsheet or painting frame that already exists in the document, select it with the arrow pointer so handles are visible.

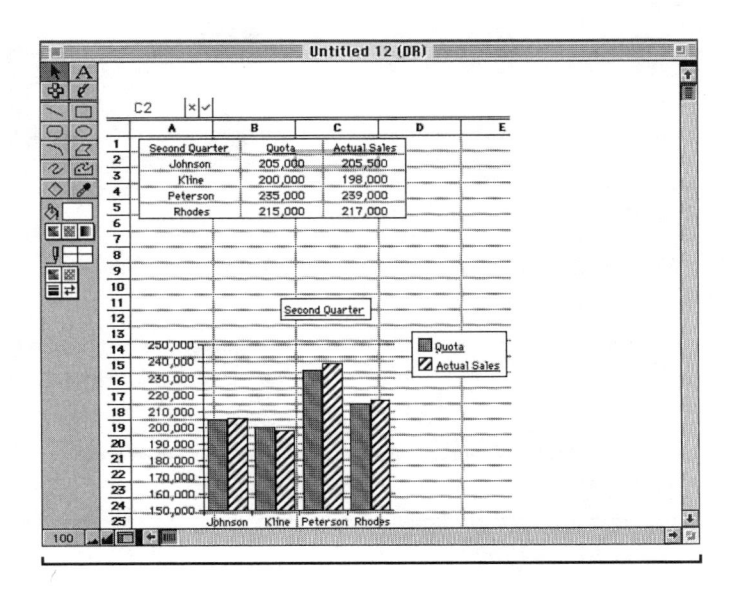

Figure 15.11
Spreadsheet frame in Open Frame view.

Chapter 15—Creating Integrated Documents

3. Choose Frame Links from the Options menu.

4. Click the Continue indicator and make another frame.

5. Add as many frames as you need by repeating step 4.

Tip
To add individual frames once you have linked frames, go back to the Options menu and deselect Frame Links.

6. Resize and move the frames to fit the data and place the frames appropriately within your document. You may need to reposition the information in the original document. You can choose Modify Frame from the Options menu. You will get a full-page view of the frame document, and editing will be easier (see fig. 15.12).

7. Click the document's close box to get back to the linked frame.

Figure 15.12
How the linked spreadsheet frames appear in a word processing document.

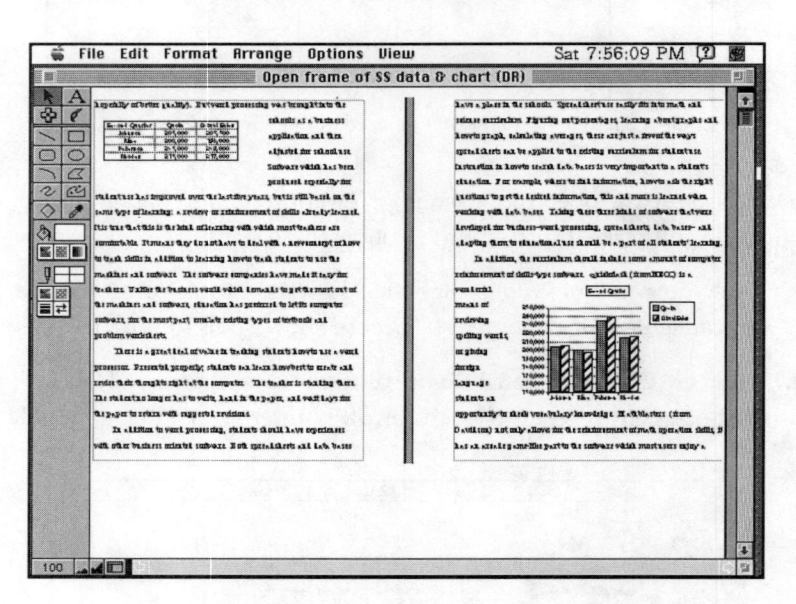

Troubleshooting Linked Frames

When I paste my copied text into the linked frames I set up, it comes in as an object, and does not flow into the linked frames.

After you create the linked frames, you must select the Text tool, and click with that tool in the first box where you want the information to begin. Then you can use the Paste command to bring it in.

I can't get my spreadsheet and chart positioned correctly into the linked frames so I get the views I want of each.

> Choose Modify Frame from the Options menu. This gives you the whole view of the spreadsheet. You can reposition your data. Be sure to place the data vertically (not horizontally). Click the close box to return to the frames within the document. You can go back and forth between views as often as necessary to position information in each frame the way you want.
>
> *I cannot make a text frame in a text document.*
>
> Hold down the Option key and then drag the Text tool to the size of the frame you want.

Combining Text, Graphics, and Spreadsheets in a Document

Integrating the various pieces from different modules does not mean having to open and close several documents to copy and paste from one file to another. With System 7.0 and above, three or four documents (depending on the amount of RAM in your computer and the amount of memory allocated to ClarisWorks) can be open at one time, allowing easy access to each and all of them.

The more you use ClarisWorks 2.1, the more possibilities you will discover for integrating one aspect of the software into another.

Working with More Than One Document

You can have several documents open and available for use at one time. The number of open documents that is possible depends on the amount of RAM installed in your machine. At the Finder (the opening screen showing the folders of software loaded onto the hard drive), you can choose About This Macintosh from the apple menu. The Total Memory number lets you know the amount of RAM in your particular machine.

Even though you may have three or four open documents, only one is active, or current, at a time. It is the active document which you can edit, add new information to, move, and resize. As you see in figure 15.13, it is easy to tell which is the active document; the ribbed lines all across the title bar are visible. Any other documents which are open show a plain white title bar with the file name in the center.

Figure 15.13
Active and inactive open documents.

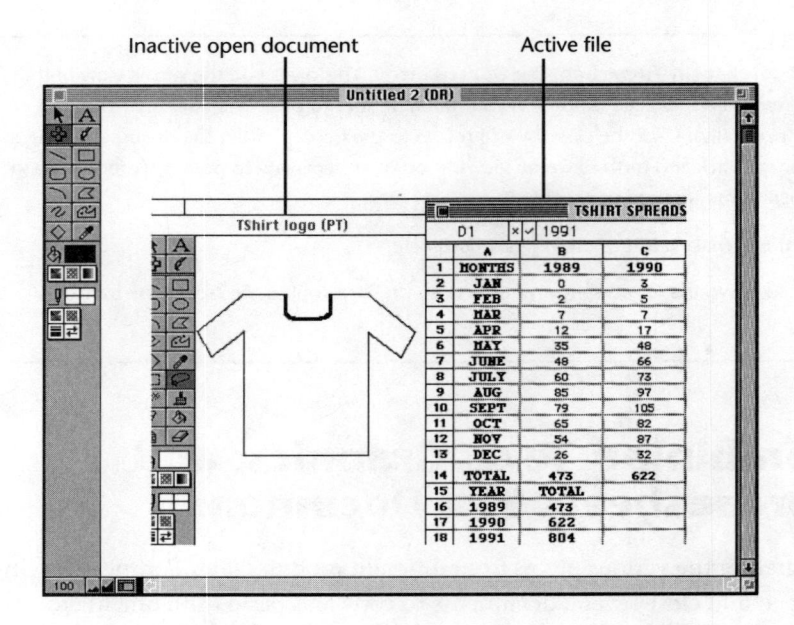

Inactive open document — *Active file*

You can move from one document to another by clicking anywhere on a document, thereby making a different document the active one. Use the resizer square at the bottom right border to vary the size of each open document. Click the title bar to reposition the document on the screen. That way, when you want to pick a different document to work with, you will be able to see at least some part of it in order to click it. Figure 15.14 shows another method of choosing a document to become active: select the icon at the top right of the screen with the arrow pointer, and position the pointer on the program you want to be active.

Figure 15.14
Desktop icon listing active and open programs.

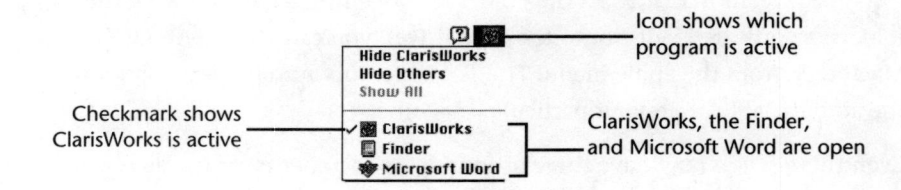

Checkmark shows ClarisWorks is active

Icon shows which program is active

ClarisWorks, the Finder, and Microsoft Word are open

Combining Text, Graphics, and Spreadsheets in a Document **329**

Combining Graphics and Spreadsheets with Text Documents

You can create and save your own graphics by working in the drawing or painting module and combining them with a ClarisWorks text file. You can also import graphics from other sources: clip-art disks, scanners, the Scrapbook (in the apple menu), and certain fonts (for example, Cairo, Mobile, and Dingbats). Even other software programs that you may install on your hard drive (for example, PrintShop, KidPix, and HyperCard) have clip art that you can copy and bring into a ClarisWorks document.

Figure 15.15 shows a graphic in a painting document that needs to be copied into a word processing document.

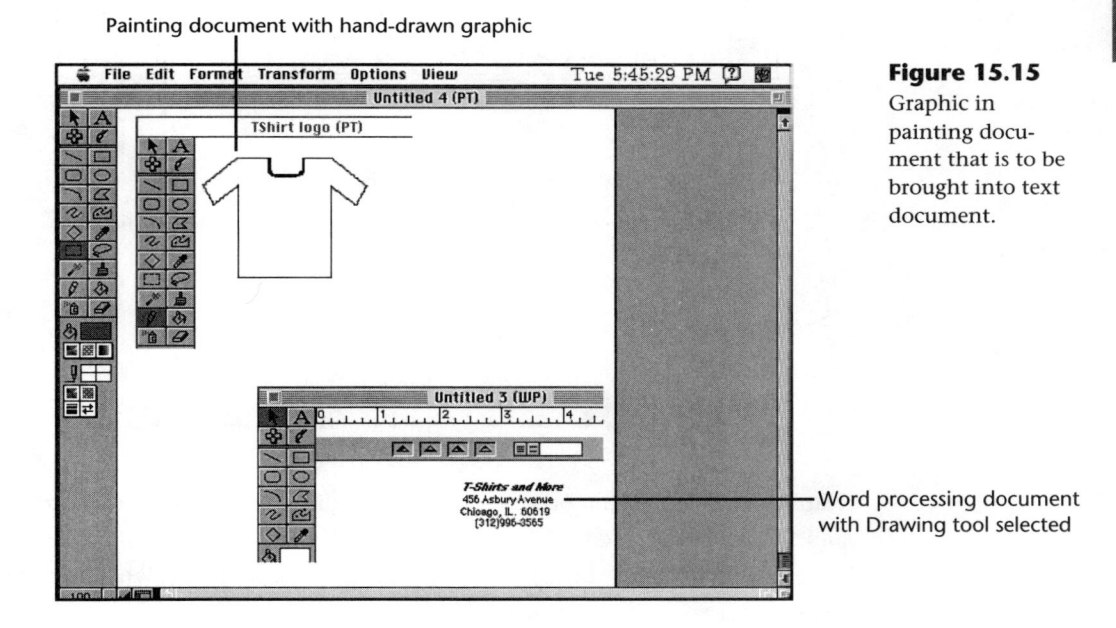

Figure 15.15
Graphic in painting document that is to be brought into text document.

The following steps show you how to place a graphic into a document:

1. Be sure that the tool palette is open in the word processing document and the Drawing tool is selected.

2. Open the file, or activate it by clicking anywhere on the document in which the graphic you want to copy resides.

3. Use either the Selection Rectangle or Lasso tool and select the graphic. (See Chapter 7 for an explanation of the differences between these two selection tools.)

4. Choose Copy from the Edit menu.

5. Click anywhere on the word processing file to make it active. If you forgot to select the Drawing tool, do so now.

6. Choose Paste from the Edit menu. The graphic appears in the word processing document (see fig. 15.16). With the handles visible, you can place it anywhere in the document or resize it.

Figure 15.16
Graphic brought into the word processing document. Handles show it can be moved and resized.

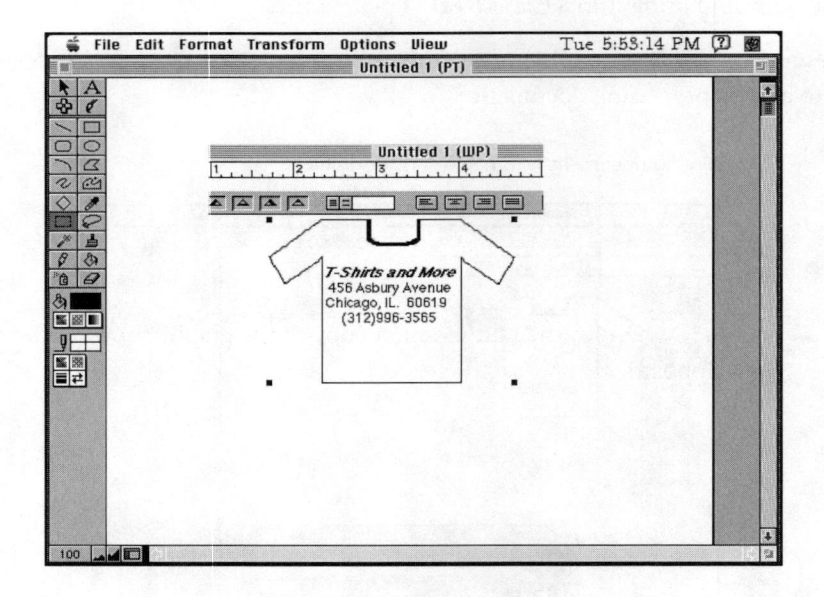

Graphics can come from other sources. Depending on what kind of file the graphic is saved as (PICT, TIFF, EPS), you may think you are unable to access it. No files may appear initially in the Open dialog box. To see what graphic files exist, change the Document Types setting to Painting (see fig. 15.17).

Figure 15.17
You can open any of the graphics files when Document Type is set to Painting.

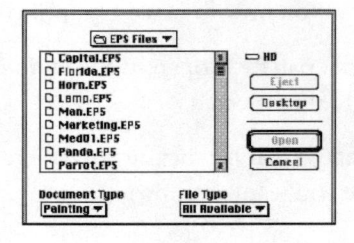

Using Graphics from Another Source

You can buy graphics disks and CDs with a variety of pictures. Looking through any discount catalog, you will find a wide selection of choices ranging from one-subject disks (for example, business clip art, holidays, sports, and so on) to a little bit of everything. Software that you already own can be another source of premade graphics. The following steps show how to copy a graphic from another source:

1. Choose Open from the File menu.

2. Select the disk or software program on the hard or floppy disk drive which contains the graphic. If you are unable to access the individual graphics in the Open menu, change the Document Type setting to Painting.

3. Select the graphic by pointing and clicking, highlighting, or using the Selection Rectangle or Lasso tool, if available.

4. Choose Copy from the Edit menu. A copy of the graphic now resides on the Clipboard.

Using Graphics from the Apple Menu. Under the apple menu, both the Key Caps and the Scrapbook commands give you access to graphics that you can include in your documents. Take a look at the Key Caps. Holding down one of the special keys, such as Option, or a combination of keys changes some of the letters on the keyboard to icons. This is how you can copy one of these icons from the Key Caps:

1. Choose Key Caps from the apple menu. Keying in a letter with the Option, ⌘, or Shift key, as well as combinations of those keys, replaces the alphabetic letter with an icon. Only certain keys show icons (i.e., holding the Option key and the number 4 key give you the cent sign).

2. Key in the icon.

3. Highlight the icon that appears in the writing bar.

4. Choose Copy from the Edit menu.

5. Close Key Caps by clicking its close box. A copy of the graphic now resides on the Clipboard.

332 Chapter 15—Creating Integrated Documents

A graphic can be copied to the Clipboard and pasted into any ClarisWorks document by selecting the Copy and Paste commands from the Edit menu. For further information regarding cutting, copying, and pasting, see Chapter 2, "Learning the Essentials."

The Scrapbook comes with seven pictures, including the graphic on the invitation shown in figure 15.18. You can add more, but remember, the Scrapbook is located in your System folder. Anything you add to the Scrapbook will take up System memory.

Follow these steps to copy and paste a Scrapbook graphic into a document:

1. Choose Scrapbook from the apple menu.
2. Go through the Scrapbook pictures by clicking the bottom scroll bar.
3. At the picture you want, choose Copy from the Edit menu.
4. Click the close box when you finish. A copy of the graphic now resides in the Clipboard, from which you can paste the graphic into a document.

Tip
Instead of going to the Edit menu for copy and paste commands, you can use keyboard commands: ⌘-C will copy a selected object or text, ⌘-V will paste the object or text.

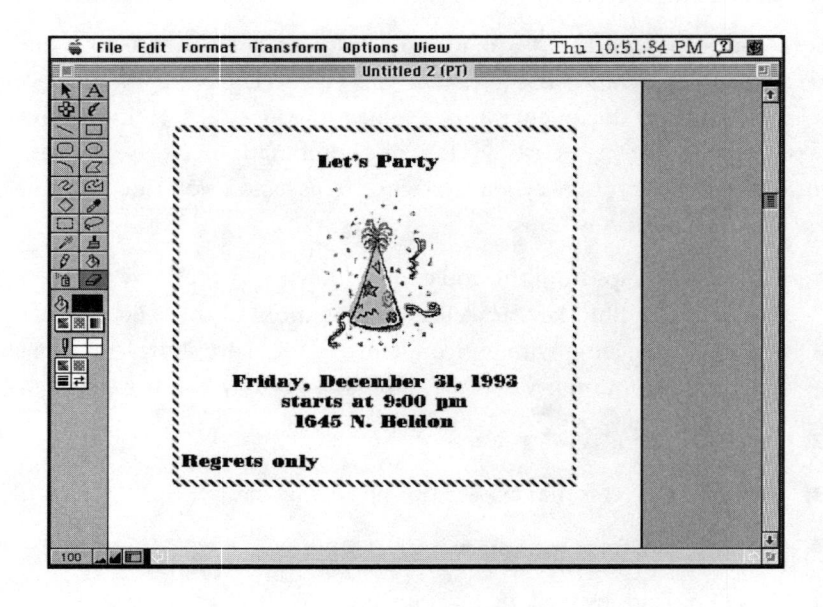

Figure 15.18
Scrapbook graphic copied and pasted into a word processing document.

Using Graphics from Fonts. Several fonts come with the Macintosh System. Two of them, Cairo and Mobile, show icons when you key in the characters. There is one set of icons for lowercase and one set for uppercase (see fig. 15.19).

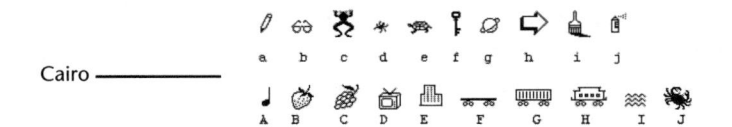

Cairo

Mobile

Figure 15.19
Examples of uppercase and lowercase fonts.

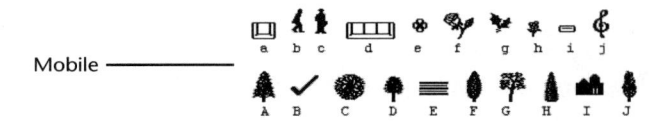

You can buy additional font packages, which may have a font similar in nature to Cairo and Mobile. This is how you can copy from one of these fonts:

1. Change the font to Cairo, Mobile, or any other font you have whose letters become icons.

2. Key in the icon you want, and highlight it.

3. Choose Copy from the Edit menu. A copy of the graphic now resides on the Clipboard.

Caution

There is only room to copy one graphic to the Clipboard at a time. If you use the Copy command a second time, you overwrite the first graphic with the second.

Troubleshooting Graphics

Why does my graphic come into a spreadsheet or text document with no handles?

Before you paste a copy of a graphic (or spreadsheet data, chart, or any text) you must choose the drawing tool and then choose Paste from the Edit menu. Only then will handles be available for moving and resizing the object.

(continues)

Tip
To save any graphic for use again, place a copy of it in the Scrapbook. Select the graphic, use the Copy command, open the Scrapbook, and use the Paste command.

> (continued)
>
> *When I have three or four documents open at the same time, I can't always find the one I want in order to make it the active document. How do I find it?*
>
> Click the Finder icon at the far right end of the menu bar. Highlight the program Application menu in which your file is created. When you let go of the mouse button, the file will come to the forefront of all the open documents.

Making a Slide Presentation

ClarisWorks 2.1 lets you place information from several documents together into one document (using Copy and Paste) so you can present them in a slide-show format. By plugging the computer into an LCD panel or large monitor, you have the capacity to enhance a speech or present a new product with visuals, illustrate a lesson, have a self-running demonstration, or show the results of a research project.

Any kind of document can become part of a slide show, except a document created in the communications module. Which module you use to create the slide show will depend on what is to be included. Keep in mind that if you are going to have multiple slides in a painting document, you may need more than the default memory allotted to ClarisWorks. Check your ClarisWorks Installation Guide, if necessary.

There is one slide for each page within the document. Before you begin to set up the slides, you will want to go through the document and make sure pages end where you want. You can always force the end of a page by choosing Insert Break from the Format menu. Once you have the document complete, creating the slide presentation takes just a few steps:

1. Open the document from which you will make the slides.

2. Choose Slide Show from the View menu. The Slide Show dialog box appears (see fig. 15.20).

There are a number of decisions you need to make to format the look of your slide show:

- You can rearrange the order of the pages by clicking the double arrow pointer on a page and dragging it to another position.

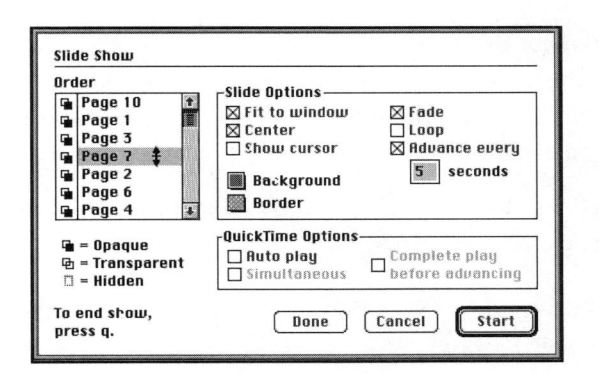

Figure 15.20
The Slide Show dialog box.

- All pages default to the Opaque view. You can change any one to Transparent (see-through effect to overlay one page on another, as in building a model), or a page can be Hidden. Click the Opaque icon to change to Transparent, click again to change from Transparent to Hidden, and click one more time to get back to Opaque.

- Decide which choices you want in the Slide Options section. One click in a box either removes a default X or places an X in the box to choose it. If you place an X in the Advance Every box, you may want to highlight the Seconds box and place a different number. Any number from 1 to 60 is acceptable.

- Click the Background box to change the default color of the background. In this case, Background means the white area of the page your information is on. Lighter colors work better if there is any amount of text.

- If you want a border around the page, click the Border box and then make your choice.

- To include a QuickTime movie, you must be sure the QuickTime extension is installed on the hard drive (if not installed, the QuickTime options are dimmed). The Auto Play option plays the movie when its slide appears. If you have more than one movie and want to show them at the same time, click Simultaneous. Complete Play before Advancing plays the entire movie before going on to the next slide. The Complete Play option overrides any timed setting you make for the slides.

- To get out of the slide show and return to the document without saving any of the options, click Cancel. To see the slide show, click Start. When finished with the slide show and you want your options to stay as they are, click Done.

- When the slide show is set to Loop and you want to get back to the dialog box, press ⌘-period (.).

If you click Done and save your document, you will save all the options in the Slide Show dialog box.

Using Form Letters and Mail Merge

A form letter is practical for many businesses and personal matters. It is a useful way of dispensing the same information to many people with ease and swiftness. A business sending a letter of confirmation to clients is one example of how using a form letter would be applicable. The written contract signed by an individual or company is another example of handling the same text over and over, and therefore calling for the use of a form. A person writing one Christmas letter, duplicating it, and sending copies to all his/her friends is another mode of the form letter.

Normally, people prefer receiving information in a more personal manner than a form letter. Merging a database with the form letter accomplishes that end. The specific information regarding each client or friend which can be inserted enhances the letter, while the form itself continues to fulfill the need of using that kind of communication.

Setting Up the Database

The first thing you need to have on file is a database. This database is going to consist of all the names and addresses of the people who will receive the form letter. If such a database does not exist, take some time to think of all the fields you will want to include. A field is a general category that will appear in each record. Fields you might want to include in a database which will be used with a form letter are:

 Title
 First Name
 Last Name
 Address
 City

State
ZIP
Phone
Birthday
Anniversary
Child/Birth
Child/Birth
Child/Birth
Modem/Fax #

This database can be useful, not only to merge with a form letter, but to create a mailing label. By rearranging the necessary field names in the Layout view, and choosing the type of label on which the information will be printed, the database does double duty. For more information about creating databases and mailing labels, see Chapter 12, "Database Basics," and Chapter 13, "Creating Layouts."

Creating the Form Letter

You want to create a letter that is generic, yet personal enough to encourage the addressee to read it. You may want to make up a series of these letters. You can merge them with the appropriate database when it comes time to send them. The following are samples of the kinds of information you might want to merge into a form letter:

- A company logo or letterhead

- Today's date

- Salutation

- An invoice amount, date of an event, or other variable in the body of the letter

- The closing and your name

Once you write the letter, you are ready to place the fields (First Name, Address, ZIP, and so on) in the appropriate places. When the letter prints, the field names will be replaced by the field variables (Harry, 253 Ridge Road, 60092, and so on). Each letter has the same basic information but is addressed to a different person with information relevant to that person. Follow these steps to open the appropriate documents so database information can be merged with a word processing document:

338 Chapter 15—Creating Integrated Documents

1. Open the database document that you want to merge with the form letter.

2. If not already open, open the word processing form letter document. This must be the active document. It can be an existing file into which you are going to insert the field names, or you can create the letter as you insert the field names.

3. Choose Save As from the File menu, and give the file a name that indicates it deals with the merging of two files. An example would be naming the file CustConfirm MM. You may want to change the Save As setting to Stationery so the document will be easy to locate.

4. Choose Insert Date from the Edit menu. Using the Insert Date command instead of typing the date allows the computer to insert the current date every time you use the document.

5. Choose Mail Merge from the File menu. The Mail Merge dialog box appears (see fig. 15.21). This dialog box lists all the field names in your database.

If you do not open a database before choosing Mail Merge in the File menu, you will get the following error message: A database document must be open before you can use Mail Merge.

You are now ready to place the field names in the appropriate places. Follow these steps:

Figure 15.21
Mail Merge dialog box.

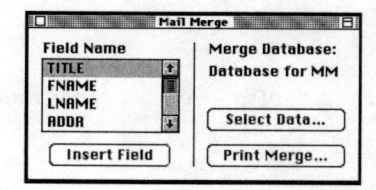

1. Place the insertion point where you want the first field name to appear.

2. Select the field name in the Mail Merge box.

3. Choose Insert Field. That name field now appears in your letter, between delimiters (i.e., << and >>). Press the space bar before adding an-

other field name or keying in any text.

4. Repeat steps 2 and 3 to insert all the necessary field names.

5. When you finish, choose OK.

Figure 15.22 shows how the names and addresses represented by field names look on-screen, with proper spacing and punctuation.

You want to be especially aware of your spacing and punctuation before and

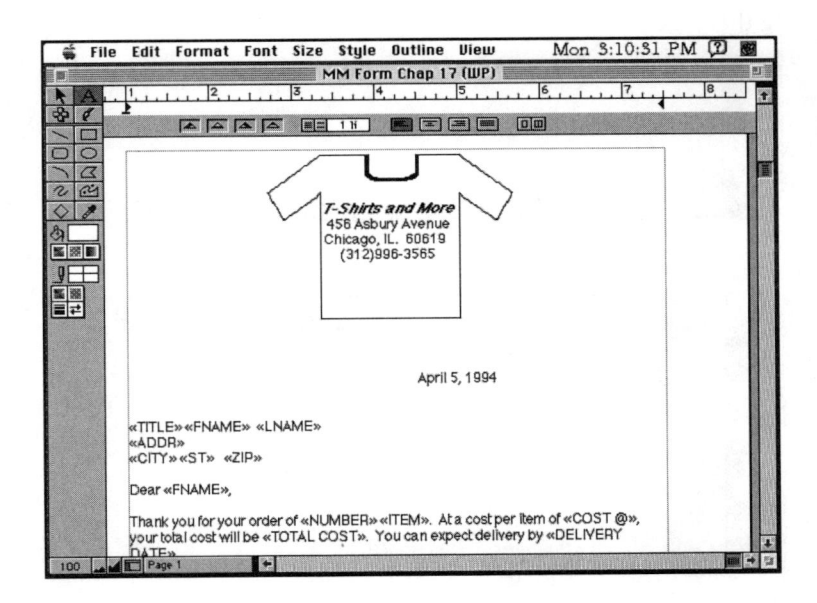

Figure 15.22
Word processing document showing proper spacing of mail merge commands.

after a Field Name with delimiters is inserted. It is easy to forget to put in a comma or to press the space bar between city, state, and ZIP field names. It is always a good idea to get a printout of the letter with the field names in it, as shown in figure 15.23. When you finish the letter, be sure to save it again, as you have added more information.

To print copies so that field variables (each person's name and address will be different) appear in each letter, choose Print Merge in the Mail Merge dialog box. If you want to print one copy with the field names and delimiters, print as you normally do (see fig. 15.24).

Figure 15.23
An example of how a template word processing document looks with mail merge commands.

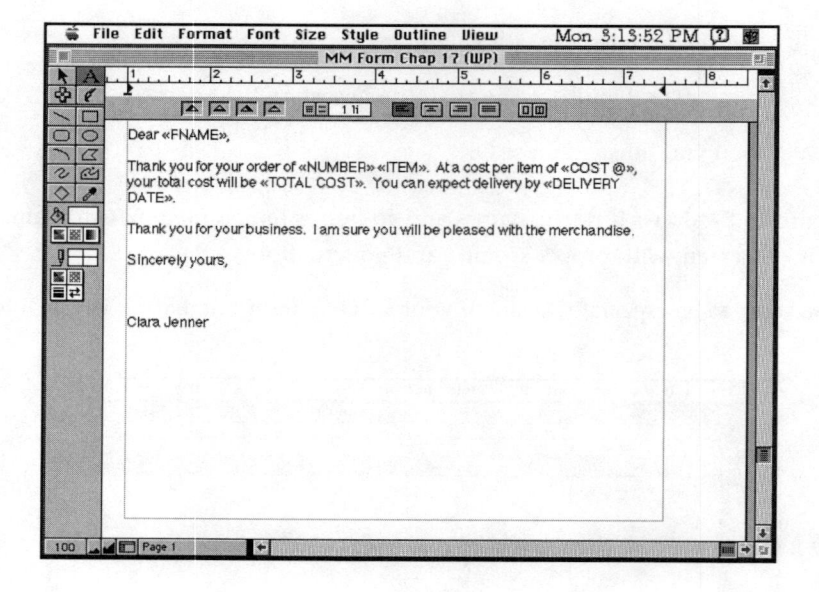

Figure 15.24
Word processing letter with merged database information.

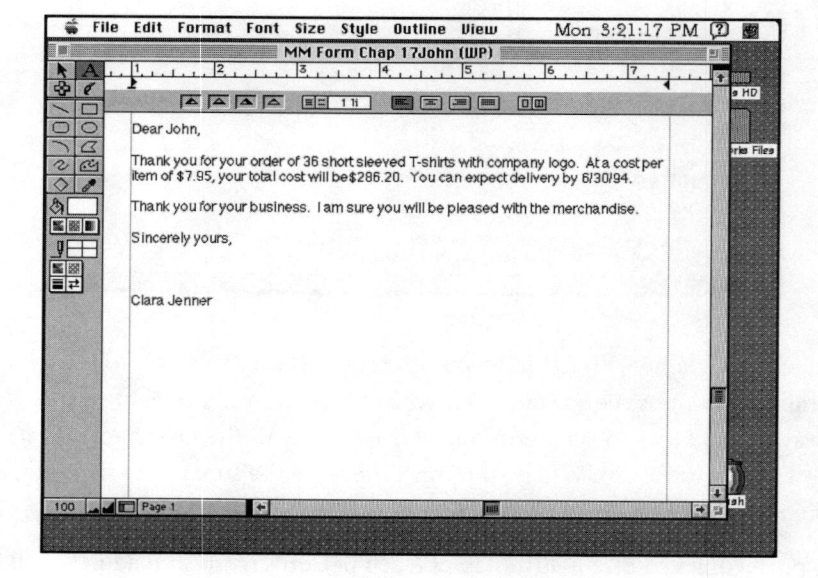

> **Troubleshooting Mail Merge**
>
> *I have to change the date on my form letter every time I use it. How do I avoid doing that?*
>
> Delete the date you keyed in. Click where you want the date to appear. Choose Insert Date from the Edit menu. The date will now be up-to-date, as the Insert Date command operates by the clock in your computer.
>
> *I cannot get my letter to print with each page having a different name. Only my mail merge commands show.*
>
> You want to choose the Print option in the Mail Merge dialog box. When you choose Print from the File menu, you get exactly what you see on-screen.

From Here...

This chapter takes you through some advanced features of ClarisWorks. It shows you how to integrate frames of one module into another kind of module, and how to create and implement linked frames. This chapter also discusses how to merge database information into a word processing document. For more information on related topics:

- Chapter 3, "Working with Text." This chapter discusses the basics of word processing.

- Chapter 6, "Drawing." The chapter explains the menus and tools you need to color and edit graphics. It also discusses frames.

- Chapter 7, "Painting." This chapter shows you how to use the menus and tools of this graphics program.

- Chapter 8, "Spreadsheet Basics." This chapter gives you information on how to create a spreadsheet.

- Part III, "Creating Databases." If you want to create labels, as well as refresh your knowledge regarding databases, see chapters 12, 13, and 14.

Chapter 16

Sharing Data with Other Documents and Applications

by Cyndie Shaffstall-Klopfenstein

The Publish and Subscribe feature of System 7 enables you to keep text and graphics updated in current documents. This feature is very much like cut/copy and paste operations. A good example of Publish and Subscribe is a company disclaimer that must appear on all company literature. You might want to store this disclaimer as a separate document (publish), to which other documents would link (subscribe). As the company changed the disclaimer, documents would update to the current version, either automatically or upon demand, at your discretion. This updating capacity makes Publish and Subscribe more powerful than a simple cut/copy and paste operation, which uses only the current version resident on the Clipboard.

In this chapter, you learn the following:

- How to publish an item
- How to subscribe to an item
- How to set Publisher and Subscriber options

Publishing an Item

You can publish and subscribe to any text or graphic object, and it need not have been created in ClarisWorks. This published item is called an *edition*. One of the most beneficial features of Publish and Subscribe is that because it is a System 7 feature, it is available in all System 7 savvy applications. This availability means that you can create a graphic in an illustration program and subscribe to it through the ClarisWorks word processing module. You also can publish items created in one ClarisWorks module and subscribe to those items through a different module.

Whether you want to Publish or Subscribe, both methods require the same steps:

1. Open an existing document, and select the item to be published. This item can be text, a graphic, or a spreadsheet.

    Figure 16.1 shows how the screen should look when you select a single graphic. Notice the *handles* (small black squares), which show that the item is selected.

Figure 16.1
This is what an item ready for publishing might look like in the ClarisWorks graphics module.

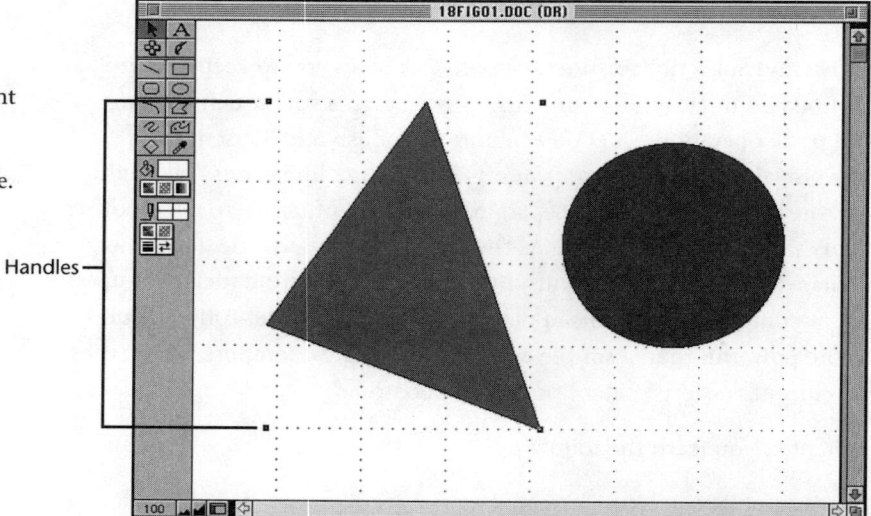

Handles

Figure 16.2 shows selected text in a word processing document. The selected text, which is highlighted, is the portion that will be published.

2. Choose Publishing from the Edit menu, and then choose Create Publisher from the submenu. The Create Publisher dialog box appears (see figs. 16.3 and 16.4). This dialog box, which could be called the destination dialog box, requests a destination and a name for the published item.

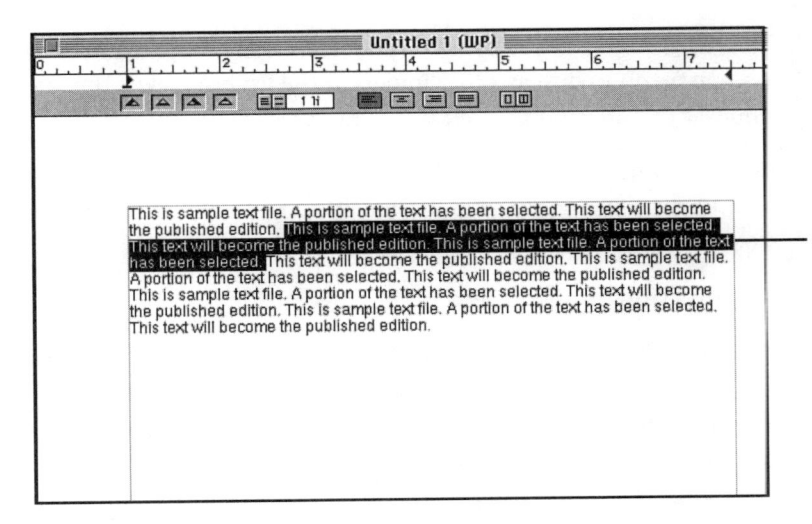

Figure 16.2
This is how text in the ClarisWorks word processing module looks when selected.

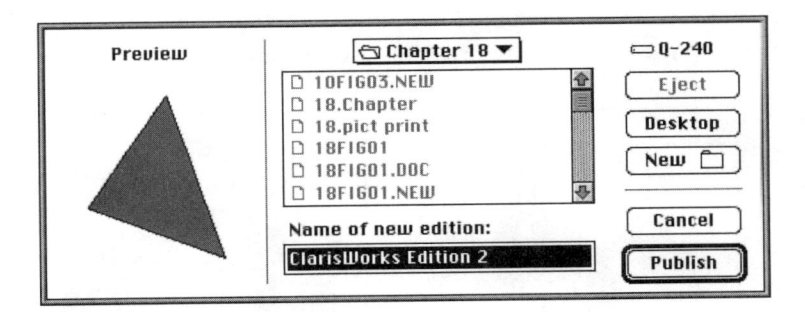

Selected text

Figure 16.3
When you choose Create Publisher, a preview of the selected object appears on the left side of the open dialog box.

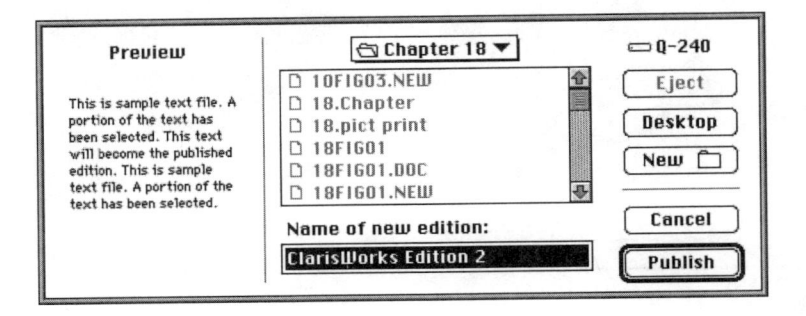

Figure 16.4
This is the Create Publisher dialog box for the selected text.

3. In the Name of New Edition text box, type a name for the file.

4. The pop-up menu above the list box shows the current folder. To save the item in this folder, choose Publish.

346   Chapter 16—Sharing Data with Other Documents and Applications

To change the folder, click the Desktop button, the drive button, or the pop-up menu to display other folders in the list box; select the folder you want to use; and then choose Publish.

To create a new folder for your published items, first select the destination, as described in step 4, and then click the New Folder command button. Type a name for the folder, and click Create.

5. Save and close the document.

You can subscribe to a document that has not been saved or closed. If you subscribe and then close the document without saving it, however, the link will be broken, and in the case of subscribed graphics, you will be unable to edit the edition.

After you publish an item, a gray box appears around it in the document (see figs. 16.5 and 16.6). The document file's icon also appears in a gray box, making the edition easy to identify in a folder or document.

Figure 16.5
A gray box appears around a published object.

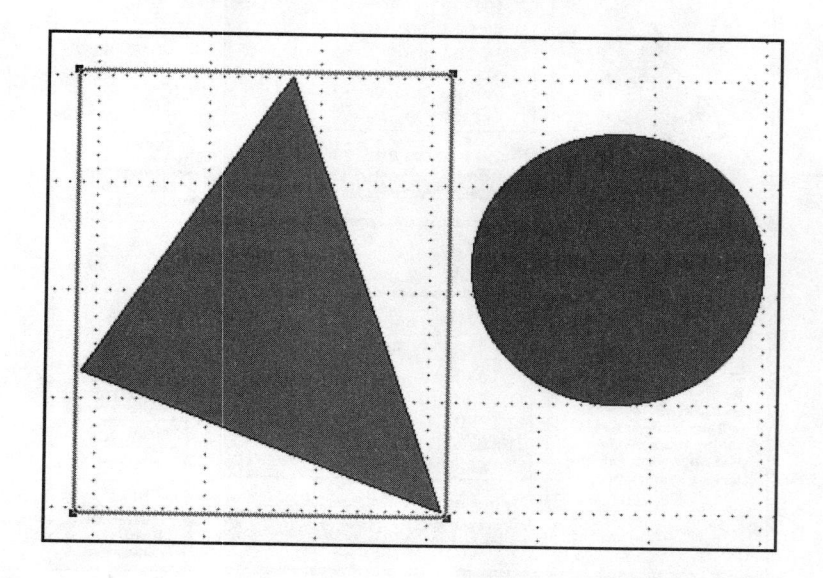

Tip
To display information about an edition file quickly, double-click that file's icon on the Desktop. Then click the Open Publisher button to open the publishing application.

If you change a published item, ClarisWorks updates all documents that subscribe to that item. Nonpublished items that are moved into the gray box (see fig. 16.7) are considered to be alterations and will appear in the subscribing documents.

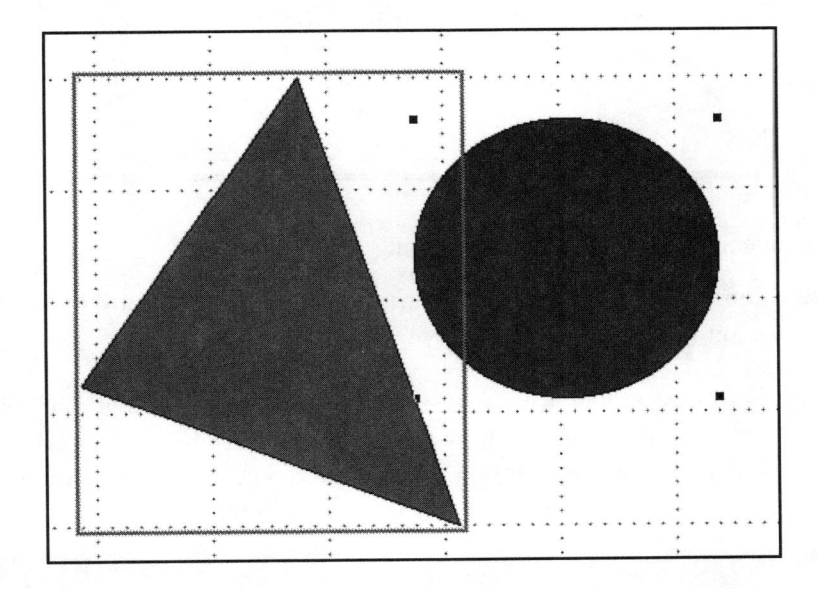

Figure 16.6
Published text is displayed with a gray box.

Figure 16.7
The portion of the item that was moved into the gray box will appear in the subscribing documents.

Subscribing to a Published Item

Subscribing to an edition—the second half of Publish and Subscribe—is the method of embedding the edition in documents to ensure that your documents have the most current version of the edition.

To subscribe to a published item, follow these steps:

1. Within a document, place the insertion point where you want to place the published item or edition.

2. Choose Publishing from the Edit menu, and then choose Subscribe To from the submenu. The Subscribe To dialog box appears (see fig. 16.8). This dialog box looks very much like the Create Publisher dialog box. The Preview area on the left side of the dialog box shows the editions to which you can subscribe.

348 Chapter 16—Sharing Data with Other Documents and Applications

> **Note**
> Any number of documents can subscribe to a published item.

Figure 16.8
The Subscribe To dialog box is similar to the Create Publisher dialog box.

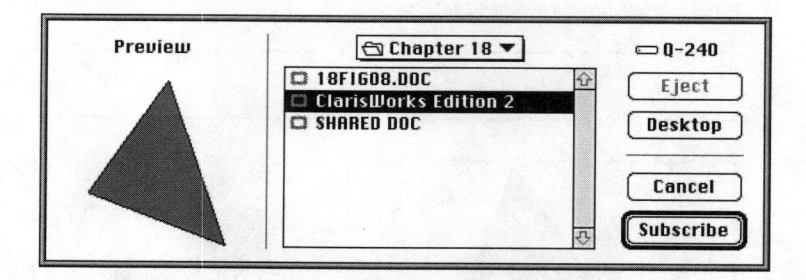

3. Select the published item or edition.

4. Choose Subscribe. ClarisWorks places the edition (surrounded by a gray box) in the document.

To view a subscribed item without the gray box, choose Publishing from the Edit menu, and then choose Hide Borders from the submenu. ClarisWorks hides the gray box. To display the box again, choose Publishing from the Edit menu again; then choose Show Borders from the submenu.

> **Note**
> The gray boxes of Publish are a lighter shade than the gray boxes of Subscribe. The difference usually is apparent only when both kinds are close together in a document.

Tip
Before you scale a subscribed graphic, choose Hide Borders from the Publishing submenu so that only the ClarisWorks graphics box is visible.

You can make the entire edition bold or change the font size, and this would apply to an updated subscriber edition. Single or selected words with style changes will be replaced with the formatting of the update.

You can scale graphics that you published to a ClarisWorks word processing document by dragging the handle of the ClarisWorks graphics box (not the gray Subscribe box). You cannot edit text published to a graphics document, however.

Changing Publisher and Subscriber Options

Both Publish and Subscribe have a set of options to which they refer in creating or updating editions. You can change these options by choosing the Publisher Options or Subscriber Options command.

The Publisher Options Dialog Box

To change the Publish options, select a published item, choose Publishing from the Edit menu, and then choose Publisher Options from the submenu. The Publisher Options dialog box appears (see fig. 16.9).

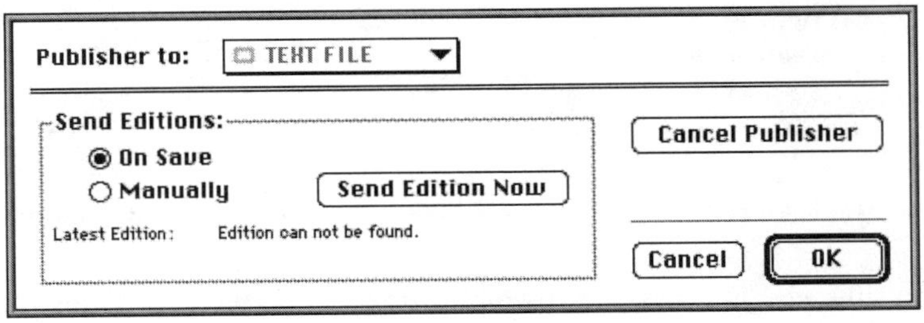

Figure 16.9
The Publisher Options dialog box enables you to make changes such as when to update.

At the top of the dialog box, a pop-up menu is available. This menu is handy for determining where an edition is saved. The menu is especially useful when you need to store subsequent editions in the same folder, or when you need to subscribe to other editions.

Tip
You also can display this dialog box by double-clicking the gray border of a published item.

In the Send Editions area, you can choose On Save or Manually. If you choose On Save, ClarisWorks sends new edition information to the subscribing documents each time you save the published edition. If you choose Manually, ClarisWorks sends new information only when you click the Send Edition Now button. (This would affect only a currently open subscriber. Other subscribers would update as they were opened.) The bottom of the Send Editions area shows the date and time when the published edition was last edited.

The button on the right side of the dialog box enables you to Cancel Publisher. This option does not delete the edition file, so it doesn't change editions already embedded in subscriber documents. You would use this option if you no longer want to maintain a link. Sometimes, an edition loses its usefulness, or perhaps it is being replaced. Either way, this option will not delete the edition from the subscribing document; it will only break the link.

If you use the Cancel Publisher button to break the link, the gray box outlining the edition will disappear when you save.

The Subscriber Options Dialog Box

Much like the Publisher Options dialog box, the Subscriber Options dialog box (see fig. 16.10) enables you to view information that is pertinent to the currently selected Subscribe edition. To display this dialog box, choose Publishing from the Edit menu, and then choose Subscriber Options from the submenu.

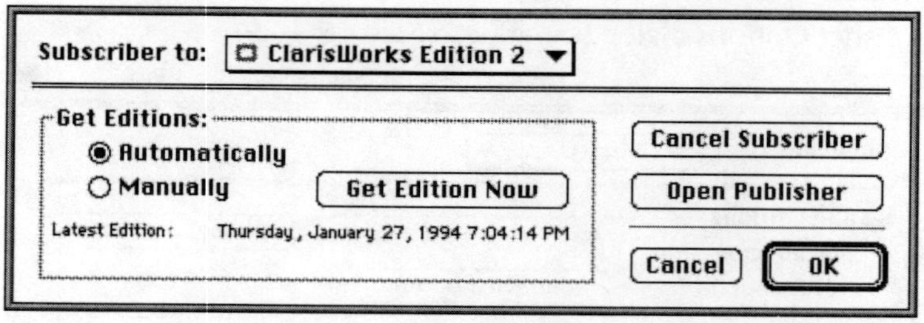

Figure 16.10
The Subscriber Options dialog box is similar to the Publisher Options dialog box.

The pop-up menu at the top of the dialog box shows the path of nested folders. This menu is useful if you want to store another edition in the same location and you've forgotten that location.

In the Get Editions area, you can choose Automatically or Manually. If you choose Automatically, ClarisWorks automatically updates editions when you make changes in the original documents. If you choose Manually, ClarisWorks accepts no new changes made in the published edition until you click the Get Edition Now button. The bottom of the Get Editions area shows the date and time of the last update.

The Allow Modification button, at the bottom of the dialog box, enables you to change a subscribed edition. As stated above, unless you make changes such as size and style for the entire edition, these changes will be overridden by changes made in the original file. You can keep this from happening by making the changes and then choosing the Update Changes Manually option. Then your changes in the subscribing document would be overridden only when you so choose.

The Open Publisher button launches the application and opens the file containing the original edition. You can edit the edition and then save it. Depending on the current settings in the Publisher Options dialog box,

ClarisWorks will update the subscribing document automatically or only when you click the Get Edition Now button in the Subscriber Options dialog box.

Rules for Using Editions

You may find that it's not very good housekeeping to save all your editions on the disk where your documents reside. An efficient storage solution might include keeping all editions on a disk just for editions. This method could substantially speed a search for a missing edition, as all editions would reside in one location.

You can store editions on other disks. But if the disk on which you stored an edition is not present when you open a subscribing document, a dialog box appears, asking that you insert the disk (see fig. 16.11). If you do not insert the disk, another dialog box appears, warning you that the edition is missing. The edition will still appear in the document, but the link will be temporarily shut down. You can update later by using the Get Edition Now button, as described in this chapter.

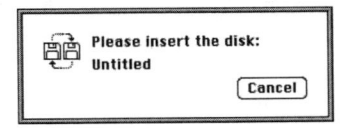

Figure 16.11
This dialog box asks you to insert the disk containing the edition file.

When you subscribe to an edition, the path name (the location from which you retrieved the edition) is embedded in the subscribing document. If you move an edition after the link has been made, the link is broken, and you cannot relink to the same edition. Although the item remains in your document, it will no longer update as an edition would. It is easy to see when this has happened; the Latest Edition line in the Options dialog box is dimmed.

To make a new link to that edition, follow these steps:

1. Open the original published document and select the edition. Although the link has been broken, the gray box remains.

2. Choose Publishing from the Edit menu, and then choose Create Publisher from the submenu.

3. In the Create Publisher dialog box, use the same name, and place it in the same location as the current edition.

4. Choose OK. A message box appears, asking whether you want to replace the existing file.

5. Choose Yes.

This method does not actually link to the same edition, but the result is essentially the same.

From Here...

For more information on specific topics, see the following chapters:

- Chapter 2, "Learning the Essentials." Refer to this chapter if you need more information on saving and opening documents.

- Chapter 4, "Enhancing Your Text." This chapter explains how to change text styles.

- Chapter 6, "Drawing." You can use the drawing module to create company logos that can be shared with other documents.

Part V

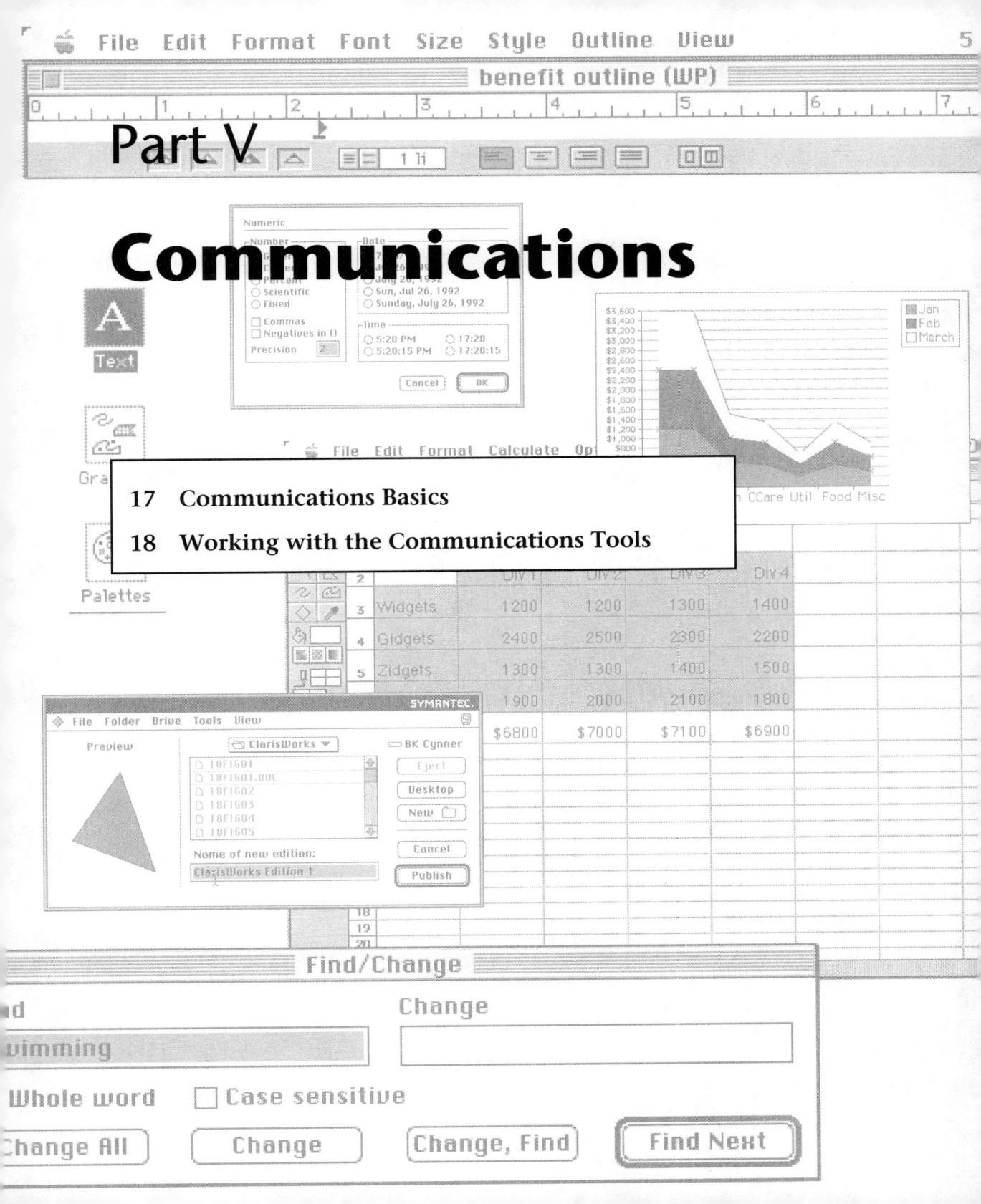

Communications

17 Communications Basics

18 Working with the Communications Tools

File Edit Format Font Size Style Outline View

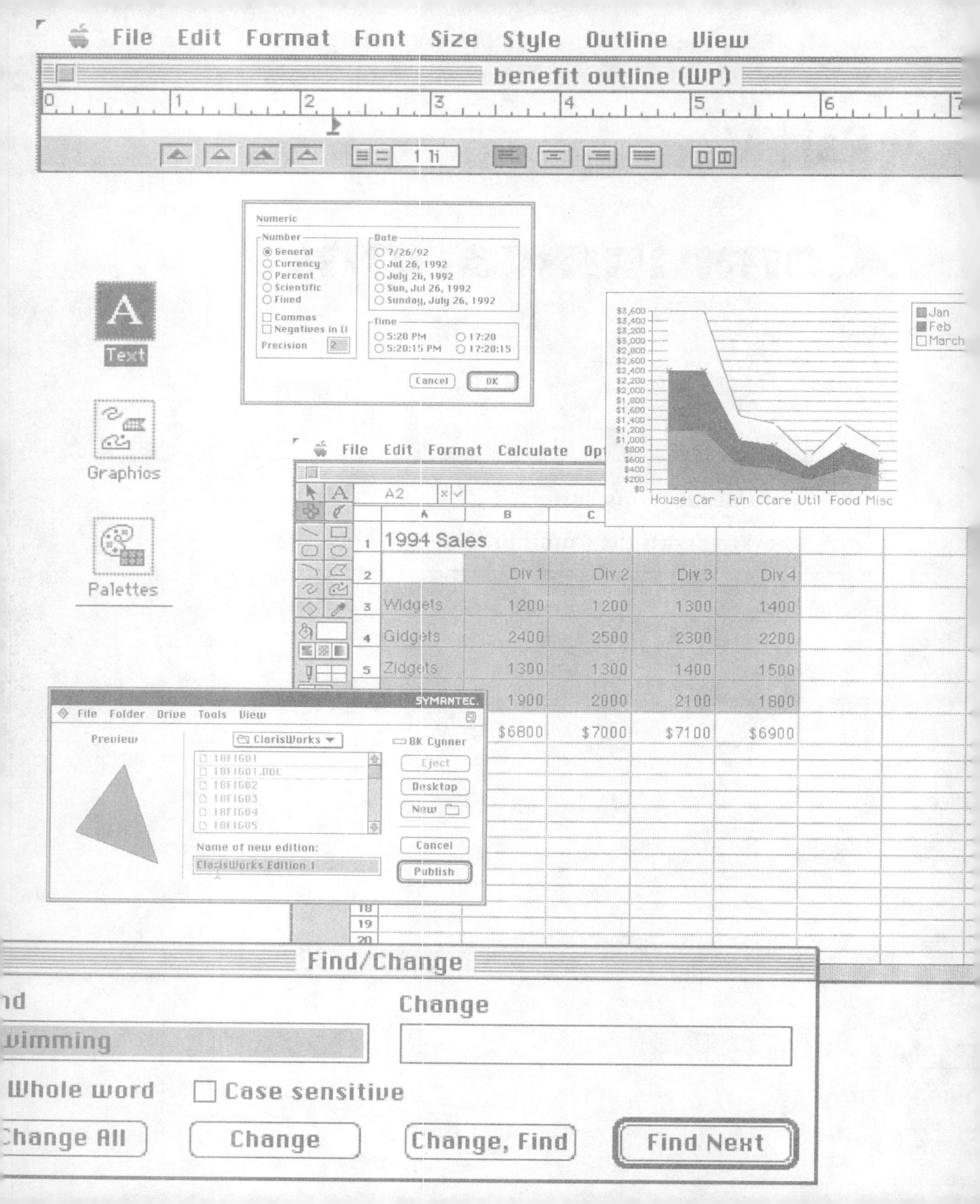

benefit outline (WP)

```
0         1         2         3         4         5         6         7
```

Numeric

Number
- ● General
- ○ Currency
- ○ Percent
- ○ Scientific
- ○ Fixed

☐ Commas
☐ Negatives in ()
Precision 2

Date
- ○ 7/26/92
- ○ Jul 26, 1992
- ○ July 26, 1992
- ○ Sun, Jul 26, 1992
- ○ Sunday, July 26, 1992

Time
- ○ 5:20 PM   ○ 17:20
- ○ 5:20:15 PM ○ 17:20:15

[Cancel] [OK]

Text

Graphics

Palettes

$3,600 / $3,400 / $3,200 / $3,000 / $2,800 / $2,600 / $2,400 / $2,200 / $2,000 / $1,800 / $1,600 / $1,400 / $1,200 / $1,000 / $800 / $600 / $400 / $200 / $0

House Car Fun CCare Util Food Misc

■ Jan
■ Feb
□ March

File Edit Format Calculate Opt...

A2

	A	B	C	D	E
1	1994 Sales				
2		Div 1	Div 2	Div 3	Div 4
3	Widgets	1200	1200	1300	1400
4	Gidgets	2400	2500	2300	2200
5	Zidgets	1300	1300	1400	1500
		1900	2000	2100	1800
		$6800	$7000	$7100	$6900

SYMANTEC

File Folder Drive Tools View

Preview   📁 ClarisWorks ▼   ☐ BK Cynner

- 18F1G01
- 18F1G01.DOC
- 18F1G02
- 18F1G03
- 18F1G04
- 18F1G05

[Eject]
[Desktop]
[New 📁]
[Cancel]
[Publish]

Name of new edition:
ClarisWorks Edition 1

18
19
20

Find/Change

nd   Change

wimming

Whole word   ☐ Case sensitive

[Change All]   [Change]   [Change, Find]   [**Find Next**]

Chapter 17
Communications Basics

by Cyndie Shaffstall-Klopfenstein

Unlike the other modules of ClarisWorks, communications does not work alone; it must have supporting hardware other than just the Macintosh. For *remote connections* (communication with computers away from your location), you need a modem, a phone line, and proper cabling. A *modem* is a piece of equipment that might be outside or inside your computer. It works very much like a fax machine in that it sends data to other modems over the phone line. The difference between a fax and a modem is that the modem sends data without actually printing it to a page. This data is a text file that other computers can read. For *local connections* (communication with computers in the same office or building), you can use a cable connected directly to the serial ports of both computers.

Local connections are not as common because there are many other ways to connect local (in the same area) computers. Using the Macintosh System 7 integrated network, for example, is simpler than using the ClarisWorks communications module. The real strength of ClarisWorks comes in connecting to remote systems—for example, to on-line services such as CompuServe and America Online. An *on-line service* is a remote computer that stores a great deal of data that you can access with your modem. Some on-line services operate on subscriptions; you pay a fee each month for the amount of time you spend connected to the service. You also can connect with other private-party computers to exchange data between corporate field offices or just to send a recipe for apple pie to your sister in Georgia.

Modems are not exclusive to the business environment. This fact is even more apparent when you *log on to* (connect with) on-line services. The types of *forums* (areas of specific information) available through on-line services include encyclopedias, daily newspapers, stock-market reports, self-help groups, and games. The ClarisWorks communications module and your Macintosh open the entire electronic world for you.

In this chapter, you learn the following:

- The hardware and software requirements for communications
- Setup options
- How to make a connection
- How to send files

Setting Up

In communications, both computers must use the same *protocol* (language). With the many different protocol options available in ClarisWorks, you should be able to connect to nearly every type of computer out there. You are not limited to connecting only to another Macintosh, or even to receiving only files created on a Macintosh. The modem and software don't care about the origin or destination of information; it's all bits to them.

> **Note**
>
> Even though you can receive data from different types of computers, you may not be able to read or use certain types of data, depending on the software used to create the data and the software used to read the data. Files saved in Text format can almost always be opened in a word processing application.

Using the Hardware and Software

Before attempting to make a connection with ClarisWorks, go through the following table, making sure that you have everything you need and that the equipment is connected or installed according to the manufacturers' specifications. The great majority of transmission struggles are caused by improperly installed equipment, and there's no sense in creating problems before you start.

Table 17.1 Equipment Requirements

Remote Connections	Local Connections
Modem	Serial-to-serial (null modem) cable
Phone line	
Phone cable	

Remote Connections	Local Connections
Modem power cable	
Modem-to-serial cable	
ClarisWorks software	ClarisWorks software
Macintosh with at least 1M of RAM (2M for System 7)	Macintosh with at least 1M of RAM (2M for System 7)
Apple Communications Toolbox	Apple Communications Toolbox
System software (Version 6.0.5 or later)	System software (Version 6.0.5 or later)

The connection should look something like figure 17.1.

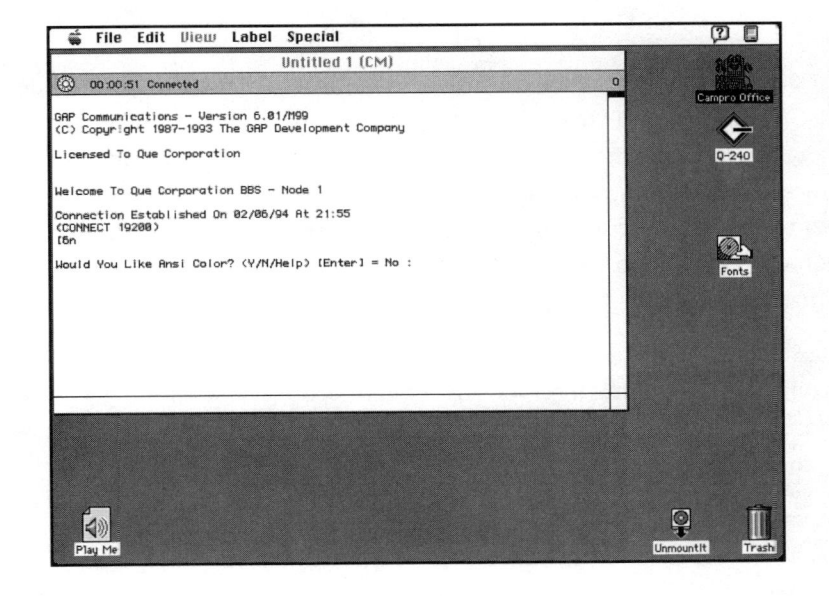

Figure 17.1
This is how a typical remote and local connection would look.

You can have a telephone in the loop of a remote connection; it's not necessary, but it does keep you from having to install a second phone line near your computer. A second phone line is more convenient, though. It allows you to connect to the remote computer and have a discussion at the same time—especially handy if you're having difficulty connecting. It will also prevent an incoming call from interfering with a connection. This is especially a problem for phone lines with call waiting.

Most modems these days have an internal speaker, which is close to a necessity. A speaker allows you to hear the terminal connecting and could alert you to any difficulties with the phone line.

Learning the Menus

For this chapter, assume that you will be making a remote connection. Two menus in the communications module will have the most effect on these types of connections: the Settings menu and the Session menu.

> **Note**
>
> The Preferences dialog box (discussed in detail in Chapter 20, "Customizing ClarisWorks") also can affect communications. You don't need to change any of the settings in that dialog box, but as you become expert in communications, you will see how certain changes can expedite the process.

The Settings menu contains controls for the protocol—the way your modem acts. These settings dictate information such as the number to dial, how many bits to use to make a character (*data bits*), and how many bits to use to indicate the end of a character (*stop bits*). Each computer to which you connect will have a different protocol. You (or the other user) must change the protocol so that both computers match. Do this for each system to which you connect.

The Session menu contains the options for just the current session. These settings are for sending files, waiting for connections, and scrolling received data. These tasks are much simpler and have less to do with making a successful connection.

Adjusting the Settings

You adjust the communications settings in the Connection Settings dialog box (see fig. 17.2). To display this dialog box, choose Connection from the Settings menu.

Although all the options in this dialog box play a role in successful connection, file retrieval, or file transmission, ClarisWorks has preset the options to the most common settings used. You can attempt to make a connection without changing any of these options, and because the default settings are common, you will probably succeed.

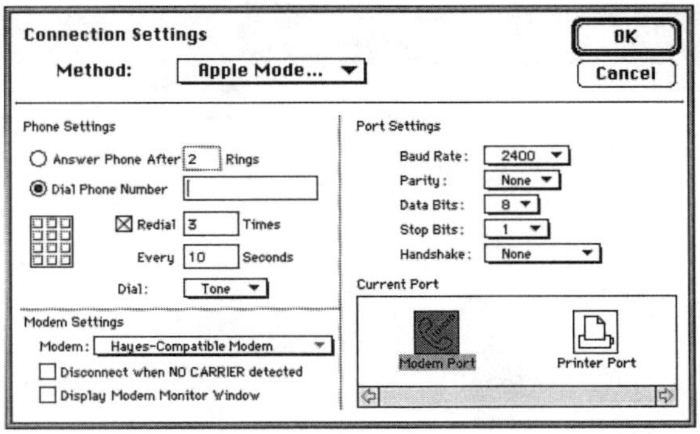

Figure 17.2
The Connection Settings dialog box.

If you have difficulty connecting, sending, or receiving, talk to the person at the remote site, usually referred to as the *SysOps* (system operator). This person is responsible for the operation of a specific terminal. The SysOps will be able to tell you which protocol settings will match the other computer; you should change your protocol to match. Table 17.2 will help you make the right choices.

Table 17.2 Connection Settings

Field	Option	Description
Method	Apple Modem Tool	Permits communication with most Hayes-compatible remote modems.
	Serial Tool	Permits communication with a local computer.
Phone Settings		
Answer Phone After ___ Rings		Instructs your modem to answer the phone after the indicated number of rings.
Dial Phone Number _____		Instructs your modem to dial the indicated number. Hyphens in the phone number don't affect the modem but do make the number easier for you to read. Use commas to insert pauses between numbers, such as when you need to dial 9 to get an outside line.

(continues)

Table 17.2 Continued

Field	Option	Description
Redial _____ Times		Indicates how many times the modem should try to make a connection after a busy signal or incomplete call.
Every _____ Seconds		Indicates how long the modem should wait to redial.
Dial	Tone	Indicates that your phone line is TouchTone.
	Pulse	Indicates that your phone line is rotary/pulse.

Modem Setting

Modem	Hayes-Compatible Modem (and so on)	Indicates the type of modem you have. If your modem is not listed, select Hayes-Compatible Modem, which is the industry-standard setting.

Disconnect When NO CARRIER Detected

	Unchecked	Prevents the modem from automatically disconnecting if it cannot make a successful connection to the remote computer.
	Checked	Instructs the modem to disconnect automatically if it cannot connect to the remote computer.

Display Modem Monitor Window

	Unchecked	Specifies that this window will not appear.
	Checked	Specifies that this window will appear.

Port Settings

Baud Rate	110, 300, 1200 2400, 4800, 9600 19200, 38400, 57600	Specifies the speed, or *baud rate*, at which data is to be sent. Both modems must be set at the same baud rate. You cannot use a baud rate higher than your modem can achieve.

Field	Option	Description
Parity	None Even Odd	Specifies *parity*, or the modem's method of checking the data. Both computers must have the same parity setting. The most common setting is None.
Data Bits	5, 6, 7, 8	Specifies the number of bits used to make up a single character. The most common setting is 8.
Stop Bits	1, 1.5, 2	Specifies the number of bits used to indicate the end of a character. The most common setting is 1.
Handshake	None XON/XOFF DTR/CTS DTR Only CTS Only	Controls the flow of data between your computer and the remote site. The most common setting is None. XON/XOFF works only if the remote computer understands that setting. A *handshake* is a communication between the two modems that establishes the settings of each modem so that one modem is receiving data as the other is sending.
Current Port	Modem Port	Tells the software that you are using the external modem port for the connection.
	Printer Port	This indicates that the modem is connected to the external printer port. If the wrong port is selected, the software will not be able to communicate with the modem.

The next menu command is Terminal. (Your Macintosh is your terminal.) This command opens the Terminal Settings dialog box (see fig. 17.3), which enables you to control the display on your monitor. This dialog box has options in four categories: General, Screen, Keyboard, and Character Set. Icons representing these four categories appear on the left side of the dialog box. Click the icon that represents the options you want to see; these options appear on the right side of the dialog box.

Figure 17.3
The Terminal Settings dialog box.

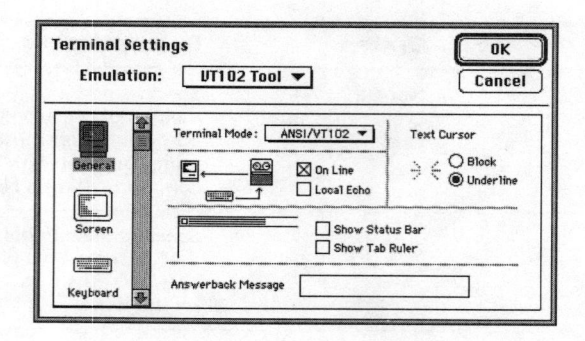

Sometimes you will want your terminal to *emulate* (act like) the terminal to which it connects. There are settings for this also.

Table 17.3 describes the Terminal Settings options.

Field	Option	Description
Table 17.3 General Terminal Settings (VT102 Tool)*		
Terminal Settings		
Emulation	VT102 Tool	This emulation mode, which is compatible with VT100 terminals, instructs your Macintosh to emulate a VT102 terminal.
	TTY Tool	This mode sets the options for the most common communications settings.
General		
Terminal Mode	ANSI/VT102 VT52	These options describe the mode you will work in. VT52 is a mode exclusive to Digital Equipment Corporation's VT52 terminal. Use this mode only when connecting to a computer (terminal) of that type.
On Line	Checked Unchecked	When checked, this option enables your Macintosh to transfer and receive data. When this option is unchecked, your computer still can connect to the remote computer, but no data transfer will take place.

Field	Option	Description
Local Echo	Checked Unchecked	When checked, this option will display your keystrokes as you type them. If you are typing a message to the remote terminal, you probably will want to be able to see the text. If you are not typing messages, you will not need Local Echo.
Show Status Bar	Checked Unchecked	When checked, this option creates a status bar in the communications window, displaying some of your settings choices at the left side of the bar. The remote computer uses the right side of the status bar to display indicators.
Show Tab Ruler	Checked Unchecked	When checked, this option displays a tab ruler at the top of your communications window. ClarisWorks provides a default eight-character tab stop; if you want to change the tabs, you must display the tab ruler.
Answerback Message		Some computers require an answerback message when they send an inquire character (basically, "Hello, are you out there?") to your terminal. If you want to provide a message, type it in the text box.
Text Cursor	Block Underline	The cursor is a blinking icon where text will be inserted. Choose Block to make the cursor a small black box; choose Underline to make it a small, blinking underline.

*VT102 is the default mode, and the default settings currently match this mode. If you choose TTY, the options change to those most commonly encountered for the TTY Tool. Most settings will remain the same as for VT102 unless your on-line service specifically requires otherwise. The VT102 tool is sensitive to some data in a communications session and responds to certain character sequences that the remote computer may send. This situation can create a problem with sessions. To reset your settings, choose Reset Terminal from the Session menu. This command changes the options in the Terminal Settings dialog box to those that you last chose.

The next tables assume that you will be using the VT102 Tool. To display screen options for this mode, click the Screen icon on the left side of the Terminal Settings dialog box (see fig. 17.4).

Figure 17.4
This is the Terminal Settings dialog box when the Screen icon is selected.

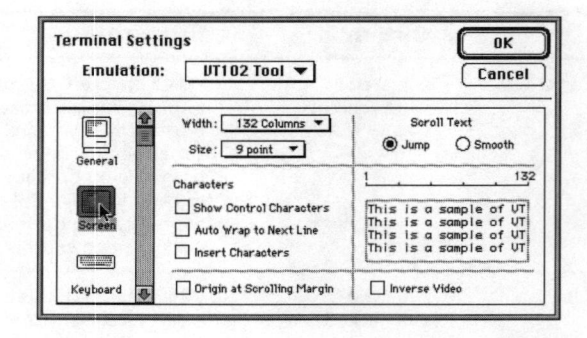

Use Table 17.4 to determine the best screen settings.

Table 17.4 Screen Terminal Settings (VT102 Tool)

Field	Option	Description
Width	80 Columns 132 Columns	This option determines how many columns wide the text will be. 80 Columns is best for a small monitor; the lines will not wrap around to a second line. 132 Columns is the right width for a two-page monitor. Make the communications window wider if you cannot see all the text.
Size	9 12	This option determines the size at which text will be displayed. Size 12 uses more screens to display the same amount of text, but the text will be easier to read.
Characters		(Watch the window to the right of this area to see how the choices you make will appear in the communications window.)
Show Control Characters	Checked Unchecked	Choose this option only if you believe that you will need to see the control characters that are transmitted.
Auto Wrap to Next Line	Checked Unchecked	Choose this option if you chose a Width option wider than your monitor's capabilities.

Field	Option	Description
Insert Characters	Checked Unchecked	When checked, this option Unchecked enables you to insert characters into text lines. If you do not check this box, text will be replaced as you type over characters.
Scroll Text	Jump Smooth	As you receive incoming text, the screen will scroll in one of two manners. Jump advances the text a screen at a time. Smooth advances the text one line at a time. If you do not need to read the text as you receive it, choose Jump. (If you choose Smooth, try selecting an XON/XOFF Handshake in the Connection Settings dialog box to ensure a cleaner transmission.)
Inverse Video	Checked Unchecked	When checked, this option displays text in white letters on a black background. (The default is black letters on a white background.)

The next icon on the left side of the Terminal Settings dialog box is the Keyboard icon. Click this icon to display options that affect the way text appears as you type it (see fig. 17.5).

Figure 17.5
The Terminal Settings dialog box, with the Keyboard icon selected.

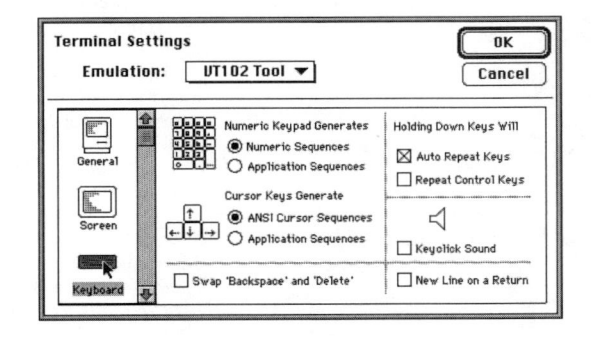

Use Table 17.5 for help in choosing the right settings.

Table 17.5 Keyboard Terminal Settings (VT102 Tool)

Field	Option	Description
Numeric Keypad Generates	Numeric Sequences Application	Numeric Sequences instructs ClarisWorks to use the keypad to type numerals. Application Sequences implements special keystroke-invoked commands that include the Escape key as specified by Digital Equipment Corporation.
Cursor Keys Generate	ANSI Cursor Sequences Application Sequences	These options control the arrow keys on your keyboard. If you use these keys and get unexpected results, you may need to change this setting. ANSI Cursor Sequences is the default; Application Sequences uses the cursor functions specified by Digital Equipment Corporation.
Swap Backspace and Delete	Checked Unchecked	Two types of Macintosh and keyboards currently are available: the Macintosh Plus keyboard and the ADB keyboard. Since the introduction of the Plus keyboard, Apple has reassigned the Backspace key to be the Delete key. This option enables you to control the keystroke when using this key.
Holding Down Keys Will	Auto Repeat Keys Repeat Control Keys	If you choose Auto Repeat Keys, non-control keys are repeated if you hold the key down. (Some keys, including Tab and Return, repeat automatically, whether or not you change this setting.) Choose Repeat Control Keys if you want control keys to repeat when you hold them down.
Keyclick Sound	Checked Unchecked	Choose this option to add sound (a click) to any pressed key. You can use the Macintosh Control Panel to lower the volume.
New Line on a Return	Checked Unchecked	When checked, this option advances the cursor one line whenever you press Return.

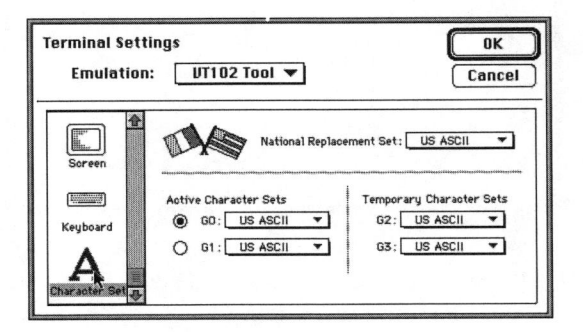

To move to the last area of the Terminal Settings dialog box, scroll down to the Character Set icon and click it. Now the dialog box displays options for the text characters themselves (see fig. 17.6).

Figure 17.6
The Terminal Settings dialog box when Character Set is selected.

Table 17.6 describes the Character Set options.

Table 17.6 Character Set Terminal Settings (VT102 Tool)		
Field	**Option**	**Description**
National Replacement Set	UK ASCII US ASCII Other Languages	From this pop-up menu, choose the character set that you want to use for your keyboard. UK ASCII and US ASCII are similar; the only difference is that the UK option replaces number signs (#) with pound-sterling symbols (£). f you choose Other Languages, the rest of the options in this dialog box will include additional languages.
Active Character Sets	US ASCII Graphics Other Languages	Use these pop-up menus to choose an active character set (G0) and an alternate character set (G1).
Temporary	US ASCII Graphics Other Languages	Use these pop-up menus to choose a temporary character set (G2) and an alternate temporary character set (G3).

The File Transfer Settings command in the Settings menu displays the dialog box shown in figure 17.7. In the File Transfer Settings dialog box, you set the data-transfer protocol, the data-transfer method, the timing options, and the transfer options.

Figure 17.7
The File Transfer Settings dialog box contains the final set of options.

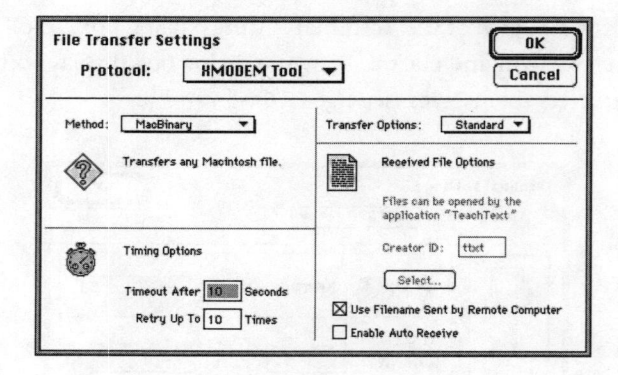

After you choose the settings in this dialog box, you will be ready to begin communicating with a remote system. If you have trouble understanding any of these settings, it's best to leave them alone; ClarisWorks automatically uses the most common settings as the default. These settings will maintain any changes you make until you change them again.

Table 17.7 describes the options in the File Transfer Settings dialog box. These are the variations of the XModem file-transfer system. Other options in this dialog box are affected by the choice you make here. As usual, ClarisWorks suggests the most common setting. Change a setting if you're sure that the change is what you need or if you are having difficulty connecting.

Table 17.7 File Transfer Settings

Field	Option	Description
Protocol	XModem Tool Claris Kermit Tool Text Tool	Most of the time, if not always, you will use XModem Tool, a simple, stable protocol that nearly all communications software packages can use. Choose another option only if the remote computer cannot use XModem Tool.
Method	MacBinary	Use MacBinary (a Macintosh protocol) for sending any file to or receiving any file from another Macintosh that is using the binary XModem Tool protocol.
	MacTerminal 1.1	Use this option only if the remote computer supports MacTerminal 1.1 with automatic file reception.

Field	Option	Description
	Straight XModem	Use this option to transmit files without converting the carriage returns (a Return key sent will be received as a Return key; paragraphs will retain their endings). This procedure is known as sending only the *dcta fork* of files. Straight XModem takes up less disk space than MacBinary.
	XModem Text	This option is for sending text only. Returns are converted to space bars depending on the direction (sending or receiving).
Timing Options	Timeout After ____ Seconds	This option automatically stops the transfer of data if the remote computer does not respond properly within the specified number of seconds. Set this number high (about 30, but no higher than 32,767) if the remote computer generally is slow to respond.
	Retry Up To ____ Times	This option instructs ClarisWorks to continue to attempt to send a block of data when the receiving computer is not responding properly. If you have a bad connection or a large file, set this number high (about 30, but no higher than 32,767).
Transfer Options	Standard	CRC-16 is a mathematical function used to detect errors. Because Standard does not support CRC detection, choose this option only when the other options do not work.
	CRC-16	This option sends data in 128-byte blocks. CRC-16 is used.
	1K Blocks	This option sends data in 1K (1,024-byte) blocks. CRC-16 is used.

(continues)

Table 17.7 Continued

Field	Option	Description
	CleanLinks	Choose this option, which uses CRC-16, when you know that you have clean transmissions. This option is faster than the others because it doesn't wait for the receiving computer to acknowledge that it received the block error-free. If you use this method and the receiving computer does detect an error, the file will cancel, and you will need to resend from the beginning.
Received File Options	Creator ID	To use this option, you must have chosen XModem or XModem Text from the Method pop-up menu. You will also need to type the name of the application to be launched when a file of this application type is received. For example, if you are going to receive a file created in ClarisWorks, type **ClarisWorks** so that ClarisWorks will start when you receive the file.
Use Filename Sent by Remote Computer	Checked Unchecked	To use this option, you must have chosen MacBinary or MacTerminal 1.1 from the Method pop-up menu. If you are receiving a file for which the name is an integral part of the file (as with font files), choose this option. If you want the opportunity to rename files that you receive, do not choose this option.
Enable Auto Receive	Checked Unchecked	This option enables your terminal to receive files automatically—if your computer and modem are turned on and the ClarisWorks software has been launched.

Now that you've completed your selections for the File Transfer Settings dialog box, click OK to apply the changes. Click Cancel to dismiss the dialog box without making the changes. You are ready to begin a communications session, and you should have an empty document window open.

Making a Connection

To start a session, choose Open Connection from the Session menu. A window appears, indicating the progress of the connection and any errors, such as an incorrectly connected modem. The first message is that ClarisWorks is initializing the modem, as shown in figure 17.8.

> **Note**
>
> You will need to have typed a phone number in the Dial Phone Number field of the Connection Settings dialog box. If you did not, you will be asked to do so now.

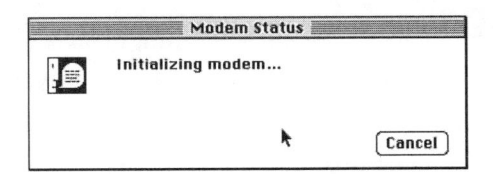

Figure 17.8
As you begin a communications setting, this dialog box appears.

Depending on what type of system you have just logged on to (connected with), you will see a wide variety of responses at this time—anything from a blank screen to a detailed graphical welcome screen sent by the system to which you've connected. The first message to appear in your window should say something like `Connect 9600 baud`. (This message will vary from connection to connection.) The modem will have whistled several times but should now be silent. Nonetheless, you will have made a successful connection. Chapter 18, "Working with the Communications Tools," shows you how to make this connection work.

Troubleshooting Making a Connection

I can't connect. What's wrong?

Check all the cables, and make sure that the modem is on. Also make sure that your phone line is suitable for file transfer. Not all phone lines can accommodate modems; you may have to call your local telephone company for help.

I still can't connect!

Check the options and the protocol settings in the Connection and Terminal dialog boxes, making sure that they match the settings of the remote computer.

Sending Files to Remote Computers

Now that you're connected, it's fairly simple to transfer files. To send a file, choose Send File from the Session menu. The Send File dialog box appears. Double-click the name of the file you want to send, and then choose OK. Click Cancel to close the dialog box without sending the file.

From Here...

In this chapter, you learned that connecting to other modems with your modem can open an entire world for you. Making a connection can be as simple as dialing the number. The modem settings you choose help make your transmissions clean and error-free. For related information, see the following chapters:

- Chapter 18, "Working with the Communications Tools." Now that you've read about the settings, go on to Chapter 18 to learn how to use them.

- Chapter 20, "Customizing ClarisWorks." This chapter describes the Preferences dialog box, which contains options that can help you automate the connection process.

Chapter 18
Working with the Communications Tools

by Cyndie Shaffstall-Klopfenstein

In Chapter 17, you explored all the connection options. Now you are ready to learn how to send, receive, store, and use communications data.

In this chapter, the quest for remote data continues. You learn the following:

- How to work in the communications window
- How to send files to remote computers
- How to capture, save, and print incoming data
- How to automate your communications tasks

Understanding the Communications Window

Before you use the options for working with the data, you need to understand how the communications window works. Like all Macintosh windows, it can be moved, resized, and closed. Although you can resize the window, you can expand it to the number of columns you chose in the Terminal Settings dialog box (Width option). If you have a large monitor and the window resists your efforts to stretch it, you probably set the Width option to 80 columns rather than 132.

The default communications window is simple; it contains a status bar (to keep you informed of progress during the transmission of data) and a Phone Book control (for editing the phone list). You can display another status bar that contains information about your settings and the remote terminal's operations. To display this status bar, choose Terminal from the Settings menu to display the Terminal Settings dialog box. Click the General icon, and then choose the Status Bar option.

Figure 18.1 shows a communications window with both status bars displayed.

Figure 18.1
Different options in the Terminal Settings dialog box enable you to control the status bar and the cursor shape.

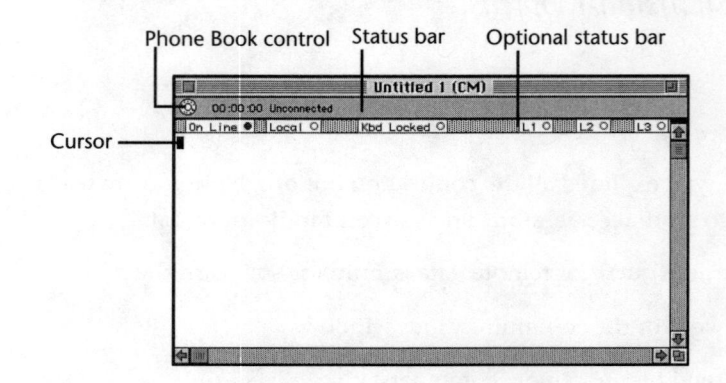

Accessing the Phone Book

The Phone Book is a great way to store commonly called remote computers. You can store the entire number-dialing sequence right down to dialing 9 for an outside line and pausing to wait for the remainder of the number.

To use the Phone Book, click the Phone Book control and hold down the mouse button to display the pop-up menu. Then choose Edit Phone Book from the pop-up menu. The Edit Phone Book Entry dialog box appears (see fig. 18.2).

Figure 18.2
The Edit Phone Book Entry dialog box enables you to create a list of numbers that you frequently call.

Type the appropriate information in the Name and Number fields. The Type box will change depending on the connection tool. In figure 18.2, the Apple Modem Tool was selected, so the type must be PhoneNumber (no space). Choose OK to add the listing to the Phone Book pop-up menu. Click Cancel to close the dialog box without adding the listing.

If you choose OK, the Phone Book dialog box appears (see fig. 18.3).

> **Note**
> You can display the Phone Book dialog box at any time by choosing Phone Book from the Settings menu.

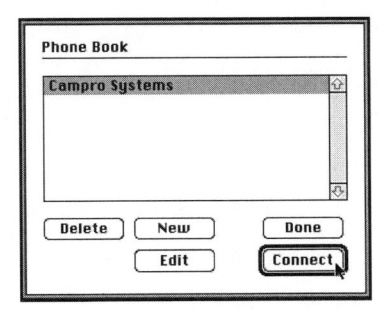

Figure 18.3
The Phone Book dialog box stores numbers. Scroll up or down if the entry you are looking for is not visible.

This dialog box contains several options for the listing that you just added and for all other existing listings. Select the entry you want to delete (permanently remove from the list) or edit (change), and then click the Delete or Edit button. Click New to create a new listing (you will return to the Edit Phone Book dialog box). Click Done if you are finished editing and do not want to connect now. To connect immediately, select a name in the list and then click the Connect button.

The name that you just typed in the Edit Phone Book dialog box appears in this dialog box, already selected. The command buttons afford you additional options. After a listing has been entered into the Phone Book, it appears in the pop-up Phone Book menu in the status bar. When you choose a listing from this menu, ClarisWorks immediately dials this listing and displays a dialog box showing the progress. Click Cancel in this dialog box if you do not want to make the connection.

Watching the Clock

The Connection Clock (see fig. 18.4) displays the elapsed time while you are connected to another terminal.

Figure 18.4
The Connection Clock displays the time elapsed during a connection.

Connection Clock

Most on-line services charge for elapsed time. This clock keeps you aware of time slipping away while you are connected. Click the clock to reset it.

Using the Optional Status Bar

If it is not already present, you can display the second status bar by checking the Show Status Bar box in the Terminal Settings dialog box. Follow these steps:

1. Choose Terminal from the Settings menu. The Terminal Settings dialog box appears.

2. If it is not already selected, click the General icon to display the General options.

3. Click the Show Status Bar check box.

4. Choose OK. The second status bar appears in the communications window (see fig. 18.5).

Figure 18.5
The optional status bar appears directly below the default status bar.

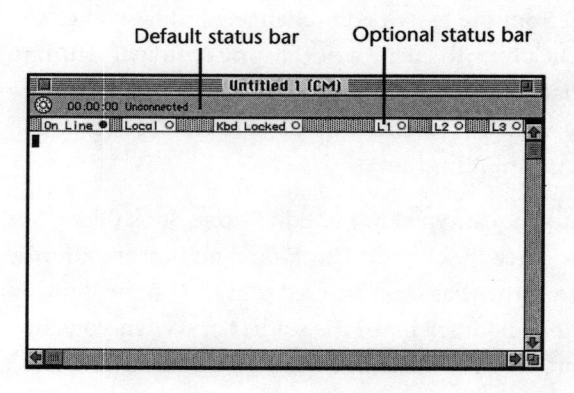

Default status bar   Optional status bar

The new status bar features seven status indicators. The first three indicators show the status of your computer; the last four show the status of the remote computer. The following table describes your computer's three indicators.

Indicator	Description
On Line	Indicates whether your computer is on-line or off-line. Your computer can be off-line and data cannot be sent or received but the connection remains.
Local	Indicates whether Local Echo is on or off. Turn on Local Echo if you need to see the text characters as you type them.
Kbd Locked	Indicates whether or not the keyboard is locked.

Using the Tab Ruler

The tab ruler is another type of status bar, displayed below both of the other status bars (see fig. 18.6). Use the tab ruler to set tab stops for your text. Click the eraser icon to delete all tab stops. Click the small ruler icon to reset the default tab stops (every eight characters).

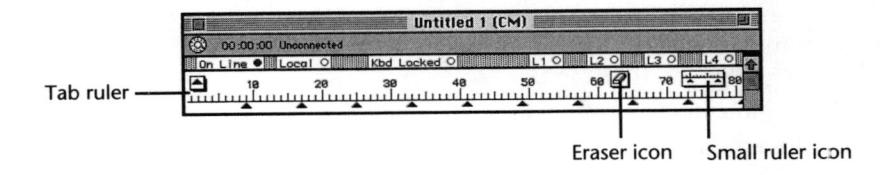

Figure 18.6
The Tab Ruler appears below the status bars.

Troubleshooting the Document Window

I can't get my window to stretch across my large-screen monitor. How can I make the window wider?

You need to open the Terminal Settings dialog box and set the Width option to 132 columns (see Chapter 17, "Communications Basics").

How can I update a phone number in the Phone Book?

Choose Phone Book from the Settings menu. In the Phone Book dialog box, select the file you want to change. Click Edit and make your changes; then click Done or Connect.

Receiving Calls

You might find the status bars and ruler bars useful when you receive data. The data that is transmitted to your computer can be used in several different ways. You can save communications data in a file, view it on-screen, and cut and paste it into a document in a different module.

Before you can send or receive data, you must be connected with another terminal. It generally doesn't matter which terminal initiates the connection. If you need help choosing communications settings, refer to Chapter 17, "Communications Basics."

To receive a call, follow these steps:

1. Adjust all settings to match the remote computer.

2. Choose Wait for Connection from the Session menu. A window appears, showing the status of the process.

3. Wait for the remote computer's modem to call.

When the remote modem calls your modem, you will hear a shrill tone; your modem will respond with a whistle. This whistle tells a modem that it is "talking to" another modem and not to a fax line or a regular phone line. If the remote modem does not hear the proper tone, it will disconnect. After a connection has been achieved, either computer can send or receive data.

Capturing Data

When you receive incoming data, you can choose to save (*capture*) that data. If you do not choose to capture the data, it will display only on your screen. You can choose to capture at any time during a transmission.

You can capture data in either of two formats, which you specify in the Preferences dialog box. To display this dialog box, choose Preferences from the Edit menu.

The following table describes these formats.

Format	Description
Port	This format captures data verbatim, including all tab, line-feed, and form-feed characters. If you plan to paste a captured table into a spreadsheet, for example, you would need to capture all the tab keystrokes as well as the text.
Screen	This format captures data as it appears on-screen, without tab, line-feed, and form-feed characters. You might use this format if you want to use captured text in a letter with margins different from those of the communications document.

To capture all or part of the data for future use, follow these steps:

1. Choose Capture to File from the Session menu. A dialog box appears, asking you to name the file and choose a destination for the captured data.

2. Name the file and choose a destination, using standard Macintosh methods.

3. Click Save to save the data to a file.

4. To end a file capture, choose Stop Capture from the Session menu.

Putting Scrollback to Work

If you do not plan to reuse the data you are receiving, but just want to read it on-screen, you have several options for receiving the data in this way. The scrollback feature is used for exactly this situation. (Scrollback, however, uses more RAM memory than Capture to File because it does not store the file on the hard disk.)

When you receive text from a remote site, the text scrolls away as the screen fills. The area to which the text scrolls is the *scrollback pane*. You can use this portion of the window to capture data that you don't need to save permanently.

380 Chapter 18—Working with the Communications Tools

To use this feature, choose Save Lines Off Top from the Session menu. This command instructs ClarisWorks to store the top lines of incoming text in the scrollback pane. When you save the document, the text in the scrollback pane is saved with it. Until you choose the Save command, however, you risk losing the text if your computer crashes or locks up. If you intend to save the text, it is better to choose Capture to File.

You can control the display of the scrollback pane in two ways. The first way is to click and drag the black bar of the window that is directly above the top scroll arrow. This bar is the *pane control*. When you move the pane control, the window divides into two parts. The top part of the window is the scrollback pane, and the bottom part is the terminal pane (see fig. 18.7).

Figure 18.7
Click and drag the pane control to adjust the sizes of the scrollback and terminal panes.

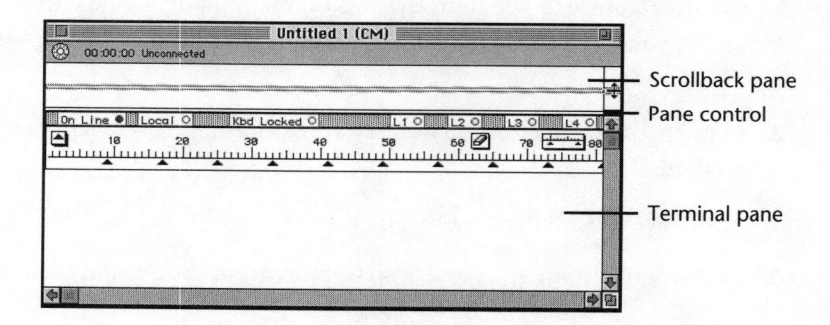

[Figure showing Untitled 1 (CM) window with labels: Scrollback pane, Pane control, Terminal pane]

Tip
Press ⌘-L to toggle quickly between Show Scrollback and Hide Scrollback.

The second way to control the display of the scrollback pane is to choose a command from the Settings menu. To display the pane, choose Show Scrollback; to hide the pane, choose Hide Scrollback.

After you have received data and that data appears in the document window, choose Save Current Screen from the Session menu. This command places a copy of any text in the terminal pane in the scrollback pane as well. If you want to delete the data in the scrollback pane but not in the terminal pane, choose Clear Saved Lines from the Session menu. When the warning dialog box appears, click OK.

> **Caution**
>
> Remote terminals can send a screen-clearing command to your terminal, deleting all text in the terminal pane. To safeguard this text, choose Save Screen Before Clearing in the Preferences dialog box. (For help with this feature, see Chapter 20, "Customizing ClarisWorks.")

You can save all data in the scrollback and terminal panes at any time by choosing Save or Save As from the File menu.

> **Troubleshooting Receiving Data**
>
> *My text is disappearing from the top of the screen. Why?*
>
> If Save Lines Off Top is selected in the Session menu, the text is scrolling into the scrollback pane. You can save this text to a file or view it on-screen.
>
> *The data that I am receiving is jumbled in my document window. What can I do?*
>
> Disconnect, and then place a telephone call to the receiving party. Compare the protocol settings—especially the baud rate—to ensure that both computers are using the same protocol.

Using Captured Data

You can use captured communications data in any of the other ClarisWorks modules. Tables can be pasted into spreadsheets, for example; text can be imported into word processing, database, and drawing documents. After you place captured data in a different module, you can edit that data.

Using Captured Data in a Spreadsheet

If the text you receive is in table format, and if you chose the Port format in the Preferences dialog box, you can paste the table directly into a spreadsheet document. Follow these steps:

1. In the communications module, choose Copy Table from the Edit menu.

2. Choose New from the File menu. The New Document dialog box appears.

3. Click the Spreadsheet button. A blank spreadsheet document appears.

4. Choose Paste from the Edit menu. The table appears in the document.

5. Edit and save the spreadsheet document.

Printing Data

Printing a communications document is exactly the same as printing documents in other ClarisWorks modules. Choose Print from the File menu to open the Print dialog box; select a page range, if necessary; and then click Print.

Automating Communications

There are several different ways to simplify the processes of logging on, sending, and receiving files. Using macros for storing log-on procedures (the process of calling remote terminals and identifying yourself) is a great way to automate the repetitive procedures of calling on-line services. Macros are discussed in greater detail in Chapter 19, "Automating Your Work."

Using Macros

A log-on macro is a way of storing the log-on process in a single keystroke. The log-on process might include typing your name, your protocol, and your password. This log-on procedure tends to be tedious if you have to perform it several times a week.

To create the macro, follow these steps:

1. Open a communications document in ClarisWorks.

2. Choose Shortcuts from the File menu, and then choose Record Macro from the Shortcuts submenu. The Record Macro dialog box appears (see fig. 18.8).

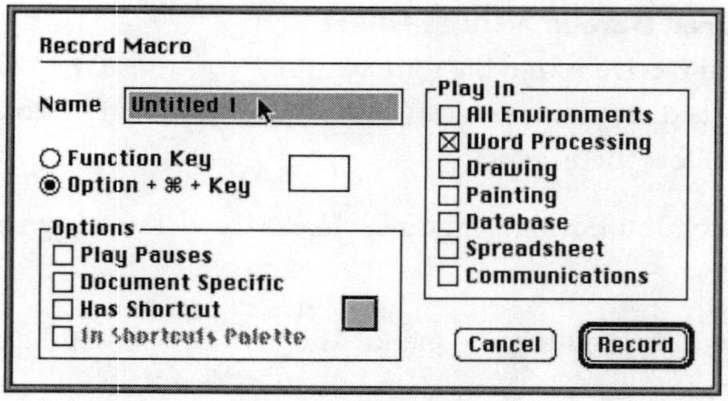

Figure 18.8
The Record Macro dialog box is used to begin the process of storing a macro.

3. Type a name and a key equivalent, or type a function key.

4. Make sure that the Communications box is selected. This box means that the macro is for use in the communications module.

5. Click Record. From this point on, the ClarisWorks macro system will record your actions.

To continue recording the macro, follow these steps:

1. Choose Connection from the Settings menu. The Connection Settings dialog box appears.

2. Type the phone number to call and the baud rate, and make any other necessary choices.

3. When you finish, choose OK. You return to the communications window.

4. Choose Shortcuts from the File menu, and then choose Macro Wait from the submenu. The Macro Wait dialog box appears (see fig. 18.9).

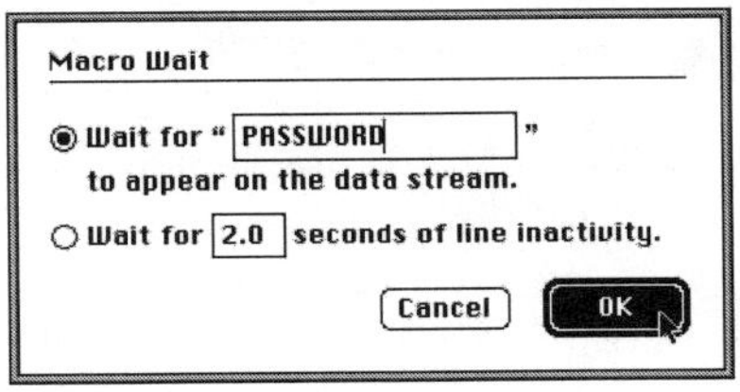

Figure 18.9
The Macro Wait dialog box instructs the macro to wait for a specific prompt or to wait for a specified period before executing the remaining steps stored in the macro.

5. Type the remote computer's prompt, character for character (matching uppercase and lowercase letters). This prompt might be your name or your password.

    or

    If the prompt varies, or if you don't know what it is, you can instruct the macro to pause for a specified period. Choose Wait for ___ Seconds of Line Inactivity, and then type the amount of time you want ClarisWorks to wait for the prompt.

6. Choose OK to save the Macro Wait information.

7. Wait for the prompt that you chose in Macro Wait to appear, and then type your name or password exactly as you want the macro to type it.

8. Continue performing the actions that you want to store in the macro.

9. When you finish, choose Shortcuts from the File menu, and then choose Stop Recording from the submenu.

The macro is ready for use. To run it, press the key combination that you entered in the Record Macro dialog box.

Using Other Shortcuts

The Preferences dialog box has a section dedicated to communications. You learn more about this dialog box in Chapter 20, "Customizing ClarisWorks." Use the automation features of the Preferences dialog box to set defaults so that you don't have to repeat the setup process each time you make a communications connection.

Using the Stationery feature, for example, enables you to save a stationery document for each on-line service or modem that you log on to regularly. This document would contain all the connection, terminal, and file-transfer options you would set to connect to a remote system. This feature is particularly handy because you can make all the desired changes in settings options, preferences, and connection options and then save the document. To make a stationery document for a remote modem, follow these steps:

1. Set all options and preferences to the desired settings. (See chapters 17 and 20 if you need help with any settings.)

2. Choose Save As from the File menu. The Save As dialog box appears.

3. Type a name for the file.

4. Choose Stationery from the pop-up menu.

5. Choose OK.

To use these settings to connect to a remote terminal, choose Open from the File menu. When the Open dialog box appears, select the stationery document that contains the settings you want to use. The document opens, and you can begin the connection sequence. (For more information on the Stationery feature, see Chapter 2, "Learning the Essentials.")

However you send or receive documents, ClarisWorks affords you many options and automation procedures for doing the work quickly, efficiently, and painlessly.

From Here...

After you've read chapters 17 and 18, you're well on your way to sharing and receiving data from all sorts of on-line services and other computers. Information in the following chapters also can help you make simple, clean connections.

- Chapter 2, "Learning the Essentials." Using the Stationery feature of ClarisWorks enables you to save all the settings and preferences. Return to Chapter 2 for additional help.

- Chapter 17, "Communications Basics." Making a clean connection can mean the difference between usable and unusable text files. Make sure that your protocol and settings match those of the computer to which you are connecting. Chapter 17 reviews each of these settings in detail.

- Chapter 19, "Automating Your Work." You can use a macro to record the log-on process. In Chapter 19, the use of macros is covered step by step.

- Chapter 20, "Customizing ClarisWorks." The options in the Preferences dialog box can be used to further automate communications procedures. See Chapter 20 for help on setting Preferences options for your documents.

Part VI

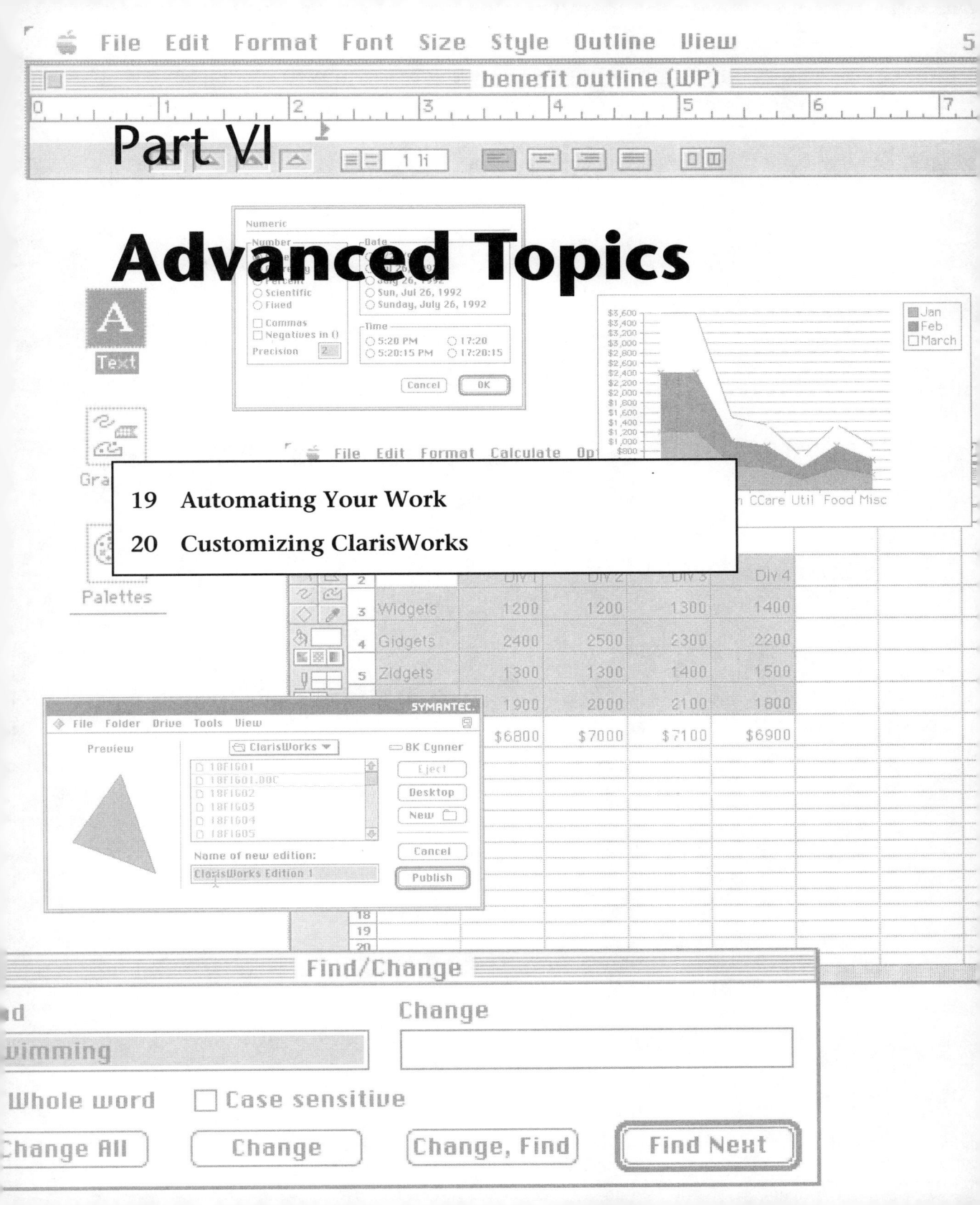

Advanced Topics

19 Automating Your Work

20 Customizing ClarisWorks

File Edit Format Font Size Style Outline View

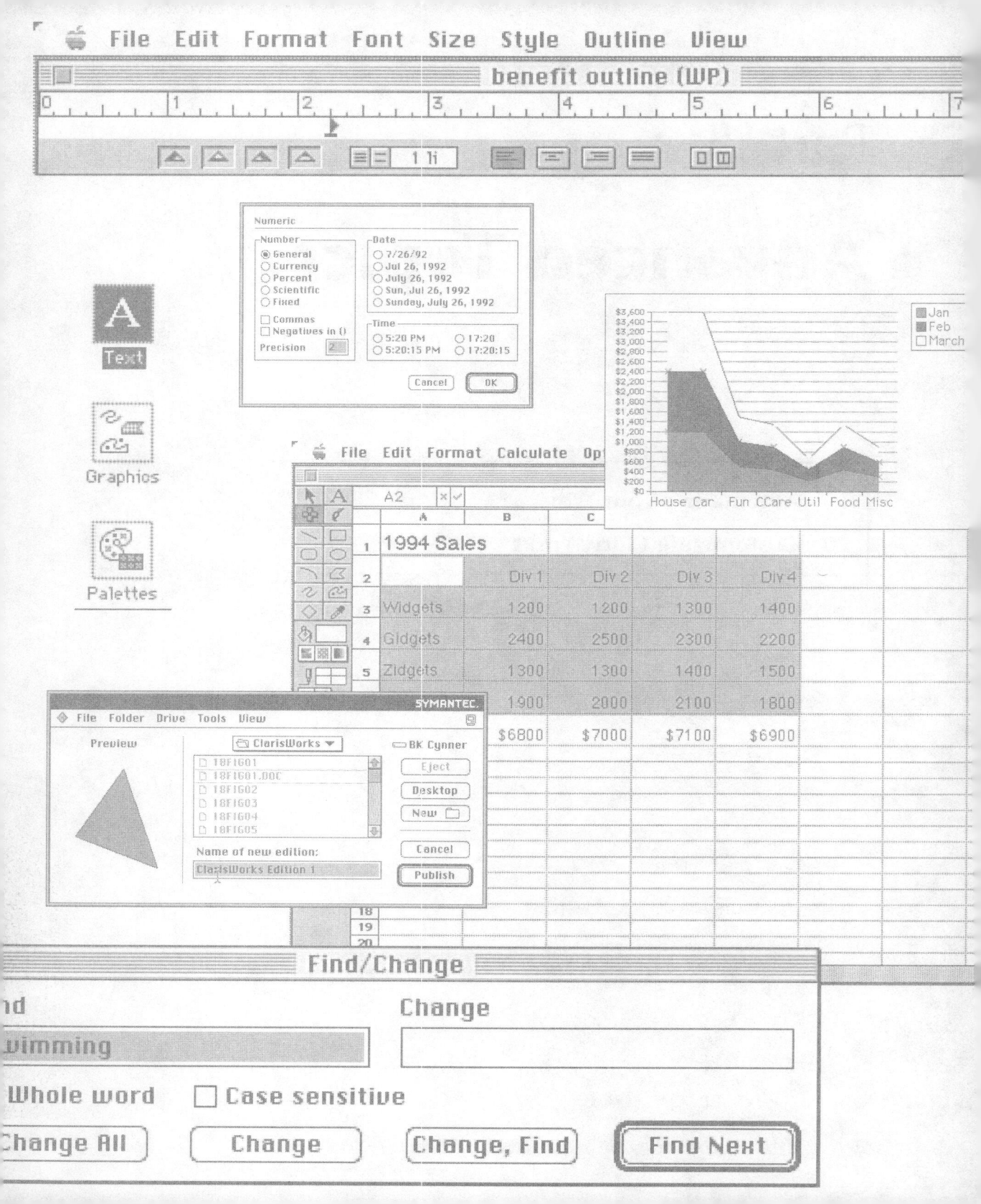

benefit outline (WP)

Numeric

Number
- ● General
- ○ Currency
- ○ Percent
- ○ Scientific
- ○ Fixed

☐ Commas
☐ Negatives in ()
Precision 2

Date
- ○ 7/26/92
- ○ Jul 26, 1992
- ○ July 26, 1992
- ○ Sun, Jul 26, 1992
- ○ Sunday, July 26, 1992

Time
- ○ 5:20 PM   ○ 17:20
- ○ 5:20:15 PM ○ 17:20:15

[Cancel] [OK]

Text

Graphics

Palettes

File Edit Format Calculate Op

A2

	A	B	C	D	E
1	1994 Sales				
2		Div 1	Div 2	Div 3	Div 4
3	Widgets	1200	1200	1300	1400
4	Gidgets	2400	2500	2300	2200
5	Zidgets	1300	1300	1400	1500
		1900	2000	2100	1800
		$6800	$7000	$7100	$6900

SYMANTEC

File Folder Drive Tools View

Preview: ClarisWorks ▼
- 18FIG01
- 18FIG01.DOC
- 18FIG02
- 18FIG03
- 18FIG04
- 18FIG05

☐ BK Cynner

[Eject]
[Desktop]
[New]
[Cancel]
[Publish]

Name of new edition:
ClarisWorks Edition 1

Find/Change

Find: wimming

Change:

☐ Whole word   ☐ Case sensitive

[Change All] [Change] [Change, Find] [**Find Next**]

Chapter 19

Automating Your Work

by Cyndie Shaffstall-Klopfenstein

The automation features of ClarisWorks help increase the efficiency and productivity with which you create documents. ClarisWorks includes everything from simple cut and paste buttons to complex macros. You can choose most menu selections from a movable palette of buttons; you need not travel repeatedly to the menu bar to click, drag, and choose options. Automation is a powerful tool to assist even the novice in becoming a ClarisWorks expert.

Using ClarisWorks Shortcuts

You can access a Shortcuts pop-up submenu from the File menu, as shown in figure 19.1. You can use the Shortcuts options in this submenu to automate ClarisWorks. In this chapter, you learn to use and customize these options to suit your requirements.

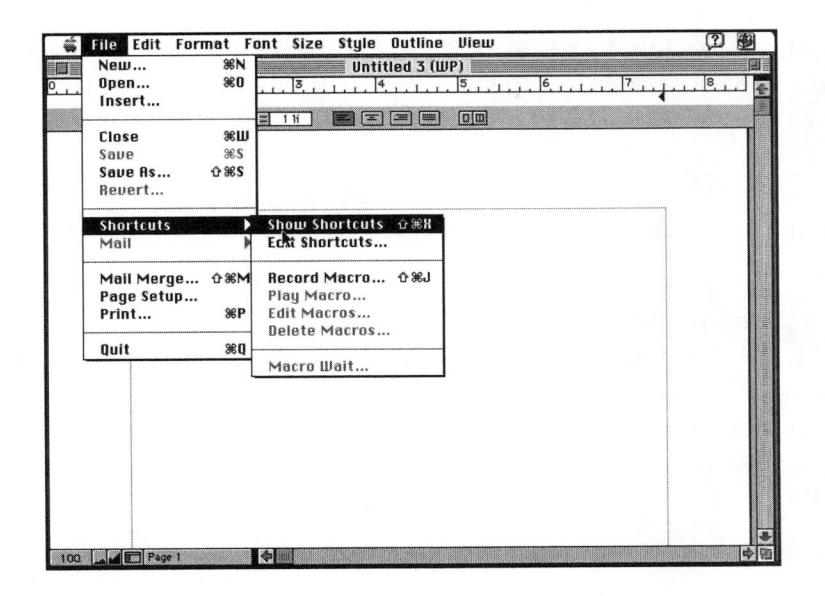

Figure 19.1
You access the Shortcuts submenu through the File menu.

Shortcuts and macros are closely related. Both are designed to help you to create documents quickly and efficiently. In this chapter, you use both to their best advantage as you learn the following:

- How to use palettes when you create different types of ClarisWorks documents
- How to hide, show, and move palettes for convenient use
- How to customize palettes to reduce returns to the menu bar
- How to record macros to automate repetitious functions such as style changes
- How to recognize situations in which automation is practical

Finding Your Way around the Shortcuts Palette

The first option in the Shortcuts submenu is the Hide/Show Shortcuts toggle command. When the Shortcuts palette is displayed (even when collapsed), the available option in this menu is Hide Palette; when the Shortcuts palette is hidden, this option is Show Palette. This Hide/Show feature is available in most Macintosh applications.

Figure 19.2 shows the Shortcuts palette.

Figure 19.2
You can place the Shortcuts palette anywhere in the Desktop area.

Close box ——————— Collapse/expand box

While the palette is displayed, the collapse/expand button appears in the top right corner. Clicking this button causes the palette either to collapse to a small window or to expand to its full size. If the submenu displays Hide when you attempt to Show Palettes, the palette window probably is collapsed and is patiently resting in an obscure area of the Desktop, waiting for use (see fig. 19.3). After you locate the palette, click the expand button to show the entire window.

Other features, such as the close box and the title bar, are common elements of Macintosh windows. Click the close box to dismiss the window, or click and drag the title bar to move the window. From the File menu and the Shortcuts submenu, choose Show Shortcuts to bring the window back to the Desktop after it has been closed.

Using ClarisWorks Shortcuts **391**

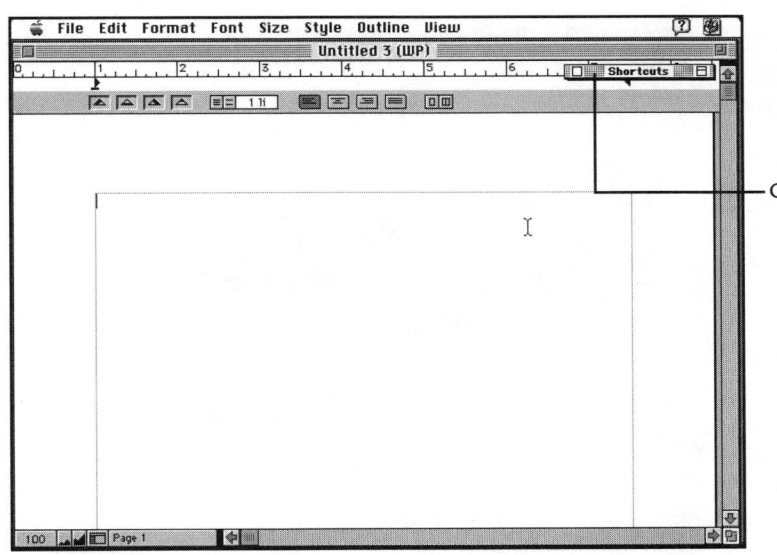

Figure 19.3
When collapsed, the palette can be difficult to locate on the Desktop.

Collapsed Shortcuts palette

Note

Keyboard shortcuts are another beneficial and timesaving feature. These shortcuts are listed beside the equivalent commands and options in the menus. You can issue the Save command, for example, by pressing ⌘-S; Save As by pressing ⌘-Shift-S; and Show Shortcuts by pressing ⌘-Shift-X.

Tip
Keep palettes out of the way but still convenient by using the collapse/expand button instead of closing the window. This practice saves you the trouble of returning to the menu bar to display the palette.

Using the Shortcut Palette

After you choose Show Shortcuts, ClarisWorks displays a palette. The nature of the palette varies in accordance with the ClarisWorks module in which you are working. The palette also changes in accordance with what is selected or active. For example, if you have text selected, the palette will display only tools available for text. A palette also may change during your work in a document, depending on what is selected.

For a look at how palettes work, open the Shortcuts palette in a ClarisWorks word processing document, select text, and click the Cut button (see fig. 19.4). The text is cut and moved to the Clipboard just as it is when you choose Cut from the Edit menu.

VI

Advanced Topics

392 Chapter 19—Automating Your Work

Figure 19.4
Select a section of text and click the Cut button.

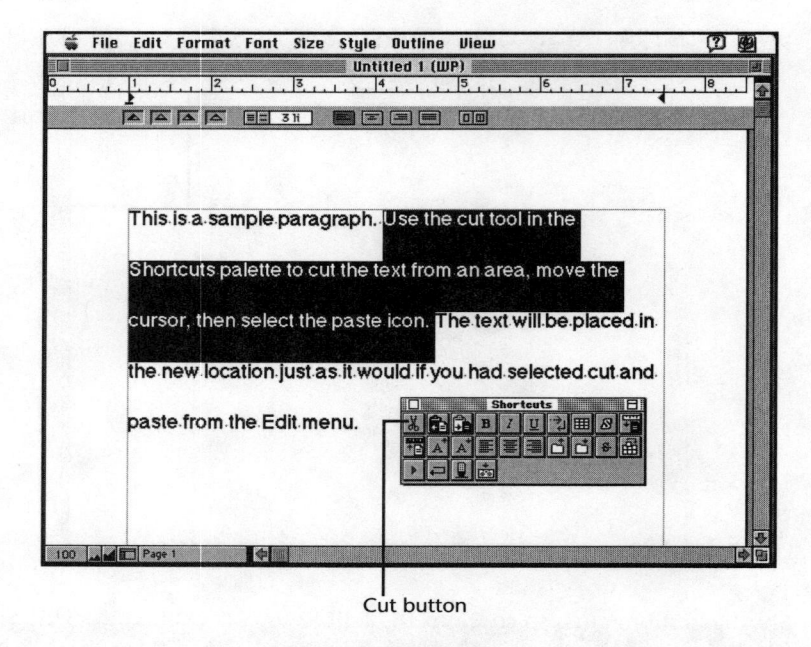

Cut button

Now move the insertion point in the document, and click the Paste button (see fig. 19.5). The text moves to its new location.

Figure 19.5
Move the insertion point and click the Paste button.

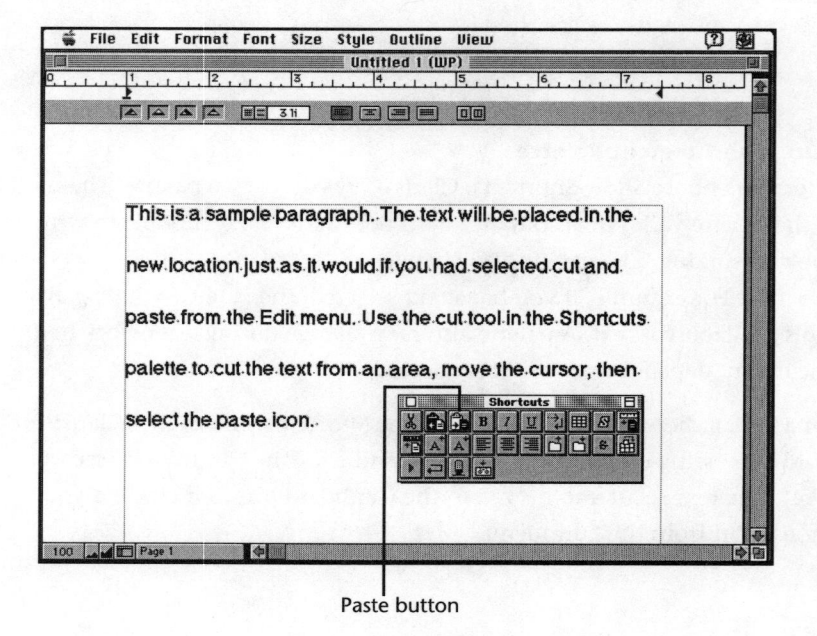

Paste button

Using ClarisWorks Shortcuts **393**

> **Note**
>
> Your Shortcuts palette may have these buttons in locations other than those shown in figures 19.4 and 19.5.

The Cut and Paste buttons are available in the default Shortcuts palette, and you can use them without touching the keyboard or returning to the menus (you use the mouse).

> **Note**
>
> If a button's function is not clear to you, you can find a description of its function in the Edit Shortcuts window, as discussed in the next section, "Editing the Shortcut Palette."

Editing the Shortcut Palette

The Shortcuts submenu also contains the Edit Shortcuts command, which opens the Edit Shortcuts dialog box (see fig. 19.6). In this dialog box, you can customize the Shortcuts palette by selecting buttons to be *added* to or *removed* from the existing palette in the current document or in the entire ClarisWorks application. This feature stores commonly used selections that you otherwise must access through the menu bar. Save the selections so that they are available in all six modules of ClarisWorks (Application button) or just in the current document (Document button).

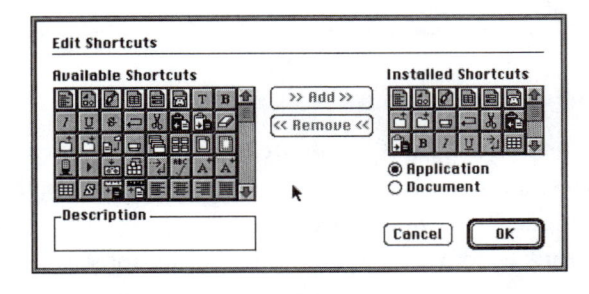

Figure 19.6
The Edit Shortcuts dialog box enables you to customize the palette.

> **Note**
>
> Buttons that are not applicable to the currently running ClarisWorks module will not be added to the palette in that document, even if you click Add.

394 Chapter 19—Automating Your Work

The Available Shortcuts section of the Edit Shortcuts dialog box displays buttons that represent all the application-accessible shortcuts. To display a description of a shortcut, click the shortcut's button in the Available Shortcuts window. The description appears in the Description field (see fig. 19.7).

Figure 19.7
Click a button and check the Description field for a brief explanation of the shortcut's function.

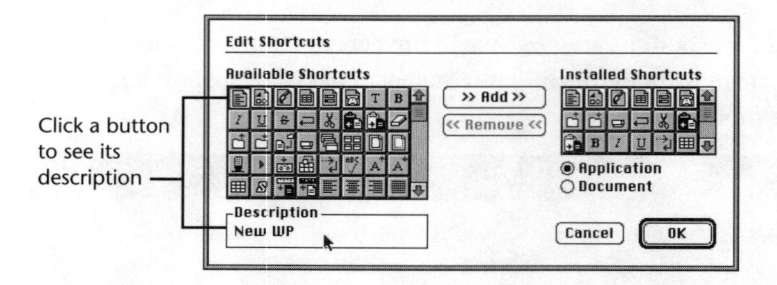

If you do not see a button for the shortcut that you want to use, scroll to move the buttons up or down until the desired button appears anywhere in the window. (Both scroll bars are visible in fig. 19.8.) Click the button to display its description.

Figure 19.8
The scroll bars move the lists of buttons up and down so you can make your selection.

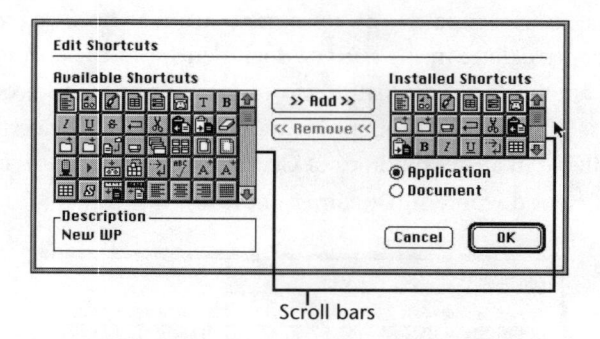

To the left, below the title Installed Shortcuts, is another window and scroll bar. Below the window and the scroll bar are two buttons: Application and Document. In figure 19.8, the Application button is selected; therefore, the Installed Shortcuts window contains all the same buttons as the Available Shortcuts window. By default, ClarisWorks uses all available shortcuts. Click the Document button to display all shortcuts used by the current document. Until you edit the palette for the current document, the Installed Shortcuts window is empty like the one shown in figure 19.9.

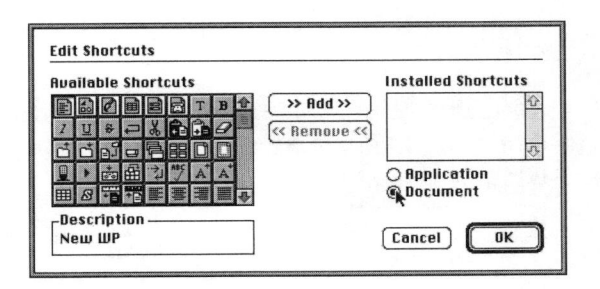

Figure 19.9
If you have not edited the Shortcuts palette for the current document, the Installed Shortcuts window is empty when you click the Document button.

In the Available Shortcuts window, click the button of the shortcut you want to install. Check the Description field to ensure that you have selected the correct button. Click the Add button in the center of the dialog box (see fig. 19.10), and repeat this process until all desired buttons have been added to the Installed Shortcuts window. These buttons appear below the current buttons of the palette, separated from the current buttons by a black bar. Use the Application (available in all ClarisWorks modules) or Document (available only in this document) button to determine which Shortcuts palettes will contain the new buttons.

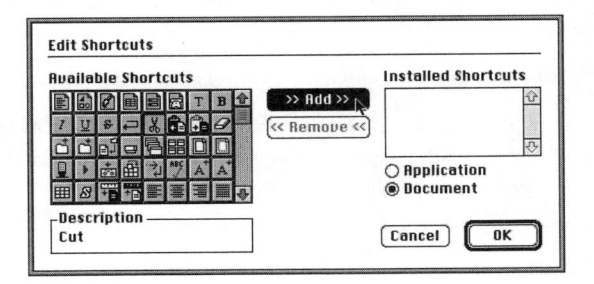

Figure 19.10
Click Add to place a button in the Installed Shortcuts window.

To remove current buttons, you reverse the process. In the Installed Shortcuts window, click the button to be removed, and then click Remove. Figure 19.11 shows that the Cut button will be removed from the document Shortcuts palette.

Tip
Don't hunt and peck through the palette; prioritize shortcuts before adding. The Shortcuts palette displays buttons in the order in which you added them. Display the shortcuts you use most often first in the palette.

Figure 19.11
Click the button to be removed, and then click Remove.

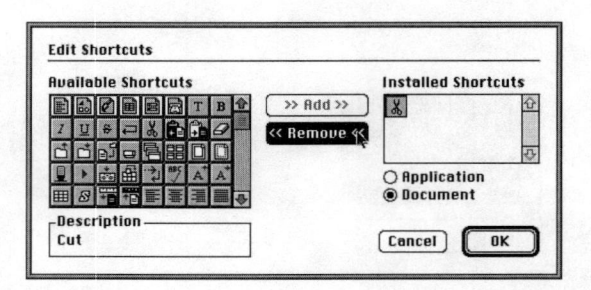

> ### Troubleshooting Shortcuts
>
> *I can't find my Shortcuts palette, and the menu says Hide Shortcuts.*
>
> The Shortcuts palette has been collapsed and is so small that it is difficult to find on your screen. Choose Hide Shortcuts and watch the screen carefully. You will see movement as ClarisWorks hides the palette. Choose Show Shortcuts to find the palette.
>
> *I can't move the palette around my work area.*
>
> Be sure to click and drag the title bar at the top of the palette. The Shortcuts palette is like other Macintosh windows; clicking and dragging the title bar is the only way to move the palette.
>
> *I inadvertently deleted some buttons from the application Shortcuts palette.*
>
> Choose Edit Shortcuts to display the Edit Shortcuts dialog box. In the Available Shortcuts window, click the button you want to reinstall, click the Application button, and then click Add. Repeat until you have replaced all deleted buttons.

Using Macros

Macros offer another extremely simple method of automating. Unlike Shortcuts, however, they are far more definable. You can record macros to perform mundane functions such as making complex style changes, adding text, or changing paragraph formatting. To make a macro, you instruct ClarisWorks to "watch" what you do and then repeat your actions.

Practicing Macro Making

To get an idea of how macros work, create a simple macro that makes a style change. Open the Shortcuts palette so that it can be used in this macro, and then follow these steps:

1. Type some sample text, and select a portion.

2. Choose Shortcuts from the File menu, and then choose Record Macro from the Shortcuts submenu (see fig. 19.12). The Record Macro dialog box appears.

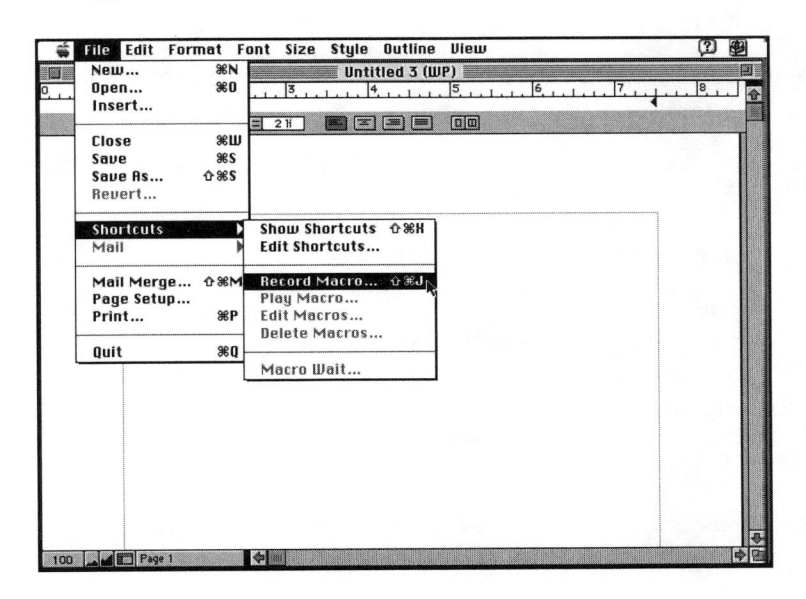

Figure 19.12
To begin recording a macro, choose Record Macro from the Shortcuts submenu.

Tip
Name macros appropriately. Assume that someone else may need to edit your document and use your macros. Then, if you forget what a macro does, its name is likely to remind you.

3. Type a name for the macro in the Name box (see fig. 19.13).

Figure 19.13
In the Record Macro dialog box, you name and store the macro.

4. Directly below the Name box, you can choose a keyboard shortcut (a series of keystrokes used to invoke the macro). If you have an extended keyboard, you can choose the Function Key button. For a standard keyboard, use the Option+⌘+Key button.

Chapter 19—Automating Your Work

5. If you chose Function Key, ClarisWorks displays an unused function key in the box next to the button. You can accept this one or press the function key you prefer.

    If you chose Option+⌘+Key, type the key that you will use in conjunction with the Option and ⌘ keys.

6. Choose the options you want to use (see the paragraphs following these steps for details about the options).

7. In the Play In box, choose in which environments the macro will be used.

8. Click Record to begin recording the macro.

    The next series of steps will be recorded until you choose Stop Recording. Recording is indicated by a blinking microphone that replaces the apple menu during recording.

9. In the Shortcuts palette, click a series of icons to change the formatting of the text.

10. Choose Shortcuts from the File menu, and then choose Stop Recording from the submenu, as shown in figure 19.14.

Tip
Use the keyboard equivalent, ⌘-Shift-J, to start and stop the macro recorder.

Figure 19.14
Choose Stop Recording from the Shortcuts submenu.

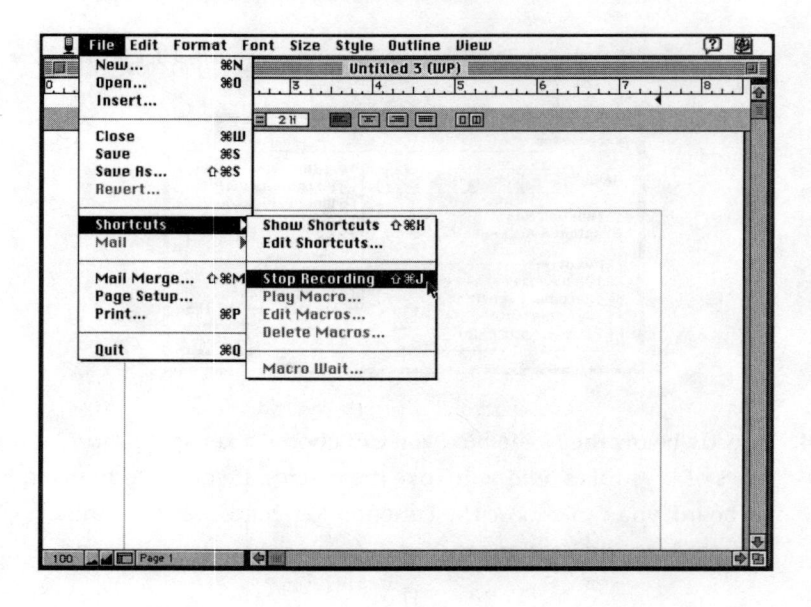

Your macro is finished and ready for use. Try selecting a different portion of the sample text, but this time use the small icon that you created (which now appears as the last entry in the Shortcuts palette) to run the macro.

Choosing Macro Options

The Record Macro dialog box contains several options you can apply to your macro. Choose the ones that will make your macro the most useful.

- *Play Pauses* inserts a pause or stops the replay of a macro to give you time to insert characters or perform other manual functions. It stops and waits for the amount of time that you pause when recording.

- *Document Specific* indicates that this macro is used for this document only.

- *Has Shortcut* indicates that there is a keyboard equivalent for this option.

- *In Shortcuts Palette* is dimmed unless you choose Has Shortcut. When you activate the Has Shortcut and In Shortcuts Palette options, you can click the small box to the right to display the Edit Button Icon dialog box.

- *Edit Button Icon*: This dialog box is called a *bitmap tablet*. In a bitmap tablet, you use *pixels* (squares that appear when you click a white area) to draw. A pixel is either on or off. A pixel that is on is colored. To edit your icon drawing, simply click each pixel to turn it on. Click on a color in the palette to color pixels with that tint. Click a colored pixel to turn it off or to erase it.

A to-scale rendition of the icon is displayed in the top-right corner of the dialog box, like the one shown in figure 19.15. When you are satisfied with the drawing, click OK. The drawing appears in the small box and in the Shortcuts palette.

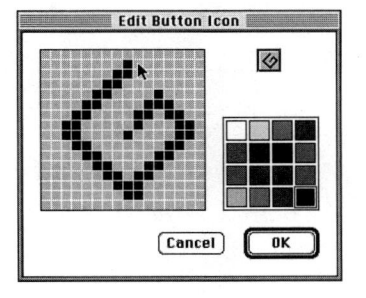

Figure 19.15
Use the Edit Button Icon dialog box to customize a button.

Tip
If your icon gets too complicated and you want to start over, click Cancel to stop, and then click the small box again to restart. This method is easier than turning all the pixels off and restarting.

Tip
To quickly save and print a document, store a macro that executes a Save, Print, and Return-key sequence.

Figure 19.16
Play Macro executes the macro.

- *Play In:* The right side of the Record Macro dialog box shows where the macro will be used. It can be used in all the modules or in any combination of modules. Click the check box of each module in which you plan to use the macro.

Macros prove very useful in modules such as the database. Perhaps once each month, for example, you print a letter to all customers in the state of Colorado. You can record a macro that sorts the database by ZIP code, performs a mail merge, and prints the letters. Each of these steps, from sorting to opening the word processing module to printing, can be recorded and subsequently executed with a single keystroke.

Using Macros from the Menu

You can implement, from the File menu, any macros that lack an icon or keyboard equivalent. Choose Play Macro from the Shortcuts submenu. A dialog box like the one shown in figure 19.16 appears, listing the names of all macros applicable to the current document. Select the macro you want to implement, and click OK to execute it.

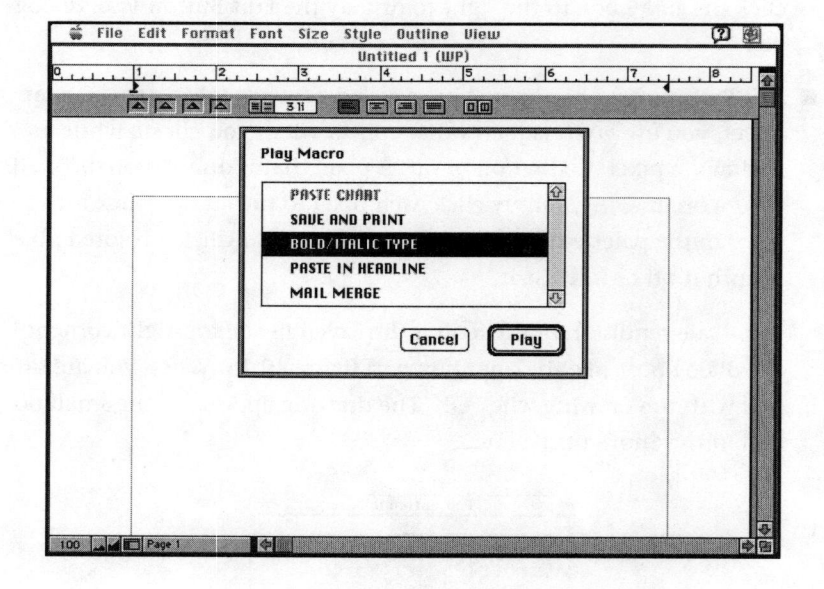

> **Note**
>
> You may have other macros recorded that you chose not to have available in this environment. For example, you might create a macro that totals columns in the spreadsheet module; it would not be very helpful in the word processing module.

Tip
Double-clicking a macro in the play list is the same as choosing a macro and then clicking OK.

Editing a Macro

In many cases, you may need to go back to a recorded macro and make changes in it. You may want to change the keyboard equivalent or the function-key assignment, or perhaps the modules that can access the macro. You can change the options of a macro without deleting the entire recording and starting over. To edit specific steps of the macro, you will need to rerecord.

To edit your macro, choose Shortcuts from the File menu and Edit Macros from the Shortcuts submenu. The Edit Macros dialog box appears (see fig. 19.17). All recorded macros for this environment are listed in the Macro pop-up menu.

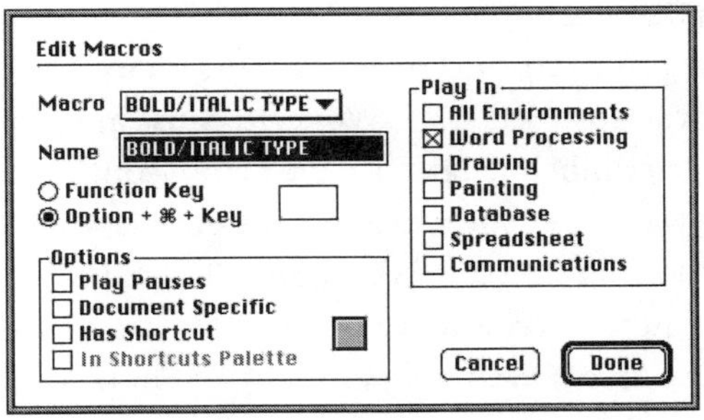

Figure 19.17
Make changes in existing macro options through the Edit Macros dialog box.

Select the macro you want to edit, make the necessary changes to the options, and click OK. The macro is changed. If you edited the icon, the new icon appears in the Shortcuts palette.

If you have recorded a macro with a mistake, a missing step, or too many steps, delete the macro (as discussed in the next section) and record a new one.

Removing Macros

The most common reason for deleting macros is that there is an error in the recording. Sometimes you may forget that you're recording, and you add too many steps. If you don't plan your recording ahead of time, you might not be able to find the options to record. Either way, you will need to delete the old recording and make a new one.

To delete a macro, choose Shortcuts from the File menu and then choose Delete Macros from the Shortcuts submenu. A dialog box like the one shown in figure 19.18 appears.

Figure 19.18
You can delete more than one macro from this dialog box.

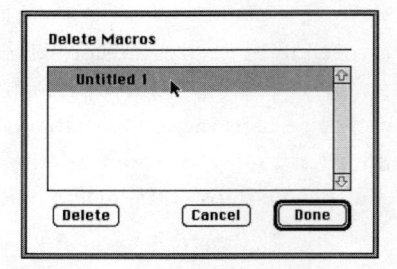

Click the macro you want to remove, and then click Delete. Continue choosing and deleting to remove all unwanted macros. When you finish, click Done.

Using Macro Wait

The Macro Wait option is available only when you use the communications module. Macro Wait instructs ClarisWorks to pause and wait for a particular prompt or for a determined length of time before continuing to execute the macro. You may want to create a macro, for example, that logs you on to an on-line service. Most on-line services require that you type your name at a specific prompt and then type your password. When you record the log-on macro, you choose Macro Wait and, in the Wait For box, type the prompt exactly as it appears from the on-line service.

To experiment with this option, you must be properly connected to a modem, and the modem must be connected to an active phone line. For the purposes of this example, assume that your macro is to log on to a typical on-line service. Before you record the macro, open a document in the communications module. Then follow these steps to record the macro:

1. Choose Connection from the Settings menu. The Connection Settings dialog box appears.

2. Type in the phone number to call, and choose the baud rate.

3. Click OK.

4. Choose Shortcuts from the File menu, and then choose Record Macro from the Shortcuts submenu. The Record Macro dialog box appears.

5. Name the macro, and click OK.

6. Choose Shortcuts from the File menu, and then choose Macro Wait from the Shortcuts submenu. The Macro Wait dialog box appears (see fig. 19.19).

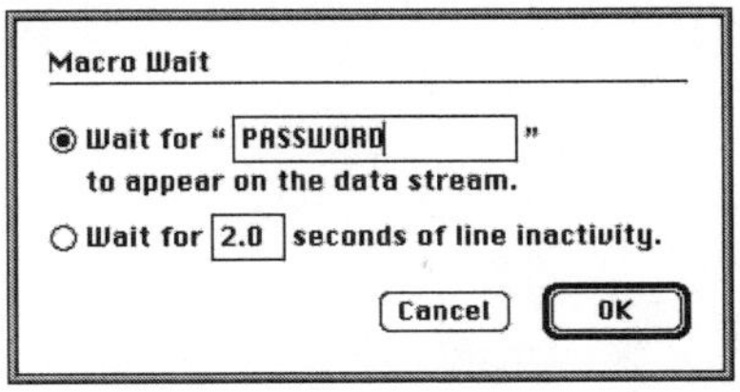

Figure 19.19
The Macro Wait option enables you to delay the response time of a macro or to wait for a specific prompt.

7. In the Wait For box, type the prompt exactly as it is given by the remote computer (match the uppercase and lowercase letters and all spaces). This prompt might be your name or your password.

   If the prompt varies, or if you don't know what it is, you can instruct the macro to pause for a determined length of time. This will give you time to type the correct response to the prompt. Type the amount of time you want the macro to wait rather than the name of the prompt to wait for.

8. Click OK to save the Macro Wait command.

9. Continue recording the remainder of the macro.

10. Choose Shortcuts from the File menu, and then choose Stop Recording from the Shortcuts submenu.

Troubleshooting Macros

When I create a new macro, ClarisWorks beeps and displays the message `A macro with that key equivalent has already been defined.`

Click OK in the message dialog box, and type a different function key in the box provided.

(continues)

> (continued)
>
> *The macro that I recorded does not perform as I expected.*
>
> Delete the macro, using the Delete Macros option, and rerecord.
>
> *When I play the macro, it moves very slowly.*
>
> You probably checked the Play Pauses option when recording. Turn it off in the Edit Macros dialog box.

From Here...

Shortcuts and macros are designed to help you to move much more quickly through document creation. When you begin using them, you will soon realize the immense time savings they can afford you. Turn to the following chapters for ways to use shortcuts and macros:

- Chapter 3, "Working with Text." The Shortcuts palette is quite helpful when you are creating the first draft of a document.

- Chapter 10, "Using Spreadsheet Functions." Macros in spreadsheets are great ways to speed the use of functions. See Chapter 10 for a refresher course on the use of spreadsheets.

Chapter 20
Customizing ClarisWorks

by Cyndie Shaffstall-Klopfenstein

Similar to the shortcuts discussed in the preceding chapter, preferences automate certain repetitive tasks. You can use preferences to set defaults for such options as smart quotes, the colors contained in palettes, and the placement of uploaded files. These defaults tell ClarisWorks how to execute specific functions. Using preferences to set defaults eliminates the need to reset a standard each time you implement a particular option. In ClarisWorks, you also can choose to set the preferences for one-time use, rather than as the default for each consecutive use.

Setting Preferences

If you are new to ClarisWorks, get a feel for how the application works before you attempt to set preferences. By familiarizing yourself with the application, you can see how the defaults affect the documents.

As you progress through this chapter, you will learn the following things:

- How to set preferences
- How to change the look of the Shortcuts palette
- How to edit the colors available in the color palettes
- How to use custom text styles

Preferences affect documents as they are opened. Launch ClarisWorks, and then choose Preferences from the Edit menu. The Preferences dialog box appears, displaying icons that represent the different groups of preferences (see fig. 20.1). A scroll bar separates these icons from the actual preferences settings.

Figure 20.1
The Preferences dialog box.

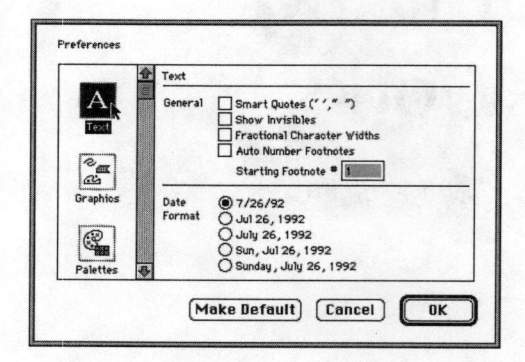

To display the preferences for a module or option, click the icon for that module or option (the icon darkens when you choose it). The preferences for the chosen module or option appear in the area to the right of the scroll bar, and the module or option's name appears above the list. In figure 20.1, the Text icon is selected and the preferences for the word processing module are shown. To see preferences for one of the other modules or options, click that icon. Use the scroll bar to move the list up or down if you do not see the module or option for which you want to adjust preferences.

The bottom of the dialog box has three buttons: Make Default, Cancel, and OK. These buttons are present regardless of which icon you choose. The Make Default button saves the settings you choose in this dialog box. Until you change these settings again, ClarisWorks refers to them each time you launch the application. Use the Cancel button to dismiss the dialog box without saving changes made in any of the preferences. Click OK to save the changes for the current session only and to dismiss the dialog box.

Setting Text Preferences

The preferences that apply to text will change the look of some characters, the spacing of others, and sometimes whether or not text is included on a page. All these preferences help make your documents more professional-looking and all-around easier to create.

General Text Preferences. The following list describes the first section of preferences:

- *Smart Quotes.* This option instructs ClarisWorks to use *smart quotes*, also referred to as *typesetter's quotes*. In figure 20.2, notice the curve of the quotation marks as opposed to the straight inch (") symbol. Using the Smart Quotes option tells ClarisWorks to use curved quotation marks and apostrophes, rather than the straight inch and foot symbols often used to indicate these punctuation marks.

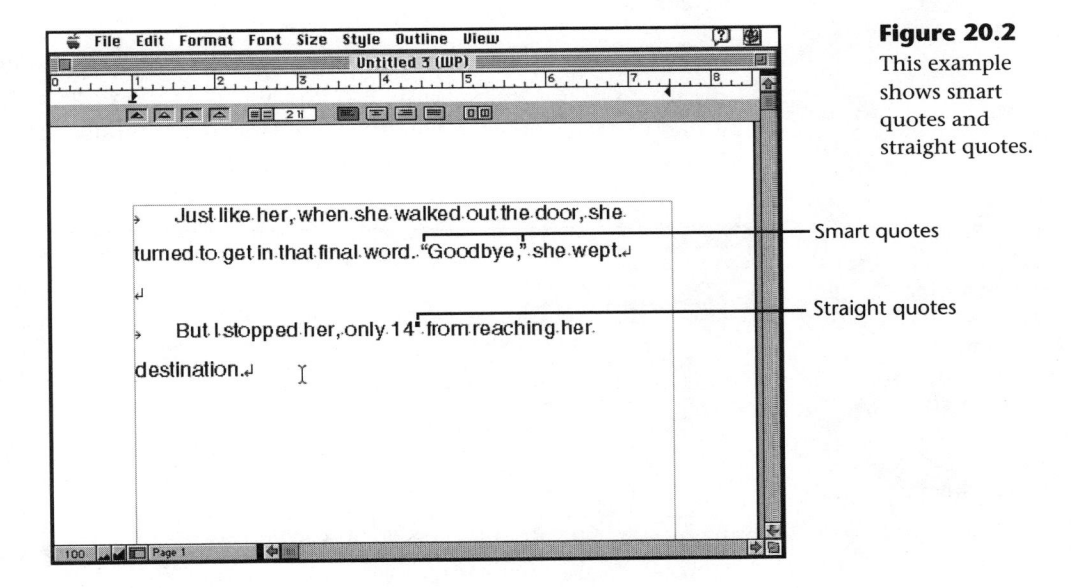

Figure 20.2
This example shows smart quotes and straight quotes.

- *Show Invisibles.* If you choose this option, ClarisWorks displays all normally invisible characters, such as carriage-return symbols, tab symbols, and space bars. These symbols do not print, even when visible in the document.

- *Fractional Character Widths.* Each character requires an amount of space that it occupies when displayed on-screen or on a printed page. This space is called the *character width*. Because characters are not an exact pixel width (they can include a fraction of a pixel), you can decide whether ClarisWorks accurately displays widths on-screen or on the printer. Using Fractional Character Widths instructs ClarisWorks to display character widths accurately by using fractions of pixels to render characters. Characters look normal, and spacing between words appears uniform. Characters may not display exactly the way they print.

Without Fractional Character Widths, there is non-uniform spacing and letters may appear crunched. But line endings are accurately matched to the printout.

- *Auto Number Footnotes.* In the Format menu, Insert Footnote is an automatic option. ClarisWorks places a footnote at the bottom of the current page when you choose this menu option. The Auto Number Footnotes option tracks each footnote and automatically places the next consecutively numbered footnote when you choose the Insert Footnote option.

- *Starting Footnote #.* In this box, type the number with which the current document's footnotes are to begin. If this document is a second chapter or one part of a large chapter, you may need to start at a number other than 1. A sample footnote is shown in figure 20.3.

Figure 20.3
The Insert Footnote option places footnotes at the bottom of the page automatically. The Starting Footnote # option makes numbering automatic as well.

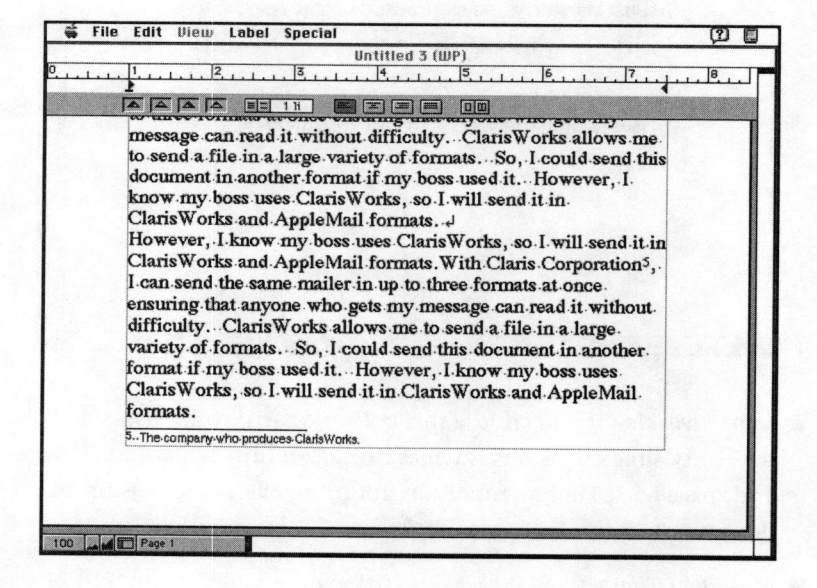

Date Format. At the bottom of the Text Preferences section are the Date Format settings. Choose from the options shown in figure 20.4 the format you prefer for the date line.

Choosing the Insert Date option from the Edit menu automatically inserts the date in the format you have chosen. The document in figure 20.5 shows how a date line might look.

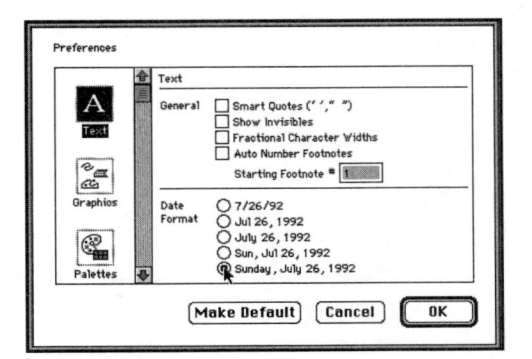

Setting Preferences **409**

Figure 20.4
You can choose a date format in the Preferences dialog box.

> **Note**
>
> The date line displays the time and date according to the internal clock of the Macintosh. If the date and time displays are incorrect, you can change them in the General Controls section of the Macintosh Control Panel.

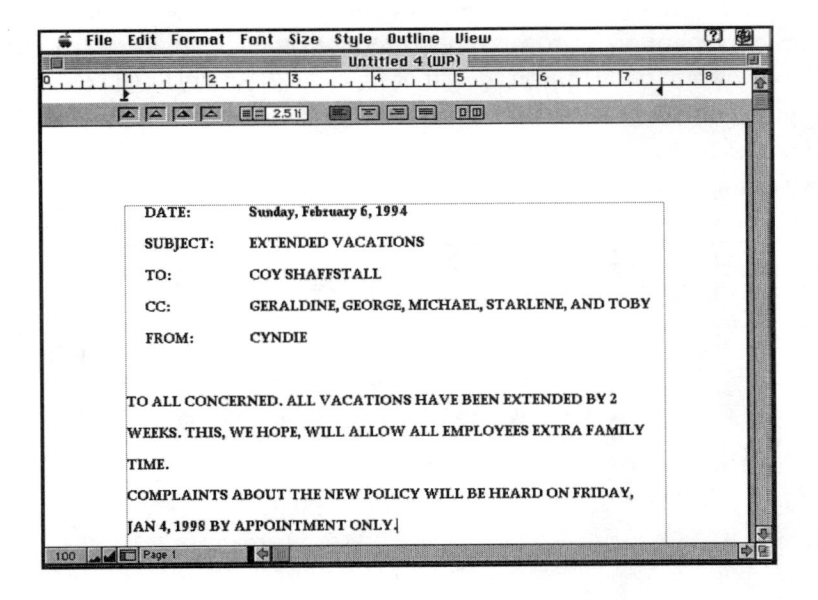

Figure 20.5
The date, in the format you chose in the Preferences dialog box, is inserted in a document when you choose Insert Date from the Edit menu.

Setting Graphics Preferences

When you choose the Graphics icon, the preferences list for the graphics modules appears (see fig. 20.6).

410 Chapter 20—Customizing ClarisWorks

Figure 20.6
The graphics preferences store default settings for the drawing module.

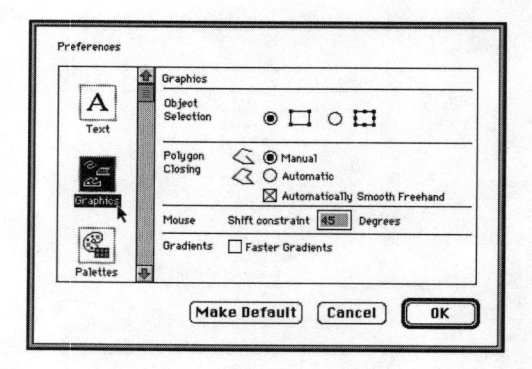

Object Selection. Use the Object Selection preferences to designate how many selection handles appear on a graphics object in the drawing module. Using four handles enables you to make changes to size from a corner only. Using eight handles enables independent size changes to the width or height.

Polygon Closing. The drawing module contains a tool for drawing irregular straight-sided shapes called *polygons*. You can fill a polygon with a color, shade, or pattern. An open polygon, however, may fill in an unwanted manner, as shown in the shape on the left of figure 20.7. An unclosed polygon will just connect the beginning and end of the shape with a straight line; it will not include the outline or stroke. The shape on the right was closed with another angle.

Figure 20.7
The polygon on the left is unclosed; it might fill in an unexpected manner. A closed polygon (such as the one on the right) always fills its internal area if you have a fill selected.

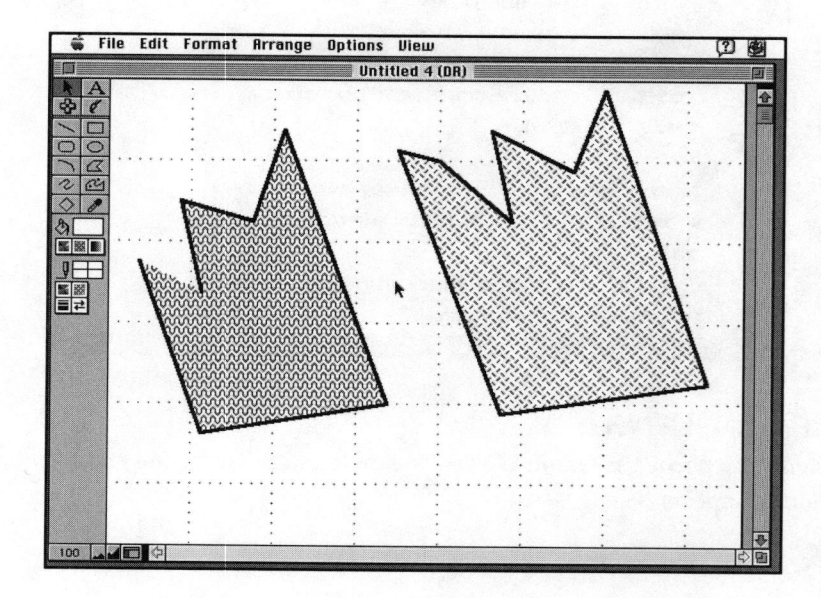

In the drawing module, lines drawn with the Freehand tool often are quite ragged. You can see this in figure 20.8. The Automatically Smooth Freehand option in the Preferences dialog box smoothes these lines and makes them more fluid.

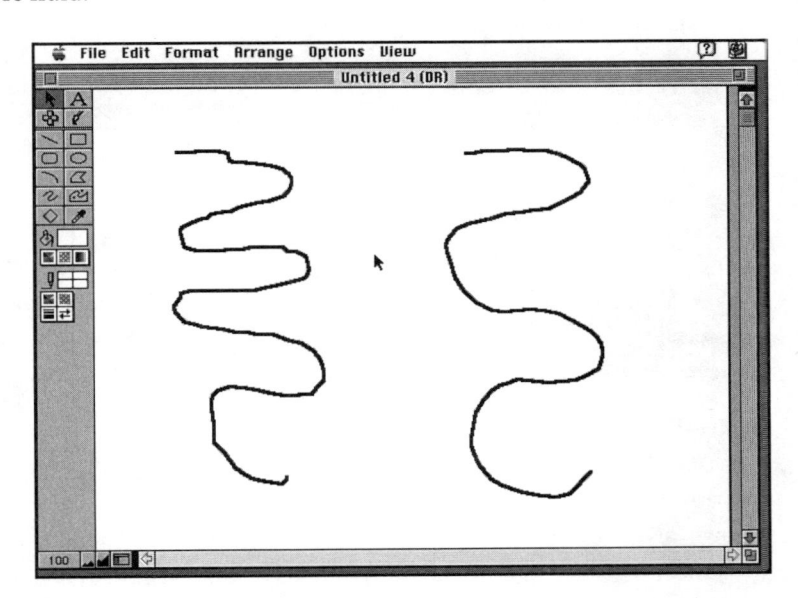

Figure 20.8
The freehand line on the left was drawn without smoothing; the one on the right, with smoothing.

Mouse Preferences. The Shift Constraint option causes mouse-drawn lines to snap to exact multiples of 45 degrees when the Shift key is pressed and held. This option also constrains the Oval tool to perfect circles and the Rectangle tool to perfect squares.

Gradients. Choosing Faster Gradients enables ClarisWorks to draw gradients faster (but less smoothly) in the drawing modules.

Setting Palette Preferences

Palettes in the drawing and painting modules are like the Shortcuts palette discussed in Chapter 19, "Automating Your Work." The palettes in the drawing and painting modules are mini-Macintosh windows that can be moved, collapsed, expanded, or closed. These palettes are especially handy because they keep colors, fills, and gradients close at hand.

412   Chapter 20—Customizing ClarisWorks

The palettes in these modules are known as *tear-off palettes*; you first click the icon representing the palette you need, and then drag the palette away from the icon. As you drag, a dotted outline appears (see fig. 20.9). This line is the outline to the palette. Drag the outline to where you want to place the palette, and release the mouse button.

Figure 20.9
Click the palette icon, hold the mouse button down, and drag to place the tear-off palette on the page.

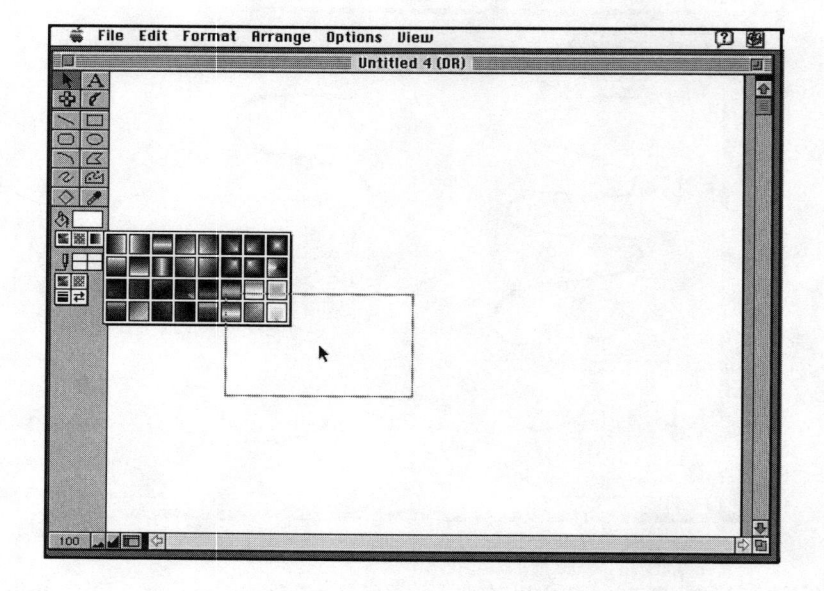

Color. Figure 20.10 shows the Preferences dialog box as it is displayed when you click the Palettes icon.

Figure 20.10
Click the Palette icon to display palette preferences.

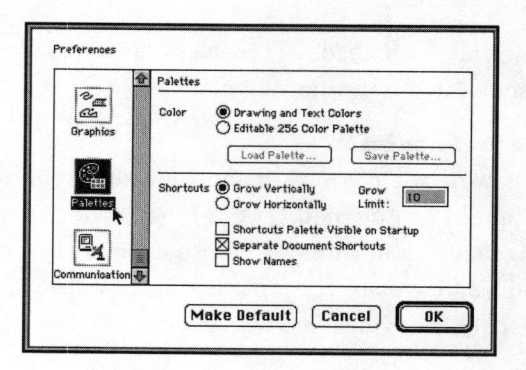

The Drawing and Text Colors option loads the default ClarisWorks limited color palette. The Editable 256 Color Palette option uses the expanded 256-color selection (this palette is editable, although not from a monochrome monitor). Click the Editable 256 Color Palette button to display the dialog box shown in figure 20.11.

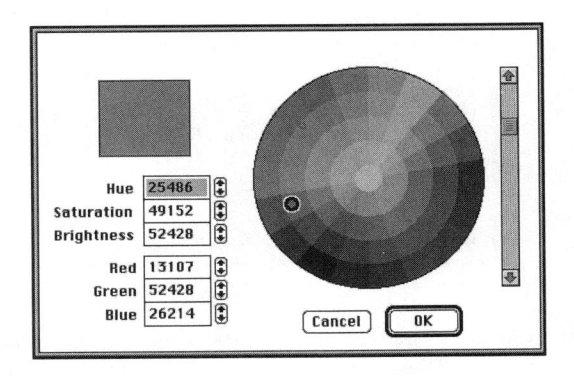

Figure 20.11
Double-click a color from the color palette to bring up the color wheel.

To fully benefit from preferences, you generally should set them before creating documents. This way, the preferences are available in each new document you create. Color palettes, however, are somewhat of an exception in that the preference is saved from within a document. With color palettes, you can create custom palettes that can be used in other documents. You also can make the custom palette the default palette by clicking the Make Default button at the bottom of the Preferences dialog box.

When you want to create a custom palette of colors (as would be the case if your company colors need to be used on all company literature), open a document, choose a palette to edit, and double-click the color you want to change. Then follow these steps:

1. Choose a new color from the color wheel, or type values in the Hue, Saturation, and Brightness boxes to change the look of the color wheel. Values typed in the Red, Green, or Blue box change the location of the selector on the wheel and display the sample of the new color at the top of the color swatch. The preceding color is at the bottom of the color swatch.

2. Click OK to make the change in this document's palette.

414 Chapter 20—Customizing ClarisWorks

3. To save the palette while the document is still open, return to the Preferences dialog box, click the Palette icon, and choose Editable 256 Color Palette.

4. Click the Save Palette button. The Save dialog box appears, as shown in figure 20.12.

Figure 20.12
In this familiar Macintosh dialog box, you can name and store your new palette.

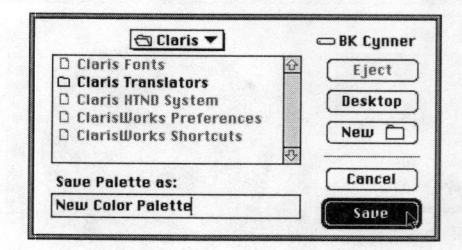

5. Type a name for the palette, choose a location, and click Save. (Refer to Chapter 2, "Learning the Essentials," if you need help with saving, naming, and opening documents.)

This palette is now ready for use by any other ClarisWorks document. It will be available in each of the modules in the same area where you would customarily find a color palette.

To load a saved palette while in a document, return to the Preferences dialog box, and then follow these steps:

1. Click the Palettes icon.

2. Choose Editable 256 Color Palette.

3. Click the Load Palette button. The Open dialog box appears, as shown in figure 20.13.

Figure 20.13
To load a previously saved palette, choose the Load Palette option. This dialog box appears, and you can choose the palette.

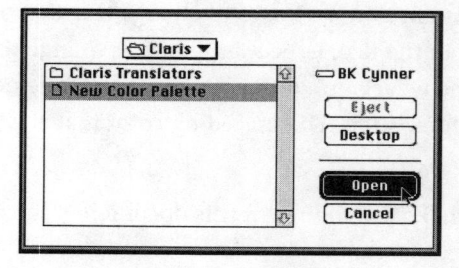

4. Return to the folder where the saved palette was stored.

5. Double-click the title of the desired palette. That palette is now available in all color palettes in all modules.

6. Click the Make Default button if you want to designate this palette as the default (the default palette opens each time you start a new ClarisWorks session).

Shortcuts. Shortcuts is another palette available in the ClarisWorks modules. It is a method of simplifying the task of using the menus to make changes or create data in your documents. Use the icon representations of menu listings to apply functions. For example, you can click the scissors icon to cut a selected item and place it on the Clipboard. In the Preferences dialog box, you can customize the Shortcuts palette by choosing any of the following options:

- *Grow Vertically.* With the Grow Vertically option selected, the Shortcuts palette adds new buttons that you select to expand the depth of the palette. In figure 20.14, when the Text tool icon was added, a third row was added; hence, the palette grew vertically.

Figure 20.14
The Shortcuts palette with Grow Vertically selected. Notice the added button below the black horizontal rule. This rule is the Separate Document Shortcuts feature.

- *Grow Horizontally.* With Grow Horizontally selected, the Shortcuts palette adds new buttons to the width.

- *Grow Limit.* The number you enter for this option limits the growth of the Shortcuts palette to a specific number of buttons. Using a small number, such as 2, creates a vertical palette, because the buttons can only expand to 2 across. Using a larger number, such as 10, creates a horizontal palette like the palette shown in figure 20.14.

- *Shortcuts Palette Visible.* This option automatically launches the Shortcuts palette when you create a document.

- *Separate Document Shortcuts.* Use this option if you want the black horizontal rule to separate those buttons you add from the default buttons (refer to fig. 20.14).

- *Show Names.* This option removes the buttons in the Shortcuts palette and replaces them with the names found in the Description field of the Edit Shortcuts dialog box. Figure 20.15 shows how your palette might look when displayed in this manner.

Figure 20.15
The Shortcuts palette can display names rather than buttons.

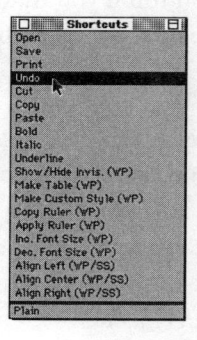

Setting Communications Preferences

Using a modem to connect to other computers, on-line services (such as CompuServe and America Online) or electronic bulletin-board systems (EBS or BBS) is generally referred to as *communications*. You can *upload* (receive) files, *download* (send) files, and even send and receive faxes. ClarisWorks provides for both short-distance (local) and long-distance (remote) communications.

The preferences for communicating simplify repetitious connections. Protocols, the settings used for connecting, are widely varied. Your protocol must match that of the system to which you are connecting in order to have a clean, error-free transmission. There's no need to continually reset your most common protocol; simply make the changes in the Preferences dialog box (see fig. 20.16) and then click the Make Default button.

Figure 20.16
The Preferences dialog box with Communications selected.

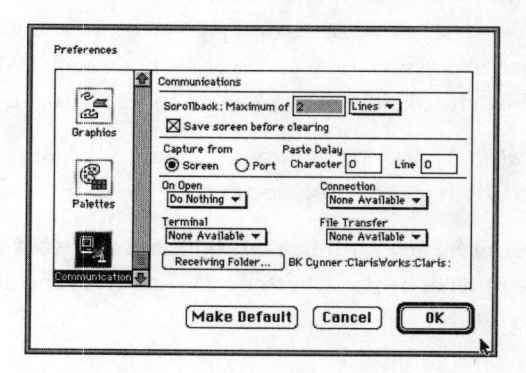

Use the following list for help in choosing the best preferences for your communications documents:

- *Scrollback.* The scrollback option determines how much data is saved so that you can scroll backward to re-read the information. The choices are Unlimited, Lines, Kilobytes, and Screens. After you choose a scrollback measure, you can enter a number in the Maximum text box (for example, you can choose Lines and type **2**).

- *Save Screen Before Clearing.* This option saves each screen of the scrollback pane before the screen clears. You may want to choose this option if you are using an on-line or bulletin board service that clears your computer's screen display before sending each message.

- *Capture From.* This option indicates the type of text that will be saved. Sometimes you will want to save text with all codes embedded. (Codes are characters such as tabs and carriage returns.) If you want to use tabbed text as a table pasted into a spreadsheet, you would want the tabs; if you were to use the text for a letter, you probably would not. If you use the Port option, it will capture codes; Screen will not.

- *Paste Delay.* Occasionally, data that is sent from your computer to the remote computer will paste (when you choose Paste) faster than the remote computer can receive it. This problem is apparent if you paste and nothing shows up on your screen. Slow the speed at which your computer sends this information by using the Paste Delay option. The number 1 equals 1/60 of a second. Try different settings until you find one that works.

- *On Open.* This preference instructs ClarisWorks when to begin a communications document or connection. If you choose Automatically Connect, ClarisWorks attempts to connect to a remote computer as soon as you start a communications document. Choose Wait for Connection if you want to create a communications document when a remote computer calls you. Choose Do Nothing if you do not want to automate either of these processes.

- *Connection.* In the communications module, you can connect to a remote computer by using the phone line or to a local computer by using a cable extending from the serial port of your Macintosh to the serial port of the other computer. To tell your Macintosh that you are connecting to a remote computer, choose Apple Modem Tool. This option enables you to connect to most Hayes-compatible modems. (Hayes is an industry-standard modem technology.)

- *Terminal*. To choose a terminal type, click this pop-up menu. The choices are VT102 and TTY Tool. Your computer must match the remote computer's type. Choose VT102 for most VT100-type modems. Choose TTY if the on-line service requires TTY emulation.

- *File Transfer*. This option sets the protocol (the language) in which your files are transmitted and received.

- *Receiving Folder*. This option sets the destination of the files you receive, automating the save process.

Troubleshooting Preferences

I am using smart quotes, but now I want to type foot and inch symbols.

Return to the Preferences dialog box and turn off Smart Quotes. Click OK and type the characters you need.

I have dots between all my words.

These dots are present because you selected Show Invisibles in the Preferences dialog box. The dots will not print. To turn them off, deselect Show Invisibles.

The date and time in my date line are incorrect.

The internal clock of the Macintosh is set wrong. Refer to your Macintosh user's guide if you need help in resetting the clock.

I can't edit my color palettes.

You may be working from a monochrome monitor. You cannot edit them from this system setup.

The chapter keeps referring to the Shortcuts palette. I can't find mine.

To display the Shortcuts palette, choose Shortcuts from the File menu, and then choose Show Shortcuts from the Shortcuts submenu. (For additional help, refer to Chapter 19, "Automating Your Work.")

I don't hear a dial tone from my modem.

Your modem may not be hooked up properly. Check the cable connections. For additional help, refer to the user's guide for your modem.

Also, your modem may not have an internal speaker.

Using Custom Text Styles

For creating complex documents (and even simple ones), there's no better way to automate than to use the Define Styles option. Formatting headlines, captions, body copy, and difficult tables deserves barely a passing glance as you slide through the document, applying styles for a professional, finished polish.

The primary reason why most new users choose not to use Define Styles is that they don't understand how simple styles can be. The trick is to save them as you format. Type the entire document with no formatting at all. Plain double-spaced text is perfect for formatting. It also makes the text very legible while proofing. After you finish typing the text, move on to the next step, making it shine.

Choosing Styles to be Defined

You can use a style every time you apply more formatting than you want to repeat. An example of such a situation may be a headline with several specific style attributes that took you 15 minutes to get to look just right, or a table with meticulous measurements, or a body-copy paragraph that you use throughout the document.

Defining Styles

For practice, create a sample document similar to the one shown in figure 20.17. *How To Type* is a section headline, *Teaching Kids To Type* is a chapter headline, and *The hand movements* is a subhead. The text following each of the three types of headlines is body copy. As you create documents, keep these styles in mind. You might also have styles for captions, tables, notes, tips, and so on.

Type the text, spell-check, proof, and print. Check your work carefully before you begin to define styles, especially when you're working with an actual project. When you are certain that the text is clean, scroll to the beginning of the document. You now are ready to define styles.

Select the first line of the document's text. This line should be the section head. Change the font to Times (or whatever you prefer), the size to 48, the alignment to centered, and the style to bold.

Set the paragraph style to your liking. Watch the formatting to make sure that the section head looks appealing. Especially watch line spacing so that lines don't overlap.

Chapter 20—Customizing ClarisWorks

Figure 20.17
This sample document is ready for styles.

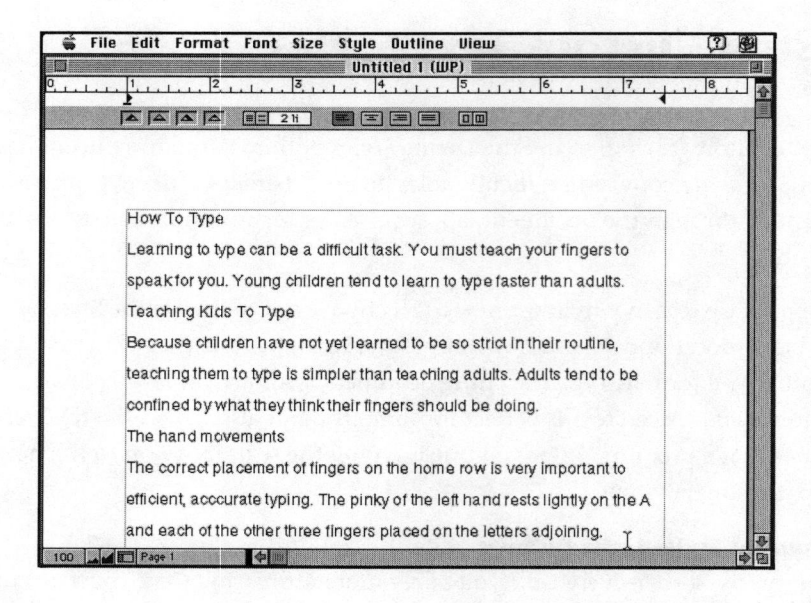

Tip
Double-click a word to select the word. To select an entire line of text, triple-click the line. To select an entire paragraph, click it four times.

While the text is highlighted, choose Define Styles from the Style menu. The Define Custom Styles dialog box appears. The first box contains a list of all currently stored styles. If this is the first time you have defined any styles, the box is empty. When you save the section head style, its name will appear in this field.

Directly below the list of styles is the Name box. The default name is the font name and the size. You can use the default name or type one of your own. In figure 20.18, the style name is Section Head.

Figure 20.18
The Define Custom Styles dialog box shows all currently stored styles and the attributes for the currently selected text. Here, the section head is Times, 48 point.

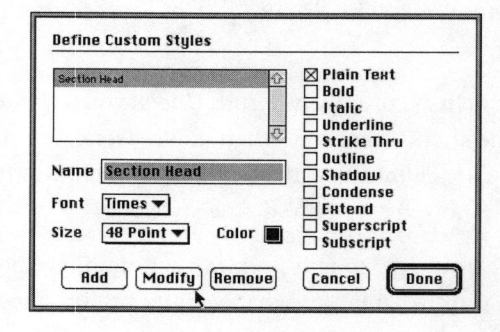

Notice that all the attributes marked in this dialog box match the attributes assigned to the section head. You can make changes in these attributes if you do not like the way the section head looked; otherwise, click Add. Click Done to move to the next style. Click Cancel to dismiss the dialog box without saving a style.

Move to the next section of text. This section is the body copy directly below the section head. Format this text. (If you need help with formatting, refer to Chapter 3, "Working with Text.") Don't forget to format line spacing, spaces before and after paragraphs, indents, and so on. Make any additional changes in the style by clicking the appropriate button. When you finish, return to the Style menu and choose Define Styles. Name the style Body Copy. Click Add, and then click Done. Notice that the Section Head and Body Copy styles are now listed.

Repeat the process with the chapter head.

Applying Stored Styles

Place your insertion point in the body copy below the chapter head; then choose Body Copy from the bottom portion of the Style menu. Watch what happens. Perfect automation! This demonstration may convince you that you want to use Define Styles. You can go all the way through the document, formatting new styles, adding them, and applying them when a paragraph uses a current style.

Modifying Styles

Occasionally, you may want to change a style's attributes after you store the style. To modify a style, first choose Define Styles from the Style menu. In the Current Styles list, choose the style you want to edit; that style's attributes appear. Make the desired changes, and then click Modify. These changes do not affect currently applied styles; you must go back through the document and reapply the new style.

Tip
Use the key equivalents (listed to the right of the style name in the Style menu) to apply styles to a selected paragraph.

Deleting Styles

You delete styles in much the same manner as you modify styles. Choose Define Styles from the Style menu. In the Current Styles list, choose the style you want to delete, and then click Remove. Click Cancel to dismiss the dialog box without deleting the style. Click Done to close the dialog box and save the changes.

> **Troubleshooting Custom Styles**
>
> *When I apply a style, it doesn't change the paragraph.*
>
> Make sure that your insertion point is in the paragraph you are trying to change. Check to make sure that the style you are applying differs from the current style of the paragraph.
>
> *The style that I applied is wrong. What can I do?*
>
> Choose Define Styles from the Style menu. When the Define Custom Styles dialog box appears, click the name of the style you are using. Check your parameters for errors.

From Here...

Now that you have worked through a chapter dedicated to making your ClarisWorks session simple and painless, you are well on your way to becoming a power user. Not enough can be said about practice, but sometimes the best practice is actual production. You learn best when a tip helps you automate an actual job. This chapter is full of practical production help. The following chapters provide additional help.

- Chapter 3, "Working with Text." Define Styles is best when used in conjunction with basic text skills. Return to Chapter 3 for help with using text in a document.

- Chapter 6, "Drawing." Using preferences for color palettes is great for editing the palettes used in the drawing module of ClarisWorks.

- Chapter 17, "Communications Basics." The communications preferences will assist you in getting good, clean transmissions. Turn to this chapter for help with making a transmission.

Appendix A
Functions

by Shelley O'Hara

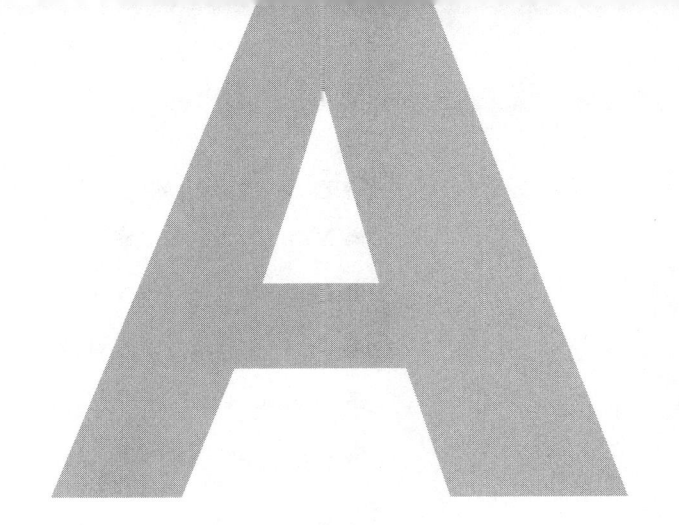

Functions are predefined formulas that you can use in a worksheet. You can use functions to perform tasks such as figuring a loan payment and averaging a series of numbers.

ClarisWorks groups its functions into eight categories:

- Business and financial
- Date and time
- Information
- Logical
- Numeric
- Statistical
- Text
- Trigonometric

When you enter a function, you must enter the parts of the formula in the correct order. The format for a function is called the *syntax*. A function consists of these parts:

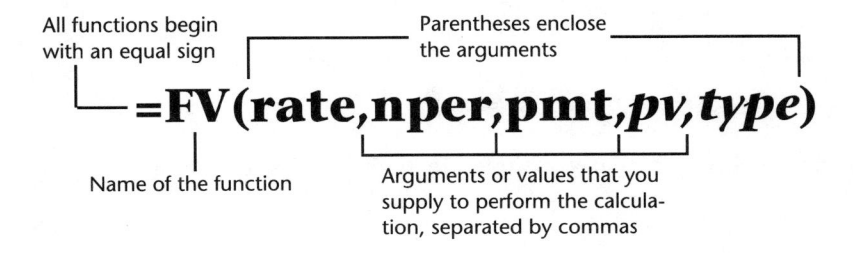

$$=FV(rate, nper, pmt, pv, type)$$

All functions begin with an equal sign

Parentheses enclose the arguments

Name of the function

Arguments or values that you supply to perform the calculation, separated by commas

For arguments, you can enter the following:

- Value (date, number, logical expression)
- Number (numeric value)
- Text (alphanumeric characters enclosed in quotation marks)
- Logical (TRUE or FALSE)
- Cell (reference to a cell or range)

Some arguments are optional; others are mandatory. In this appendix, optional arguments are bold italic, and mandatory arguments are bold.

Function Reference

The following function reference arranges functions by category and then lists them alphabetically within each category.

Business and Financial

Business and financial functions are useful for calculating loan amounts and present and future values of investments. The following arguments are used in business and financial functions:

FV (rate, nper, pmt, *pv*, *type*). Calculates the future value of an investment. For example, if you save $500 a month for 5 years at an interest rate of 6 percent, how much will you have saved?

Example:

A1	Savings Plan	
A2	.06	(rate, or interest rate)
A3	60	(nper, or number of periods; here, 5 years * 12 months)
A4	−500	(pmt, or the amount you save)
A5	=FV(A2/12,A3,A4)	

The result is $34,885.02.

IRR (range, *guess*). Calculates an approximate internal rate of return on an investment.

Function Reference **425**

> **Note**
> You cannot use this function in a database document.

Example:

A1	Cash Flows
A2	–5,000
A3	2,000
A4	3,000
A5	1,500
A6	=IRR(A2..A5)

The result is 14.92%.

MIRR (safe, risk, values, ...). Calculates a modified rate of return, given safe and risky investment rates.

Example:

A1	Investment
A2	–25,000
A3	2,000
A4	3,000
A5	=MIRR(5%,8%,A2..A4)

The result is 43.67%.

NPER (rate, pmt, pv, fv, type). Calculates the number of periods of an investment.

Example:

A1	Number of Periods	
A2	.10	(rate)

A3	−400	(pmt)
A4	32,000	(pv, or present value)
A5	=NPER(A2/12,A3,A4)	

The result is 132 payments.

NPV (rate, payment1, payment2, ...). Calculates the net present value of an investment.

Example:

A1	Net Present Value	
A2	.12	(rate)
A3	−4000	(payment 1)
A4	1000	(payment 2)
A5	2000	(payment 3)
A6	=NPV(A2,A3,A4,A5)	

The result is −$553.48.

PMT (rate, nper, pv, *fv*, *type*). Figures the payment on a loan.

Example:

A1	Car Loan	
A2	.08	(rate)
A3	48	(nper, or number of payments; here, 4 years *12 months)
A4	32,000	(pv, or amount of loan)
A5	=PMT(A2/12,A3,A4)	

The result is −$781.21.

PV (rate, nper, pmt, *fv*, *type*). Calculates the present value of an investment. Can start with the amount of money you can afford to pay monthly and then figure backward to tell you how much you can afford to borrow.

Example:

A1   Monthly Payment

A2   .10   (rate)

A3   48   (nper)

A4   324   (pmt)

A5   =PV(A2/12,A3,A4)

The result is ($12,774.72).

RATE (fv, pv, nper). Calculates the interest rate required for a future value to grow to a certain amount.

Example:

A1   Interest Rate

A2   50,000   (fv, or future value)

A3   10,000   (pv, or present value)

A4   48   (nper)

A5   =RATE(A2,A3,A4)

The result is 3.41%.

Date and Time

Date and time functions are useful for working with dates—for example, converting dates to text and vice versa.

DATE (year, month, day). Returns the serial number for the specified date.

Example:

A1   =DATE(94,2,13)

The result is –661044.

DATETOTEXT (serial_number, *format_number*). Converts the serial number to a text date. You can specify the following optional formats:

0 or none   2/13/94

1   Feb 13, 1994

2   February 13, 1994

3   Sun, Feb 13, 1994

4   Sunday, February 13, 1994

DAY (serial_number). Returns the number of the day of the month from the serial number.

Example:

A1   2/14/94

A2   =DAY(A1)

The result is 14.

DAYNAME (number). Calculates the name of a specified day. The **number** argument can be a number from 1 to 7.

Example:

A1   7

A2   =DAYNAME(A1)

The result is Saturday.

DAYOFYEAR (serial_number). Returns the number of days of the year from the serial number.

Example:

A1   2/13/94

A2   =DAYOFYEAR(A1)

The result is 44.

HOUR (serial_number). Converts the time portion of a serial number to the number of the hour.

Example:

A1   =HOUR(.1200)

The result is 2.

MINUTE (serial_number). Calculates the number of minutes in a serial date.

Example:

A1   =MINUTE(.1200)

The result is 52.

MONTH (serial_number). Returns the month number from the serial number (1 = January, 12 = December).

Example:

A1   2/13/94

A2   =MONTH(A1)

The result is 2.

MONTHNAME (number). Calculates the name of the month from the number. The **number** argument can be a number from 1 to 12.

Example:

A1   =MONTHNAME(2)

The result is February.

NOW (). Returns the current date and time.

SECOND (serial_number). Calculates the number of seconds from a serial number.

Example:

A1   =SECOND(.1200)

The result is 48.

TEXTTODATE (date_text). Returns the serial number of the **date_text** argument.

Example:

A1   =TEXTTODATE ("February 13, 1994")

The result is 32916.

TEXTTOTIME (time_text). Returns the serial number of the **time_text** argument.

Example:

A1   =TEXTTOTIME ("9:00AM")

The result is .375.

TIME (hour, minute, second). Calculates the serial number of the time.

Example:

A1   =TIME (1,30,10)

The result is 6.2615740e–2.

TIMETOTEXT (serial_number, *format*). Converts the serial number to a text time. You can specify the following optional formats:

0 or none	2:00 PM
1	2:00:45 PM
2	14:00
3	14:00:45

WEEKDAY (serial_number). Returns the number for the day of week (1 = Sunday, 7 = Saturday) of the serial number.

Example:

A1   =WEEKDAY(32916)

The result is 1 (Sunday).

WEEKOFYEAR (serial_number). Returns the week number from the serial number.

Example:

A1   =WEEKOFYEAR(32916)

The result is 8.

YEAR (serial_number). Returns the year for the serial number.

Example:

A1   =WEEKOFYEAR(32916)

The result is 1994.

Information

Information functions return information about the current cell or worksheet. You also can use information functions to look up information in a table.

ALERT (value). Displays a message in a dialog box.

> **Note**
>
> You cannot use this function in a database document.

Example:

A1   "You have made a mistake. Try again!"

A2   =ALERT(A1)

You see a dialog box that says You have made a mistake. Try again!

BEEP (). Plays the alert sound.

CHOOSE (index, value1, value2, ...). Searches a list of values for the values specified by **index**.

Example:

A1   =CHOOSE(2,"A","B")

Because the **index** value is 2, the result is B, which is the second item in the list.

COLUMN (*cell*). Returns the column number (not letter) of the current cell. If you enter a cell, returns the column number of that cell.

> **Note**
>
> You cannot use this function in a database document.

Example:

A1   =COLUMN(C5)

The result is 3.

ERROR (). Returns the error value #ERROR!.

HLOOKUP (lookup_value, compare_range, index, *method*). Looks horizontally through the rows specified in **compare_range** for **lookup_value**. If found, the function adds the index to the row number of the found cell and returns that value.

INDEX (range, row, column). Returns the value of the cell that is the specified number of rows and columns away from the range.

Example:

A1   5

B1   7

A2   =INDEX(A1..B1,1,2)

The result is 7.

LOOKUP (lookup_value, compare_range, result_range, *method*). Looks through the rows specified in **compare_range** for **lookup_value**. Returns the value of the corresponding cell in the cell in **result_range**.

> **Note**
>
> You cannot use this function in a database document.

MACRO (text). Executes the macro named.

> **Note**
>
> You cannot use this function in a database document.

MATCH (lookup_value, compare_range, *type*). Looks through **compare_range** for **lookup_value**. If found, returns the position of that value in relation to the start range.

> **Note**
>
> You cannot use this function in a database document.

NA (). Returns the error value #N/A!. Use this function to enter the error message into cells that currently are not available.

> **Note**
>
> You cannot use this function in a database document.

ROW (cell). Returns the row number of the current cell or the cell named.

> **Note**
>
> You cannot use this function in a database document.

Example:

A1   =ROW(B7)

The result is 7.

TYPE (value). Returns a number that represents one of the following values:

1   Blank

2   Logical

3   Number

4   Text

VLOOKUP (lookup_value, compare_range, index, *method*). Looks vertically through the columns specified in **compare_range** for **lookup_value**. If found, the function adds the index to the column number of the found cell and returns that value.

Logical

Logical functions evaluate statements as TRUE or FALSE.

AND (logical1, logical2, ...). Evaluates the arguments and returns TRUE if *all* arguments are true. Returns FALSE if one or more arguments are false.

IF (logical, true_value, false_value). Performs the **logical** test and returns **true_value** if TRUE or **false_value** if FALSE.

Example:

A1   100

A2   =IF(A1=100,"Perfect Score," "Good Try!")

The result is Perfect Score.

ISBLANK (value). Returns TRUE if the value is blank or FALSE if the value contains an entry.

Example:

A1   100

A2   =ISBLANK(A1)

The result is FALSE.

ISERROR (value, *error_type*). Returns FALSE when the named value does not contain an error. Returns TRUE when an error does occur. If you specify an error type, ClarisWorks checks only for the named error. (See Chapter 8, "Spreadsheet Basics," for a list of error messages.)

ISLOGICAL (value). Returns TRUE if the value contains a Boolean expression; returns FALSE if it doesn't.

ISNA (value). Returns TRUE if the value contains #N/A!; otherwise, returns FALSE.

> **Note**
> You cannot use this function in a database document.

ISNUMBER (value). Returns TRUE if the value is a number and FALSE if it isn't.

NOT (logical). Evaluates the **logical** test. If TRUE, returns FALSE; if FALSE, returns TRUE.

OR (logical1, logical2, ...). Evaluates the arguments and returns TRUE if *any* arguments are true. Returns FALSE if all arguments are false.

TEXT (value). Returns TRUE if the text is a number and FALSE if it isn't.

Numeric

Numeric functions are useful for operations such as rounding numbers and returning a random number.

ABS (number). Returns the positive number of the **number** argument, which can be an actual number or a cell reference.

Example:

A1   −7

A2   =ABS(A1)

The result is 7.

EXP (number). Calculates e to the power of the number entered. The **number** argument can be an actual number or a cell reference.

Example:

A1   2

A2   =EXP(A1)

The result is 7.389056....

FACT (number). Calculates the factorial of a number. The **number** argument can be an actual number or a cell reference.

Example:

A1   4

A2   =FACT(A1)

The result is 24.

FRAC (number). Calculates the fractional part of a number. The **number** argument can be an actual number or a cell reference.

Example:

A1   5.95

A2   =FRAC(A1)

The result is .95.

INT (number). Returns the integer closest to the number. The result cannot be greater than or equal to the number. The **number** argument can be an actual number or a cell reference.

Example:

A1   6.5

A2   =INT(A1)

The result is 6.

LN (number). Calculates the natural logarithm of a positive number. The **number** argument can be an actual number or a cell reference.

Example:

A1   2

A2   =LN(A1)

The result is 3.010299e–1.

LOG (number, base). Calculates the logarithm of a number to the base entered. The **number** argument can be an actual number or a cell reference. The number must be positive. You can enter a base if you want; it must be positive and not equal to 1. If you don't enter the base, ClarisWorks uses base 10.

Example:

A1   2

A2   =LOG(A1,2)

The result is 1.

LOG10 (number). Calculates the logarithm of a number to base 10. Number can be an actual number or a cell reference. The number must be positive.

Example:

A1   100

A2   =LOG10(A1)

The result is 2.

MOD (number, divisor_number). Returns the remainder of the number after dividing by **divisor_number**. The **number** argument can be an actual number or a cell reference. You cannot use 0 as **divisor_number**.

Example:

A1   100

A2   =MOD(A1,6)

The result is 4.

PI(). Calculates the value of pi (Π). You enter only the parentheses; this function uses no arguments.

RAND (number). Returns a random number. The **number** argument is optional. If you specify an argument, the function returns a whole number between 1 and the number you enter.

Example:

A1   20

A2   =RAND(A1)

The result is 11.

ROUND (number, number_of_digits). Rounds the number to the number of digits you specify. The **number** argument can be an actual number or a cell reference.

Example:

A1   23.4589

A2   =ROUND(A1,2)

The result is 23.46.

SIGN (number). Returns 1 when the number is positive and –1 when the number is negative. The **number** argument can be an actual number or a cell reference.

Example:

A1   –9

A2   =SIGN(A1)

The result is –1.

SQRT (number). Calculates the square root of a number. The **number** argument can be an actual number or a cell reference.

Example:

A1   9

A2   =SQRT(A1)

The result is 3.

TRUNC (number). Lops off the fractional part of a number and returns only the integer. The **number** argument can be an actual number or a cell reference.

Example:

A1   6.5

A2   =TRUNC(A1)

The result is 6.

Statistical

Use statistical functions for tasks such as counting the items in a list, figuring an average, or returning the minimum or maximum value in a list.

AVERAGE (number 1, number 2, ...). Averages numbers. The **number** arguments can be specific values, cells, or a range.

Example:

A1   Test Scores

A2   100

A3   90

A4   80

A5   =AVERAGE(A2..A4)

The result is 90.

COUNT (value 1, value 2, ...). Counts the values. The values can be specific values, cells, or a range.

Example:

A1	Task Completed
A2	4/4/94
A3	4/6/94
A4	
A5	4/7/94
A6	
A7	=COUNT(A2..A6)

The result is 3.

COUNT2 (searchvalue, value1, ...). Counts the number of times that **searchvalue** occurs in a value.

Example:

A1	Test Scores
A2	100
A3	90
A4	88
A5	100
A6	98
A7	=COUNT2(100,A2..A6)

The result is 2.

MAX (number1, number2, ...). Returns the largest value in a range.

Example:

| A1 | Best Test Score |
| A2 | 99 |

A3	88
A4	87
A5	92
A6	93
A7	=MAX(A2..A6)

The result is 99.

MIN (number1, number2, ...). Returns the lowest value in a range.

Example:

A1	Worst Test Score
A2	99
A3	88
A4	87
A5	92
A6	93
A7	=MIN(A2..A6)

The result is 87.

PRODUCT (number1, number2, ...). Calculates the product of the numbers in a list.

Example:

A1	20
A2	30
A3	10
A4	=PRODUCT(A1..A3)

The result is 6000.

STDEV (number1, number2, ...). Calculates the standard deviation of a population.

Example:

A1   20

A2   30

A3   10

A4   =STDEV(A1..A3)

The result is 10.

SUM (number1, number2, ...). Sums the numbers in parentheses. The **number** arguments can be specific values, cells, or a range.

Example:

A1   120

A2   120

A3   240

A4   =SUM(A1..A3)

The result is 480.

VAR (number1, number2, ...). Calculates the variance of a population.

Example:

A1   20

A2   30

A3   10

A4   =VAR(A1..A3)

The result is 100.

Text

To work with text, use text functions that can perform tasks such as changing the case of a text entry, returning only part of a text entry, and combining entries.

CHAR (number). Returns the ASCII character that corresponds to **number**.

Example:

A1   100

A2   =CHAR(A1)

The result is d.

CODE (text). Returns the numeric ASCII character for the text.

Example:

A1   X

A2   =CODE(A1)

The result is 88.

CONCAT (text 1, text 2, ...). Combines text.

Example:

A1   Mildred

A2   McDaniel

A3   =CONCAT(A1, " ", A2)

The result is Mildred McDaniel.

EXACT (text1, text2). Returns TRUE if **text1** and **text2** are identical; otherwise, returns FALSE.

FIND (find_text, in_text, *start_offset*). Searches for **find_text** in **in_text**. Optionally, you can specify where to start the search.

LEFT (text, number_of_characters). Returns **number_of_characters** starting from the left in the text you specify.

Example:

A1   =LEFT("Michael", 3)

The result is Mic.

LEN (text). Calculates the number of characters in text.

Example:

A1   =LEN("Michael")

The result is 7.

LOWER (text). Converts the text to lowercase.

Example:

A1   HELLO

A2   =LOWER(A1)

The result is hello.

MID (text, start_position, number_of_characters). From **start_position**, returns **number_of_characters** in text.

Example:

A1   =MID("Michael Raymond", 1, 7)

The result is Michael.

NUMTOTEXT (number). Interprets a number as text.

PROPER (text). Capitalizes the first character of each word.

Example:

A1   happy birthday

A2   =PROPER(A1)

The result is Happy Birthday.

REPLACE (old_text, start_num, num_chars, new_text). Starting at **start_num**, replaces **num_chars** in **old_text** with **new_text**.

REPT (text, #_of_times). Repeats text the number of times specified.

Example:

A1   =REPT(!,7)

The result is !!!!!!!.

RIGHT (text, number_of_characters). Counting from the right, returns **number_of_characters** in text.

Example:

A1   Raymond

A2   =RIGHT(A1,4)

The result is mond.

TEXTTONUM (text). Converts text to a number.

TRIM (text). Removes any extra spaces in text or any leading and following zeros in numbers.

UPPER (text). Converts text to uppercase.

Example:

A1   Wow

A2   =UPPER(A1)

The result is WOW.

Trigonometric

Trigonometric functions are useful for figuring trigonometric equations, such as sin, tan, and cosine.

ACOS (number). Calculates the arccosine, or inverse of cosine, of an angle.

ASIN (number). Calculates the arcsine, or inverse of sine, of an angle.

ATAN (number). Calculates the arctangent, or inverse of a tangent, of an angle.

ATAN2 (x_number, y_number). Returns the angle between the positive x-axis and a line that starts at the origin and passes through the x and y coordinates.

COS (number). Calculates the cosine or inverse of sine of an angle. The **number** argument is the angle in radians.

DEGREES (radians_number). Converts radians to degrees.

RADIANS (degrees_number). Converts degrees to radians.

SIN (number). Calculates the sine of a number. The **number** argument is an angle in radians.

TAN (number). Calculates the tangent of a number. The **number** argument is an angle in radians.

Index

Symbols

& (ampersand) in formulas, 176
* (asterisk) in formulas, 176
+ (plus sign) in formulas, 176
– (minus sign)
    formulas, 176
    PMT functions, 224
/ (slash) in formulas, 176
< (less than)
    database searches, 263
    formulas, 176
<> (not equal to) in formulas, 176
= (equal sign)
    database searches, 263
    formulas, 175
> (greater than)
    database searches, 263
    formulas, 176
^ (caret) in formulas, 176
    (less than or equal to) in formulas, 176
    (greater than or equal to) in formulas, 176
1K Blocks setting, 369
3-D charts, 229

A

About This Macintosh command (apple menu), 327
ABS function, 435
ACOS function, 444
active cells, 17
Active Character Sets setting, 367
Add Page Break command (Options menu), 42, 211
ALERT function, 431
Align Objects command (Arrange menu), 133
aligning
    paragraphs, 84
    worksheet data, 205-206
Alignment command (Format menu), 205
Alignment Wrap command (Format menu), 206
ampersand (&) in formulas, 176
AND function, 433
Answer Phone setting, 359
Answerback Message setting, 363
apple menu commands
    About This Macintosh, 327
    Chooser, 44
    Help, 33
    Key Caps, 331-336
    Scrapbook, 331-336
Apply Ruler command (Format menu), 90
applying stored styles, 421
Arc tool, 118, 123
area charts, 230
#ARG! error message, 182
arguments, 179, 213
Arrange menu commands
    Align Objects, 133
    Flip Horizontal, 134
    Flip Vertical, 134
    Group, 135
    Lock, 141
    Move Back, 130
    Move Backward, 130
    Move Forward, 130
    Move to Back, 98
    Move to Front, 130
    Rotate, 134
    Ungroup, 135
    Unlock, 141
ASIN function, 444
asterisk (*) in formulas, 176
ATAN function, 444
ATAN2 function, 444
Auto Calc command (Calculate menu), 179, 218
Auto Number footnotes option (Preferences dialog box), 408
Auto Wrap to Next Line setting, 364
Autogrid (drawing module), 133
automatic hyphenation, 16
Automatically Smooth Freehand option (Preferences dialog box), 411
AVERAGE function, 217, 438
Avery mailing labels, 278
axes (charts), 240-242
Axis dialog box, 240

B

backing up documents, 30-31
Bad Formula dialog box, 220
Bad Formula error message, 181
Balloon Help, 33
Balloon Help icon, 15
bar charts, 230
Baud Rate setting, 360
BEEP function, 431
Bezigon tool, 119, 127-128

Blank layout

Blank layout, 279
Blend command (Transform menu), 163
blending colors, 163
boldface type, 82
borders (worksheets), 204
Borders command (Format menu), 204
Browse view, 36, 39, 272, 281-283
Brush Editor dialog box, 151
Brush Shape command (Options menu), 150
Brush tool (painting), 144, 150-151
business functions, 424-427
buttons (Shortcuts palette), 391-393

C

Calculate menu commands
    Auto Calc, 179, 218
    Calculate Now, 179, 215
    Delete Cells, 192
    Fill Left, 188
    Fill Right, 188, 224
    Insert Cells, 191
    Move, 185
    Sort, 195
Calculate Now command (Calculate menu), 179, 215
calculating worksheets, 178-179
    Auto Calc, 218
calculation fields, 248-250, 296-298
calculation precedence, 178
Capture From option (Preferences dialog box), 417
Capture to File command (Session menu), 379
capturing data (communications), 378-381
caret (^) in formulas, 176
case-sensitive searches, 68
cells (spreadsheets), 170
    active cells, 17
    copying contents, 186-187
    deleting cell contents, 185
    deleting cells, 192-196
    editing, 183
    formulas, 175-178
changing text, 69-71
CHAR function, 442

character set terminal setting, 367
Characters setting, 364
Chart Options dialog box, 228, 234
charts, 16
    3-D charts, 229
    area charts, 230
    axes, 240-242
    bar charts, 230
    chart series, 235-236
    colors, 237-238
    creating, 227-230
    deleting, 230, 234
    editing, 233-234
    formatting data, 235
    frames, 318-321
    high-low charts, 233
    legends, 239-240
    line charts, 231
    modifying chart type, 234-235
    moving, 233
    pictograms, 232
    pie charts, 231
    scatter charts, 232
    sizing, 233-234
    stacked area charts, 231
    stacked bar charts, 230
    stacked pictograms, 232
    titles, 238-239
    troubleshooting, 230, 241
    x-y line charts, 233
    x-y scatter charts, 233
CHOOSE function, 431
Chooser dialog box, 44-45
circular references, 193
circular sweep (gradients), 139
CleanLinks setting, 370
Clear command (Edit menu), 129
Clear Saved Lines command (Session menu), 380
Clipboard, 47-48, 65, 94
close box, 14
Close command (File menu), 32
closing documents, 32
CODE function, 442
Collapse command (Outline menu), 110
collapsing Shortcuts palette, 390
Color Editor, 135-136
colors
    blending, 163
    charts, 228, 237-238

    customizing, 413-414
    Drawing and Text Colors option (Preferences dialog box), 413
    editing, 136
    objects (drawing module), 128, 135-136
    painting module, 163
    reversing, 163
    shading, 163
    text, 82-83
    worksheets, 203-207
COLUMN function, 431
Column Width command (Format menu), 208
Columnar Report layout
    creating, 274-276
    fill order, 277-278
columns, 99-101, 170
    column breaks, 101
    Columns dialog box, 100-101
    deleting, 192-196
    headings, 193
    height, 207-209
    inserting, 191
    locking
        columns, 37
        titles, 193
    rulers, 100
    selecting, 184
    text, 101
    width, 208
Columns command (Format menu), 100
Columns dialog box, 100-101
commands
    apple menu
        About This Macintosh, 327
        Chooser, 44
        Help, 33
        Key Caps, 331-336
        Scrapbook, 331-336
    Arrange menu
        Align Objects, 133
        Flip Horizontal, 134
        Flip Vertical, 134
        Group, 135
        Lock, 141
        Move Back, 130
        Move Backward, 130
        Move Forward, 130
        Move to Back, 98
        Move to Front, 130
        Rotate, 134
        Ungroup, 135
        Unlock, 141

commands

Balloon Help menu, 33
Calculate menu
    Auto Calc, 179, 218
    Calculate Now, 179, 215
    Delete Cells, 192
    Fill Left, 188
    Fill Right, 188, 224
    Insert Cells, 191
    Move, 185
    Sort, 195
Edit menu
    Clear, 129
    Copy, 48, 65, 131
    Copy Format, 207
    Copy Table, 381
    Cut, 48, 65
    Duplicate, 131
    Duplicate Record, 259
    Find/Change, 67, 182
    Insert Break, 101
    Insert Date, 44, 94, 338, 408
    Insert Page #, 44
    Insert Page Number, 92
    Insert Time, 44, 94
    New Request, 265
    Paste, 48, 65, 131
    Paste Format, 207
    Paste Function, 179, 215
    Paste Special, 189
    Preferences, 76, 104, 405-418
    Publishing, 344
    Reshape, 125
    Select All, 64, 88, 129
    Smooth, 126
    Undo, 65
    Undo Distort, 158
    Undo Flip, 162
    Undo Move, 129
    Undo Perspective, 159
    Undo Rotate, 160
    Undo Scale, 161
    Undo Shear, 158
    Undo Sort, 196
    Unsmooth, 126
    Writing Tools, 72, 75, 94, 261
File menu
    Close, 32
    Insert, 49-50
    Mail Merge, 338
    New, 27, 63
    Open, 28
    Page Setup, 45
    Print, 46
    Quit, 52
    Revert, 31
    Save, 30
    Save As, 29, 50
    Shortcuts, 59, 171-173, 382, 389-396
Font menu, 81
Format menu
    Alignment, 205
    Alignment Wrap, 206
    Apply Ruler, 90
    Borders, 204
    Column Width, 208
    Columns, 100
    Copy Ruler, 90
    Document, 39-40, 91
    Font, 200
    Insert Break, 42, 62
    Insert Footer, 44, 92
    Insert Footnote, 103, 408
    Insert Header, 44, 92
    Number, 198, 216
    Paragraph, 85
    Remove Footer, 92
    Remove Header, 92
    Resolution and Depth, 165
    Row Height, 209
    Rulers, 41, 132
    Size, 201
    Style, 202
    Tab, 88
    Text Color, 203, 309
keyboard shortcuts, 59-61
Layout menu
    Define Fields, 253, 293
    Delete Layout, 281
    Find, 262
    Insert Field, 286
    Insert Part, 300-302
    Layout, 273
    Layout Info, 277
    New Layout, 274
    Tab Order, 258, 311
Options menu
    Add Page Break, 42, 211
    Brush Shape, 150
    Default Font, 200
    Display, 192
    Field Format, 293
    Frame Links, 322
    Go To Cell, 183
    Gradients, 137
    Hide Graphics Grid, 133
    Lock Title Position, 37, 194
    Make Chart, 228, 319
    Modify Arc, 123
    Modify Chart, 234
    Modify Frame, 321
    Object Size, 132
    Paint Mode, 166
    Patterns, 137
    Polygon Sides, 126
    Print Range, 211
    Protect Cells, 190
    Remove All Breaks, 211
    Remove Page Break, 42, 211
    Round Corners, 122
    Scale Selection, 122
    Show Graphics Grid, 133
    Spray Can, 151
    Text Wrap, 96
    Turn Autogrid Off, 133
    Unprotect Cells, 190
Organize menu
    Go To Record, 260
    Hide Selected Records, 262
    Hide Unselected Records, 262
    Match Records, 265
    Show All Records, 262
    Sort Records, 266
Outline menu
    Collapse, 110
    Edit Custom, 114
    Expand, 110
    Expand To, 111
    Move Above, 109
    Move Below, 109
    Move Left, 109
    Move Right, 109
    New Topic Left, 108
    New Topic Right, 108
    Outline Format, 113
    Outline View, 107, 112
    Raise Topic, 109
    Topic Label, 112
Session menu
    Capture to File, 379
    Clear Saved Lines, 380
    Open Connection, 371
    Reset Terminal, 363
    Save Current Screen, 380
    Save Lines Off Top, 380
    Stop Capture, 379
    Wait for Connection, 378
Settings menu
    Connection, 358, 383, 402
    File Transfer Settings, 367
    Hide Scrollback, 380
    Phone Book, 375

450 commands

Show Scrollback, 380
Terminal, 361
Size menu, 81
Style menu
    Define Styles, 420
    Plain Text, 83
    Text Color, 82
Transform menu
    Blend, 163
    Darker, 163
    Distort, 158
    Fill, 147, 162
    Flip Horizontal, 162
    Flip Vertical, 162
    Free Rotate, 159
    Invert, 163
    Lighter, 163
    Perspective, 159
    Pick Up, 163
    Resize, 161
    Scale Selection, 161
    Shear, 158
    Tint, 163
View menu
    Hide Rulers, 58
    Hide Tools, 34
    New View, 36, 282
    Open Frame, 318
    Page View, 39, 141
    Show Rulers/Hide Rulers, 34
    Show Tools, 34, 58, 237
    Slide Show, 334
    Stack Windows, 38
    Tile Windows, 37
communications module, 19-20, 355-356
    connections, 371-372
    file transfer settings, 368-370
    hardware, 356-358
    local connections, 355
    macros, 382-383
    on-line services, 355
    preferences, 416-419
    printing captured data, 381
    protocol, 356
    receiving calls, 378
        capturing data, 378-381
        scrollback, 379-381
    remote connections, 355
    scrollback option, 417
    sending files, 372
    Session menu, 358
    settings, 358-370
    Settings menu, 358
    shortcuts, 384

software, 356-358
Stationery feature, 384
SysOp (system operator), 359
terminal settings
    character set, 367
    general, 362-363
    keyboard, 366
    screen, 364-365
troubleshooting
    receiving calls, 381
    window, 377
windows, 373-377
    Connection Clock, 376
    Phone Book, 374-375
    status bar, 376-377
    tab ruler, 377
CONCAT function, 442
Connection Clock, 376
Connection command (Settings menu), 358, 383, 402
Connection option (Preferences dialog box), 417
Connection Settings dialog box, 358-370, 383
connections (communications), 371-372
Copy command (Edit menu), 48, 65, 131
Copy Format command (Edit menu), 207
Copy Ruler command (Format menu), 90
Copy Table command (Edit menu), 381
copying
    cell contents, 186-187
    graphics, 94
    images, 156-157
    layouts (databases), 279-280
    objects, 130-131
    paragraph formats, 89-90
    records (databases), 259
    text, 47, 65-66
    worksheet formats, 207
COS function, 444
COUNT function, 439
COUNT2 function, 439
CRC-16 setting, 369
Create Publisher dialog box, 344
Current Port setting, 361
Cursor Keys Generate setting, 366
Custom Percentage dialog box, 35

customizing
    ClarisWorks, 405-418
    communications module, 416-419
    fields (databases), 250-254
    footnotes, 104-105
    graphics, 409-411
    installation, 11
    outlines, 114-116
    page settings, 40-41
    painting module
        Brush shape, 151
        resolution and depth, 165
        Spray Can, 151
    palettes, 411-416
    text, 406-409, 419-422
    word processor, 76-77
Cut command (Edit menu), 48, 65
cutting text, 47, 65

D

Darker command (Transform menu), 163
Data Bits setting, 361
databases, 17, 245-246
    designing, 246
    editing, 254-256
    fields, 17, 246-248
        automatic data entry, 250-251
        calculation fields, 248-250, 296-298
        customizing, 250-254
        date fields, 247
        defining, 248-249, 255
        deleting, 255-259
        input lists, 253-254
        inserting, 255
        number fields, 247
        summary fields, 296-298, 301
        text fields, 247-248
        time fields, 248
        verifying entries, 252
    form letters, 336-341
    formatting
        date format, 294-295
        number formats, 293-294
        time format, 295-296
    layouts
        Blank layouts, 279
        Browse view, 272, 281-283

dialog boxes 451

closing spaces, 289-290
Columnar Report layout, 274-277
copying, 279-280
deleting, 281
deleting parts, 304
designing, 270-271
fields, 284-286
Find view, 272
footers, 299-300
grand summary parts, 304
headers, 299-300
Label layout, 277-279
Layout view, 272, 281-283
naming, 280-281
printing, 288-289
Standard layout, 273
sub-summary parts, 301-303
text, 307-312
tools, 305-307
records, 246
copying, 259
deleting, 262
editing, 260-261
hiding, 262
inserting, 259
navigating, 260
selecting, 261
sorting, 266-268
saving, 254
searching, 262-266
Spelling Checker, 261
troubleshooting, 254
data entry, 258-259
editing, 256
layouts, 287-289, 311-312
records, 262
sorting, 268
viewing pages, 39
#DATE! error message, 182
date fields, 247
date format (databases), 294-295
DATE function, 427
date functions, 215-217, 427-431
dates, 44, 94
word processor, 71
worksheets, 173-174
DATETOTEXT function, 216, 427
DAY function, 428
DAYNAME function, 428

DAYOFYEAR function, 428
Decrease Column icon, 100
Default Font command (Options menu), 200
Define Fields command (Layout menu), 253, 293
Define Fields dialog box, 246-248
Define Styles command (Style menu), 420
defining
calculation fields, 249-250
fields, 248-249
text styles, 419-421
DEGREES function, 444
Del key, 61
Delete Cells command (Calculate menu), 192
Delete Layout command (Layout menu), 281
Delete macros command (Shortcuts submenu), 402
deleting
cell contents, 185
cells (spreadsheets), 192-196
charts, 230, 234
columns (spreadsheets), 192-196
Eraser tool, 156
fields
databases, 255-259
layouts, 285
footers, 92
footnotes, 103
headers, 92
layouts (databases), 281
macros, 401-402
objects, 129
page breaks, 42
parts (layouts), 304
pictures, 96
records (databases), 262
rows (spreadsheets), 192-196
tabs, 88
text, 66
text styles, 421-422
density (Spray Can tool), 151
designing
databases, 246
layouts, 270-271
Dial Phone setting, 359
Dial setting, 360
dialog boxes
Axis, 240
Bad Formula, 220
Borders, 204

Brush Editor, 151
Brush Shape, 150
Chart Options, 228, 234
Chooser, 45
Column Width, 208
Columns, 100-101
Connection Settings, 358-370, 383
Create Publisher, 344
Custom Percentage, 35
Define Fields, 246-248, 293
Display, 192
Document, 39-40, 91
Easy Install, 11
Edit Macros, 401
Edit Phone Book Entry, 374
Edit Shortcuts, 393
Enter Formula, 249
Enter Match Records, 265
Entry Options, 251
File Transfer Settings, 367
Find/Change, 67
Go To, 260
Go To Page, 39
Gradient Editor, 137-139
Help, 32-33
Insert, 50
Insert Cells, 191
Insert Part, 300-302
Label Layout, 279
Labels, 238
Layout Info, 277
Level Format, 114
Macro Wait, 383, 403
Mail Merge, 338
New Document, 12, 26, 51
Number Format, 216, 294, 319
Numeric, 198
Open, 48
Page Setup, 45
Painting Mode, 166
Paragraph, 85
Paste Function, 179, 215
Pattern Editor, 136-137
Preferences, 76
communications module, 358, 378, 416-419
footnotes, 104
freehand objects, 126
graphics, 409-411
object color, 135
palettes, 411-416
polygons, 125
text, 406-409
troubleshooting, 418

452 dialog boxes

Printer, 46
Publisher Options, 349
Record Macro, 382, 397
Resolution and Depth, 165
Row Height, 209
Rulers, 41
Save As, 29
Select Dictionary, 74
Series, 236
Set Field Order, 274
Size, 132, 308
Slide Show, 334
Sort, 195
Sort Records, 266
Spelling, 73
Subscribe To, 347
Subscriber Options, 350-351
Tab, 88-89
Tab Order, 258
Terminal Settings, 361, 377
Text Wrap, 96
Values, 253
Word Finder Thesaurus, 76
Disconnect when NO CARRIER detected setting, 360
Display command (Options menu), 192
Display Modem Monitor Window setting, 360
Distort command (Transform menu), 158
#DIV/0! error message, 181
Document command (Format menu), 39-40, 91
Document dialog box, 39-40, 91
Document Specific macro option, 399
documents, 25-32
   backing up, 30-31
   closing, 32
   columns, 99-101
   communications module, 19-20
   copying text/graphics, 47-48
   creating, 26-28
   cutting text/graphics, 47-48
   databases, 17
   dates, 44, 94
   drawing, 17-18
   editions
      guidelines, 351-352
      linking, 351
      options, 349-352
      publishing, 343-346
      subscribing, 347-348

exporting, 50-51
footers, 43-44, 92-93
footnotes, 103-105
frames
   charts, 318-321
   editing, 317
   importing data, 325-326
   inserting, 316-317
   linking, 321-327
   painting frames, 324-327
   spreadsheet frames, 324-327
   switching environments, 317-318
   text frames, 322-323
   troubleshooting, 326-327
   viewing, 318
graphics, 98-99, 329-330
headers, 43-44, 92-93
help, 32-33
hyphenation, 93-94
importing, 48-49
inserting, 49-50
line spacing, 86-87
loading saved palettes, 414-415
multiple documents, 28, 327-328
opening, 28-29
pages
   margins, 91-92
   navigating, 39-40
   page breaks, 42
   page numbers, 44, 92-93
   page options, 45
   page settings, 40-41
   title pages, 92
   viewing, 39
   WYSIWYG (What You See Is What You Get), 39
painting module, 18-19, 143-144
   deleting, 156
   resolution, 165-166
   sizing, 164
paragraphs
   aligning, 84
   copying formats, 89-90
   indenting, 84-86
   spacing, 87
   troubleshooting, 90
pasting text/graphics, 47-48
printing, 44-47, 59
QuickTime movies, 335
restoring, 31
rulers, 41-42

saving, 29-30
setting tabs, 87-89
slide presentations, 334-336
spreadsheets, 16-17
Stationary, 51-52
tables, 102-103
templates, 51-52
text
   color, 82-83
   columns, 101
   formatting, 79-83
   wrapping, 96-98
times, 44, 94
windows
   multiple views, 36
   rescaling contents, 34-35
   rulers, 34
   splitting, 36-37
   stacking, 38
   tiling, 37
   tools, 34
word processing, 14-16
   editing, 63-66
   saving, 62-63
   troubleshooting, 63, 66
dpi (dots per inch), 165
Drawing and Text Colors option (Preferences dialog box), 413
drawing module, 17-18
   Autogrid, 133
   Color Editor, 135-136
   drawing tool, 22
   Gradient Editor, 137-139
   handles, 120
   multiple pages, 140-141
   objects
      arcs, 123
      Bézier curve, 127-128
      colors, 128
      copying, 130-131
      creating, 120-128
      deleting, 129
      filling, 121
      flipping, 134
      freehand objects, 126-127
      grouping, 134-135
      lines, 121-123
      locking, 141
      moving, 129-134
      ovals, 121-123
      overlapping, 130
      polygons, 124-125
      rectangles, 121-123
      regular polygons, 125-126
      rotating, 134

fields **453**

rounded rectangles, 121-123
rounding corners, 122
selecting, 128-129
sizing, 121-122, 132
Pattern Editor, 136-137
ruler settings, 132
saving documents, 141
tools, 22, 118-119
troubleshooting, 119-120
windows, 117-120
Duplicate command (Edit menu), 131
Duplicate Record command (Edit menu), 259

E

Easy Install dialog box, 11
Edit Button Icon: macro option, 399
Edit Custom command (Outline menu), 114
Edit Macros command (Shortcuts submenu), 401
Edit Macros dialog box, 401
Edit menu commands
Clear, 129
Copy, 48, 65, 131
Copy Format, 207
Copy Table, 381
Cut, 48, 65
Duplicate, 131
Duplicate Record, 259
Find/Change, 67, 182
Insert Break, 101
Insert Date, 44, 94, 338, 408
Insert Page #, 44
Insert Page Number, 92
Insert Time, 44, 94
New Request, 265
Paste, 48, 65, 131
Paste Format, 207
Paste Function, 179, 215
Paste Special, 189
Preferences, 76, 104, 405-418
Publishing, 344
Reshape, 125
Select All, 64, 88, 129
Smooth, 126
Undo, 65
Undo Distort, 158
Undo Flip, 162
Undo Move, 129
Undo Perspective, 159

Undo Rotate, 160
Undo Scale, 161
Undo Shear, 158
Undo Sort, 196
Unsmooth, 126
Writing Tools, 72, 75, 94, 261
Edit Phone Book Entry dialog box, 374
Edit Shortcuts dialog box, 393
editing
arcs, 123
cells, 183
charts, 233-234
colors, 136
databases, 254-256
data entry, 256-259
records, 259
troubleshooting, 256
fields
deleting, 255-259
field definitions, 255
inserting, 255
layouts, 284-285
formulas, 176
frames, 317
functions, 179-181
gradients, 137
macros, 401
outlines, 108-110
paintings, 154-157
records (databases), 260-261
Shortcuts palette, 393-396
text styles, 421
word processing documents, 63-66
worksheets, 173-174
electronic mail, 10, 19
Emulation setting, 362
Enable Auto Receive setting, 370
Enter Formula dialog box, 249
Enter Match Records dialog box, 265
Entry Options dialog box, 251
environment tools, 22
equal sign (=)
database searches, 263
formulas, 175
equipment requirements, 10
Eraser tool (painting), 145, 156
#ERROR! error message, 182
ERROR function, 432
error messages
#ARG!, 182
Bad Formula, 181

#DATE!, 182
#DIV/0!, 182
#ERROR!, 182
Frame too small to draw chart, 234
#NUM!, 182
#REF!, 182, 185
Some cells are locked, 190
#TIME!, 182
#USER!, 182
#VALUE!, 182
Every _____ Seconds setting, 360
EXACT function, 442
EXP function, 435
Expand command (Outline menu), 110
Expand To command (Outline menu), 111
expanding Shortcuts palette, 390
exporting documents, 50-51
Eyedropper tool, 119, 128, 156-157

F

FACT function, 435
Faster Gradients option (Preferences dialog box), 411
Field Format command (Options menu), 293
fields
databases, 246-248
automatic data entry, 250-251
calculation fields, 248-250, 296-298
customizing, 250-254
date fields, 247
defining, 248-249
deleting, 255-259
field definitions, 255
input lists, 253-254
inserting, 255
number fields, 247
summary fields, 296-298, 301
text fields, 247-248
time fields, 248
verifying entries, 252
layouts
deleting, 285
editing, 284-285
inserting, 285-286

454 fields

    outlining, 306
    shading, 306
    tab order, 311-312
File menu commands
    Close, 32
    Insert, 49-50
    Mail Merge, 338
    New, 27, 63
    Open, 28
    Page Setup, 45
    Print, 46
    Quit, 52
    Revert, 31
    Save, 30
    Save As, 29, 50
    Shortcuts, 59, 171-173, 382, 389-396
File Transfer option (Preferences dialog box), 418
file transfer settings, 368-370
File Transfer Settings command (Setting menu), 367
files
    backing up, 30-31
    opening, 12, 59
    saving, 59
Fill Color palette, 238
Fill command (Transform menu), 147, 162
Fill Indicator palette, 146-147
Fill Left command (Calculate menu), 188
Fill palette, 23
Fill palette tool, 119, 122, 145
Fill Right command (Calculate menu), 188, 224
filling
    objects, 121
    patterns, 162
    pictures, 146-147
    ranges (spreadsheets), 187-188
financial functions, 220-224, 424-427
Find command (Layout menu), 262
FIND function, 442
Find view, 272
Find/Change command (Edit menu), 67, 182
Find/Change dialog box, 67
finding, *see* **searching**
Flip Horizontal command
    Arrange menu, 134
    Transform menu, 162

Flip Vertical command
    Arrange menu, 134
    Transform menu, 162
flipping
    images, 161-162
    objects, 134
floppy disks
    backups, 30-31
    locking, 10
    retrieving documents, 28
focus (gradients), 138
Font command (Format menu), 200
Font menu, 81
fonts, 79-81
    graphics, 333-334
    layouts (databases), 307
    type size, 81
    type styles, 81-82
    worksheets, 199-201
footers, 43-44, 92-93, 299-300
footnotes, 103-105
    Auto Number Footnotes option, 408
    finding, 71
form letters
    creating, 337-341
    setting up database, 336-337
    troubleshooting, 341
Format menu commands
    Alignment, 205
    Alignment Wrap, 206
    Apply Ruler, 90
    Borders, 204
    Column Width, 208
    Columns, 100
    Copy Ruler, 90
    Document, 39-40, 91
    Font, 200
    Insert Break, 42, 62
    Insert Footer, 44, 92
    Insert Footnote, 103, 408
    Insert Header, 44, 92
    Number, 198, 216
    Paragraph, 85
    Remove Footer, 92
    Remove Header, 92
    Resolution and Depth, 165
    Row Height, 209
    Rulers, 41, 132
    Size, 201
    Style, 202
    Tab, 88
    Text Color, 203, 309

formatting
    charts
        axes, 240-242
        chart series, 235-236
        colors, 237-238
        data, 235
        legends, 239-240
        modifying chart type, 234-235
        titles, 238-239
    databases
        date format, 294-295
        layouts, 305-307
        number formats, 293-294
        time format, 295-296
    lines, 86-87
    margins, 91-92
    outlines, 112-116
    paragraphs
        alignment, 84
        copying formats, 89-90
        indenting, 84-86
        spacing, 87
        tabs, 87-89
    text, 79-81
    worksheets, 191-192
        aligning data, 205-206
        borders, 204
        color, 203-207
        columns, 207-209
        copying formats, 207
        fonts, 199-201
        number format, 197-199
        rows, 207-209
        troubleshooting, 203, 209
        type size, 201
        type styles, 202-203
formulas (spreadsheets), 173-176, 193, 213
    absolute cell references, 177
    calculation precedence, 178
    circular references, 193
    editing, 176
    functions, 179, 213
        arguments, 179, 213
        AVERAGE, 217
        business functions, 424-427
        date functions, 215-217, 427-431
        DATETOTEXT, 216
        editing, 179-181
        financial functions, 220-224, 424-427
        FV (Future Value), 220
        HLOOKUP, 226
        IF, 219

hyphenation **455**

IRR, 222
logical functions,
 219-220, 433-434
lookup functions,
 225-226
MAXIMUM, 217
MINIMUM, 217
MIRR, 222
NOW, 215
numeric functions,
 435-438
PMT, 222-224
statistical functions,
 217-218, 438-441
text functions, 441-444
time functions, 427-431
trigonometric functions,
 444-445
troubleshooting, 218
VLOOKUP, 225-226
mixed cell references, 178
relative cell references, 177
troubleshooting, 182
FRAC function, 435
Fractional Character Widths
 (Preferences dialog box), 407
Frame Links command
 (Options menu), 322
Frame too small to draw chart
 error message, 234
frames, 20-21
 charts, 318-321
 editing, 317
 environment tools, 22
 importing data, 325-326
 inserting, 316-317
 linking
  painting frames, 324-327
  spreadsheet frames,
   324-327
  text frames, 322-323
 spreadsheets, 102
 switching environments,
  317-318
 troubleshooting, 326-327
 viewing, 318
Free Rotate command
 (Transform menu), 159
Freehand tool, 119, 126-127
freezing values, 189-190
functions, 213
 arguments, 179, 213
 AVERAGE, 217
 business functions, 424-427
 date functions, 215-217,
  427-431
 DATETOTEXT, 216

editing, 179-181
financial functions, 220-224,
 424-427
FV (Future Value), 220
HLOOKUP, 226
IF, 219
IRR, 222
logical functions, 219-220,
 433-434
lookup functions, 225-226
MAXIMUM, 217
MINIMUM, 217
MIRR, 222
NOW, 215
numeric functions, 435-438
PMT, 222-224
statistical functions,
 217-218, 438-441
text functions, 441-444
time functions, 427-431
trigonometric functions,
 444-445
troubleshooting, 218
VLOOKUP, 225-226
FV (Future Value) function,
 220, 424

G

general terminal settings,
 362-363
Go To Cell command (Options
 menu), 183
Go To Page dialog box, 39
Go To Record command
 (Organize menu), 260
Gradient Editor dialog box,
 137-139
Gradients command (Options
 menu), 137
grand summary parts
 (layouts), 304
graphics, 94-99
 copying, 47
 cutting, 47
 fonts, 333-334
 Key Caps, 331-336
 layering, 98-99
 overlapping, 166-167
 pasting, 47
 preferences, 409-411
 rulers, 41
 Scrapbook, 331-336
 software, 331-336
 text, 329-330

troubleshooting, 98-99,
 333-334
worksheets, 209
greater than (>)
 database searches, 263
 formulas, 176
greater than or equal to ( ) in
 formulas, 176
grids (spreadsheets), 193
Group command (Arrange
 menu), 135
grouping objects, 134-135
Grow Horizontally option
 (Preferences dialog box), 415
Grow Limit option
 (Preferences dialog box), 415
Grow Vertically option
 (Preferences dialog box), 415

H

handles, 120
Handshake setting, 361
hanging indents, 86
hard disks, 31
hardware (communications
 module), 356-358
Has Shortcut macro option,
 399
headers, 43-44, 92-93, 299-300
help, 32-33
Hide Graphics Grid command
 (Options menu), 133
Hide Rulers command (View
 menu), 58
Hide Scrollback command
 (Settings menu), 380
Hide Selected Records
 command (Organize menu),
 262
Hide Tools command (View
 menu), 34
Hide Unselected Records
 command (Organize menu),
 262
hiding records (databases),
 262
high-low charts, 233
HLOOKUP function, 226, 432
HOUR function, 428
hyphenation, 93-94

456 icons

I-J

icons
    Balloon Help, 33
    Decrease Column, 100
    Increase Column, 100
IF function, 219, 434
images, 18
importing
    documents, 48-49
    to frames, 325-326
In Shortcuts Palette macro option, 399
Increase Column icon, 100
indenting paragraphs, 84-86
INDEX function, 432
input lists (databases), 253-254
Insert Break command
    Edit menu, 101
    Format menu, 42, 62
Insert Cells command (Calculate menu), 191
Insert Characters setting, 365
Insert command (File menu), 49-50
Insert Date command (Edit menu), 44, 94, 338, 408
Insert dialog box, 50
Insert Field command (Layout menu), 286
Insert Footer command (Format menu), 44, 92
Insert Footnote command (Format menu), 103, 408
Insert Header command (Format menu), 44, 92
Insert Page # command (Edit menu), 44
Insert Page Number command (Edit menu), 92
Insert Part command (Layout menu), 300, 302
Insert Time command (Edit menu), 44, 94
inserting
    cells (spreadsheets), 191
    column breaks, 101
    columns (spreadsheets), 191
    dates, 94
    documents, 49-50
    fields
        databases, 255
        layouts, 285-286
    footers, 44, 92-93
    footnotes, 103-104
    frames, 316-317
    headers, 44, 92-93
    page breaks, 42
    pictures, 96
    records (databases), 259
    rows (spreadsheets), 191
    times, 94
insertion point (word processor), 58
installing ClarisWorks, 10-11
INT function, 436
integrating modules, 20-21
Inverse Video setting, 365
Invert command (Transform menu), 163
investment planning, 220-222
invisible characters, 71-72
IRR function, 222, 424
ISBLANK function, 434
ISERROR function, 434
ISLOGICAL function, 434
ISNA function, 434
ISNUMBER function, 434
italic type, 82

K-L

Key Caps, 331-336
keyboard shortcuts, 59-61, 391
keyboard terminal settings, 366
Keyclick Sound setting, 366

Label layout, 277-279, 288
Label Layout dialog box, 279
Labels dialog box, 238
landscape orientation, 45
Lasso tool (painting), 144, 155
Layout command (Layout menu), 273
Layout Info command (Layout menu), 277
Layout menu commands
    Define Fields, 253, 293
    Delete Layout, 281
    Find, 262
    Insert Field, 286
    Insert Part, 300-302
    Layout, 273
    Layout Info, 277
    New Layout, 274
    Tab Order, 258, 311
Layout view, 36, 39, 272, 281-283
layouts (databases)
    Blank layout, 279
    Browse view, 272, 281-283
    closing spaces, 289-290
    Columnar Report layout
        creating, 274-276
        fill order, 277-278
    copying, 279-280
    deleting, 281
    deleting parts, 304
    designing, 270-271
    fields
        deleting, 285
        editing, 284-285
        inserting, 285-286
        outlining, 306
        shading, 306
        tab order, 311-312
    Find view, 272
    footers, 299-300
    grand summary parts, 304
    headers, 299-300
    Label layout, 277-279, 288
    Layout view, 272, 281-283
    naming, 280-281
    printing, 288-289
    Standard layout, 273
    sub-summary parts, 301-303
    troubleshooting, 287-289, 311-312
leading grand summary parts, 304
LEFT function, 442
legends (charts), 239-240
LEN function, 443
less than (<)
    database searches, 263
    formulas, 176
less than or equal to ( ) in formulas, 176
Level Format dialog box, 114
Lighter command (Transform menu), 163
line charts, 231
Line tool, 118, 121-123
lines (word processor)
    line breaks, 71
    selecting, 64
    spacing, 86-87
linking
    editions, 351
    frames, 21
        painting frames, 324-327
        spreadsheet frames, 324-327
        text frames, 322-323
LN function, 436

objects **457**

loading saved palettes, 414-415
loan payments, 222-224
local connections, 355
Local Echo setting, 363
Lock command (Arrange menu), 141
Lock Title Position command (Options menu), 37, 194
locking
    column titles, 193
    columns, 37
    objects, 141
    row titles, 193
    rows, 37
LOG function, 436
LOG10 function, 436
logical functions, 219-220, 433-434
LOOKUP function, 432
lookup functions, 225-226
LOWER function, 443

M

MACRO function, 432
Macro Wait command (Shortcuts submenu), 402-404
Macro Wait dialog box, 383
macros
    communications module, 382-383
    deleting, 401-402
    editing, 401
    Macro Wait option, 402-404
    options, 399-400
    playing, 400-401
    recording, 396-399
    troubleshooting, 403-404
Magic Wand tool (painting), 144, 155-156
Mail Merge command (File menu), 338
Make Chart command (Options menu), 228, 319
margins
    page breaks, 42
    widths, 40
    word processor, 58
MATCH function, 432
Match Records command (Organize menu), 265
MAX function, 439
MAXIMUM function, 217

memory, 327
menu bars, 58
menus, 13, 33
Method setting, 368
MID function, 443
MIN function, 440
MINIMUM function, 217
minus sign (–)
    formulas, 176
    PMT functions, 224
MINUTE function, 429
MIRR function, 222, 425
MOD function, 437
modems, 20, 355
    settings, 359-361
Modify Arc command (Options menu), 123
Modify Chart command (Options menu), 234
Modify Frame command (Options menu), 321
MONTH function, 429
MONTHNAME function, 429
mouse, 63
Move Above command (Outline menu), 109
Move Back command (Arrange menu), 130
Move Backward command (Arrange menu), 130
Move Below command (Outline menu), 109
Move command (Calculate menu), 185
Move Forward command (Arrange menu), 130
Move Left command (Outline menu), 109
Move Right command (Outline menu), 109
Move to Back command (Arrange menu), 98
Move to Front command (Arrange menu), 130
moving
    cell contents, 185
    charts, 233
    fields (layouts), 284
    fills (painting), 155-156
    objects, 129-134
    pictures, 96
multiple document views, 36
multiple-page drawings, 140-141

N

#N/A! error message, 181
NA function, 433
naming layouts (databases), 280-281
National Replacement Set setting, 367
navigating
    multiple documents, 328
    pages, 39-40
    records (databases), 260
    word processor, 61-62
    worksheets, 183
New command (File menu), 27, 63
New Document dialog box, 12, 26
    Stationery option, 51
New Layout command (Layout menu), 274
New Line Return setting, 366
New Request command (Edit menu), 265
New Topic Left command (Outline menu), 108
New Topic Right command (Outline menu), 108
New View command (View menu), 36, 282
not equal to (<>) in formulas, 176
NOT function, 434
NOW function, 215, 429
NPER function, 425
NPV function, 426
#NUM! error message, 182
Number command (Format menu), 198, 216
number fields, 247
Number Format dialog box, 216, 294, 319
Numeric dialog box, 198
numeric functions, 435-438
Numeric Keyboard Generate setting, 366
NUMTOTEXT function, 443

O

Object Size command (Options menu), 132
objects, 18
    arcs, 123
    Bézier curve, 127-128

458 objects

colors, 128, 135-136
copying, 130-131
creating, 120-128
deleting, 129
filling, 121
flipping, 134
freehand objects, 126-127
gradients, 137-139
grouping, 134-135
lines, 121-123
locking, 141
moving, 129-134
ovals, 121-123
overlapping, 130
patterns, 136-137
polygons, 124-125
rectangles, 121-123
regular polygons, 125-126
rotating, 134
rounded rectangles, 121-123
rounding corners, 122
selecting, 128-129
sizing, 122, 132
On Line setting, 362
On Open option (Preferences dialog box), 417
on-line services, 355
Opaque mode (painting), 166
Open command (File menu), 28
Open Connection command (Session menu), 371
Open dialog box, 48
Open Frame command (View menu), 318
opening
documents, 28-29
files, 12, 59
multiple documents, 28
painting documents, 143-144
word processor, 12
operators, 175-176
Options menu commands
Add Page Break, 42, 211
Brush Shape, 150
Default Font, 200
Display, 192
Field Format, 293
Frame Links, 322
Go To Cell, 183
Gradients, 137
Hide Graphics Grid, 133
Lock Title Position, 37, 194
Make Chart, 228, 319
Modify Arc, 123
Modify Chart, 234
Modify Frame, 321
Object Size, 132
Paint Mode, 166
Patterns, 137
Polygon Sides, 126
Print Range, 211
Protect Cells, 190
Remove All Breaks, 211
Remove Page Break, 42, 211
Round Corners, 122
Scale Selection, 122
Show Graphics Grid, 133
Spray Can, 151
Text Wrap, 96
Turn Autogrid Off, 133
Unprotect Cells, 190
OR function, 434
Organize menu commands
Go To Record, 260
Hide Selected Records, 262
Hide Unselected Records, 262
Match Records, 265
Show All Records, 262
Sort Records, 266
Outline Format command (Outline menu), 113
Outline menu commands
Collapse, 110
Edit Custom, 114
Expand, 110
Expand To, 111
Move Above, 109
Move Below, 109
Move Left, 109
Move Right, 109
New Topic Left, 108
New Topic Right, 108
Outline Format, 113
Outline View, 107, 112
Raise Topic, 109
Topic Label, 112
Outline View command (Outline menu), 107, 112
outlines
creating, 107-108
customizing, 114-116
formatting, 112-116
topic levels
changing levels, 108-109
changing symbols, 112
moving, 109-110
troubleshooting, 116
viewing, 110-112
outlining fields (layouts), 306
outlining type, 82
Oval tool, 118, 121-123
overlapping
graphics (painting), 166-167
objects, 130

P

Page Setup commands (File menu), 45
Page Setup dialog box, 45
Page View command (View menu), 39, 141
pages
margins, 91-92
navigating, 39-40
page breaks, 42
finding, 71
word processor, 62
worksheets, 210-211
page guides, 39, 58
page numbers, 44, 71, 92-93
page options, 45
page settings, 40-41
title pages, 92
viewing, 39
WYSIWYG (What You See Is What You Get), 39
Paint Bucket tool (painting), 144, 152-153
Paint Mode command (Options menu), 166
painting module, 18-19
blending colors, 163
copying images, 156-157
customizing, 151
Eraser tool, 156
Fill Indicator palette, 146-147
filling patterns, 162
flipping images, 161-162
frames, 324-327
moving fills, 155-156
opening documents, 143-144
overlapping graphics, 166-167
painting tool, 22
Pen Indicator palette, 147
Perspective command, 159
pictures, 145-149
resolution, 165-166
reversing colors, 163
rotating images, 159-160
selecting images, 147, 154-155

records (databases)   459

shading colors, 163
shearing, 158
sizing
    documents, 164
    images, 160-161
    stretching images, 158
    tools, 23, 144
        Brush, 150-151
        Paint Bucket, 152-153
        Pencil, 149
        Spray Can, 151-152
    transferring colors, 163
    zoom controls, 148
Painting tool, 118
palettes
    loading saved palettes,
      414-415
    preferences, 411-416
    Shortcuts, 390-393, 415-416
Paragraph command (Format menu), 85
Paragraph dialog box, 85
paragraphs
    aligning, 84
    copying formats, 89-90
    finding paragraph returns, 71
    indenting, 84-86
    selecting, 64
    spacing, 87
    troubleshooting, 90
parentheses in formulas, 178
Parity setting, 361
Paste command (Edit menu), 48, 65, 131
Paste Delay option (Preferences dialog box), 417
Paste Format command (Edit menu), 207
Paste Function command (Edit menu), 179, 215
Paste Special command (Edit menu), 189
pasting text, 47, 65
Pattern Editor dialog box, 136-137
Patterns command (Options menu), 137
Pen Indicator palette, 147
Pen palette, 23, 119, 122, 145
Pencil tool (painting), 144, 149
percentage box, 14, 35
Perspective command (Transform menu), 159
Phone Book, 374-375

Phone Book command (Settings menu), 375
PI function, 437
Pick Up command (Transform menu), 163
pictograms, 232
pictures, 94-99
    creating, 145-149
    deleting, 96
    Fill Indicator palette, 146-147
    inserting, 96
    moving, 96
    Pen Indicator palette, 147
pie charts, 231
Plain Text command (Style menu), 83
Play In: macro option, 400
Play Macro command (Shortcuts submenu), 400
Play Pauses macro option, 399
playing macros, 400-401
plus sign (+) in formulas, 176
PMT function, 222-224, 426
Polygon Sides command (Options menu), 126
Polygon tool, 119, 124-125
portrait orientation, 45
Preferences command (Edit menu), 76, 104, 405-418
Preferences dialog box, 76
    communications module, 358, 378, 416-419
    footnotes, 104
    freehand objects, 126
    graphics, 409-411
    object color, 135
    palettes, 411-416
    polygons, 125
    text, 406-409
    troubleshooting, 418
Print command (File menu), 46
Print Range command (Options menu), 211
Printer dialog box, 46
Printer Port setting, 361
printing, 46-47
    captured data, 381
    documents, 59
    landscape orientation, 45
    layouts (databases), 288-289
    page options, 45
    portrait orientation, 45
    selecting printers, 44-45
    worksheets, 210-212
PRODUCT function, 440

PROPER function, 443
Protect Cells command (Options menu), 190
protecting cells, 190-191
protocol, 356
Protocol setting, 368
Publish and Subscribe
    publishing items, 343-346
    publishing options, 349-350
    subscribing items, 347-348
    subscribing options, 350-351
Publisher Options dialog box, 349
Publishing command (Edit menu), 344
PV function, 426

Q-R

QuickTime movies, 335
Quit command (File menu), 52
quitting ClarisWorks, 52

RADIANS function, 444
Raise Topic command (Outline menu), 109
RAM (Random Access Memory), 52
RAND function, 437
Random Access Memory (RAM), 52
ranges (spreadsheets), 170
    charts, 227
    filling, 187-188
    selecting, 183-184
    transposing, 188-189
RATE function, 427
Received File Options setting, 370
receiving calls
    capturing data, 378-381
    scrollback, 379-381
    troubleshooting, 381
Receiving Folder option (Preferences dialog box), 418
Record Macro command (Shortcuts submenu), 397
Record Macro dialog box, 382, 397
recording macros, 382-383, 396-399
records (databases), 246
    copying, 259
    deleting, 262
    editing, 260-261

records

hiding, 262
inserting, 259
matching records (searches), 265-266
navigating, 260
selecting, 261
sorting, 266-268
troubleshooting, 262
Rectangle tool, 118, 121-123
Redial _____ Times setting, 360
#REF! error message, 182, 185
registering ClarisWorks, 11
Regular Polygon tool, 125-126
remote connections, 355
Remove All Breaks command (Options menu), 211
Remove Footer command (Format menu), 92
Remove Header command (Format menu), 92
Remove Page Break command (Options menu), 42, 211
REPLACE function, 443
REPT function, 443
rescaling window contents, 34-35
Reset Terminal command (Session menu), 363
Reshape command (Edit menu), 125
Resize command (Transform menu), 161
resolution, 165-166
Resolution and Depth command (Format menu), 165
restoring documents, 31
Retry Up To _____ Times setting, 369
reversing colors, 163
Revert command (File menu), 31
RIGHT function, 444
Rotate command (Arrange menu), 134
rotating
    images, 159-160
    objects, 134
Round Corners command (Options menu), 122
ROUND function, 437
Rounded Rectangle tool, 118, 121-123
ROW function, 433
Row Height command (Format menu), 209

rows (spreadsheets), 170
    deleting, 192-196
    headings, 193
    height, 207-209
    inserting, 191
    locking
        rows, 37
        titles, 193
    selecting, 184
ruler (word processor), 58
rulers, 41-42
    columns, 100
    drawing module settings, 132
    indenting paragraphs, 84
    line spacing, 86
    setting tabs, 88
Rulers command (Format menu), 41, 132
Rulers dialog box, 41

S

Save As command (File menu), 29, 50
Save As dialog box, 29
Save command (File menu), 30
Save Current Screen command (Session menu), 380
Save Lines Off Top command (Session menu), 380
Save Screen Before Clearing option (Preferences dialog box), 417
saving
    capturing data, 378-379
    databases, 254
    documents, 29-30, 62-63
    files, 59
    worksheets, 174
Scale Selection command
    Options menu, 122
    Transform menu, 161
scatter charts, 232
scientific notation, 174
Scrapbook, 331-336
screen terminal settings, 364-365
scroll bars, 14
Scroll Text setting, 365
scrollback (communications), 379-381
scrollback option (Preferences dialog box), 417

scrolling records, 260
searching
    databases, 262-266
    invisible characters, 71-72
    text, 67-72
SECOND function, 429
Select All command (Edit menu), 64, 88, 129
Select Dictionary dialog box, 74
selecting
    columns, 184
    fonts, 81
    images, 147
        Lasso tool, 155
        Selection Rectangle tool, 154-155
    objects, 120, 128-129
    printers, 44-45
    ranges, 183-184
    records (databases), 261
    rows, 184
    text, 63-65
Selection Rectangle tool (painting), 144, 154-155
sending files (remote computers), 372
Separate Document Shortcuts option (Preferences dialog box), 415
Series dialog boxes, 236
Session menu commands
    Capture to File, 379
    Clear Saved Lines, 380
    Open Connection, 371
    Reset Terminal, 363
    Save Current Screen, 380
    Save Lines Off Top, 380
    Stop Capture, 379
    Wait for Connection, 378
Set Field Order dialog box, 274
setting tabs, 87-89
Settings menu commands
    Connection, 358, 383, 402
    File Transfer Settings, 367
    Hide Scrollback, 380
    Phone Book, 375
    Show Scrollback, 380
    Terminal, 361
shading
    colors, 163
    fields (layouts), 306
shadow type, 82
shadows (charts), 228
Shear command (Transform menu), 158

spreadsheets **461**

shearing images, 158
Shift Constraint option (Preferences dialog box), 411
shortcut palette, 59-61
Shortcuts command (File menu), 59, 171-173, 382, 389-396
Shortcuts palette
    customizing, 415-416
    editing, 393-396
    options, 390-391
    removing buttons, 395
    troubleshooting, 396
Shortcuts Palette Visible (Preferences dialog box), 415
Show All Records command (Organize menu), 262
Show Balloons command (Balloon Help menu), 33
Show Control Characters setting, 364
Show Graphics Grid command (Options menu), 133
Show Invisibles option (Preferences dialog box), 407
Show Names option (Preferences dialog box), 416
Show Rulers/Hide Rulers command (View menu), 34
Show Scrollback command (Settings menu), 380
Show Shortcuts command (Shortcuts submenu), 418
Show Status Bar setting, 363
Show Tab Ruler setting, 363
Show Tools command (View menu), 34, 58, 237
Show/Hide Tools control, 14
SIGN function, 437
SIN function, 445
Size command (Format menu), 201
Size dialog box, 132, 308
Size menu, 81
Size setting, 364
sizing
    charts, 233-234
    fields (layouts), 284
    images, 160-161
    objects, 121-122, 132
    painting module documents, 164
    windows, 14
slash (/) in formulas, 176
slide presentations, 334-336

Slide Show command (View menu), 334
smart quotes, 77, 407
Smooth command (Edit menu), 126
software
    communications module, 356-358
    graphics, 331-336
Some cells are locked error message, 190
Sort command (Calculate menu), 195
Sort Records command (Organize menu), 266
sorting
    records (databases), 266-268
    worksheets, 194-196
spacing
    lines, 86
    paragraphs, 87
special effects (painting)
    blending colors, 163
    depth, 159
    flipping images, 161-162
    reversing colors, 163
    rotating images, 159-160
    shading colors, 163
    shearing, 158
    sizing images, 160-161
    stretching images, 158
    transferring colors, 163
    troubleshooting, 167
Spelling Checker, 72-75, 261
Spelling dialog box, 73
splitting windows, 36-37
Spray Can command (Options menu), 151
Spray Can tool (painting), 145, 151-152
Spreadsheet tool, 118
spreadsheets, 16-17
    active cells, 17
    captured data, 381
    cells, 170
        absolute cell references, 177
        copying contents, 186-187
        deleting cell contents, 185
        deleting cells, 192-196
        editing, 183
        formulas, 175
        inserting, 191
        mixed cell references, 178
        moving contents, 185

        protecting, 190-191
        relative cell references, 177
    charts
        3-D charts, 229
        area charts, 230
        axes, 240-242
        bar charts, 230
        chart series, 235-236
        colors, 237-238
        creating, 227-230
        deleting, 230, 234
        editing, 233-234
        formatting data, 235
        frames, 318-321
        high-low charts, 233
        legends, 239-240
        line charts, 231
        modifying chart type, 234-235
        moving, 233
        pictograms, 232
        pie charts, 231
        scatter charts, 232
        sizing, 233-234
        stacked area charts, 231
        stacked bar charts, 230
        stacked pictograms, 232
        titles, 238-239
        troubleshooting, 230
        x-y line charts, 233
        x-y scatter charts, 233
    columns, 170
        deleting, 192-196
        headings, 193
        height, 207-209
        inserting, 191
        locking titles, 193
        selecting, 184
        width, 208
    error messages, 181-182
    formulas, 175-176, 193, 213
        calculation precedence, 178
        circular references, 193
        editing, 176
        functions, 179, 213-224, 423-445
    frames, 102, 324-327
    grids, 193
    page breaks, 42
    ranges, 170
        charts, 227
        filling, 187-188
        selecting, 183-184
        transposing, 188-189

462 spreadsheets

rows, 170
   deleting, 192-196
   headings, 193
   height, 207-209
   inserting, 191
   locking titles, 193
   selecting, 184
Shortcuts command, 171-173
spreadsheet tool, 22
text, 329-330
tools, 169-172
troubleshooting
   charts, 241
   data entry, 175, 190
   formulas, 182
   functions, 218
   windows, 172
windows, 169, 192-196
see also worksheets
SQRT function, 438
Stack Windows command (View menu), 38
stacked area charts, 231
stacked bar charts, 230
stacked pictograms, 232
stacking windows, 38
Standard layout, 273
start up, 11-12
Starting Footnote # option (Preferences dialog box), 408
Stationery documents, 51-52, 384
statistical functions, 217-218, 438-441
status bar, 376-377
STDEV function, 441
Stop Bits setting, 361
Stop Capture command (Session menu), 379
Straight setting, 369
stretching images, 158
strikethrough type, 82
Style command (Format menu), 202
Style menu commands
   Define Styles, 420
   Plain Text, 83
   Text Color, 82
styles (text)
   applying, 421
   defining, 419-421
   deleting, 421
   editing, 421
   troubleshooting, 422
sub-summary parts (layouts), 301-303

Subscribe To dialog box, 347
Subscriber Options dialog box, 350-351
subscribing items, 347-348
subscripts, 82
SUM function, 441
summary fields, 296-298, 301
superscripts, 82
Swap Backspace setting, 366
switching environments (frames), 317-318
SysOp (system operator), 359
System 7 (Publish and Subscribe), 343-351

T

Tab command (Format menu), 88
Tab dialog box, 88-89
Tab Order command (Layout menu), 258, 311
tab ruler (communications), 377
tables, 102-103
tabs, 87-89
TAN function, 445
telecommunications, 19
templates, 51-52
Temporary setting, 367
Terminal command (Settings menu), 361
Terminal option (Preferences dialog box), 418
terminal settings
   character set, 367
   general, 362-363
   keyboard, 366
   screen, 364-365
   Terminal Mode setting, 362
Terminal Settings dialog box, 361, 377
text
   columns, 101
   copying, 47, 65-66
   cutting, 47, 65
   deleting, 66
   formatting, 79-83
   graphics, 98-99, 329-330
   pasting, 47, 65
   preferences, 406-409
   rulers, 41
   searching, 67-72
   selecting, 63-65
   smart quotes, 77, 407

   spreadsheets, 329-330
   styles, 4`9-422
   text fields, 247, 248
   text frames, 322-323
   text functions, 441-444
   text tool, 22, 118
   troubleshooting, 422
   typing, 61
   worksheets, 173
   wrapping, 96-98
Text Color command
   Format menu, 203, 309
   Style menu, 82
Text Cursor setting, 363
TEXT function, 434
Text Wrap command (Options menu), 96
Text Wrap dialog box, 96
TEXTTODATE function, 429
TEXTTONUM function, 444
TEXTTOTIME function, 430
Thesaurus, 75-76
Tile Windows command (View menu), 37
tiling windows, 37
#TIME! error message, 182
time fields, 248
time format (databases), 295-296
TIME function, 430
time functions, 427-431
times, 44, 94
   word processor, 71
   worksheets, 173-174
TIMETOTEXT function, 430
Timing Options setting, 369
Tint command (Transform menu), 163
Tint mode (painting), 166
title bars, 14, 27
title pages, 92
titles (charts), 238-239
tool palette, 21
tools, 34
   Balloon Help, 33
   databases, 305-307
   drawing module, 118-119
   drawing tools, 22
   environment tools, 22
   Fill palette, 23-24
   painting module, 23, 144, 149-153
   Pen palette, 23-24
   Shortcuts palette, 59-61
   spreadsheet, 169-172
   tool palette, displaying, 58
   troubleshooting, 119-120

windows **463**

Topic Label command (Outline menu), 112
topic levels (outlines)
  changing, 108-109
  changing symbols, 112
  collapsing, 110
  expanding, 110
  moving, 109-110
trailing grand summary parts, 304
Transfer Options setting, 369
transferring colors (painting), 163
Transform menu commands
  Blend, 163
  Darker, 163
  Distort, 158
  Fill, 147, 162
  Flip Horizontal, 162
  Flip Vertical, 162
  Free Rotate, 159
  Invert, 163
  Lighter, 163
  Perspective, 159
  Pick Up, 163
  Resize, 161
  Scale Selection, 161
  Shear, 158
  Tint, 163
Transparent mode (painting), 166
transposing ranges, 188-189
trigonometric functions, 444-445
TRIM function, 444
troubleshooting
  communications module
    receiving calls, 381
    window, 377
  databases, 254
    data entry, 258-259
    editing, 256
    layouts, 287-289, 311-312
    records, 262
    sorting, 268
  drawing module, 119-120
  form letters, 341
  formatting
    paragraphs, 90
    text, 83
    worksheets, 203, 209
  frames, 326-327
  graphics, 98-99, 333-334
  macros, 403-404
  outlines, 116
  painting module, 167
  Preferences dialog box, 418

printing worksheets, 212
searches, 72
Shortcuts palette, 396
spreadsheets
  charts, 230, 241
  data entry, 175, 190
  formulas, 182
  functions, 218
  windows, 172
text, 422
windows, 60
word processing documents, 63, 66
TRUNC function, 438
Turn Autogrid Off command (Options menu), 133
TYPE function, 433
type size (worksheets), 201
type styles (worksheets), 202-203
typesetter's quotes, *see* smart quotes

U

underlining, 82
Undo command (Edit menu), 65
Undo Distort command (Edit menu), 158
Undo Flip command (Edit menu), 162
Undo Move command (Edit menu), 129
Undo Perspective command (Edit menu), 159
Undo Rotate command (Edit menu), 160
Undo Scale command (Edit menu), 161
Undo Shear command (Edit menu), 158
Undo Sort command (Edit menu), 196
Ungroup command (Arrange menu), 135
Unlock command (Arrange menu), 141
Unprotect Cells command (Options menu), 190
Unsmooth command (Edit menu), 126
UPPER function, 444
US Hyphenation dictionary, 16

Use Filename Sent by Remote Computer setting, 370
#USER! error message, 182
user dictionary, 74-75

V

#VALUE! error message, 182
Values dialog box, 253
VAR function, 441
View menu commands
  Hide Rulers, 58
  Hide Tools, 34
  New View, 36, 282
  Open Frame, 318
  Page View, 39, 141
  Show Rulers/Hide Rulers, 34
  Show Tools, 34, 58, 237
  Slide Show, 334
  Stack Windows, 38
  Tile Windows, 37
viewing
  frames, 318
  outlines, 110-112
  pages, 39
views (databases)
  Browse, 272, 281-283
  Find, 272
  Layout, 272, 281-283
VLOOKUP function, 225-226, 433

W

Wait for Connection command (Session menu), 378
WEEKDAY function, 430
WEEKOFYEAR function, 430
Width setting, 364
window components, 13-14
windows
  communications module, 373-377
  databases, 281-283
  drawing module, 117-120
  multiple views, 36
  rescaling contents, 34-35
  rulers, 34
  sizing, 14
  splitting, 36-37
  spreadsheets, 169, 192-196
  stacking, 38
  tiling, 37

464 windows

tools, 34
troubleshooting, 60, 172
word processor, 57-62
Word Finder Thesaurus dialog box, 76
word processor, 14-16
  columns, 100-101
  customizing, 76-77
  documents
    creating, 60-63
    editing, 63-66
    opening, 59
    printing, 59
    saving, 59, 62-63
    troubleshooting, 63, 66, 72
    typing text, 61
  footers, 92-93
  footnotes, 71, 103-105
  graphics, 94-99
  headers, 92-93
  margins, 91-92
  navigating, 61-62
  objects, 96-98
  opening, 12
  outlines
    changing topic levels, 108-109
    creating, 107-108
    customizing, 114-116
    formatting, 112-116
    moving topic levels, 109-110
    viewing, 110-112
  pages
    formatting, 90-93
    page breaks, 62
    page numbers, 93-96
  paragraphs
    aligning, 84
    indenting, 84-86
    spacing, 87
  pictures, 94-99
  screen display, 57-60
  smart quotes, 77, 407
  Spelling Checker, 72-75
  tables, 102-103
  tabs, 87-89
  text
    copying, 65-66
    cutting, 47, 65
    deleting, 66
    formatting, 79-83
    pasting, 65
    searching, 67-72
    selecting, 63-65

Thesaurus, 75-76
US Hyphenation dictionary, 16
user dictionary, 74-75
word wrap, 96-98
worksheets, 16-17
  calculating, 178-179, 218
  cells
    copying contents, 186-187
    deleting cell contents, 185
    deleting cells, 192-196
    editing, 183
    inserting, 191
    moving contents, 185
    protecting, 190-191
  columns
    deleting, 192-196
    headings, 193
    height, 207-209
    inserting, 191
    locking titles, 193
    selecting, 184
    width, 208
  dates, 173-174
  editing, 173-174
  error messages, 181-182
  finding data, 182
  formatting, 191-192
    aligning data, 205-206
    borders, 204
    color, 203-207
    copying formats, 207
    fonts, 199-201
    number format, 197-199
    troubleshooting, 203, 209
    type size, 201
    type styles, 202-203
  formulas, 173-176, 193
    absolute cell references, 177
    calculation precedence, 177
    circular references, 193
    editing, 176
    functions, 179
    mixed cell references, 178
    relative cell references, 177
  freezing values, 189-190
  graphics, 209
  navigating, 183
  numbers, 173
  page breaks, 210-211
  printing, 210-212

  ranges
    filling, 187-188
    selecting, 183-184
    transposing, 188-189
  rows
    deleting, 192-196
    headings, 193
    height, 207-209
    inserting, 191
    locking titles, 193
    selecting, 184
  saving, 174
  scientific notation, 174
  sorting, 194-196
  text, 173
  times, 173-174
  troubleshooting
    data entry, 175, 190
    formulas, 182
    functions, 218
    printing, 212
wrapping text, 96-98
Writing Tools command (Edit menu), 72, 75, 94, 261
WYSIWYG (What You See Is What You Get), 39

X–Y–Z

x-axis (charts), 240-242
x-y line charts, 233
x-y scatter charts, 233
XModem setting, 369

y-axis (charts), 240-242
YEAR function, 431

zoom controls, 14, 34, 148
zooming in/out, 34-35